LEGACY
OF GLORY

LEGACY OF GLORY

The Bonaparte Kingdom
of Spain 1808-1813

MICHAEL GLOVER

*The invasion of Andalusia will finish the
Spanish business. I leave the glory of it to you.*

NAPOLEON TO JOSEPH BONAPARTE,
11 JANUARY 1809

CHARLES SCRIBNER'S SONS
NEW YORK

CONTENTS

List of Illustrations

Maps

PREFACE

THE history of the Bonaparte kingdom of Spain is a drama in which the leading role was played almost wholly *in absentis*. It is as if Lady Macbeth, having instigated the murder of Duncan and established her husband on the throne of Scotland, retired to a long and absorbing tour of Europe during which she devoted such time as she could spare from her other interests to bombarding her husband with nagging letters, full of specious advice based on misconceptions of the actual situation in his kingdom. Unfortunately for France, Napoleon was not only the leading character in his Spanish tragedy. He insisted on retaining the functions of producer and stage manager.

While the outward story of the French occupation of Spain is a military one, underlying everything is the discord between the Emperor Napoleon and King Joseph. In legal terms the situation could be described as Napoleon Bonaparte *versus* Joseph Bonaparte, Lord Wellington and the Spanish people intervening. Thus this book is largely a study of the relationship of the two Bonaparte brothers. Nevertheless, since this fraternal struggle was conducted against a background of war, much space has had to be devoted to military history, chiefly, since he was the most dangerous antagonist, to the operations of Wellington and his Anglo-Portuguese army. It can fairly be said that too little space is devoted in these pages to the doings of the Spanish forces, regular and irregular. This is intentional. To have included any detailed account of their operations would have complicated the story beyond endurance. The Spanish armed effort was inefficient throughout but it was all-pervasive. It is as if King Joseph's operations were conducted in a fog. While it must always be stressed that the fog was there and exerted its influence at all times, it would be confusing and pointless to describe its swirlings in detail.

Up to 1807 Napoleon's career had been one of astonishing triumph. There seemed to be no limits to his success. Time and again he had gambled and won. He came to believe that he could not lose. Increasingly he came under the influence of what a great French historian has defined as "the heroic urge to take risks, the magic lure of the dream, the irresistible impulse of his flashing temperament."[1] This led him to embark on the two ventures which cost him his throne—the attempts to conquer Spain and Russia. For the Russian campaign of 1812 he made enormous, if inadequate preparations. Four years earlier he had attempted to conquer Spain by legalistic manipulations backed, in the first instance, by an improvised army, inadequate in numbers, in training, in commanders. He made a brief personal appearance, an eleven weeks tour de force. This intervention had all the appearance of a triumph but was, in fact, an ineffective promenade. For the rest of the war he paid for his overconfidence with a constant, crippling strain on his resources. Leaving aside the cost in money and equipment, the Spanish venture cost France, in dead, disabled and troops who could not be withdrawn, more than six hundred thousand men, almost all of them native Frenchmen. The entire army which set out for Moscow in 1812 was only half a million strong, of whom two-fifths were drawn from Austria, Prussia, and France's subject states. It was these who bore the brunt of the casualties. As a recent biographer of Napoleon has recorded, "Half of the casualties sustained in Russia were suffered by Bavarians, Württembergers, Saxons, Prussians, Poles and Italians."[2] Dire though the French losses in Russia were, it was the Spanish campaign which bled the French army so white that it could not defend the natural frontiers of the home country in 1814. The greatest loss to Napoleon on his expedition to Moscow was his personal legend of invincibility. It may have been to preserve this legend that he declined to take over the command of his armies in Spain in 1810–1811.

Unwilling to take the supreme command himself, Napoleon declined, until too late, to allow anyone else to hold it. He thereby ensured that his initial miscalculation should turn out to be a disaster. The blame for this he threw on his unfortunate, well-meaning brother Joseph. By no stretch of the imagination could King Joseph be considered as the hero, or even the villain, of the Spanish tragedy. With all his good qualities, he was not cast in the heroic mold. He has been harshly treated by historians and, judged by results, his reign was uniformly disastrous. In justice it can only be held against him that he was unfortunate in being the brother of a man of almost unrivaled brilliance whose judgment, in later life, began to deteriorate and who was prepared ruthlessly to use his relations for his own ends while scarcely bothering to conceal his contempt for them.

The spelling of Spanish and Portuguese place names presents a difficult problem to any historian. In the early nineteenth century they were spelled with reckless abandon even by the literate inhabitants. To make matters worse, the French used their own variants of many names (e.g., Salamanque, Valence), while the British, notoriously bad linguists, tended to use their own phonetic versions. Even the meticulous and multilingual Wellington did not manage to be wholly consistent. Difficulties in deciphering handwriting are another hazard, and to this day the battle honors on the colors of British regiments commemorate the error of a War Office clerk who read Roliça as Roleia. I have tried to be consistent in using the spelling used on modern maps except where another version is so widely accepted as to make the "correct" spelling absurd. It would be affected to refer to Lisbon as Lisboa or to call the River Douro the Duero where it runs through Spanish territory.

In the references I have given locations of quotations from English translations where these are reasonably easily available. I have, however, not scrupled to make my own translation where the published translation has not seemed to me to be satisfactory.

I would like to express my gratitude for help received to Professor Richard Glover, to my former colleague Guy Sells,

Preface

to Dr. Gonzalez Lopez, to the library staff at the Royal United Service Institution, especially Miss Stephanie Glover, and to the London Library.

Most of all my thanks go to my wife, without whose help and encouragement this task, and most of my life, would not have been worthwhile.

London, 1970.

PROLOGUE

IN the sixteenth and early seventeenth centuries Spain could claim to be the greatest world power. In the seventeenth century her strength passed its zenith, yielding first place to the France of Louis XIV, but she remained decidedly a factor to be reckoned with in European politics. Her army had lost the preeminence it had once enjoyed; her navy had never fully recovered from its defeat at the hands of the English and the weather in 1588. She had been forced to acknowledge the independence of Holland and to restore that of Portugal. Nevertheless, her territory remained enormous. Apart from mainland Spain and the Balearics, her possession of Naples, Sardinia, Sicily, and Milan made her the predominant power in Italy. The Spanish Netherlands still comprised an area larger than modern Belgium. Greatest of all was her overseas empire, which consisted of the whole of Central and South America, excluding only Brazil and a few small trading posts in the Guianas, and in addition, California, Florida, the Philippines, Cuba, and the Canary Islands.

Far gone in senility, Charles II, last of the Hapsburg kings of Spain, died in November 1700. There was no direct heir, and the statesmen of Europe had been trying for years to arrange a division of the Spanish inheritance between the two strongest claimants, Philip, duke of Anjou, grandson of Louis XIV of France, and the Archduke Charles, younger son of the Emperor Leopold of Austria. In his will, however, King

I

Charles insisted that his dominions should pass entire to his heir, whom he named as Philip of Anjou. It would have taken a less ambitious man than Louis XIV to refuse for his grandson so glittering a legacy, an accretion of power which would make France unassailably the predominant world power. Despite his earlier agreement to the principle of partition, Louis determined to claim all the Spanish possessions for Philip.

The rest of western Europe could not accept such an arrangement. Austria, whose candidate for the Spanish throne had, in legal terms, a marginally stronger case, refused to submit to Louis's breach of faith. The British and the Dutch, both dependent on their overseas trade, could not afford to see the French established across the sea routes to the Baltic, to the Levant, to the Indies, and to the Americas. A Franco-Spanish union would permanently tilt the balance of power against them.

There followed the twelve years of the War of the Spanish Succession (1701–1713), ending with the Treaty of Utrecht in which a partition not dissimilar to that planned before the death of Charles II was agreed. The French prince was acknowledged as King Philip V of Spain and secured the colonial empire. The Spanish Netherlands and the Spanish hegemony over Italy went to Austria. One part of Spain did not pass to Philip, however; the British captured and retained Gibraltar.

Louis XIV claimed, "Henceforward, there are no Pyrenees," and it was true that the long war changed Spain from France's most powerful rival to her loyal ally for almost a century. In one sense, however, the Pyrenees became a greater barrier than ever before. Shorn of her European possessions, Spain turned her back on the Continent. Her home economy had never been strong and was further weakened by a listless, precedent-ridden, incompetent bureaucracy. Increasingly she looked to her colonies for the revenue that she was too poorly equipped to produce and too poorly governed to collect. She turned her eyes westward and, in consequence, failed to realize what was going on behind her back. As one of her leading savants commented, Spain missed the eighteenth century.

In France, Britain, Switzerland, and even in Austria and Germany, the eighteenth century was the age of ideas, the age of education. The ideas and the education were confined to a small segment of the upper classes, but the century planted a seed which was to blossom in the centuries which followed. Spain stayed in the attitudes of the seventeenth century. Even if there was nothing to rival the decree of one of her Hapsburg kings which restricted the publication of books on the grounds that there were already too many, she stagnated mentally, militarily, and governmentally, immobilized by the pressures of the entrenched Catholic church, by the traditional privileges of the aristocracy and the guilds, by the sheer ineptitude of the governmental machine.

Only for twenty-nine years, the reign of Charles III (1759–1788), was any attempt made to bring Spain up to date. Charles was a worthy, forward-looking king with a genuine concern for the welfare of his subjects, especially his poorer subjects. His ministers were enlightened men determined to make the machinery of government equal to the tasks it had to perform. They failed because Charles was an Anglophobe, determined above all else to regain Gibraltar. Twice he was drawn by his hereditary alliance with his French cousins into war with Britain.

Nothing could have suited Spain worse than the hostility of Britain. The French alliance had secured her land frontier with Europe, but war with the strongest naval power not only laid open her long coastline but put the whole of her colonial empire at risk. From the Seven Years' War (1756–1763) and from her intervention in the American Revolution (1779–1783) she gained nothing but the recapture of Minorca (1781).* To obtain this meager return, Charles further weakened the Spanish economy and heightened his subjects' tendency to turn in on their own domestic concerns. He did not even manage to extract Gibraltar from Britain's defeat in America.

When Charles III died in 1788, the throne passed to his

* In 1763 she also obtained Louisiana from France but, finding it unattractive, returned it.

3

second son, Charles IV, who was not a dynamic ruler, and all reform, all urge to efficiency, ground to a halt. When, therefore, the French Revolution burst upon the world in 1789, Spain would seem to have been more than usually open to the contagion of *liberté, fraternité, egalité.* In no part of western Europe were these ideals so conspicuously lacking. In fact, Spain was immunized by her backwardness. Revolutionary thinking, to a country still mentally in the seventeenth century, was more repulsive than attractive. The people of all classes rallied around their king and church and gave freely and generously to the treasury. When in 1793, during a period in which the revolutionary government was much given to declaring war on established governments, France opened hostilities against Spain, Spanish armies crossed the frontier, occupied Hendaye, and momentarily invaded Roussillon.

Peace was reestablished in 1795 and Spain returned to her French alliance, again setting her eyes on Gibraltar, again without success. Her system of government was quite unaffected by the political convulsions in France. The French, indeed, made little or no effort to convert their southwestern neighbor from her ancient ways. The revolutionary government was too concerned with holding off the dangers that threatened France on every other front and with combatting their own internal problems to wish to fish in the turgid waters of Spanish politics. Spain was allowed to purchase domestic peace by paying an annual tribute to the coffers of Paris and by using her still considerable navy to distract British attention from the French fleet.

The situation could not last. Napoleon Bonaparte pacified and united France. He imposed his will on his eastern enemies. It was not to be expected that he would long tolerate a potentially hostile neighbor to his rear. Spain had only one valuable military asset, her navy. From 21 October 1805, when Nelson smashed the Franco-Spanish fleet off Cape Trafalgar, there was nothing of consequence that she could offer to the alliance. From that day forward Spain was on risk.

Chapter 1

THE CONFIDENCE

TRICK

Once you have behaved as a knave, you must never behave as a fool.

NAPOLEON

IN July 1807 Napoleon Bonaparte reached the apex of his power. Fifteen years before, he had received his promotion to the rank of captain in the artillery.* Now he was recognized as the greatest commander, the most enlightened lawgiver, and the dominant political figure of his age. From the chaotic legacy of the Revolution he had imposed on France stable and efficient government. He was emperor of the French, king of Italy, mediator of Switzerland, and protector of the Confederation of the Rhine. One of his brothers was king of Holland; another, king of Naples. Spain was his long-standing ally. His good relations with Turkey were cemented by the exotic fact that his wife's cousin was the most favored inmate of the sultan's harem. In the three preceding years his victories at Ulm

---

* The promotion was back-dated by five months and he simultaneously held the rank and pay of a lieutenant colonel of Corsican Volunteers.

(19 October 1805), Austerlitz (2 December 1805), Jena (14 October 1806), and Friedland (14 June 1807) had crushed the military power of Austria, Prussia, and Russia. He had dictated peace in Vienna and Berlin. On 7 July 1807 he concluded, at Tilsit, an alliance with Alexander I, Czar of all the Russias. By this treaty, the whole of Europe from the Atlantic to the Urals was to be united for a single purpose—the defeat of England.

England had consistently opposed Napoleon. Her military efforts had been, at best, inept, but she possessed one incomparable weapon, the Royal Navy. Napoleon led a vast and magnificent army, but between its outposts and the coast of England lay twenty-two miles of saltwater. In 1805 Napoleon had hoped, under cover of the combined fleets of France and Spain, to secure command of the Channel long enough to transport his army to the English beaches. However, his attention had been diverted by war with Austria and, while Ulm was being fought, Lord Nelson smashed the combined fleets off Cape Trafalgar.

Aware that his empire could never be secure while England was undefeated, Napoleon determined to unite Europe against her. England was to be weakened by the prohibition of her trade and France was to acquire a navy which would enable the *Grande Armée* to cross the Channel. Already every port under his control had been closed by the Berlin Decrees (November 1806). At Tilsit the czar agreed to close the ports of Russia and to declare war on England. There remained only three European countries with which the British could do business—Sweden, Denmark, and Portugal—and at Tilsit it was resolved to bring them into line. Sweden was forced to yield Swedish Pomerania and to cede the island of Rügen, but metropolitan Sweden could only be reached, on land, by the Russians, and the czar contented himself with filching Finland. Denmark and Portugal lay within the reach of the French army and Napoleon turned his mind to their subjugation. It so happened that these two countries possessed fleets which could tip the balance of naval power.

The Royal Navy had an average strength of 108 ships of the line.* The combined French and Dutch fleets possessed 75 comparable ships in varying states of repair. The Spaniards could add 24 and the Russians 30. Their combined strength of 129 was a clear numerical superiority, but the French were too realistic not to realize that the British would have an enormous qualitative advantage. The Royal Navy had been at sea continuously throughout the war and had a long tradition of victory. The French, Dutch, and Spanish fleets had seldom ventured outside their harbors and when they had done so, they had usually been defeated. A contemporary French appreciation of the naval situation justly declared, "We shall be able to make peace with safety when we have 150 ships of the line."[1] The Danish fleet had 17 battleships, the Portuguese 10. If these squadrons could be brought under French control, the disposable force would amount to 156 ships of the line, and the invasion of England would be a practical possibility.

The British government, whose sources of information about the secret arrangements made at Tilsit were both accurate and rapid, saw its danger and, for once, reacted quickly and efficiently. On 3 August a combined expedition, twenty-seven ships of the line and 26,000 troops, arrived off Copenhagen and demanded that the Danish navy be handed over to their safekeeping until the end of the war. Not unnaturally, the Danes refused this demand, whereupon Copenhagen was invested and bombarded until they changed their minds. Thirteen battleships and fourteen frigates, all that could be got ready for sea, were sailed to England with British crews, and the rest of the fleet, together with several ships which were building, was burned. French troops occupied Denmark soon afterwards, but the seventeen battleships had gone forever.

Napoleon worked up a considerable head of synthetic indignation at this high-handed British act. The real cause of

---

* At the time of Tilsit there were only 103 ships in commission. In the following year the strength went up to 113, the highest point for the whole war.

his anger was that he had been forestalled, and his moral position was weakened by the fact that he was, at that moment, attempting to bully the prince regent of Portugal into handing over not only his fleet but, in effect, his country to France. The prince, an irresolute, timid character, wished to cling to the long-standing British alliance but realized that he was unlikely to be allowed to do so. In desperation, he played for time, making partial concessions to France while trying to convince Britain of his goodwill. This was not a technique likely to be successful against so ruthless a potentate as Napoleon. Nor was the British government prepared to allow the Portuguese to side with their enemy without suffering the consequences, as their prince regent begged that they be allowed to do. The British could not, at that time, provide enough troops to defend Portugal against Napoleon, but her navy could blockade the Portuguese coasts and bring the country to economic ruin. They made it clear that they would not hesitate to do so.

While the British were threatening Portugal with starvation, Napoleon was planning the physical submission of the country. To reach Portugal, French troops would have to pass through the territory of their ally Spain, and Napoleon took the opportunity to involve the Spaniards in his aggression. This was not difficult. There was between Spain and Portugal what a British general described as "a long standing enmity. . . which is more like that of cat and dog than any thing else, and of which no sense of common danger, or common interest, or any thing else, can get the better."[2] Nor were the Spaniards averse to striking an indirect blow at the British, whom they had just defeated in an inept invasion of the Spanish colonies at Buenos Aires and Montevideo.

To ensure Spanish cooperation, Napoleon held out substantial bribes. Portugal was to be partitioned. The provinces north of the Douro were to be made into a "Kingdom of Northern Lusitania," which was to be awarded to a kinsman of the king of Spain. South of the Tagus the provinces of Alemtejo and Algarves were to be established as a sovereign principality for Manuel de Godoy, first minister of Spain. Lisbon and the central part of Portugal was to remain under French occupation until a general peace, when its future would be decided. Meanwhile, the king of Spain was to be recognized as having a general suzerainty over Portugal and the grandiose title of Emperor of the Two Americas. On these terms, the Spaniards were more than ready to assist and, by the Treaty of Fontainebleau (27 October 1807), they agreed to permit a French corps of 28,000 men to march across Spain and to support it with three Spanish divisions, one to act under French command in the main drive on Lisbon while the other two occupied the "Kingdom of Northern Lusitania" and the "Principality of the Algarves."

Nine days before the Treaty of Fontainebleau was signed, Gen. Androche Junot at the head of the Army of Observation of the Gironde, 25,000 strong, crossed into Spain. The troops were enthusiastically received by the Spanish people. "Our march," wrote the chief of staff, "was the occasion of a holiday for them and a triumph for us."[3] Fêted all the way, the army reached Salamanca on 12 November.

On that day Junot received a dispatch from Paris urging him to hurry his march. The emperor, knowing that the British had evacuated Copenhagen in mid-October, assumed that their troops would be sent immediately to Lisbon and was determined that Junot should forestall them. In the interests of speed, he was ordered to abandon the main road through Ciudad Rodrigo and Coimbra, march south over the Pass of Perales to Alcantara, whence he was to follow the line of the Tagus, moving on Lisbon by way of Abrantes. This was an absurd decision. In order to shorten the distance to be marched within the Portuguese frontier, the army was commited to moving by tracks, some of which consisted of no more than a line on a map.* For much of the route the country was so rugged as to be almost uninhabited. Food was

* Tomás López's atlas of the Peninsula, on which the French chiefly relied for maps, marks a road along the north bank of the Tagus from Alcantara to Abrantes which did not exist. Junot had to go north to Castello Branco to advance at all.

9

unobtainable. Napoleon was aware of this but commented casually that "20,000 men can feed themselves anywhere, even in a desert."[4] Before he had reached Alcantara, while crossing the Pass of Perales in pitiless rain, Junot lost half his horses and most of his guns. The Spanish division, which was supposed to come under his orders at Alcantara, was, in typical Spanish fashion, quite unready to march. Junot took from it its ammunition, its rations, and a troop of horse artillery and pushed on alone. He entered Portugal on 19 November and reached Lisbon, after appalling hardships, on the thirtieth. The gates of the city were opened to him by the chief of police, a French *emigré*. Not a shot had been fired since he crossed the border.

It was as well for Junot that he was unopposed. In the words of his chief of staff, he "took possession of Lisbon, and of the entire kingdom, without having in hand a single trooper, a single cannon, a single cartridge which would fire—with nothing indeed save the 1,500 grenadiers remaining from the four battalions of his advanced guard. Fagged-out, unwashed, ghastly objects, these grenadiers no longer had the strength even to march to the beat of the drum. The rest of the army came in at intervals over the next two days in even worse condition, some falling dead at the gates."[5]

Junot had taken Portugal, but he had ruined his army in doing so. Napoleon had taken a calculated risk and had won, but by a desperately small margin. Portugal had an army which, on paper, had 30,000 men in the ranks. If as much as a brigade of these had opposed the French in any of the excellent defensive positions available to them, Junot must have been defeated with ignominy. He could not have defended himself. All the French powder was so soaked with rain that they could not have fired a shot. Napoleon had played his luck to the limit. It was the last major piece of good luck that he had.

Even so, it was largely an empty victory. The prince regent of Portugal had gone to every length to appease France. He had declared war on England on 20 October. He had seized the goods and persons of those English merchants rash enough to stay in Oporto. On 25 November, he realized that even this would not save him. On that day, he received, via the British ambassador, who was lying off the coast in a man-of-war, a copy of the *Moniteur*, the official French newspaper, dated 13 October. In it he read Napoleon's unequivocal statement, "The House of Braganca has ceased to reign in Europe." That day Junot was at Abrantes, ninety miles from Lisbon. Realizing that he had, at last, to make a decision, Prince John gave orders for his mad mother, the queen regnant, the state coffers, the royal archives, and all the panoply and personnel of his court to be embarked. As Junot approached Lisbon, the prince regent sailed out of the Tagus bound for the Brazils. With him went his fleet, six battleships, and nine frigates.* Escorting the whole was a British naval squadron under Rear Adm. Sir Sydney Smith.**

Junot was to rule in Lisbon for nine months. He made attempts, probably with the best intentions, to reconcile the Portuguese to French occupation, but it was an impossible task. French occupation, quite apart from the affront to national pride, exposed Portugal to the full rigors of the British blockade. This could only be disastrous to a country dependent on overseas trade and the importation of food. The rich ports of Lisbon and Oporto stagnated. Blockade alone would have tipped Portugal's precarious home economy into poverty but orders from the Paris made the situation desperate. Napoleon insisted on Portugal's being treated harshly. Hearing of Junot's attempts to govern justly, he wrote, "You are in a conquered country and you carry on as if you were in Burgundy."[6] "Do not seek popularity in Lisbon, or try to please the populace; to do so would be to lose sight of your

---

* Four ships of the line could not be made ready for sea and had to be left behind. These were recovered by the Portuguese crown in September 1808.

** Despite the importance Napoleon put on capturing the Portuguese fleet in his orders to Junot, he realized that it might be impossible. On 2 November he ordered naval officers to be sent overland to Lisbon to take over the port and the ships "if we are lucky enough to seize them" (NC, xvi, 13,320).

objective, would embolden the people and lay up troubles for yourself."[7]

Apart from paying and feeding his army, now rechristened the Army of Portugal, at the expense of the Portuguese, Junot was ordered to confiscate for the French treasury all the property of the royal family and of the *"seigneurs"* who had accompanied it into exile. Beyond that he was to levy an extraordinary tax of one hundred million francs,[8] some fifty gold francs for every man, woman, and child of the population. Meanwhile, the Portuguese army was to be disbanded except for 6,000 men who were to be marched across Europe to swell the French armies of occupation on the shores of the Baltic and the Adriatic.[9] The remnant of this forlorn force was pressed into service in the Russian campaign of 1812 and died, almost to a man, in the snows of the retreat from Moscow.

The Portuguese had been conquered by sheer effrontery. For a time they suffered the occupation in sullen silence, punctuated by a few minor outbreaks of mob violence. By the spring of 1808 there were signs everywhere that the country was ripe for revolt.

It is possible that if Napoleon had contented himself with occupying Portugal and reinforcing his army there to at least twice the strength which Junot had brought with him, the country might have been forced to remain amenable. Spain was not an effective ally but it was improbable that she would, of her own accord, rise to support either Portugal or Britain. A French army of 50,000 or 60,000 men in Portugal would have been too much for the British to tackle alone. Nevertheless, behind all the French operations in Portugal there was a hidden, overriding purpose, the subjugation of Spain. Around France's eastern and southeastern frontiers, from Holland to Piedmont, there lay a cordon of subject states. Now the southwestern, the only remaining land frontier, was to be secured by bringing Spain under direct control. This was a further step in the process Napoleon had outlined to a small group of his close associates in August 1804 when he said that "there will be no peace in Europe until she is under only one head—an Emperor, who will distribute kingdoms to his lieutenants."[10] A year later in Verona, while talking to Marshal Jean Baptiste Jourdan, he had pursued the same theme, stressing the need to re-create the western empire of Charlemagne, "as much to consolidate the position of his own dynasty as for the security of France, repeating several times that a Bourbon on the throne of Spain was too dangerous a neighbour."[11]

His Most Catholic Majesty Charles IV, king of Spain and the Indies, was, indeed, a third cousin once removed of the executed King Louis XVI of France, but it is a feat of the imagination to cast him in the role of a danger to any human being. A passion for hunting was almost the only Bourbon characteristic which he had inherited. He preferred almost anything to having to make a decision. The government, such as it was, was dominated by his queen, Maria Luisa of Parma, his first cousin. She, in turn, was wholly under the influence of Mañuel de Godoy, who twenty years earlier, as a handsome guards officer, had achieved the double eminence of being the king's first minister and the queen's lover. In 1807 he still performed in both capacities.

Godoy, who had been awarded the title of Prince of the Peace, was a deplorable figure. He had little education but much native wit, excellent taste, an admirable memory, great personal charm, and limitless avarice. The French ambassador described him as "frightened, timid, exceedingly ill-informed, overwhelmingly covetous, insatiable. Most of the gold of Spain and the Indies belongs to him. He takes bribes on all sides and sells all the public appointments. His only administrative talent lies in not keeping his word; he is incapable of making a plan and plunges into each new project with great enthusiasm—until something else comes along and makes him forget about it. Unreliable, crafty and wheedling, he can only be influenced by fear. Flighty, indiscreet, pleasure-seeking, slothful, his principle is to have no principles. Money is his lodestone and falseness is his policy."[12] Under his rule, Spain had taken a long step on the downward path that she had followed since her sixteenth-century greatness. The ambassador added, "It is beyond understanding how this government can continue without governing, how it can support itself with an empty Treasury and without foreign credit. All Spain is longing for things to change. Everyone is waiting patiently for the day when the Emperor will turn his attention to this country so that things may be put right."[13]

Godoy was the most hated man in Spain. He had also given gratuitous offense to Napoleon. In October 1806, when France was engaged in a campaign against Prussia and Russia, Godoy had issued a windy proclamation to the Spanish people calling upon "all good and loyal subjects to assist their sovereign" in increasing the army. The only country with which Spain was at war was Britain, and war with Britain was almost wholly a matter of sea power. Godoy's proclamation made no mention of the navy and laid great stress on the need for cavalry. "Will the kingdom of Andalusia, favored by nature in the provision of horses suitable for light cavalry work, the province of Estremadura, which gave such valuable services to King Philip IV, see with indifference the cavalry of the King of Spain reduced and incomplete? No. I trust not."[14] If the proclamation meant anything, the inference was that Godoy intended to invade southern France if the emperor got into difficulties in the east. Certainly Napolean read it in that light and was far from convinced by Godoy, who, greatly embarrassed by the overwhelming victory at Jena, tried to explain that all he had in mind was an expedition against the emperor of Morocco.

Napoleon, however, was content with pretending to accept Godoy's explanation, at least until he had secured his eastern frontiers by the Treaty of Tilsit in July 1807. He was prepared to plot with the Spanish minister the dismemberment of Portugal and to dangle before him the prospect of a territorial principality. He also secured, under the terms of the long-standing Franco-Spanish alliance, the services of 15,000 Spanish troops for garrison duties around the Baltic. The mobilization of these troops led to the final ruin of the Spanish regular army. To complete these regiments fully in men and equipment meant drawing heavily on every unit that remained in Spain. So heavy was the requirement for horses that few of the cavalry regiments remaining in Spain could mount more than one trooper in three. Those units of the Spanish army which were still close to battle-worthiness had to be concentrated around the coasts to guard the naval bases of Ferrol, Vigo, Cádiz, and Cartagena or to man the lines for the wholly ineffective seige of British-held Gibraltar. No effective military force remained to garrison the center of Spain or the line of the Pyrenees.

By November 1807, Napoleon had decided to put into operation his long-considered plan to take over Spain. In that month he first offered the Spanish crown to one of his brothers.[15] He also gave orders for the rearming of the fortresses on the Franco-Spanish frontier. At the same time an opportunity was offered him to meddle in the Spanish government.

The opposition to Godoy found its focus in the heir apparent, Ferdinand, prince of the Asturias, a man as worthless as his parents but redeemed in Spanish eyes by his hatred of the Prince of the Peace. In an attempt to build up support for himself against the all-pervasive influence of the favorite, Ferdinand appealed to Napoleon for a bride of the Bonaparte family. In doing so he had the support, quite unauthorized from Paris, of the French ambassador. Godoy's agents having intercepted Ferdinand's letter to Napoleon, the king was induced to imprison his son for conspiring to gain the throne. He was only released, on 5 November 1807, after he had written, at Godoy's dictation, a humiliating letter begging for pardon.

Napoleon, thereupon, set about strengthening his military force in Spain. Under the Treaty of Fontainebleau, the French were permitted to march a further 40,000 men through Spain to reinforce Junot in Portugal. It was, however, laid down that "this new corps shall not enter Spain until the High Contracting Parties agree that it should do so." In November 1807 there was nothing happening in Portugal which could require large reinforcements. The Portuguese were sullenly submissive. The British, having secured the Portuguese navy, seemed to have lost interest in the Peninsula and were planning a major military campaign in South America. Nevertheless, before Junot had even occupied Lisbon, a further French corps moved unannounced into Spain. On 22 November General Dupont, at the head of 25,000 men, the "Second Corps of Observation of the Gironde," marched into Spain. They seemed in no hurry to reinforce Junot; they contented themselves with taking up comfortable quarters in Biscay and stayed there until early January, when they advanced to Burgos and Valladolid, where they again billeted themselves. Their place in Biscay and Navarre was taken by Marshal Adrien Moncey at the head of the "Corps of Observation of the Ocean Coast," 35,000 strong. A month later, at the other end of the frontier, General Duhesme with the "Army of Occupation of the Eastern Pyrenees", 14,000 French and Italian troops, occupied the city of Barcelona. The road to Barcelona seemed a roundabout way of reinforcing Lisbon.

Faced with a steadily increasing army of occupation, King Charles and Godoy had no idea of how to proceed. Protest was clearly futile. To strengthen their own position, they proposed that Napoleon should give to the prince of the Asturias a bride of the Bonaparte family. This request was the very one that Ferdinand himself had made a few weeks before, only to be imprisoned for his pains. Having left the proposal unanswered for two months, the emperor rejected it with contempt.

To add to Godoy's disquiet, the *Moniteur*, Napoleon's mouthpiece, started a campaign against him, and he heard from his agents in Paris that it was the French intention to annex all Spain north of the Ebro and give to the king central Portugal in compensation. Worse was to follow. On 16 February, French troops, under cover of a friendly snowball fight with the garrison, seized the fortress of Pamplona. In the next four weeks, by threats or subterfuges, the French gained control of the fortresses of San Sebastián, Barcelona, and Figueiras. In March, yet another French army, the "Corps of Observation of the Pyrenees," 30,000 men under Marshal Jean Baptiste Bessières, crossed into Spain. With them came Marshal Joachim Murat, grand duke of Berg and Napoleon's brother-in-law, who was armed with a commission as lieutenant of the emperor and commander in chief of the French armies in Spain. He had been dispatched from the palace of the Tuileries at a few hours' notice. He was furnished with only the vaguest instructions and it was not until he reached Burgos that anything like an order reached him. From that city, which he reached on 13 March, he issued a proclamation stating that the emperor "sought only the good and happiness of Spain."

Murat's orders, when they reached him, were precise on the military side. On 17 March, the French ambassador was to present to the Spanish government a demand that 50,000 French troops should be permitted to march through Madrid.[16] Irrespective of the answer given, the French army was to march on Madrid and take up positions in and around it. "I hope," wrote Napoleon, "that there will be no war."[17] If asked for explanations, Murat was to "give reassurances to the Prince of the Peace, to the King, to everyone. . . . Say that your intentions are peaceable, say that you are marching to Cadiz, to Gibraltar."[18] No political instructions were given. The emperor intended to reach Madrid on the heels of his troops. Then he decided to temporize. "I am obliged to delay my departure for a few days, but I will arrive promptly when it is necessary."[19]

Things did not work out as the emperor expected. Before the French demand for passage through Madrid reached the capital, Godoy lost his nerve. With Murat's troops drawing nearer daily, the Prince of the Peace convinced himself that he could hope for nothing but disgrace at Napoleon's hands. He also knew that, save for a handful of his personal adherents, every Spaniard hated him and believed that it was he who had invited the French army to march on Madrid. Rumors circulated that vast stores of gold bullion were being sent out

of the capital towards Cádiz to be shipped for safekeeping in
South America or, perhaps, in England. An even more dangerous story was going around that Godoy, notorious for his
meanness, was handing out money to his personal guards and
to a Swiss regiment in the Spanish service.

The court was at Aranjuez, a small town on the Tagus
twenty-five miles south of Madrid where both the king and
Godoy had palaces. There, on 15 March, Godoy issued in the
king's name a proclamation denying any intention of moving
the royal family to the safety of Seville. On the evening of
the seventeenth, it was clear to the crowd hanging about
outside Godoy's palace that all his baggage was being loaded
into wagons. Similar activity was noticed outside the royal
palace. Only Prince Ferdinand gave no sign of trying to slip
away; indeed, he took care to have word circulated in the
town that whatever his parents and their minister might do,
he had no intention of deserting his people. The crowd around
Godoy's palace built up, swelled by refugees from Madrid. It
became increasingly menacing. Troops tried, without enthusiasm, to disperse it. A few shots were fired. In an effort
to save his minister, the king dismissed him from all his offices.
Regarding this as a sign of weakness, the mob on 18 March
swarmed into the fallen favorite's palace and sacked it. It was
an orderly sacking. Godoy's unfortunate wife was not only
unmolested but commiserated with on her unhappy lot.
Godoy's art treasures were looted or destroyed, but not a soul
crossed the threshold of the room in which his child slept.

Meanwhile, the Prince of the Peace hid under a pile of rub-
bish in an attic. He lay there undetected for thirty-six hours
until thirst drove him into the open, where he was recognized
and set upon. With difficulty he was rescued by soldiers. The
Saxon chargé d'affaires wrote that "when he passed my window, between two mounted guardsmen holding him by the
collar, he had been wounded in the face near the right eye.
It was a miracle that the soldiers managed to get him safely
to the Guards barracks. According to one of the surgeons a
horse had trodden on his feet."[20]

Brought before Prince Ferdinand, he fell on his knees, bleeding and weak from loss of blood, and begged forgiveness. The prince replied, "Mañuel, I forgive you for all the injuries you have done to me, but for the wrongs you have done to Spain you shall answer to the Council of Castille. They will be your judges."[21]

Besotted by their affection for Godoy, the king and queen were terrified for his safety. In a desperate attempt to save his life, the king agreed to abdicate in Ferdinand's favor. "Since my increasing infirmities make it impossible for me any longer to sustain the burden of the government of my realm, and needing, for the sake of my health, to retire into private life in a warmer climate, I am resolved, after mature consideration, to abdicate my crown to my much loved son, the Prince of the Asturias. Given at Aranjuez, this nineteenth day of March 1808." Immediately after this became known in the town, the crowd, which had been so menacing, gave itself over to rejoicing, feasting, and shouting *vivas* for King Ferdinand VII.

Meanwhile, Murat was approaching Madrid. Murat, without political instructions, was the last man to deal with the situation in which he found himself. He had been sent as a commander in chief in a campaign in which no fighting was expected. His qualifications were that he was a superb leader of cavalry in battle and that he was the emperor's brother-in-law. "He is," said Napoleon, "a brave man on the battlefield, but he has no head. He likes only intrigues, and is always taken in by them."[22] Intrigues he was certainly going to find. Beauharnais, the French ambassador, whose main qualification was that he was the empress's brother-in-law, had been an active partisan of Prince Ferdinand against the king and Godoy. Now he believed that he had secured a major triumph for his imperial master. Having dashed from Aranjuez to Madrid to be ready to meet Murat, he wrote, "Calm in the heart of the storm, Your Majesty may rely on his ambassador. . . . A mariner without a compass, I have reached port safely, receiving the homage of an exasperated people."[23] Even Murat could understand that the situation was not one for rejoicing and self-congratulations. As soon as he heard of the abdication he wrote to Paris, "I must not disguise from Your Majesty my distress. Bloodshed is likely and Europe will not fail to blame France for it. I command your armies. I am your representative here and no one in Europe will believe that I could be here without knowing your plans."[24]

Nevertheless, on 23 March Murat made a formal entry into the Spanish capital in the midst of a parade which had all the appearance of the celebration of a great military triumph. At the center of it, surrounded by a gilded staff and a hundred men of the light cavalry of the Imperial Guard, rode Murat himself. His jacket was of green velvet frogged with gold, his sash of silk, his boots of red leather. In his cocked hat was a white eagle's plume, which stirred gently in the spring breeze. The Spanish crowd in the streets was, perhaps, drawn more by curiosity than by enthusiasm, but it was not unfriendly even if the procession smacked more of conquest than alliance. During the previous night, posters urging the populace to welcome the "allies of Ferdinand VII" had been placarded all over the town at the new king's orders.

The next day Ferdinand came to Madrid to meet his ally. His entry was the greatest, perhaps the only, triumph of his life. He rode to the palace amid a whirlwind of enthusiasm. From the surrounding country the peasants had streamed into the capital to catch a glimpse of their new king. With a sense of occasion which came to him only once in his life, he disdained the military pomp that had characterized Murat's entry. Instead, escorted only by four Horse Guards, he rode alone on a white horse. His brother and his uncle followed in a closed coach. Nothing could have been more effective. Never had the people of Madrid given a more unambiguous demonstration of devotion to any of their monarchs.

· Murat refused to see him. Instead he sent the French ambassador, who, retreating from his former advocacy for Ferdinand's accession, addressed him pointedly as "Prince" instead of "Your Majesty," as he had done three days earlier. Through him, Ferdinand sent to Murat a renewal of his request for a

Bonaparte bride. Murat made no answer. His aide-de-camp was at Aranjuez persuading King Charles to withdraw his abdication. Urgently pressed by the queen, and knowing that French troops had Godoy safely in their keeping, the king was more than anxious to go back on his word and regain his throne. King Ferdinand threw himself on the emperor's mercy.

The revolution at Aranjuez upset all Napoleon's plans. He wrote to Murat, "I am gravely perplexed. . . . Should I go to Madrid? Should I appear as the Great Protector and arbitrate between father and son? It would seem difficult to put Charles IV back on his throne: his government and his favorite are so unpopular that his restoration would not last three months. On the other hand Ferdinand is the enemy of France: that is why they have made him king."[25] For a moment he had an insight into the consequences of imposing a king by force of French arms. He advised Murat not to imagine that he was "attacking a defenseless people or that you have only to show troops in order to subdue Spain. The revolution shows that the Spaniards have spirit. You are dealing with a rejuvenated people. Spain is full of courage and you will find there all the enthusiasm that is aroused in people unused to political passions. The aristocracy and the clergy are supreme in Spain. If they fear for their privileges and for their lives, they will raise the country against us and cause a war which would go on for ever. I have some supporters in Spain but, if I appear as a conqueror, I shall lose them."[26] This realistic insight had no sooner come than it was gone. On 29 March, the same day that he cautioned prudence to Murat, he offered the crown of Spain to one of his brothers.

It appeared that the game was now completely in the emperor's hands. His troops held the two principal cities and the roads leading to them. Both the new king and the old submitted to his arbitration. Believing that fate had opened the road for him to extend his domains, Napoleon decided to play his advantage to the full. By the end of April both kings, the queen, and Godoy were assembled, by a mixture of threats and cajolery, on French soil at Bayonne. There they were confronted by the emperor in person. Ruthlessly he played one king off against the other until, on 6 May, Ferdinand was forced to return the throne to his father.* He was immediately confronted with a treaty, concluded the previous day, by which King Charles had made over his realm to Napoleon as "the only person who, in the existing state of affairs, can re-establish order." Charles had made only two stipulations: that the territory of Spain should remain intact and that the Roman Catholic religion should remain the only one recognized in Spain. He was also given a handsome pension.

Four days later Ferdinand was bullied into ceding his rights of succession, and on 10 May, both ex-kings set out for comfortable exiles in separate French chateaux. King Charles lived until 1819 but never returned to Spain. Ferdinand, to the great misfortune of the Spanish people, returned as king in 1814 after a British general, at the head of an army composed of British, Portuguese, and Spanish troops, had liberated his country. Godoy, astonishingly, lived on in exile until 1851.

In Madrid, the government was nominally in the hands of a regency presided over by Ferdinand's uncle Don Antonio, a foolish old man much concerned with other people's morals. Real power resided with Murat. Napoleon could not have had a worse representative. "He is," said the emperor, "ambitious and ridiculously vain. He is under the delusion that he is gifted with political gifts to a superior degree whereas, in fact, he is destitute of any such thing."[27]

Feeling against the French was growing steadily higher as baseless rumors of what was going on at Bayonne were whispered in the streets. Anger erupted when Murat sent Godoy off to France, thus avoiding his promised trial. This Murat could plead he had done on the emperors orders. There could be no such excuse for his filching from the royal amory the sword of Francis I, the French king who had been captured by the Spaniards at Pavia in 1525. The theft of this treasured

---

* One of the arguments used to extort this renunciation was the queen's statement that King Charles was not, in fact, Ferdinand's father.

relic gave mortal offense and set an example which the French troops were not slow to follow.

In the last days of April, the regency received, by a secret messenger from Prince Ferdinand, some impression of the maneuvers of Napoleon in Bayonne, and this news greatly heightened the anti-French feeling. The final spark, however, was Murat's order on 1 May that the remaining members of the royal family, except Don Antonio, were to leave for France on the following day. When, on 2 May, the coaches were being prepared for the royal departure, the mob rose in earnest and murdered every French soldier on whom they could lay hands. This was the famous *Dos de Mayo*, immortalized in Goya's paintings. It was not, in fact, a very major riot, being totally unpremeditated, and, while Murat had large and well-disciplined forces on hand to quell the disturbance, the Spanish troops in Madrid, with the honorable exception of some forty artillerymen, stayed in their barracks. Thirty-one Frenchmen and about two hundred Spaniards lost their lives, but within four hours it was all over. Murat proceeded to execute a hundred Spaniards without trial, but by the following day all was quiet and Murat was able to issue a proclamation attributing the whole affair to "the machinations of our common enemy, the English government."

On 4 May, Don Antonio, having borrowed 25,000 francs from Murat, set off on his own accord for France, resigning the presidency of the Council of Regency to Murat. Thus, even before Charles and Ferdinand had been persuaded to abdicate, the legal government in Spain was in French hands. As soon as he held the strings of power, the grand duke sent out orders designed to cripple the military strength of Spain. The six Swiss regiments in the Spanish army were ordered to join the French army and take an oath of allegiance to the emperor. The fleet at Cádiz was ordered to sail for Toulon. Most of the troops in Andalusia were ordered to embark for Buenos Aires. So low had twenty years of Godoy's rule brought the standards of Spanish public life that most of the officials charged with these orders were prepared to carry them out.

This they were not permitted to do. Spanish officialdom might be rotten to the core, but the spirit of the people and the minor nobility was quite otherwise. Spanish pride had been mortally offended. The king of Spain and his minister might be worthless. The queen might be vicious. Nevertheless, they were the legal rulers of Spain and it was a national insult for a foreigner to abuse and dismiss them. Moreover, Napoleon had thought that by seizing Madrid he would seize Spain. In this he was mistaken. To occupy Vienna might be to conquer Austria. To occupy Berlin might be to conquer Prussia. But Madrid held no such dominating position in Spanish sentiment. It was an administrative convenience, a new town raised to capital status in the sixteenth century because of its central position. As a city, it ranked lower in Spanish regard than Valladolid and half a dozen other towns. Deprived of their royal family and capital city by the foreign invader, the Spaniards turned instinctively to their age-old provincial loyalties. Despite more than two centuries of centralized despotism, Spain was, at heart, little more than a federation. It was to the constituent parts of the federation that the Spanish people now turned.

In every province, even in those under French occupation, local juntas sprang into being. The principality of the Asturias led the way. On 25 May, the Asturian junta declared war on France, although it had no more military resources than one regular regiment of infantry and one of militia. It ordered the raising of 18,000 troops within its own borders, and on 30 May dispatched two envoys to seek arms and money from London. On the same day its westerly neighbor, Galicia, burst into spontaneous revolt. There the local commander in chief, Captain General Filanghieri, who showed a disposition to obey orders from Murat, was murdered by his own troops, and the Galician junta found itself at the head of a substantial force. The heavy garrisons of the seaports of Coruña, Vigo, and Ferrol provided an army of thirty-two battalions, more than half of them regulars, the remainder militia. In Andalusia, which had an even larger force of regular troops, the outbreak was signaled by the bombardment and capture of the five French battleships which had been sheltering in Cádiz since Trafalgar.* Solano, the captain general of Andalusia, was murdered by the mob for attempting to direct the popular fury against the English fleet lying off the port. A source of future frustration was the determination of the junta at Seville to arrogate to itself the title of "Supreme Junta of Spain and the Indies," an implicit claim that the other local juntas refused to accept.

Even in Catalonia, where French troops already controlled Barcelona and the main centers, a junta was established. Catalonia, moreover, had a very particular tradition of separatism, and the uprising there, sustained by the ancient tradition of calling out guerrilla fighters, the *somatenes*, those called out by the ringing of the church bells, was the most effective and long lasting of the popular resistance movements. In many places the uprisings were marked by murderous violence against stray Frenchmen, supposed French supporters, and ancient enemies of all kinds. The most appalling outbreak was in Valencia, where the whole of the French merchant colony—338 men, women, and children—were murdered by a mob led by a fanatical priest. It is to the credit of the Valencian junta that as soon as it assumed power, it seized and executed the priest and his principal supporters.

The uprising spread over the frontier to Portugal. In Oporto the Spanish troops handed over control of northern Portugal to an improvised junta headed by the bishop of the town and marched for Galicia, taking with them a French general and his escort. In the south, the Spanish troops in the Algarves marched to join their compatriots in Andalusia. Junot managed to imprison all but a thousand of the Spanish troops in central Portugal, but his position became precarious in the extreme. Even with 4,000 reinforcements which had reached him from France, he could muster only 26,500 men, and everywhere beyond the range of his cannon, Portugal flared into revolt.

* A further French survivor of Trafalgar fell into Spanish hands at Vigo.

Murat, who as late as 18 May had been assuring his master that "the country is tranquil, the state of public opinion in the capital far happier than could have been hoped and the native soldiery showing an excellent disposition," took to his bed at the end of the month, beset with a fever. He left Spain, never to return, in the middle of June and traveled across France giving to those he met "a very alarming account of the state of Spain." One intelligent friend, bound for Madrid, to whom he spoke at this time, got the impression "that he thought himself lucky to have escaped."[28]

Both Napoleon and Murat publicly blamed the outbreaks in Spain on the work of English agents and agitators, and they may well have believed what they said. The fact of the matter was, however, that the British government and people were in almost total ignorance of events in Spain; their only sources of information were the French newspapers and such information as the governor of Gibraltar could glean from his friendly contacts with the general who commanded the Spanish army besieging him. The first of these sources was closely controlled by the emperor. The second was frequently inaccurate and, since to sail from Gibraltar to England took two or three weeks, consistently late. A high proportion of the British troops who could be spared from home defense were in the Baltic, and the remainder, about 7,500 infantry, were being collected and equipped at Cork for the expedition to Latin America, for which they were to be joined by a strong brigade of about 4,000 men from Gibraltar. Such paring of the home garrison as might be immediately possible could release rather more than 6,000 further men within six weeks, but the government was reluctant to spare too many troops as there was a steady undercurrent of industrial unrest, especially among Lancashire cotton weavers, and in the absence of a police force, only troops were available to deal with mob violence. Moreover, the government, headed by the old and ailing duke of Portland, was a weak one which stayed in office less because of any public admiration for its talents than because the Opposition was not a credible alternative, being factious and more than suspected of wishing to appease Napoleon. Only two of the ministers, George Canning, the foreign secretary, and Lord Castlereagh, secretary of state for war and the colonies, were men of ability, and they were on the coldest terms with each other.

Britain was at war with Spain and the news of the deposition of the royal family was received with resignation rather than hailed as an opportunity. The newspapers, which were only slightly worse informed than the government, reported a number of isolated anti-French outbursts in Spain, but as late as 7 June a leading article in the *Morning Chronicle* asserted, "It does not appear that any party or person of consequence in Spain has yet ventured to erect a standard of resistance to Bonaparte."

The next day the situation changed abruptly. The *Sun*, a government evening paper, reported: "This morning about seven o'clock, two Spanish noblemen, viz. Viscount Materosa and Don Diego de la Vega, arrived at the Admiralty accompanied by Captain Hill of the 'Humber'. These noblemen landed at Falmouth from the 'Stag' privateer, to which vessel they had made their way in an open boat from Grijon, a sea port in the province of the Asturias and offered the captain five hundred guineas to convey them to England. The intelligence they bring is of the utmost importance. . . . It appears that, in consequence of the outrageous and barefaced conduct of the French tyrant, the whole province of the Asturias has risen in arms, and 40,000 men had been embodied into an army."

The delegates brought with them a letter from the General Assembly of Representatives of the Asturias addressed to "The Magnanimous Monarch of Great Britain," which announced that the province had taken "arms in their defense to recover the Monarchy, although they cannot recover the persons of their sovereigns. . . . The Principality, therefore, through its Deputies furnished with full powers, presents itself to solicit from your Majesty the succours necessary for their present situation, . . . and they hope your Majesty will deign to attend to their earnest solicitations.

"May the Lord preserve the important life of your Majesty."[29]

Canning, as foreign secretary, immediately assured the delegates that "His Majesty is disposed to afford every assistance and support to an effort so magnanimous and praiseworthy."[30]

There was a most unusual unanimity in the press in support of the Spanish cause. Opposition papers, normally bitter in their attacks on ministers, came somewhere near to civility in encouraging the government to act, and as early as 10 June were announcing that the troops at Cork were to sail for Spain as soon as their designated commander, Sir Arthur Wellesley, could reach Cork from London where, as a junior minister, he was calmly piloting the Dublin Police Bill through the House of Commons. That talented officer, aware that the troops could not be ready to sail for some weeks, went quietly on with his job and did not set off from London until 16 June.

Meanwhile, delegates from the other provincial juntas were flooding into London, to be received with great popular enthusiasm and turtle feasts. The information they brought was frequently contradictory. On one point, nevertheless, they spoke with one voice: they needed money, arms, and ammunition. They did not require British troops in Spain.

On 5 July, a declaration signed by King George III put an end to the long-standing war with Spain.

Having disposed of the Bourbon dynasty, Napoleon was faced with the problem of finding a king for Spain. He determined from the start to appoint a member of his own family, although he had no high opinion of them. "They are all," he said, "insanely ambitious, ruinously extravagant and devoid of talent."[31] Nevertheless, being a Corsican, he had a strong sense of family obligation, and since Spain was the largest realm he was likely to be able to bestow, his instinctive reaction was to give it to his elder brother Joseph, the natural head of the family. As early as 2 December 1807, Joseph, then king of

Naples, had been summoned to Venice and persuaded to accept the Spanish crown.[32]

Later the emperor had second thoughts. As soon as he heard that Charles IV had abdicated at Aranjuez, he offered the throne to his morose younger brother Louis, king of Holland. "I have determined to put a French prince on the throne of Spain. The Dutch climate does not suit you. Holland can never rise again from its ashes. . . . Things being so, I was thinking of you for the throne of Spain. There you will be sovereign of a generous nation of 11,000,000 souls, and of important colonies overseas. . . . Tell me definitely what you think of the plan. If I appoint you King of Spain, do you accept? Can I count on you? . . . Don't mention the subject of this letter to a soul. A thing like this must be done before one admits to having thought of it."[33] King Louis wisely declined the offer, and Napoleon's choice reverted to Joseph who had, of course, never heard of the offer to his brother.

It is easy to see why Napoleon sought an alternative to Joseph. Guiseppe Napoleone the First, king of Naples, was not designed by nature to play a leading role. In other circumstances, he might have passed a peaceable, unexceptionable life as a country gentleman. He was gentle and cultured, a good conversationalist, a collector of pictures, and a patron of the drama and the opera. Born on 7 January 1768, nineteen months before Napoleon, he was at first destined for the church; but although he distinguished himself in his clerical training at Autun, he decided to abandon it and for a time intended to become a soldier, a course strongly opposed by his domineering younger brother. The death of his father, Count Carlo, in 1785 left him Count Giuseppe Buonaparte, head of the family, and he returned to Corsica to run the family estates and support his mother and his younger brothers and sisters, the youngest of whom, Jerome, was born soon after Carlo's death. He found time, nevertheless, to travel and study in Italy and received a doctorate of law from the University of Florence, which earned him a post in local government on his return to Ajaccio.

The French Revolution stirred up all the latent anti-French feeling in Corsica, and under the veteran patriot Paoli, the island declared its independence and sought British protection. The entire Bonaparte family, notorious Francophiles, had to fly to mainland France, where they lived as penurious refugees. Two things restored their fortunes: Napoleon, as a captain of artillery, became a public hero for his part in regaining Toulon from the Royalists, the British, and other foreign allies; and in August 1794, Joseph married Julie Clary, the co-heiress of a silk merchant.* In their straightened circumstances, the size of Julie's dowry was more significant than Napoleon's fame. Her father's influence was also useful in setting up Joseph as a merchant in Genoa, where, financially, the Bonaparte fortunes were firmly established. From this point onward, Joseph never had to worry about money. He was a rich man and lived as such. In between his commercial activities, he acted as French consul general in Genoa and wrote a romantic novel, *Moïna, the Nun of Mont Cenis.*

Meanwhile, in Paris and at the head of the army of Italy Napoleon was working his way up to a position of dominance in France. Some of his new greatness rubbed off on Joseph, who was employed first as part of the restored French administration in Corsica, then as minister to Parma and as the French representative in Rome. By the time that Napoleon had established himself as the predominant figure in France by the coup d'état of 18 Brumaire (November 1799), Joseph had a good deal of public experience of a minor sort and bought a country estate at Mortefontaine, within reach of Paris, where he and his wife entertained on a large scale. Napoleon did everything that he could for his elder brother. He sent him as plenipotentiary to negotiate and sign the Peace of Amiens with England in 1804. Between these two dates he appointed him colonel of the Fourth Regiment of Infantry of the Line and sent him to serve with it at Boulogne so that he might learn

* According to some authorities Monsieur Clary's occupation was that of soap boiler. His other daughter, Desirée, married Marshal Bernadotte, prince of Ponte Corvo, and became in time queen of Sweden and the ancestor of the present Swedish royal family.

the elements of soldiering. In January 1805 Napoleon offered Joseph the kingdom of Lombardy but Joseph refused since acceptance was conditional on his resigning his rights to the French imperial throne, to which, through Napoleon's childlessness, he was heir presumptive. The following year he accepted the crown of Naples, to which no such conditions were attached, and accompanied the army which seized the continental territory of that country from King Ferdinand Bourbon.

Joseph did well as king of Naples. Largely disregarding Napoleon's draconian instructions for the conduct of the government, he succeeded in introducing many liberal reforms, in greatly improving the legal system, in increasing the royal revenue by insisting on honest tax-gathering methods, and in founding a system of public education. Apart from the occasional British incursion and the brigandry which was endemic in the south, he largely pacified the country and achieved a wide measure of popularity, although this may have been due to the contrast between his own charm and the detestable character of his predecessor and his consort. He was helped in his task by the natural indolence and lack of national pride of the Neapolitans and by the fact that Napoleon was too busy in his concerns in eastern Europe to have time to interfere with Joseph's rule.

Count Miot de Melito, a lifelong friend and minister of the interior in Naples, wrote of his first meeting with Joseph that "his mild and refined countenance, affable manners and polished conversation predisposed me in his favor."[34] There is no doubt that Joseph was a kindly man, loyal to his friends and anxious to do his best for his subjects. Unfortunately, his character was flawed by a number of weaknesses: he was utterly under the domination of his younger brother; he was ambitious— not, like Napoleon, for power and glory, but for wealth and comfort; worst of all, like so many men who are both kindly and ambitious, he was almost totally ineffective. As Miot said, "He was strongly opposed to all measures of severity. He was of sanguine disposition and, flattering himself that he would be able, by his speeches, by his pleasant words and gracious manners, to win all hearts, he always refused to recognize enemies in those about him."[35]

He had the intelligence and the instincts to know the right course to pursue but he had neither the determination nor the ability to pursue it. His reign in Spain is punctuated by his pressing sensible and proper courses of action upon his brother, frequently backed by the threat of his own abdication. Napoleon consistently overruled or ignored these proposals, but Joseph could never bring himself to carry out his threat to resign. The most revealing commentary on his character was the reaction of the Spanish people. As *Il Re Intruso*, the uninvited king, he symbolized everything that the Spaniards detested and against which they fought with every resource at their disposal. As a person, they regarded him with no more than an amused contempt. They nicknamed him *"Pepe Botellas,"* Joey Bottles.

Between Napoleon and Joseph there existed a strange love-hate relationship. The emperor was fond of his brother. As children they had been close companions and a genuine affection remained between them throughout their lives. Napoleon admired Joseph for his charm, his culture, his success with women, but he had no illusions about his effectiveness in public life. When he appointed Joseph king of Naples, he sent him a verbal message saying, "Tell him that I am making him King of Naples, but tell him that the slightest hesitation, the slightest vacillation will ruin him utterly. In my own mind, I have another appointed in his place if he declines this crown. . . . Every natural affection must yield to the welfare of the state. I only recognize as kinsmen those who are useful to me. Fortune is not attached to the name of Bonaparte, but to that of Napoleon. I can only love those I esteem. Joseph must forget all the ties and affections of childhood. He must win esteem! He must acquire glory! He must get wounded in a battle! I can esteem him then. Let him prove himself worthy of my gifts."[36]

Joseph's view of Napoleon veered sharply from unqualified

admiration to bitter reproach. In November 1802 he said of his brother, "He is a wonderful man and each day I am more and more amazed at the depth, the extent and the boldness of his projects."[37] But in the following year he burst out, "He shall deceive me no longer. I am sick of his tyranny, of his repeated promises, so often repeated and never fulfilled. . . . Let him leave me in my privacy or offer me a position which will secure power to me when he is gone. For that I would bind myself, I would pledge myself. Is not the fatal power that he exercises over France and over Europe, which his insatiable ambition has disturbed, enough for him that he must drag me after him as his slave?"[38]

For better or for worse, Joseph was the man whom Napoleon chose to rule in Spain. In early May, therefore, Murat devoted his energies to cajoling, with 50,000 armed men at his back, the regency and the council of Castille into petitioning the emperor to give them his brother as king. It proved not overly difficult although, in an excess of servility, the council referred to Joseph by all the titles held by the Hapsburg and Bourbon kings over the centuries. These, apart from the title of king of Jerusalem, which could be considered no more than an interesting historical anomaly, included king of Corsica, duke of Burgundy, duke of Brabant, and duke of Milan, all titles to territories over which Napoleon himself ruled in person. For good measure, the list included king of the Two Sicilies, a dignity which Joseph already claimed to hold in his role as king of Naples. A hasty adjustment had to be made, and Joseph was eventually declared to be no more than king of Spain and the Indies.

Joseph received his marching orders on 21 May. He was to choose a regency for Naples and ride post to Bayonne. He was to tell no one in Naples of his new throne. Among the loyal addresses which reached him at Bayonne was one from the Spanish marquis de la Romaña, commander of the Spanish troops which Napoleon had sent to the Baltic, which expressed on behalf of his division "the assurance of our complete submission and our unchangeable devotion to your person."[39] The new king, a man of great natural optimism, must have been touched by this spontaneous declaration. While he was reading it, La Romaña, on the Danish island of Fünen, was arranging with a British agent for the whole Spanish force in the Baltic to be embarked by the Royal Navy and returned to Spain to fight against the French.

Even Joseph's sanguine nature must have been sickened by another letter he received at Bayonne. Prince Ferdinand, from his exile in France, wrote congratulating him on his accession and "pledging the allegiance I owe to the King of Spain."[40] Even the Spanish Bourbons never sank lower than this.

Chapter 2

THE CROWN
IN HIS POCKET

At this time the Spaniards were saying 'Joseph has put the crown in his pocket but he cannot put it on his head.'

MIOT DE MELITO

THE emperor had decreed that a junta of a hundred and fifty Spaniards should be at Bayonne to welcome their new sovereign. Their first task was to present an address of loyalty to him, and the emperor was anxious that his brother should appear to his new subjects in the most favorable light. "Prepare your answer," he wrote. "You must speak of the sadness which recent events in Spain have caused you; of your sorrow that it has been necessary to use force to reach a conclusion which could have been reached by reason and discussion alone. Tell them of your desire to be amongst your subjects in order to reconcile all factions and to commence your reign by acts of pardon and clemency. You will be well advised to make your speech rather long and elaborate."[1]

The junta did not come up to imperial expectations. The

hundred and fifty members were to have been elected in series of complicated indirect ballots to represent twenty-four classes of propertied or influential voters, including the grandees, the religious orders, the episcopate, the municipal corporations, the judiciary, and other established groups. It was difficult to induce voters to take part in the elections and even more difficult to induce those elected to set out for Bayonne. In Catalonia, elections duly took place, at the point of French bayonets, but the chosen representatives were intercepted by the *somatenes*. Some returned to Barcelona; most sought sanctuary at the monastery of Poblet, near Tarragona. Eight archbishops were bidden to attend. Four refused, two declined to answer the summons, and only the archbishop of Burgos, whose seat was on the French line of communications, presented himself at Bayonne. Naturally no elections were held in the provinces beyond the range of the French artillery.

By conscripting the grandees and officials who had accompanied the old royal family to France and who had not permitted to return to Spain, ninety-one members were scraped together to form the junta. They could not be held to be representative of the country, and many of them were far from enthusiastic about complying with their instructions. Many of them later rendered loyal and devoted service to the cause, which Napoleon insisted on referring to as that of "the rebels."

The meeting of King Joseph and his new subjects started badly. The deputies, having been harangued by Napoleon on the benefits which he intended to impose on Spain, were expected to make suitable reply. The duke of Infantado, the senior grandee present, was the first to respond. His speech was courtly in the extreme but made no reference to the change of dynasty. Instead, he pronounced that the junta must wait "until the Spanish people had made their views known and authorised us to give full rein to our feelings." This was too much for the emperor, who burst out angrily against the unfortunate duke and "told him that, far from being a statesman, he was fit only for the soft life of Paris (where he had stayed on several occasions), threatened him with the gallows, accused him of being responsible for all the trouble amongst the peasants. 'Why not be honest?' he demanded; 'Go and lead the rebels! I will give you a safe conduct.' "[2] Infantado did not avail himself of this offer immediately. Instead, he continued to play his part in Joseph's court until it was safe to leave. Before the end of the year, he was commanding a "rebel" army.

There was a series of meetings at which, in theory, a new constitution for Spain was hammered out. In fact, the junta had little part in its devising. The draft had been prepared in the French Foreign Ministry two months before and had then been submitted for modification to the French embassy in Madrid, which advised on points of Spanish usage. Few further modifications were made at Bayonne. The final constitution as proclaimed on 6 July, made numerous obeisances toward democracy but was little more than an absolute monarchy, thinly disguised. There were clauses guaranteeing the freedom of the press and the freedom of the individual from arbitrary arrest but the implementation of these provisions was specifically deferred. There was to be a Senate to watch over the implementation of the constitution, but, apart from the king's nonexistent male children, it was to consist of twenty-four members appointed by the king from among the ministers, generals, admirals, ambassadors, and privy councillors, all offices in the king's gift. All the senators were to be over forty years of age. At least once in three years a Cortes was to be called. This was to be a large body consisting of twenty-five archbishops and twenty-five grandees "who must enjoy an income of not less than twenty thousand *reals** a year, or have rendered long and important services to the state in a civil or military capacity." There were also to be a hundred and twenty-two representatives of the people. Sixty-two of these were to represent the provinces of Spain and the Indies, with one deputy for every 300,000 inhabitants chosen by indirect election. Thirty more were to represent the principal towns

---

* The real was worth about thirty centimes in France or seven cents U.S.

and were to be chosen by the municipal corporations. Deputies from both provinces and towns could be eligible only if they held landed property. Fifteen more deputies were to represent business and commerce. These were to be nominated by the king from lists submitted to him by the Chambers of Commerce. The remaining fifteen were to be "the deputies of universities, *savants* or men distinguished by their personal merit, in either the arts or the sciences."

All this is of purely academic interest. None of these worthy bodies ever came into being. The only parts of the constitution ever to be implemented were those establishing a cabinet, consisting of a secretary of state and seven to nine ministers, and a privy council of between thirty and sixty members, a purely consultative body which met under the king's chairmanship. There was also, in Clause 124, a provision that "there will be a perpetual alliance, offensive and defensive, on sea and on land, between France and Spain.

On 7 July, Joseph, in the presence of the archbishop of Burgos, gave the oath prescribed in the constitution: "I swear, by the Holy Evangelists, to respect and enforce respect for our Holy Religion, to observe and to enforce the observation of the constitution, to maintain the integrity and the independence of Spain and its overseas possessions, to respect and enforce respect for individual liberty and for property, and to govern with the sole aim of establishing the welfare, happiness and glory of the Spanish nation." Then the king and the junta went to pay their respects to the emperor, who treated them to a speech lasting three-quarters of an hour full of threats and long pauses.

On 9 July the emperor rode with his brother down to the bridge at Behobie, which spanned the Bidassoa, the river which separates France from Spain at the western end of the Pyrenees. Then, followed by his new ministers and the members of the junta, King Joseph entered Spain. He went first to San Sebastián to test out Spanish reaction to his accession "to see that my journey will not be wholly useless."[3] He did not get a favorable impression. "There is" he wrote, "much to

be done to gain the good opinion of this nation; it will, however, be possible to do so, especially once the rebels are beaten,
with moderation and justice."[4] The prospects for moderation
and justice did not seem bright. While in San Sabastián, he
was approached by a deputation from the neighboring town
of Santander on which, a few days earlier, Napoleon had
imposed a fine of twelve million *reals* for having subjected
the French consul to indignity. The city fathers came to Joseph
to beg for mercy. To Napoleon he wrote, "I do not think
that anyone should impose such fines without my authority.
The whole population should not be penalised in such a way.
It would suffice to identify the ringleaders and distrain on their
goods. If we take any other course we will never gain
the support of the people, without which we can never succeed."[5]

Two days later Joseph reached Victoria, where his gloom
deepened. "The townspeople are very hostile. Persons of rank
are intimidated by the threats of the mob and by reports reaching them from Saragossa. The news from the Asturias, from
Valencia, from Galicia, from Andalusia, does nothing to reassure them. No one has told Your Majesty the truth. The fact is
that, except for the handful who attended the Junta and are
travelling with me, not a single Spaniard has declared for me."[6]
On the same day, the emperor was writing from Bayonne to
assure Joseph that according to Gonzales O'Farrill, the Spanish
minister of war, "the rebels ask for nothing better than to be
permitted to surrender."[7]

The fact was that Napoleon had attempted to take over
the government of Spain under a disastrous misapprehension.
"I thought," he said in November 1808, "that troops would
only be needed to maintain public order and to garrison the
fortresses."[8] Consequently, at the moment when his chosen
monarch was entering Spain, there were only 91,000 Imperial
troops in the country.* Even these were not first-class troops.
Apart from a detachment of the Imperial Guard, nine well-
established infantry battalions, and three veteran cavalry regi-

* In addition Junot commanded 26,000 men in Portugal.

ments—about 13,000 men in all—the army consisted of newly raised conscripts in improvised units commanded by such elderly officers as could be found at short notice in the regimental depots. These were supplemented by fifteen battalions of assorted foreigners—Swiss, Prussian, and Italian. Even the marshals and generals who commanded them were, by Napoleonic standards, second rate.

Believing that French troops had only to appear for the new regime to be accepted, the emperor had dispersed them widely in small corps incapable of supporting each other. In Catalonia, General Duhesme, with 12,500 men, held Barcelona and little else. His communications with the rest of Spain were nonexistent and those with France were so tenuous that in July a further 8,000 men had to be detailed to attempt to clear the road from Barcelona to Perpignan. At the other end of the Pyrenees, Marshal Bessières was charged with keeping open the road from Bayonne to Burgos. His corps consisted of 25,000 men from which he had been ordered to detach 4,000 men to take Saragossa and a further brigade to occupy Santander. After he provided garrisons for San Sebastián and Pamplona, his field strength was no more than 10,000, while he was increasingly threatened by the Spanish armies of Galicia, the Asturias, and Castille, which, if properly coordinated, could march against him with 40,000 men, including a strong nucleus of regular infantry.

The operation against Saragossa turned out to be a disaster. Bessières's 4,000 men could do no more than fight their way up to the walls. Joseph Palafox, the twenty-eight-year-old captain general of Aragon, had less than a thousand regular troops, but the whole population of the city, 60,000 souls, were determined that the French should not enter Saragossa. This was the first time that the French experienced the full force of patriotic fury in Spain. Men, women, and children all took their part in building and holding the defenses. Assault after assault was launched against the walls. Reinforcements from France built up the assailants' strength from 4,000 to 16,000. Siege guns were brought up. In mid-August, after two months of the siege, the French had secured no more than a toehold within the walls and had lost 3,500 men.

The bulk of the French strength was based around Madrid. This consisted of two corps, those of Marshal Moncey and General Dupont, which, with the detachment of the guard, amounted to 53,000 men. From this total two large detachments had been ordered. Moncey, with 8,000 men, was sent southeast to occupy Valencia and Cartagena. Dupont's orders were to occupy Cordova, Seville, and Cádiz. From Madrid to Cádiz is four hundred miles. Dupont, a brave soldier but quite untried in independent command, was allocated 13,000 men for this task. Of these only one battalion, the marines of the guard, was a regular French unit.

Both these expeditions failed. Moncey arrived at the walls of the city of Valencia but, having no siege train, could make no impression on the armed townspeople manning the walls. He fell back to the Tagus, having lost a fifth of his strength. Dupont found less opposition. He crossed the Sierra Morena with scarcely a shot fired and sacked Cordova on 7 June. Then, hearing that Gen. Xavier Castaños was organizing an army in Audalusia to oppose him, he fell back to the southern foothills of the sierra and called for reinforcements. Six thousand men were sent up to him from Madrid, reaching him on 27 June, but the emperor was not greatly concerned about him. "If General Dupont suffers a setback, it will not matter much. All that will happen is that he will have to come back over the Sierra."[9]

Even the main road to Madrid from France was not clear, and the king's progress to the capital was delayed while Bessières, reinforced from Madrid up to 14,000 men, routed 22,000 men of the Spanish northern armies at Medina de Río Seco on 14 July. It was not until 20 July that Joseph reached Madrid. Every day he was becoming more despondent about the situation. "The opposition is everywhere. Even where it is not in arms, it is lurking underground. The task before us is immense and to complete it will require immense means." Before he had been ten days in Spain, his letters took on a constant, nagging refrain: "Fifty thousand more men and fifty million francs are needed within the next three months."[10] He was not comforted by the emperor's reiterated but useless advice, "Keep fit. Have courage and gaiety and never doubt that we shall be completely successful."[11]

Another source of discontent to Joseph was the emperor's arrangements, or lack of them, for the overall command of the armies in Spain. "I beg Your Majesty to give his orders on this point clearly and precisely. . . . Whoever commands the French army is master of such parts of Spain as we occupy. At my age, and in my position, I must have councillors but not masters in Spain."[12] Napoleon was quick to reassure him. "You are in command. I have told you so. I will put it in orders. . . . You might have saved yourself the trouble of writing a page of nonsense."[13] This reassurance was worthless. Although the king received the nominal command and was allowed to have his friend Marshal Jourdan as chief of staff,* the emperor had no intention of allowing Joseph, Jourdan, or anyone else to exercise supreme command in Spain. He embarked on a system of sending orders directly to subordinates, which, as much as anything else, ensured that the French must ultimately be defeated in Spain.

Meanwhile, such central military direction as was exercised in Madrid was in the hands of General Anne Jean Marie René Savary, one of the emperor's aides-de-camp, who had been sent hurriedly as Napoleon's representative when Murat's health broke down. He had only moderate pretensions to the higher military skills, and his temporary appointment had gone badly to his head. He insisted on being treated with all the ceremony and deference that had been given to Murat as grand duke of Berg and the emperor's brother-in-law. He gave great offense to the Spaniards by being accommodated in the apartments belonging to Prince Ferdinand at the royal palace. Worse than this was, in the words of Count La Forest, the new French ambassador, the way he was always speaking of "plunder, arson and massacre. I am ashamed to repeat

* Jourdan did not join Joseph until 21 August.

the excesses of this kind which escape him at every moment and which are always claimed to be 'in the name of the Emperor'. These indiscretions are overheard by young officers, by servants, by Spaniards. Reports of them are passed round the town and cause fear without helping to subdue the people. Many of the troops take them as authority for acts of useless violence."[14]

It was into an atmosphere poisoned by this kind of French arrogance that Joseph made his formal entrance into Madrid on 20 July. "All the ancient customs were observed. The King entered the town at the Alcala gate and thus crossed the town at its widest extent to reach the palace. At the foot of the grand staircase he was received by the Great Officers of the Household who conducted him to his apartments. Deputations of the Councils of State came to pay him homage and, on 23rd July, he was proclaimed king in the squares and principal streets with all the ceremonies observed at the accession of a Spanish king."[15] His own view of popular reaction was not overly pessimistic. "I was not received as well here as I was in Naples, but it was less bad than might have been expected from this very ill-disposed town."[16] His friend Count Miot, now superintendent of the household, took a more gloomy view. "It was a melancholy scene. The silence and disdainful looks of the inhabitants were all the more significant since so much solemnity was given to the ceremonial."[17]

For a few days the king was engrossed in getting his government on its feet, but he could not overlook the mounting tide of hostility against him. He was reminded of the early days of the French Revolution nearly thirty years earlier. "All classes of the populace are leaving the city; it is just as it was in '89. Even the servants of the Duke del Parque have left him, writing to him that they have gone to join the Spanish army. . . . We must have fifty thousand more men and fifty million francs within three months. Respectable people here have no more use for me than the rabble has. You are making a mistake, Sire; your glory will not avail you in Spain. I shall fail and the limits of your power will be exposed, since no one doubts your affection for me. Things can only be set right with fifty thousand more men and fifty million francs. . . . Only this can save the country and the army."[18]

On 26 July, only six days after Joseph's entry into Madrid, the situation took a serious turn for the worse. Although he had been pleased that morning at the reactions of a deputation of the clergy whom he had addressed for an hour, it was noticeable that, with one exception, the duke of Frias, all the grandees who had been with him at Bayonne ceased attending the palace. Aversion to the French in the streets suddenly became open and apparent. The town was alive with rumors from beyond the Sierra Morena. That night the king wrote that it was being reported that "Dupont had been in action against 60,000 men; certainly the enemy corps was very strong. I say once more to Your Majesty: 50,000 men and 50,-000,000 francs in the next three months will not be too much. The nation is unanimously against us. Dupont has 60,000 men against him; Bessières is still facing 40,000. Your Majesty remembers '89 and '93; there is no less determination here; no less anger."[19]

Next day the situation deteriorated, the reports were more menacing. The king wrote to France, "Most disturbing rumours are going round about Dupont's corps. I do not believe them all but it is to be feared that some will prove to be true. If they are the rebel army will be able to march on Madrid with 100,000 men. I can lead 20,000 men from here to reinforce what is left of Dupont's corps."[20]

On the evening of 28 July, an aide-de-camp from Dupont galloped into the city with bad news which surpassed even the rumors. There could be no further question of leading 20,000 men to reinforce Dupont. On 18 July, two days before Joseph had entered Madrid, Dupont, with 17,635 unwounded men, had surrendered to General Castaños at Bailén, twenty miles north of Jaén.

Suddenly Madrid was no longer surrounded by a protecting screen of French troops. It had become a part of the front line, open to attack by overwhelming numbers of Spanish troops. A few weeks as a colonel of infantry at Boulogne had not equipped King Joseph for this kind of situation. He turned for counsel to the only source available, General Savary. Savary's advice was unequivocable: they must retreat and at once. " 'You would recommend our evacuating Madrid?' asked the King. 'Unquestionably, Sire' I replied, 'The enemy now possesses a great moral superiority over us. He knows that the troops which we can bring against him do not, in numbers, exceed the forces of General Dupont. He will take special care, therefore, not to miss another opportunity of acquiring any fresh laurels which may seem to be within his grasp.' 'But what will the Emperor say?' 'No doubt the Emperor will scold, but words are not blows. What would he not say if we were to re-enact the piece played at Bailén?' "[21]

The king gave orders immediately for Madrid to be evacuated. The hospitals and depots started evacuation on the twenty-ninth. Joseph himself, with the fighting troops, nearly 20,000 of them, marched out on 1 August aiming for Burgos. "Marshal Bessières will join me there with his 17,000 men. I shall decide, according to events, whether to raise the siege of Saragossa in order to reinforce myself with the troops there. . . . I need not tell Your Majesty that it now needs 100,000 more men to conquer Spain. I must repeat that we have not a single Spanish supporter. The whole Spanish nation is exasperated and determined to fight."[22] Only five members of his Spanish cabinet retreated with Joseph. The rest pleaded urgent private business and he never saw them again. Almost to a man, the grandees and generals who had been at Bayonne moved south to take up commands in the Spanish armies.

Burgos was not far enough for Joseph to feel himself safe. His troops, never of high quality, were demoralized by the news of Bailén and by their hurried retreat. Encouraged by Bessières and Moncey, the king ordered the army back behind the Ebro, setting up his headquarters at Vitoria. To swell his numbers he ordered the siege of Saragossa to be

raised and called in the troops taking part in it to strengthen
his southern flank. Nevertheless, his thoughts were running
on the offensive. He yearned to be able to help Junot in distant
Lisbon.[23] Repeatedly he complained that he had heard nothing
from Portugal since he entered Spain. For his peace of mind
it was as well that this was so.

In London the government, with the unanimous support
of the press, had decided to send troops to help the Spanish
patriot cause and had earmarked a commander for them. Two
questions remained to be solved: where to send the troops
and how many could be sent.

Information about events in Spain was scanty. Since the
two countries had been at war for years, there was no diplomatic contact, and there were few, if any, intelligence agents
working in the Peninsula. The French seizure of Spanish central government had the effect of reinforcing regionalism as
each Spanish province looked to its own defenses and, separately, sought British aid. Information coming to London
from provincial delegates was partial and parochial, while
British gleanings from French sources reflected only the emperor's propaganda and wishful thinking. Moreover, French
information about what was occurring outside the territory
occupied by their troops was no more adequate than that
which the British were able to acquire for themselves. Perhaps
it was even less so, since Britain had a source of news in the
person of Sir Hew Dalrymple, lieutenant governor of Gibraltar who, since 1806, had been in confidential correspondence with Xavier Castaños, who, as captain general of
Andalusia, was in charge of the siege of Gibraltar. The utility
of this source was limited, however, since Castaños had no
reliable information of events outside Andalusia and since
it took at least a month for London to receive an answer to
any query raised with Gibraltar.

In London the general impression was that the Spaniards
were confident and that they would not need British troops
to complete the expulsion of the French, although they would

welcome supplies of arms and money. Nor were the Spaniards disposed to allow the British the occupation of one of their deep-water ports on the Atlantic coast, affecting to believe that the object of British assistance was the acquisition of a second Gibraltar. Since a deep-water, all-weather port was essential to continuing operations, the British resolved to base their operations in Portugal, on the incomparable harbor of Lisbon.

Since the largest part of Britain's disposable force was in Baltic waters trying to devise a satisfactory way of cooperating with Britain's only ally, the mad king of Sweden, all that could immediately be sent to Portugal were a contingent of 10,000 men from Ireland and another of 5,000 from Gibraltar. Included in the force were 14½ battalions of excellent infantry, 381 light dragoons, although only 180 had horses, and 5½ field batteries with sufficient draft horses to draw 2 batteries. No transport was provided, the government giving the specious excuse that "the great delay and expense that would attend the embarking and sending from hence all those means which would be requisite to render the army completely moveable immediately on landing, has determined His Majesty to trust in great measure to the resources of the country [i.e, Portugal] for their supplies."[24]

The intention of this small and ill-equipped expedition was, however, clearly laid down: "The entire and absolute evacuation of the Peninsula by the troops of France, being, after what has lately passed, the only security for Spanish independence, and the only basis upon which the Spanish nation should be prevailed upon to treat or lay down their arms."[25]

While the British cabinet may justly be indicted for sending to Portugal a force that was too small and was deficient in almost everything required to enable a field force to operate, it is to their credit that they put in command of it as great a soldier as has ever served in the British army. It was unfortunate that they contrived to make his appointment look as if it were a piece of political jobbery.

More than any other individual, Sir Arthur Wellesley was

responsible for the overthrow of the Bonaparte kingdom in Spain. In 1808 he was thirty-nine years old, the same age as Napoleon. In the Flanders campaign of 1793–1795 he had been, as a battalion commander, one of the few British soldiers to distinguish themselves. In India, as a major general, he had not only, at Assaye and Argaum, won two of the greatest victories in the history of British India but had acquired a mastery of logistics which was to prove invaluable in the Peninsula. At the time of his appointment to the Portuguese expedition, he was almost the junior lieutenant general on the army list, apart from being a member of Parliament and a member of the government as chief secretary for Ireland, the effective head, under the lord lieutenant of that island.

The very fact that the ministry had nominated one of its own number to command the expedition was suspect from the start. Other factors tended to heighten the impression of jobbery. Many senior generals felt entitled to the post. Nor was Wellesley's manner conciliatory. Although a man of great charm, kindness, and justice, he was exceedingly shy with strangers and openly contemptuous of the corruption and incompetence which he constantly encountered in his political life in London and Dublin. Worst of all was the public image of his family. The Wellesleys tended to stick together, and all were, to some extent, tainted with the widely felt dislike for the eldest brother, Lord Wellesley, who, for all his brilliant talents and official probity, was arrogant, extravagant, supercilious, and loose-living. William Cobbett was not alone when he publicly declared in November 1808, "Sir Arthur Wellesley, it is well known, is allied to a family, the most powerful and eminent in the country—a family raised to predominance, not by any great or shining talents, nor by actions of a sort that can be deemed even meritorious. . . . They control twelve votes in the House of Commons."[26] Little of this diatribe was true, but it was widely believed.

Sir Arthur landed the two portions of his force at Figueira da Foz, the port of Coimbra, by 8 August. While the landing was in progress, news arrived that not only was the army to be substantially reinforced but that Wellesley was to be superseded by no fewer than six senior officers. The details of this squalid maneuver are at present irrelevant, but the fact remained that in the immediate future the chief command was to be taken by Sir Hew Dalrymple, the lieutenant governor of Gibraltar and a senior lieutenant general of frighteningly little field experience, with Sir Harry Burrard, an amiable nonentity, as his second in command.

Fortunately for Wellesley and for the allied cause in the Peninsula, the French commander, General Junot, precipitated matters. Gathering together all the troops he thought could be spared from garrison duties—some 13,000 men, about half his total force—he attacked Wellesley on 21 August at Vimeiro, where the British had gone to cover the landing of 4,000 reinforcements. Wellesley, who was still in command, repulsed him, but before he could follow up his victory, Sir Harry Burrard landed from the sea and forbade pursuit. Nothing would move him from this resolve and Wellesley, in disgust, "turned his horse's head, and, with a cold contemptuous bitterness, said aloud to his aide-de-camp, 'You may think about dinner, for there is nothing more for soldiers to do this day.' "[27]

Next day, while the British still remained stationary on the battlefield, Sir Hew Dalrymple arrived. Soon afterwards an emissary from General Junot arrived in the British lines with a proposal that the French army should be permitted to evacuate Portugal and be repatriated to France in British ships. Dalrymple seized the chance eagerly, a cease-fire was agreed, and on the last day of the month the agreement known as the Convention of Cintra was concluded. The last French soldier left the Tagus estuary on 18 September.*

Junot's skill as a negotiator was in inverse proportion to the

* This date refers to the departure of Junot's field army and the garrison of Lisbon and its surroundings. The outlying garrisons of Elvas and Almeida had a long march to the coast and followed later.

military skill he had shown as a soldier at Vimeiro. The terms he won from the victorious British do him the greatest credit. The French embarked as a fighting force, complete with their artillery, their horses, and, despite the terms of the treaty, with the vast majority of the loot they had acquired during their occupation of Portugal. Elements of Junot's army were in action in Spain again before the end of the year. Even Napoleon, never disposed to accept excuses from a defeated subordinate, forgave him for losing Portugal. "You won the Convention," he said, "not by your dispositions, but by your courage. The English are right to complain that their general signed it."[28]

The British were certainly complaining. News of Vimeiro had been published in the English papers on 5 September. The victory was blown up out of all proportion to its real significance. Even the opposition papers praised the "talents of the army's gallant and most distinguished leader, Sir Arthur Wellesley," forgetful for a time that he was one of the hated ministers. The shock was, therefore, all the greater when the actual terms of the convention were published on 17 September. Led by George III, public opinion demanded an enquiry and more than hinted at severe punishment for those responsible. Dalrymple, Burrard, and Wellesley were all summoned before a Court of Enquiry.

The court met in mid-November and reported just before Christmas. As might have been expected, it came to no conclusion, contenting itself with a handsome compliment to Wellesley and drawing attention to "the extraordinary circumstances under which two commanding generals arrived from the ocean and joined the army, (the one during and the other immediately after a battle, and those successively superceding each other, and both the original commander within the space of twenty-four hours)."[29] It was probably a fair verdict. Dalrymple, although he had behaved stupidly and given more to the French than he need have done, had been placed in an intolerable position by the circumstances of his appointment, for which he could not be held responsible. Neither he nor Burrard was ever employed overseas again.

Moreover, there were positive gains. Thanks to Wellesley, Portugal was liberated. Thanks to the insistence of the Royal Navy, the Russian squadron in the Tagus came under British control until the end of the Anglo-Russian hostilities in 1812. Napoleon had, therefore, lost his original gains both in closing Portuguese ports to British trade and in adding the nine Russian battleships to his disposable fleet. The British had gained the vital all-weather port of Lisbon and, with it, the ability to intervene in the Peninsula.

The emperor was at Bordeaux on 3 August when the news of Bailén reached him. "Has there ever," he demanded of the minister of war, "been such a cowardly, stupid, idiotic business as this?"[30] "Dupont has tarnished our colours: What baseness! What stupidity!" he declared to Joseph.[31] He had no one but himself to blame. It was he who sent an untried commander with 13,000 inferior troops on an advance of four hundred miles, out of touch with all other French troops, against an enemy of unknown strength.[31] It was he who asserted that Dupont had "nothing to fear,"[33] and complained that he had unnecessarily reinforced.[34] It was he who encouraged Dupont to rashness by showering his corps with decorations for minor actions at Cordova and Jaén.[35] It is true that Dupont turned out to be a hesitant and inept commander, but it was Napoleon who chose him and gave him orders impossible to execute. Moreover, Dupont was unlucky. His opponent, Xavier Castaños, had 30,000 men and split them into three groups for a complicated encircling movement, thus exposing himself to defeat in detail. By a combination of ill chance and indecisiveness, Dupont found himself in the Spanish trap, which was not even where Castaños intended it to be. He attempted to break out, losing 2,000 men in doing so. Several of his foreign battalions disintegrated. He had no option but to surrender. Unforgivably, he agreed to surrender not only the 8,000 unwounded men still with him but another division of 9,000 men who were outside the Spanish trap and could have escaped with ease. It was the greatest Spanish victory of the whole war and was the success Spain needed to cement its determination to resist.

Bailén made Napoleon realize that the Spanish business must be taken seriously, that French rule in Spain could not be established by the mere signing of papers. Spain would have to be conquered, and for conquest, troops would be needed—veteran troops under experienced commanders. These could only come from the *Grande Armée*, still quartered in Germany. But Austria was again making bellicose moves, and before Germany could be stripped of troops, arrangements must be made to hold Austria in check. The first move, therefore, must be a meeting with the czar, which was held at Erfurt (27 September–14 October). Napoleon described Czar Alexander's attitude as "defiant and unspeakably obstinate,"[36] but the czar was persuaded to undertake to overawe Austria while the French armies were deployed in Spain. This left Napoleon free to deploy the main body of his veterans westward. At the end of August he wrote to Joseph, "10,000 of the Grande Armée have reached Mainz. By January you will have 100,000 of them, and there will not be a rebel village in the whole of Spain. . . . Do not worry."[37]

For a time Napoleon considered entrusting the chief command to one of the marshals. "I have ordered Ney to Spain," he wrote on 3 August. "He is brave, thrusting and full of spirit. He might be the man to command the army."[38] Joseph's evacuation of Madrid and retreat to the Ebro disillusioned the emperor about his subordinates. "The army," he complained, "seems to be commanded not by experienced generals but by postal inspectors."[39] He determined to take the command himself as soon as he was certain of the czar's support. On 13 October he wrote from Erfurt, "I have finished my business with the Emperor of Russia and I leave for Paris tomorrow. I shall be at Bayonne in less than a month. . . . The war can be finished by a single properly concerted operation, and I must be there to arrange it."[40]

52

If Napoleon and Joseph reacted violently to the news of Bailén, it might have been expected that the Spaniards would exert themselves to exploit their success. Instead they gave themselves over to rejoicing and political wranglings. The last of Joseph's troops left Madrid on 1 August. It was not until the thirteenth that Spanish troops entered the city. Even then, they were not men of Castaños's victorious corps, but a stray division of 8,000 men from Valencia. It was not for another ten days that Castaños managed to reach the capital. The interregnum had been wasted since the junta of Seville, the self-styled "Supreme Junta of Spain and the Indies," had insisted on his return to Seville to take part in victory celebrations. These being completed, the general had the greatest difficulty in obtaining permission to advance. It was not until he discovered that it was the junta's intention to use his troops against the neighboring junta of Granada that Castaños let it be known that he was marching against the French, with the junta's consent or without. Then they reluctantly let him cross the Sierra Morena with a single division.

There was, at this stage, a danger that Spain would disintegrate into its component provinces. In each of them, provincial juntas clung to their petty dignities and disputed for the command of their military forces with their captains general. Meanwhile the French were able to conduct their ignominious retreat unmolested. At the beginning of September only the Spanish Army of Aragon, the defenders of Saragossa, supported by a Valencian division, were in touch with the enemy. The Army of Estremadura was still beseiging the French garrison of the Portuguese fortress of Elvas, which had already surrendered to the English.

Left to themselves, the provincial juntas would have done nothing effective until the French were ready to destroy them at their leisure. The vast, inarticulate mass of the Spanish people of all classes, however, demanded action. Reluctantly, the juntas agreed to the meeting of a Supreme Central Junta, consisting of representatives from all the provinces, at Aranjuez on 25 September. The proposal that this body should meet in Madrid was vetoed by the powerful and thoroughly unsatisfactory junta of Seville. Before this assembly met, the military leaders convened a council of war of their own, which met at Madrid on 5 September. This was a difficult gathering, as many of the generals, each of them at the head of the troops of his own province, were on terms of the bitterest enmity with their colleagues from other provinces. In consequence, they failed to appoint a supreme commander and merely roughed out a scheme for holding Joseph's army on its front on the Ebro while substantial bodies turned both the flanks. Apart from the fact that the plan was far from perfectly coordinated, it suffered from the defect that Joseph's army, even without the reinforcements pouring in from Germany, outnumbered its assailants by a comfortable margin and much of the force detailed to hold the French in front was, and continued to be, hanging about in Andalusia and on the frontiers of Portugal.

At least the council of generals succeeded in drawing up some kind of plan. The Supreme Junta General achieved nothing. It devoted its time to debating proposals for a future constitution for Spain. At the best of times it would have been an unsatisfactory body for directing the war effort. There were fewer soldiers amongst its members than there were priests,* but it might have been expected that, under the circumstances, it would have devoted some of its activities to defeating the French. In fact, apart from announcing that it intended to raise an army of 500,000 foot and 50,000 cavalry, an impossible target, it devoted its energies to voting to its members an annual salary of 120,000 reals and proclaiming that, as a corporate body, it should be referred to as "Its Majesty the Supreme Junta." As the British minister commented, "Their attention is absorbed in petty pursuits and in wrangling, which impedes even the simplest arrangements."[41] The possibility of appointing an overall commander of the Spanish army was not even raised. The Supreme Junta did,

---

* There were six priests—two archbishops, one prior, and three canons—and only five soldiers, of whom three were militia officers.

however, interfere with the generals' arrangements to the extent of detaching 15,000 men from the armies of Aragon and Andalusia, where they were badly needed, to assist the Catalonian armies, which at that time could well have managed without them.

Having retreated to the Ebro and raised the siege of Saragossa, King Joseph began to recover his spirits. To the emperor, who was constantly urging him to gaiety, he replied, "I have never been so composed, so healthy or so tireless. If I envy Your Majesty the superior genius which gives him his mastery over victory, I have that in common with everyone. I need envy no one their composure and coolness."[42] He still hankered for the supreme command over the French armies in Spain. "I beg Your Majesty to give his orders only to me, and I will have them executed. Your should authorize me to deprive of their commands those who send back advice when they are given orders. You must believe that no one in the army is less indeterminate than I am. You should make me absolute master of my operations. With obedient and determined commanders under me, . . . the enemy would be defeated everywhere."[43] He resented the suggestion that anyone but himself had commanded the army since he had been in Spain. "I can hardly conceive how you can know so little of my character, to be able to think that it was the generals and not myself, who make the important decisions. . . . It was I, alone, who decided to evacuate Madrid."[44] When his brother complained that "your advisers are too cautious. Attack the enemy and do not let yourself be attacked,"[45] Joseph replied with a plan of the greatest audacity. He would leave garrisons in Pamplona, San Sebastián, Pancorbo, and Burgos and drive on Madrid with the rest of the army, 50,000 men, dropping his communications and waiting in the capital until the *Grande Armée* arrived to relieve him.[46] "If this plan is foolish, it is my own folly; no one suggested it to me. I alone should take the blame for it, just as I would have taken the honour if Your Majesty had judged it a wise plan."[47]

Napoleon, however, insisted that the army should hold its position until the reinforcements arrived. He "would have preferred that Madrid had not been evacuated and that the army had not retired as far as it has but, as things stand, it would not be right for the army to advance until it is certain of being able to hold its gains."[48] Joseph, therefore, remained on the Ebro with bridgeheads on the south bank from Miranda de Ebro to Lodosa. On his right, a corps faced north to hold off the Spanish army of General Blake, which occupied Bilbao at the end of September, was driven out, but returned in mid-October. On the French left, Moncey's corps faced south, with its headquarters at Tafalla, to guard against a Spanish thrust against Pamplona from the direction of Saragossa.

At the end of October, Joseph, who had established his headquarters at Vitoria, was in no great danger from the Spanish attempts to encircle him. Every time a Spanish force pressed forward it was driven back with ease. The king and Jourdan, his chief of staff, were, however, perturbed by the multifarious Spanish moves. They were unable to divine their enemy's plan. For this they cannot be blamed. The Spaniards had started with less of a plan than a vague idea. This was modified constantly by individual generals without reference to their colleagues. A number of advances were attempted but none of them were pressed. Nevertheless, the intentions of every Spanish commander were offensive. None of them considered the possibility that the French might be reinforced. All their plans were laid on the assumption that King Joseph's army, 75,000 strong, would sit quietly and wait until they were ready to demolish it. They did not discover that by the first days of November two fresh corps, 50,000 men, had been added to the French strength. They never dreamed that a few days later Napoleon himself would fall upon them at the head of a quarter of a million men.

Chapter 3

PERSONAL APPEARANCE

I am here with the soldiers who conquered at Austerlitz, at Jena, at Eylau.

NAPOLEON, AT VITORIA,
5 NOVEMBER 1808

ON 25 October the emperor made a farewell address to the Legislative Council in Paris. "I leave in a few days to put myself at the head of my army and, with the help of God, I will crown the King of Spain in Madrid and plant my eagles on the ramparts of Lisbon. . . . It is a special blessing that Providence, which has always watched over our armies, should have so blinded the English that they have left the protection of the sea and, at long last, exposed their troops on the continent."[1]

Five days later he left Paris riding flat out (*"à franc etrier"*). He reached Bayonne at 3 A.M. on 3 November. Two days later he joined Joseph at Vitoria. At his orders, riding horses had been stationed along the route at intervals of not more than five leagues. Outside Vitoria a small country house had

57

been requisitioned for his quarters and he insisted on arriving there after dark. "I want to reach Vitoria *incognito* and without arousing suspicion. That is why I am arriving at night; no one will know until the next day. At nine o'clock the next morning you should fire a salute of sixty guns."[2]

Next day, after the salute had announced his presence, he attended a reception given by Joseph and asked that all the Spaniards should be presented to him. According to Count Miot,

> he spoke to them all with great animation, expressing himself alternately in French and Italian, according as he thought he could best make himself understood. But the greater part of what he said was unintelligible to them . . . and he was excessively annoyed. He complained bitterly of the conduct of the Spanish people, who had stupidly failed to see the advantages of the changes he had introduced into their political system. He was especially bitter against the monks. "It is they," he complained, "who mislead and deceive you. I am as good a Catholic as they, and I am not against your religion. Your priests are paid by the English, and those English, who say they come to help you, want your trade and your colonies. That is their real design. What have you gained by listening to their advice? I am here, with the soldiers who conquered at Austerlitz, at Jena, and at Eylau. Who can withstand *them*? Certainly not your wretched Spanish troops, who do not know how to fight. . . . I shall conquer Spain in two months and thereby gain all the rights of a conqueror. Treaties, constitutions and all other agreements cease to exist. I am no longer bound by them."[3]

As he spoke, the Imperial Guard, twelve thousand strong, marched into Vitoria. The *Grande Armée* was complete and ready to move.

At this time there were 314,612 men on the muster rolls

of the French "Army of Spain." Of these, however, two corps and a few detached units were still on the north side of the Pyrenees, reducing the available strength by some 45,000. Garrison duty within Spain and on the French frontier accounted for a further 43,000 and there were 36,000 stationed in Catalonia, where they were out of touch with the main army. 38,000 were in hospitals or listed as missing. There remained 152,00 men under Napoleon's hand to defeat the Spanish armies, to march to Madrid and beyond.

Opposed to them were 87,000 Spanish troops, the majority of them untrained peasants, hastily recruited. Since the Spanish plan, such as it was, called for encircling movements around the flanks of Joseph's position on the Ebro, the two larger portions of the Spanish army were separated by ninety miles and the main strength of the French army. On the Spanish left, General Blake, with 30,000 men from the armies of Galicia and the Asturias, held Bilbao and Orduña. On the French left, the armies of Andalusia and Aragon under Generals Castaños and Palafox were in the area of Calahorra and Tudela and amounted to 45,000 men. In the wide gap between these two forces there were only 12,000 men of the Army of Estremadura. This exiguous force was stationed around Burgos and was the only body of troops between Napoleon and Madrid. Thus the French striking force had a numerical superiority of five to three, a qualitative superiority considerably greater, the advantage of a central position, and the unrivaled generalship of the emperor.

Napoleon's plan was to drive straight for Madrid through Burgos, while opposing defensive flanks to the main Spanish forces. While he advanced, he planned to dispatch corps to right and left to encircle the Spaniards who had intended to encircle him. It was a plan that might have succeeded against Austrians or Prussians, but the emperor had yet to learn that the routing of a Spanish army meant not victory but only the purchase of a few weeks' breathing space. The Spanish forces were never militarily efficient, but even their most ramshackle armies had astonishing powers of re-creating themselves, however often they were demolished in the field. The sheer persistence of the Spanish armies made them the most dangerous opponents that Napoleon had yet met.

To make matters worse, the plan was not executed as he would have wished. Before the emperor had left Paris, Blake had pressed his army forward from Bilbao, driving in the French units in front of Durango, which he occupied. The corps commander opposed to him, Marshal Pierre François Joseph Lefebvre, duke of Danzig, was a gallant veteran who before the Revolution had been a sergeant in the Royal Guards. He was under the strictest orders to remain on the defensive but he had never won a victory as an independent commander. The sight of Blake's army isolated and exposed at Durango was too much for him. He led his 20,000 men forward and attacked Blake's main body at Zornoza on 29 October. Blake was defeated but managed to extract his army without crippling loss. It was now Lefebvre who was isolated, and Marshal Claude Victor's corps was sent up to assist him. Victor inflicted a much more serious defeat on Blake at Espinosa (10–11 November) but Blake was still able to extricate the wreck of his army and retire to Reinosa, southwest of Santander. The Spaniards had suffered enormously. Although Blake had been reinforced during the campaign by 9,000 men from Denmark whom the British navy had landed at Santander (see Chapter 1, p. 27), he had only 12,000 men with the colors at Reinosa. His battle casualties had not exceeded 4,000. The remaining 16,000 had dispersed to their homes. Nevertheless, the Spanish northern army was still in being and was to prove a menace to the French for years to come. On that flank, Napoleon's encircling move had failed.

The Spaniards on the French right also escaped without total disaster. Marshal Jean Lannes, with the corps of Moncey and Ney, brought Castaños and Palafox to battle at Tudela on 23 December and routed them, taking twenty-six guns and causing 6,000 casualties. The Spaniards, however, escaped from the net, and although the two armies separated, Palafox with the Aragonese falling back on Saragossa while Castaños with the Andalusians made for Madrid, both survived and had many more battles to fight.

In the center things went better. On 10 November Marshal Nicolas Jean de Dieu Soult's corps, leading the advance, found the Army of Estremadura drawn up in front of Burgos. Its commander Count Belvedere, disdaining all assistance from fortifications or natural features, had deployed 10,000 of his men in open country behind a large wood near the village of Gamonal. The French veterans broke through without pausing and the cavalry pursued the Spanish without respite until nightfall. By that time, the leading fugitives had covered thirty miles. Belvedere, who had no military virtue except courage, lost a third of his men and all his guns. Soult's corps, which lost only fifteen killed and thirty wounded, spent the next thirty-six hours sacking Burgos.

Napoleon reached Burgos on 11 November and waited there for eleven days while the main body of his column came forward. During this time, Soult's infantry and a brigade of cavalry was marched northward to intercept Blake at Reinosa. They failed to catch him, although they captured one of his convoys comprising his sick, his baggage, and the greater part of his artillery. The Spaniard, realizing that he was beset by the corps of Lefebvre, Victor, and Soult, more than 70,000 men, fled to the north, crossed the Cantabrian Mountains, and reached the sea. There he collected some desperately needed supplies from the Royal Navy and resigned his command. He was a brave, pertinacious commander of Irish extraction, with considerable self-esteem and minimal talent. Unfortunately, he was to be reemployed on several occasions. In each case his efforts were ill conceived.

His successor in the north, the marquis de la Romaña, was a more competent commander. He led the army to the southwest, crossing the Cantabrian Mountains, and at the end of November stationed it around the town of León. Having collected some recruits, the army's numbers crept up to 15,500. The emperor considered La Romaña's army as a spent force. He ordered the corps of Lefebvre and Victor to join him for the main drive on Madrid. Soult was ordered to detach one division to hold Santander and the district around it, and, with the rest of his corps, took up a position on the river Carrión, north of Valladolid, facing west. He had 18,000 men and his orders were to be responsible for everything between the river Douro and the Bay of Biscay —a distance of a hundred and twenty miles as the crow flies.

Despite Lefebvre's headstrong insubordination, Napoleon could be satisfied with his progress in the first three weeks of November. The Spanish armies threatening his flanks had been driven back and vastly reduced in strength. His own numbers were increased as the corps of Junot and Mortier crossed the Pyrenees and closed up to his rear. No substantial force stood between his advanced guard and Madrid. The English did not appear to be intervening, and he believed that the Spanish people would be subdued if their armies were defeated. The supply situation was satisfactory. Before he left France, it had been reported to him that food would be difficult to obtain. He could now describe these reports as " 'alarmist.' . . . —I have never seen an army better fed."[4] When he had been two days in Burgos he felt sufficiently confident to write to his minister in Paris in charge of *l'administration de la guerre* ordering him to "recall the reserve of oxen and make proposals for cutting down the expense for provisions sent forward from Bayonne. I have no need of provisions; there is plenty of everything. . . . I have never seen an army so well off or one so lavishly supplied."[5] The illusion that Spain was a country well able to support large armies persisted in the emperor's mind throughout the Peninsular War. When, in the years to follow, his generals protested that they could not concentrate their armies as it was impossible to feed them, Napoleon could not understand the difficulty and attributed such failures to carry out his orders to indolence or indifference on the part of the generals.

At Burgos the imperial mood was optimistic. The main problems seemed to be those of administering the conquered provinces. Napoleon wrote to his brother that it was important that "*Corregidors* and senior magistrates, whom the people are accustomed to obey, should be appointed and that they should go to the liberated provinces making proclamations, pardoning rebels who surrender with their arms and, above all, sending instructions to *alcades* and parish priests, so that the people will know that your government is in control."[6] A prolongation of the "rebellion" seemed unlikely. He believed that "many Biscayans, who have rebelled, are coming in and asking for nothing better than to hand in their arms, if they are promised a pardon with no questions asked."[6] Once more the emperor was deceiving himself. In no part of Spain was the guerrilla to be more effective and more implacable than in Biscay.

The advance from Burgos to Madrid started on 22 November. The spearhead of the advance consisted of Victor's corps, the Imperial Guard, and a mass of cavalry, 45,000 men in all. The Spaniards could only raise 21,000 men, many of them the dispirited fugitives from Gamonal, to defend the capital. The French met opposition only at the Pass of Somosierra, where the main road crosses the Sierra de Guadarrama. If the junta could have stationed more and better troops than the 12,000 they allocated to its defense, the Somosierra should have been impregnable. On 30 November, Victor attempted to force it in conventional style by sending infantry to gain the crest beyond the flanks of the defenders. This took time and Napoleon was impatient. He ordered his escort squadron of Polish light horse to attack the position frontally. Incredibly, this tiny force achieved its objective. One hundred and fifty horsemen charged more than a mile and a half uphill. They stormed four successive batteries, some of them protected with earthworks, and reached the crest. They lost fifty-seven killed or seriously injuried. Twenty-four were more lightly wounded, and many more lost their horses during the ascent. Only a handful remained when they reached their objective, but they were enough to induce the Spaniards, already threatened by Victor's infantry, to take to their heels.

Madrid was garrisoned by 3,000 men. The city set up a

Junta of Defense under the presidency of the duke of Infantado, who a few months before had ridden into Madrid in King Joseph's entourage. The junta produced much rhetoric and the citizens raised a few earthworks in unlikely places. When some of the cartridges issued by the junta were found to be filled with sand, a marquis was beaten to death by the mob and a number of large houses looted. There was, in fact, no effective resistance, and Napoleon had hopes of entering the city on 2 December, the anniversary of Austerlitz. The advanced guard was staved off, however, until 6 A.M. on 4 December when the gates were opened to the French by agreement. Infantado, with his handful of regular troops, retreated behind the Tagus, accompanied by many citizens of Madrid who felt that their conduct during Joseph's absence would have exposed them to French reprisals. The first French occupation of Madrid had lasted three months. The second was to continue for three and a half years.

Napoleon spent eighteen days in the capital. He spent the time planning the final blow which would complete the subjugation of the whole Peninsula. Meanwhile Victor's corps marched to the Tagus, holding the bridges at Toledo and Aranjuez and thus securing the southern approaches to the capital. Lefebvre moved westward and occupied Talavera de la Reina. A large body of cavalry accompanied him and pushed on further to Oropesa and towards Almaraz. To secure the communication with France and with Soult's corps on the Carrión, small forces occupied the passes over the Guadarrama and a cavalry brigade was stationed at Ávila. On the east an infantry division, that of Dessolles, was placed at Guadalajara to secure the road to Saragossa, where Lannes, with the 34,000 men of the corps of Moncey and Mortier, was renewing the interrupted siege. From that direction, where according to every probability ample forces were available to compel a speedy surrender, Ney's corps was recalled towards Madrid to take its place in the striking force which was to make the conclusive advance. Once again the emperor's genius had triumphed. It seemed that all that remained was a mopping up operation which would culminate in triumphal entries into the capitals of Portugal and Andalusia.

The four weeks which Napoleon spent in advancing from Vitoria to Madrid were a time of humiliation for King Joseph. He had dreamed of holding an independent, responsible command in Spain. As the *Grande Armée* surged forward, the king, accompanied by his own guard, found himself relegated to the rear with the baggage. He had to be content with the occasional scraps of information that his brother or the chief of staff found time to throw to him. When the emperor was approaching Burgos, the king made a desperate appeal to him. "An irresistible sentiment tells me that I should not be at the rear of the army. Spain, France and my own feelings all demand that I should be at the post of honour, at the point of danger."[7] The emperor made no reply. It was not until the end of the month that Joseph was called forward. He was advised to bring his guard with him, as there were "brigands" in the Somosierra.

When he reached Chamartín, where imperial headquarters were established just outside Madrid, the king found that there was nothing for him to do. Napoleon, in his proclamation to the Spanish people (7 December 1908), asserted that "to the rights resigned to me by the prince of the former dynasty, you have forced me to add those of a conqueror."[8] He undoubtedly acted as if he had recalled all the rights which he had made over to his brother. Claiming that "I have broken the shackles which have weighed upon the nation. I have given you a liberal constitution; I have replaced an absolute monarchy with one that is moderate and constitutional,"[9] the emperor gave a brisk display of absolutism. Without a word to the "constitutional" monarch, he abolished all feudal rights and dues and gave orders to suppress the Inquisition and to close one-third of the monasteries.* The proceeds from both

---

* Two weeks after publishing the decree suppressing the monasteries, the emperor told Berthier, the chief of staff, to consult Joseph on which monasteries were to be put down. He stipulated only that one near the palace must be amongst those to go. (NC, xviii, 14,590)

the Inquisition and the monasteries were to be divided between the royal coffers and the pay chest of the French army. All these reforms may have been, theoretically, desirable, but at least the last two, which affected the established religion, were directly contrary to the emperor's word pledged to King Ferdinand and to King Joseph's oath on taking up the crown.

It was not only in major matters that the emperor insisted on ignoring his brother. Even in matters of municipal detail he gave his orders directly. On 17 December he wrote to Louis Alexandre Berthier, "Give an order tomorrow that all horses and corpses lying in the streets of the town and within a league outside it should be buried. A squad of townsmen should be told to do it."[10] Joseph, in consequence, refused to reenter Madrid, retiring to the old palace of the Spanish kings at El Pardo, outside the city limits. From there, having heard from one of his ministers of Napoleon's reforms, he wrote, "I am shamed in the eyes of my supposed subjects. I beg Your Majesty to accept my renunciation of all the rights you have given me to the throne of Spain. I will always prefer honor and honesty to power so dearly bought."[11] He received no answer except a brisk command to "send agents into the provinces, into Cuenca, La Mancha, Castille, Segovia and to Talavera de la Reina, which we have just occupied, to secure the coffers of the villages and towns. There is plenty of money everywhere."[12] Meekly Joseph obeyed, only stipulating that the agents should have military escorts.

The king was wise to absent himself during his brother's stay in Madrid. For all Napoleon's elaborate show of clemency towards the people of the city, the atmosphere had seriously deteriorated since Joseph's first entrance in July. An intelligent Frenchman recorded that

> hatred could be seen in the gloomy and severe faces
> of those few of the inhabitants who showed them-
> selves outside their houses. No one came to meet the
> French, no one sought to propitiate their new mas-

66

ters. Even curiosity seemed to have lost its power.
For several days no women appeared on the streets;
none could even be seen at the windows. The theatres
were reopened, on French orders, but no Spaniard
attended the performances. . . . [The Emperor] held
a review of his army on the plain between Madrid
and Chamartín. It had been announced two days be-
forehand in the hope that some of the inhabitants
might be attracted to it by curiosity, and that they
would pay some kind of homage. In this the Emperor
was disappointed: the review took place, but there
was not a single Spaniard present.[13]

The sullenness of the people of Madrid was not of great
concern to the emperor. On military grounds, however, he was
concerned at the misbehavior of his troops in the countryside.
"Pillage," he wrote on 12 December, "ruins everything, even
the army which commits it. The peasants run away from us;
this is doubly a misfortune in that it makes them into irreconcilable enemies who revenge themselves on isolated soldiers
and drives them to swell the ranks of those who plan to destroy
us. It deprives us of all information and of all means of
supply."[14]

Apart from such minor irritations, the emperor's attention
was focused on his next move. The Imperial Guard and Ney's
corps were concentrated at Madrid to strike the blow. He
made no secret of his intention. "I shall hunt the English army
out of the Peninsula," he announced to the civic dignitaries of
Madrid. "Nothing can for long withstand the fulfillment of
my wishes."[15] He was determined to march on Lisbon by way
of Talavera, Badajoz, and Elvas. A forward base was being
prepared at Talavera, where vast stores of bread were being
baked. The Spanish armies he regarded as a spent force. There
could be nothing to disturb his plans to the north of Madrid.
All that could be needed was Soult's corps, 16,000 infantry and
2,000 cavalry, which was stationed north of Valladolid and

Palencia. So confident was the emperor that his northern flank was safe that he authorized Soult to push forward a further fifty miles westward to León.[16]

Determined as he was to drive the English into the sea, Napoleon was regrettably uncertain as to their whereabouts. It seemed probable that they were near the Portuguese border to the south and southwest of Madrid. On 11 December, eight dragoons of the King's German Legion* had been captured near Talavera de la Reina, and he felt that "if the Hanoverians have been taken, the English will not be far away."[17] It was possible, he thought, that more of the English advanced posts might be found when his own forward cavalry reached Plasencia. For public consumption, however, he announced, in the Bulletin of 12 December, that "the English are in full flight towards Lisbon, and if they do not make good speed the French army may reach that capital before them." It is possible that this is what the emperor really thought the English were doing. It is certain that this was what he hoped they would do.

In fact, at the very moment that Napoleon was announcing their flight to the sea, a British army of 30,000 rank and file was marching from the area of Salamanca and Astorga against the French communications at Valladolid. On 12 December, British Hussars swept up a French cavalry patrol at Rueda, scarcely twenty miles from that city. It was largely fortuitous that the British were there. If the intentions of the British government had been carried out, the army would have been near Madrid before Napoleon crossed the Ebro. It is unlikely that it would have survived the Spanish debacle.

The public outcry over the Convention of Cintra had driven the government into giving the command to Sir John Moore. He was instructed that it was intended to employ 20,000 out of the 30,000 men in Portugal in northern Spain, "to co-operate with the Spanish armies in the expulsion of the French from

---

* The King's German Legion was a force of all arms on the strength of the British army. It was formed from the remains of King George's Hanoverian army.

that kingdom."[18] To make Moore's force up to what was intended to be a minimum of 30,000 infantry and 5,000 cavalry, a further corps of 12,000 men—three regiments of cavalry and thirteen battalions—was shipped out from Falmouth with orders to land at Coruña.

This order reached Moore at Lisbon on 6 October, and acting with remarkable swiftness, he managed to get his first battalions marching towards Spain within five days. The task was a difficult one. Owing to the inactivity of Dalrymple, no preparations had been made. "At this instant," Moore wrote three days after receiving his orders, "the army is without equipment of any kind, either for the carriage of the light baggage of the regiments, artillery stores, commissariat stores, or other appendages of the army; and not a magazine is formed in any of the routes by which we are to march."[19] Almost more disastrous, since British armies had a long tradition, forced upon them by a parsimonious treasury, of improvising their transport and supply, was a total lack of topographical intelligence. No one could give an accurate account of the roads from Lisbon to Almeida on the Portuguese-Spanish border. Opinion generally was that it was impracticable to take artillery this way. Unfortunately Moore accepted this estimate, and while the bulk of his infantry, accompanied by a single battery, moved on the line of Lisbon, Coimbra, Almeida, and Salamanca, the bulk of his artillery, seven batteries, marched eastward to Talavera, El Escurial, and Arévalo. To escort them, Moore had to detach his only two cavalry regiments and two brigades of infantry under Sir John Hope. This was a serious, if perhaps an excusable, error. Not only did it delay the concentration of the army at Salamanca, since the additional distance to be marched, 130 miles, meant that Hope's column could not reach Salamanca for a week or ten days after the main column, but, as things turned out, their deep incursion into Spain exposed them to a danger which had not been foreseen when they set out. So rapid was the French advance that at one stage the French and British outposts were only fifteen miles apart, and in the last days of November, Hope had to urge his men and draft oxen to forced marches, including one of forty-seven miles in thirty-six hours, to pass across the front of the French advance. It was not until 3 December that Hope and the precious guns reached Alba de Tormes, in close touch with the main column at Salamanca.*

There was delay also in the arrival of Sir David Baird's corps at Coruña. The infantry of this force arrived off Coruña on 13 October only to find that the junta of Galicia refused them permission to land. After some argument, they consented to send an officer to the Supreme Junta at Aranjuez to seek their agreement. This consultation with the central government was successful but took thirteen days, and it was not until 26 October that the troops began to land. Even then the Galician junta made difficulties about supplying the troops on their march inland, insisting that they should move in small bodies, well spaced. In consequence, Baird, with his 9,000 infantry, only reached Astorga on 22 November. There he heard of the Spanish defeats at Gamonal and Espinosa and was told that the French were in strength to the north of Valladolid. Realizing that there was no Spanish force between his small force of infantry and a large French army and having no cavalry with which to gather information, he resolved to halt at Astorga and seek further orders from Moore. His three regiments of cavalry, which by some incompetence were dispatched from England three weeks behind the infantry, reached Coruña only in the second week of November and did not join him until the last week of the month.

By 23 November, Moore had the whole of the main column assembled at Salamanca. He was besieged by the Spaniards with appeals, usually garnished with a wealth of tendentious information, to move forward and help them. Seeing, rightly, that to plunge forward with 15,000 infantry, no cavalry, and

---

* One useful by-product of this wasteful circular tour was that it helped to mislead Napoleon. Although in total ignorance of the size and purpose of Hope's column, the emperor judged from the eight German stragglers captured at Talavera on 11 December that the British army was in the direction of Badajoz.

only six light guns* would lead to their destruction without any compensating gains, Sir John resolutely refused to advance until his army was concentrated.

In this resolve he was confirmed by the news of Castaños's defeat at Tudela, of which a British account reached him on 28 November, the messenger, Charles Vaughan, having ridden 476 miles in six days. For the moment, Moore's spirit failed him. He determined to retreat on Portugal and sent orders for Hope to make for Ciudad Rodrigo and for Baird to retreat on Coruña. To Hope he wrote, "I have determined to give the thing up, and to retire. It was my wish to have run great risks to fulfil what I conceive to be the wishes of the people of England, and to give every aid to the Spanish cause. But they have shown themselves equal to do so little for themselves, that it would only be sacrificing this army, without doing any good to Spain, to oppose it to such numbers as must now be brought against us. A junction with Baird is out of the question, and with you, perhaps, problematical: as there must be troops at Burgos, which must now push on to intercept us. . . . This is a cruel determination for me to make, . . . but I hope you will think the circumstances such as demand it. I shall take measures for falling back; but I shall stay at this place [Salamanca] as long as possible."[20]

On purely military grounds Moore was undoubtedly right to decide to fall back. His position was dangerous in the extreme, and if, as he had to expect, the French knew where his scattered corps were, it would be suicidal to stay in Spain. Nevertheless, it went against the grain for Moore to abandon his allies, the more so since his army, and even his staff, were openly criticizing his timidity. Faced with further pleas from the Supreme Junta and an overly optimistic forecast from the British minister at Aranjuez, who claimed that Madrid would defend itself stoutly, Moore changed his mind. On 5 December he issued orders to suspend the retreat, on which so far only

* The roads had been found practicable for the bringing forward of this battery, despite all the forebodings in Lisbon.

Baird had acted, and set an advance on foot to Valladolid. "I shall," he reported to London, "threaten the French communications, and create a diversion, if the Spaniards can avail themselves of it. . . . The French force in Spain may fairly be set down at 80,000 men, besides what is in Catalonia."[21] Five days later, on 10 December, he heard that Madrid had fallen on the third. Needless to say, the news was brought by a British officer. Moore had already learned that the Spaniards never bothered to send him accounts of actual events, only of visionary schemes based on imaginary facts.

The main body started to move forward from Salamanca on 11 December and two days later, by which time Baird's cavalry stood on the line of Tordesillas and Medina del Campo, Moore had the first piece of good fortune since leaving Lisbon. Peasants murdered one of Napoleon's aides-de-camp near Segovia and took from his body a dispatch he was carrying to Soult. This dispatch, dated 10 December, was quickly forwarded to Moore's headquarters at Alaejos. From it he learned, for the first time, something of the real state of affairs in Spain. He learned that the advance of the French had reached Talavera and was expected soon to reach Badajoz; that Bessières's corps was chasing the wreck of Castaños's corps into Valencia; that Mortier's corps was moving on Saragossa and that Junot's was on the move from Vitoria to Burgos; that the emperor, and presumably his guard, was at Madrid; and that, in the emperor's view, Moore was in full march towards Lisbon. Most significantly, he learned that Soult, with two divisions of infantry and four regiments of horse, was isolated on the river Carrión. Simultaneously, he heard that the marquis de la Romaña, with 20,000 men, was at León and would be glad to cooperate with him. Moore did not hesitate. On 15 December, the main body turned northward and on the twentieth joined the infantry of Baird's corps at Mayorga on the river Cea. The commander in chief had decided to fall upon Soult's corps before it could be reinforced. The next day Lord Paget, at the head of the Hussar brigade, rode in on two of Soult's cavalry regiments at Sahagún and almost destroyed them.

Moore's determination to strike at the French communications, to destroy Soult's corps in isolation, has been much criticized. It was certainly a very rash undertaking and could have led to the most dire results. Moore had no illusions about what he was doing. "I mean to proceed bridle in hand; for if the bubble bursts . . . we shall have to run for it." What the critics overlooked was the result he achieved. Napoleon gave up his plan for the complete subjugation of the Peninsula. Nothing more was heard of the advance from Talavera to Badajoz and Lisbon. From the moment that the emperor heard that the English were on the move in León, everything was subordinated to their destruction. Writing from Coruña three days before his death, Moore said to the secretary of state for war, "Your Lordship knows that had I followed my own opinion as a military man, I should have retired with the army from Salamanca. The Spaniards were then beaten; there was no Spanish force to which we could unite, and . . . I was satisfied that no efforts would be made to aid us, or favor the cause in which they were engaged. I was sensible, however, that the apathy and indifference of the Spaniards would never have been believed; that, had the British been withdrawn, the loss of the cause would have been imputed to their retreat; and it was necessary to risk this army to convince the people of England, as well as the rest of Europe, that the Spaniards had neither the power, nor the inclination, to make any efforts for themselves. It was for this reason that I marched to Sahagún. As a diversion it succeeded: I brought the whole disposable force of the French against this army."[22]

At his headquarters outside Madrid, the emperor had all but given up hope of being able to destroy the small British army which he knew to be in the Peninsula. He would dearly have loved to have done so—it would teach the ministry in London not to meddle with his plans—but he was convinced that long before he could come to grips with them, they would have taken to their ships. So certain was he that they would be beyond his reach that he made no great effort to discover

where Sir John Moore was. On 10 December he believed that
they had earlier advanced into Spain as far as El Escurial only
to hurry back to Lisbon. Two days later, when he heard that
stragglers had been taken near Talavera and that, on the same
day, British cavalry with a few infantry had been seen near
Ávila, he saw no reason to change his opinion. In the next few
days he received reports that 14,000 English were at Astorga
and that others were moving towards Salamanca. By 17
December, he had made up his mind that such British troops
as were still in Spain would be found at Plasencia, 130 miles
west of Madrid.[23] He expected them to choose this position,
since from it they could either threaten Madrid or operate
against the flank of his advance to Lisbon by way of Badajoz.
All his efforts were by this time devoted to mounting this
advance, for which he had available at and between Madrid
and Talavera 42,000 men of the Imperial Guard and the corps
of Ney and Lefebvre.

Nothing occurred to make him change his plans until 19
December, when a message arrived from General Houssaye at
El Escurial reporting that according to the statement of three
German deserters,* 14,000 English troops had been at Sala-
manca on 14 December and did not appear to contemplate
retreat. On the same afternoon, an aide-de-camp from Soult
rode on to the grounds while the emperor was reviewing
Ney's corps. He carried a message from the marshal dated 16
December, which told that French cavalry had been attacked
at Rueda on the twelfth of the month by three squadrons of
British horse backed by at least 5,000 infantry. Rueda, on the
main road from Madrid to Coruña, is only twenty miles from
Valladolid, and this information changed the whole situation.
Far from being to the west and northwest of Madrid, the English were now shown to be almost due north of the city. In
front of them was a single isolated corps of 18,000 men which
formed the only covering force for the main road to France.
Soult was in serious danger, but the English had offered

* From the Fifth battalion, Sixtieth (Royal American) Regiment.

Napoleon a chance to destroy them. He broke off the review immediately.

At 4 P.M., Ney's corps was warned to be ready to move at dawn and Dessolles's division, which was guarding the Madrid-Saragossa road, was recalled to Madrid. Shortly afterwards the three deserters were brought in and interrogated. From their statements there could be no doubt that Moore was advancing, and, since they had left the army before the captured dispatch had reached headquarters, they belived that the British goal was Valladolid. With this information in hand, messages were sent to Lefebvre at Talavera, suspending the advance westward, and to Soult, advising him that a force was to be sent against the rear of the British. To make assurance doubly sure, reconnaissances were ordered to Plasencia and Salamanca to ensure that the English were not there.

The next morning Ney's corps, two divisions of infantry and a brigade of cavalry, about 20,000 men, was ordered to march for the Guadarrama Pass and the cavalry of the guard followed them. To increase the striking force available, Lapisse's division from Victor's corps was called up to Madrid from Toledo. At this time the emperor still had doubts about the position of the British main body; he still suspected that only their cavalry was to the northeast of Salamanca, but that afternoon a number of reports arrived which went far to convince him. The most significant was one from General Tilly, stationed at Segovia, which asserted that the British had driven his outposts from Tuleda de Douro, a few miles to the east of Valladolid. It so happened that there was no basis for this story, but it persuaded Napoleon that the time for decisive action had come. That evening the divisions of Dessolles and Lapisse were ordered to follow Ney, as were two further brigades of cavalry. Junot, the head of whose corps had reached Vitoria, was ordered to move to Valladolid to fill the gap between Soult's left and Ney's right. At noon on 22 December, the emperor left Madrid at the head of the infantry of the guard. Before leaving he scribbled a note to the Empress

Josephine. "I am just setting out to deal with the English, who seem to have received their reinforcements and to want to try their luck [*faire les crânes*]. The weather is fine; my health is excellent; do not worry."[24]

Thus, even excluding parts of Junot's corps which were too far away to be able to play a part, Napoleon had set in motion more than 70,000 men to encircle a British army which he believed to be 36,000 strong. He planned to pin them between Soult's corps, strengthened by Junot's, on one side and his own force of Ney's four divisions and the guard on the other. In this way he hoped to conclude the Spanish war at a blow. If, as he believed, Moore had been at Valladolid, he might have been right. Certainly he believed that it could be done. He wrote to Joseph twenty-four hours after leaving Madrid, "Put in the Madrid papers that 20,000 English are surrounded and lost."[25] Drafting a statement on the previous day for the Paris papers he had been somewhat more cautious. "The English have at last shown signs of life. They seem to be abandoning Portugal and taking up another line of operations. They have marched towards Valladolid. The army has been on the move for three days and is maneuvering to get on their rear. Important events must soon occur. If the English do not move towards the sea and do not outmarch us, it will be difficult for them to escape and they will pay dearly for their temerity in venturing on to the continent."[26]

In private he admitted to being puzzled.

> The English maneuver is extraordinary. It is clear that they have evacuated Salamanca. They have probably sent their ships to Ferrol, fearing that their retreat to Lisbon would not be safe since we can move on the left bank of the Tagus from Talavera and close the mouth of that river to them. There is no anchorage at Peniche. They do not feel able to embark, with all their cavalry, except with a good harbour covered by a strong fortress. Everything leads us to suppose that they have abandoned Portu-

gal and switched their communications to Ferrol, which would give them certain advantages.

Before making this retreat they may hope to strike a blow at Marshal Soult and be delaying this attack until they are certain of a clear line of retreat to the north of the Douro. They may have reasoned: If the French march on Lisbon, we can embark at Oporto and still be on our line of communications through Ferrol. Alternately, they may expect further reinforcements. But whatever the English plan may be it will lead to operations which will have a great influence on the outcome of the whole business.[27]

While Napoleon was writing that letter, before setting out from Madrid on the twenty-first, Moore was ordering his army to rest for forty-eight hours. They were to march from Sahagún at dusk on the twenty-third so as to be able to strike at Soult at Carrión at first light on the following day. The advance never took place. On 23 December, one of Moore's aides-de-camp, Colonel Thomas Graham, wrote in his diary, "Frost in the morning. Tossed by a bullock in the convent yard. Orders to march at 8 P.M. in two columns on Carrión. In the afternoon a dispatch from La Romaña with the intelligence of the enemy marching [from Madrid] determined the General to abandon the attack of Soult's corps. . . . A retreat on Astorga . . . now becomes imperiously necessary so as to prevent the enemy from cutting in on the communications with Galicia. There is not a man in the whole army who will not feel mortified and disappointed at the counter orders just issued."[28]

Instead of advancing, the main body of the British army set off on the twenty-fourth for Astorga, marching in two columns. To cover their rear, Moore left his five cavalry regiments under Lord Paget and his reserve division, 7,000 infantry, under Sir Edward Paget, the cavalry commander's younger brother. These two succeeded in presenting so firm a front to Soult that the French made no move forward until the twenty-sixth, thus gaining for Moore a start of forty-eight hours. It was as well that they did so. The main body spent Christmas marching through thick clay in heavy rain. Already they were disgruntled at not being permitted to attack the French, and their discipline was beginning to crack in the discomforts of the retreat. A private soldier wrote, "Our sufferings were so great that many of the men lost their natural activity and spirits, and became savage in their dispositions. The idea of running away, without even firing a shot, from the enemy we had beaten at Vimeiro was too galling to their feelings."[29] There was some pillaging and a certain amount of wilful damage, but at this time morale was not seriously affected. The men believed that Moore intended to stand and fight at Astorga and, with that assurance, they were little more than morose and bitter. The general, they grumbled, "intended to march them to death first and fight afterwards."[30]

By the evening of 27 December, the whole of the infantry, including the reserve, was across the Esla at Benavente and Valencia de Don Juan. On that day, however, Soult's cavalry began to press in on Lord Paget's Hussars. At first they had only the four regiments of Soult's corps opposed to them, but next day these were joined by two regiments from Ney's corps and three from the Imperial Guard. Soon there were thirteen French regiments opposing five British. Brilliantly handled by Lord Paget, the Hussars never failed. Repeatedly they turned about and drove the French back. Their greatest success was at Benavente on 29 December when Paget fell upon the cavalry of the guard which had succeeded in forcing the Esla. They were driven back in disorder having suffered 150 casualties, amongst whom was their commander, General Lefebvre-Desnoettes. So effectively did Paget do his work that Napoleon reckoned his cavalry strength at 4,000 or 5,000 against the real figure of 2,500 at the start of the fighting. The emperor gave his own cavalry strength opposed to them at 8,000.[31]

It was fortunate that the cavalry and Sir Edward Paget's rear guard did their task well. Behind them, the British position was far from happy. The three divisions of the main body reached Astorga on 30 December. There Moore found not the great stores of food that he was expecting but only enough to feed the army for two days. To make matters worse, there swarmed into the town from the east the bulk of Castaños's army. On that day its rear guard was being destroyed by Soult at Mansilla, little more than thirty miles to the east. Castaños's men numbered about 10,000, but far from being a reinforcement, they were a menace. They were starved and half naked. Most were unarmed and typhus was rampant amongst them. "They appeared," noted a Scottish doctor, "like spectres issuing from a hospital rather than an army."[32] Moore abandoned his plan to defend the passes around Astorga and determined to march for the sea. On New Year's Eve the head of his columns started to march out of Astorga and to climb the snow-covered passes over the Montes de León. "We pushed on all day without halting," recalled a rifleman of the Ninety-Fifth.

> Night came down upon us, without our having tasted food or halted, and all night long we continued this dreadful march. Men began to look into each others' faces and ask the question, "Are we never to be halted again?", and many of the weaker sort were now seen to stagger, make a few desperate efforts, and then fall to rise no more. Thus we staggered on for four days and nights before we could discover the reason for this continued forced march. The discovery was made in our company by a good-tempered fellow named Patrick McLauchlan. He inquired of an officer marching directly in his front, the destination intended. I heard him say, "By Jasus, Musther Hills, where the divil is this you're taking us to", "To England, McLauchlan," returned the officer with a melancholy smile, "If we can get there."[33]

Meanwhile, Napoleon was galloping ahead of his infantry. He reached the Douro at Tordesillas on Christmas Day and still hoped to cut off Moore from the sea. As late as 3 A.M. on the twenty-seventh he was still under the impression that Moore was facing Soult across the Carrión River, and that his own force was on the English right.[34] He now realized that Moore had shifted his base to Coruña, but he was confident of destroying them. "Put it in the newspapers and spread it about everywhere that 36,000 English are surrounded, that I am at Benavente, in their rear, and that Marshal Soult is in front of them. . . . Arrange some ceremonies to celebrate this victory."[35] In fact, the English were away to the northwest on the west bank of the Esla, and far from pursuing them on the direct road to Benavente, where he claimed already to be, the emperor moved on 28 December to Medina del Río Seco.

The last day of 1808 found the main bodies of the two French forces approaching Astorga. Soult, on the east, had taken the town of León, and Napoleon, coming up from the south, had his advanced infantry in La Bañeza. Only gross folly on Moore's part could now enable the French to entrap him. The emperor realized that the game was up. On New Year's Eve he ordered Dessolles's division to countermarch and return to Madrid. Two days later, when he reached Astorga, he turned over the pursuit to Soult, whose strength was made up with a division from Junot's corps, with Ney's corps in support. "The Guard is returning to Benavente; I myself am returning to the centre of my army. . . . Have salutes fired in celebration of all our successes against the English."[36]

All that was now possible was for Soult to chase the English back to their ships and to do them as much damage as possible before they embarked. Napoleon had no doubt that if they were hustled out of Spain in sufficiently humiliating circumstances and much reduced in numbers, they would never return to interfere in Spanish affairs. This was in line with all French experience of British interventions over the past fifteen years. He believed that Moore's army had already suffered severely. On 5 January he claimed "nearly 4,500 English prisoners,*"[37] and soon afterwards he estimated Moore's strength at 18,000. "It can be assumed that, with the men who are exhausted, sick, prisoners or hanged by the Spaniards, the English army is reduced by a third; and if, to this third are added the horses killed, which makes cavalrymen useless, I do not think that they can put in line more than 15,000 fit men and 1,500 cavalry. This is a long way from the 30,000 men with which they set out."[38]

Almost as important as the business of alarming the British cabinet by wrecking their army was the necessity for convincing the Spaniards that their British allies were a dangerous, self-seeking liability. The emperor, whose ruthlessness was notorious and whose army systematically looted throughout Europe, worked himself into a self-righteous ecstasy. "The English have not only broken the bridges, but have even blown the arches with mines, barbarous conduct and contrary to the usages of war, as it brings ruin to the countryside. They are a terror to the whole country. They seize everything— oxen, mattresses, bedding, and they have maltreated and beaten everyone. There could be no better way of pacifying Spain than to send an English army there."[39] "The town of Lugo has suffered much by being pillaged by the English, who have indulged in every conceivable excess. . . . Put this in your newspapers. See that the Madrid papers are sent to Valladolid, and that your Spanish ministers spread the word through their officials."[40]

Always with allowances for the normal imperial exaggeration, there was much truth in what Napoleon said about the excesses committed by the English, mostly against the Spaniards. Once it was known that they were not to fight at Astorga, the discipline of all but the best regiments broke down. When the cavalry rear guard passed through Villafranca, they found "the most dreadful scenes of riot and distress. Parties of drunken soldiers were committing all kinds

* The total number of prisoners who were taken by the French during the whole of Moore's campaign was, on French figures, 2,189.

of enormities; several houses were in flames; and a quantity of military stores, for which there was no means of conveyance, were burning in the piazza. The gutters were running with rum, a number of puncheons having been staved in the streets, and a promiscuous rabble were drinking and filling bottles and canteens from the stream."[41] In Bembibre, the cellars were found to be stocked with "a pernicious 'black strap' manufactured from the mountain vine which grew in the neighbourhood. The soldiers not waiting to broach the barrels in the usual way, stove them in, . . . so that, in a little time, they were wallowing in the liquor. They literally floated in lakes of wine. The men once tasting the intoxicating drink were maddened by its influence and became reckless and unmanageable. Some hours passed off in a brutal state of revelry and riot."[42]

So bad was the state of the army that Moore, the most humane general of his day, was forced to take stern measures. On 6 January, at Lugo, he issued a general order to the army:

> Generals and Commanding Officers of corps must be as sensible as the Commander of the Forces of the complete disorganization of the army.
>
> The advanced guard of the French is already close to us, and it is to be presumed that the main body is not far distant; and action may, therefore, be hourly expected. If the Generals and Commanding Officers of Regiments (feeling for the honor of their country and of the British arms) wish to give the army a fair chance of success, they will exert themselves to restore order and discipline in the regiments, brigades and divisions which they command.
>
> The Commander of the Forces is tired of giving orders, which are never attended to: he therefore appeals to the honor and feelings of the army he commands, and if these are not sufficient to induce them to do their duty, he must despair of succeeding by any other means. He was forced to order one soldier

to be shot at Villafranca, and he will order all others to be executed who are guilty of similar enormities: but he considers that there would be no occasion to proceed to such extremities if the officers did their duty; as it is chiefly from their negligence, and from the want of proper regulations in the regiments, that crimes and irregularities are committed, in quarters and upon the march.

Two things may be said in defense of the troops. Although there were many bad characters in the army who behaved disgracefully, the majority of the thousands of stragglers were men who asked nothing better than the physical strength to keep up with their regiments. One group of men, worn out by the mountain snows, by the shortage of food, and by staggering along on bare feet, was attacked by French cavalry. Sergeant Newman, of the Forty-Third Light Infantry, formed the stragglers into a "rallying square" and the French were repeatedly driven off with loss. The little group trudged on and, eventually, regained the rear guard of the army. Sergeant Newman was rewarded with a commission and a cash grant of fifty pounds from the Patriotic Fund. It was also true that whenever there was a chance that the army would be called upon to fight, the men instantly rejoined the ranks and behaved admirably. This was most noticeable at Lugo, where Moore took up a strong position and waited for Soult to attack him. Soult, whose troops had suffered from the conditions as much as the English had, declined to be drawn, and after waiting from 6 January until the early morning of the ninth, Moore continued his retreat to the sea.

By midnight on 12 January, the whole British army was in or near Coruña, only to find that their fleet of transports had not arrived. Fortunately, Soult could not immediately bring up his force. Only two divisions were up and they were both thinned by stragglers. When the fleet arrived on the fourteenth there was, therefore, time to embark the cavalry, all the artillery except nine light guns, and 3,000 sick. The remainder,

15,000 infantry,* took up a position on the low hills outside the town to wait for Soult.

On 16 January, Soult had three of his four infantry divisions, eight regiments of cavalry, and twenty guns in position to attack. Nevertheless, he did not stir throughout the morning, and about three o'clock Moore, assuming that he was again refusing battle, gave orders for the infantry to start embarking. "Now," he remarked, "if there is no bungling, I hope we shall get away in a few hours."[43] Ten minutes later the French started to advance.

A naval officer who had recently landed was struck by "the profound almost melancholy silence which prevailed amongst so many thousands of men. . . . the weary soldiers looked in such a miserable plight, that it seemed as if the enemy would have little more to do than to gallop across the valley to catch them all napping." He was even more astonished, therefore, when the French army, under a heavy cannonade, started to advance. "At the first discharge from the French battery the whole of the British troops, from one end of the line to the other, started on to their feet, snatched up their arms and formed themselves with as much regularity and apparent coolness as if they had been exercising in Hyde Park. I could scarcely believe my eyes when I saw these men spring from the ground as if touched by a magic wand, all full of life and vigor, though but one minute before they had been stretched out listless in the sun. I have already noticed the silence which reigned over the field—now there was a loud hum and occasionally a shout and many a burst of laughter, in the midst of which sound a peculiar sharp click, click, of fixing bayonets fell distinctly on the ear."[44]

Soult attacked with almost equal numbers of infantry and a great superiority in artillery. He was decisively repulsed, and had it not been that Moore was mortally wounded just as the British gained the tactical initiative, the French might have suffered a very severe reverse. As it was, Sir John Hope,

---

* Two light brigades, about 3,500 strong, had been detached from the main army at Astorga and marched westward to embark at Vigo.

on whom the British command devolved, decided to concentrate his efforts on embarking the army and halted the advance. Soult, who claimed that his aim was only to drive in the outposts and force Moore to show his strength, could claim no more than that "our troops halted on the enemy ground; but the enemy held his position, which it had not been my intention to force on that day unless a favorable opportunity offered."[45] Even this modest claim to achievement was untrue. No British position, not even the smallest outpost, remained in French hands at the end of the day. Soult asserted that his loss had been one general officer killed and 250 soldiers wounded, "many of them slightly."[46] A more reasonable estimate of the French losses would be between 1,000 and 1,500 men. It was a high price to pay for making Moore show his strength.

Next day the British embarked and sailed for England almost unmolested. The battle had cost them less than 1,000 men, probably about 750, but the whole campaign in Spain caused the loss of about 6,000 men, of whom 2,189 remained as prisoners in French hands and 300 were drowned on the voyage home. The immediate reaction in England was that the whole campaign was a disaster—the kind of disaster to which the public was only too accustomed whenever British troops ventured on to the continent.

In fact, the Coruña campaign was a triumph for the allies. Having occupied Madrid, Napoleon planned to subdue Portugal and southern Spain by a single smashing blow. He had the force to carry it out and, had he not been diverted, it is at least probable that he would have succeeded. Moore's intervention meant that the striking force of the French army was diverted to the mountainous cul-de-sac of Galicia. By the time it extricated itself, the Spaniards, Portuguese, and British had time to reorganize their forces and consolidate their resolve to resist. Napoleon had taken over the government of Spain by shock tactics; Moore bought time for the shock to wear off.

The tactics of both Napoleon and Moore have been much criticized. The emperor made sweeping plans based on his own illusions. Moore indulged in a rash, if not foolhardy, raid on the French communications, which he knew to be militarily unsound. Both committed serious faults, but in war, success is the only criterion. Moore, convinced that "we have no business to be here," created the conditions in which the French in Spain could be defeated.

It was a campaign in which chance played an unusually large part. Neither side had an effective intelligence service and, consequently, maneuvered blindfold. Moore launched his raid from Salamanca in total ignorance of the presence of Soult's corps on the line of the Carrión. Outdated and inaccurate reports led Napoleon to assume that Moore would march on Valladolid. Therefore, he aimed his counterblow fifty miles too far south. Moreover, his carelessness in allowing his aides-de-camp to ride unescorted resulted in Berthier's letter of 10 December to Soult falling into Spanish hands. Seldom can money have been better spent than when Captain John Waters paid a peasant twenty dollars for this letter giving almost the whole of the French dispositions in Spain. Without the information it contained, Moore would have been at Valladolid when Napoleon's blow fell. His army would have been surrounded and destroyed. It is hard to believe that the British cabinet, after such a catastrophe, could have summoned up either the courage or the public support to venture again into the Peninsula.

Chapter 4

THE DREAM

OF VALLADOLID

The Spanish business is finished.

NAPOLEON TO JEROME NAPOLEON,

KING OF WESTPHALIA,

16 JANUARY 1809

ON 17 January 1809, General Thiebault, the newly appointed French governor of Burgos, was driving towards his new post when "my servant told me, 'I believe the Emperor is coming'; at once I opened the carriage door in order to dismount, when . . . Savary* went past me at a flat gallop, followed by the Emperor, beating the horse of his aide-de-camp, while he dug his spurs into his own: . . . more than a minute behind them dashed Duroc** and the Emperor's Mameluke orderly; as far behind again came one of the Guides, knocking himself up trying to get closer; then four more Guides, getting ahead as best they could."[1]

* Savary, lieutenant general, duke of Rovigo, aide-de-camp to the emperor, later minister of police.
** Duroc, marshal of the palace.

87

The emperor was on his way back to Paris. On New Year's Day he had ridden up to his forward troops at Astorga, arriving there only a few hours after the last of the English Hussars had quit the town. It is said that a courier came up with him as he neared Astorga with a dispatch that determined him to return immediately to Paris. The contents of the dispatch have never come to light. According to one version, it was news of Austrian preparations for war against France; another story holds that it was information about a conspiracy in Paris. Neither version is likely to be true. Certainly Austria was intending war while Napoleon's attention was held in Spain, but this would not have been news. On the day before, he had sent instructions to Paris for his armies on the eastern front to be ready to move against Austria by March[2] and it was his view that with 400,000 in his armies of the Rhine and Italy he had "more than enough troops" should Austria move.[3] It was, in any case, improbable that Austria would move before the spring. It was equally true that there was a conspiracy afoot in Paris—there usually was. This one centered around those veteran intriguers Talleyrand, former foreign minister, and Fouché, the minister of police. It was noteworthy in that one of the principal conspirators was Caroline Napoleon, the emperor's sister, but it was scarcely of immediate significance, since the object of the plot was to proclaim Caroline's husband Murat as emperor should Napoleon die while in Spain. Since the emperor was in rude health and in no particular danger, the affair was only of academic interest and little more than an irritant.

Napoleon's real reason seems to have been his realization that there was no longer a chance of destroying Moore's army. Further harm might be done to it by a hard-pressed pursuit, but there was no hope of a shattering victory which would add glory to the imperial name. The British, or at any rate the bulk of them, would escape to their ships. It was Napoleon's view that as soon as the British were out of the Peninsula, Spain would settle down peacefully.

In the first instance, Joseph was told no more than that

"the Guard is returning to Benavente; I myself, am returning to the centre of my army."[4] Two weeks later, confidential letters were sent to the king and to Marshals Soult, Ney, and Lannes announcing that the emperor was to leave Spain, although the army was to be told that he was going to superintend the siege of Saragossa.[5] When his departure could no longer be concealed, the troops were told that he would return in "twenty or twenty-five days" and the king was confidentially informed that "before the end of October, I shall come back."[6] The country house at Chamartín outside Madrid, where Napoleon had had his headquarters, was to be kept prepared for his occupation.[7]

Late on 7 January, imperial headquarters returned to Valladolid. They remained there for ten days. The time was spent in making the necessary arrangements for the future of Spain. Command of the army was given to King Joseph, although detailed orders for future operations were given directly to each corps commander. A delegation consisting of such dignitaries as could be dispatched from Madrid was admitted to the emperor's presence. He was graciously pleased to accede to their humble petition that Joseph be restored to the throne of Spain. Thereupon, instructions were sent out ordering that every town of more than 2,000 inhabitants should send to the king a delegation with a report that every inhabitant had subscribed to an oath of loyalty on the altar of the parish church. Bishops were to be members of these delegations.

There were a few minor irritations. Marshal Lefebvre, duke of Danzig, disobeyed three written orders from Joseph and turned up at Ávila when he should have been holding Talavera. Regretfully, Napoleon relieved him of the command of Fourth Corps since "he does not know how to read his orders; . . . it is a pity since he is a brave enough fellow in action."[8] The villagers of Pinilla, near Toro, ambushed and captured some guns of the Imperial Guard. The village was burned to the ground and the culprits, or at any rate some eligible males, were hanged. The towns of Toro and Zamora opposed the entrance of French troops. They were fined half a million and a million francs respectively, and some more *mauvais sujets* were hanged. "It seems to me," the emperor wrote to Joseph, "that your kingdom is settling down."[9]

To his younger brother Jerome he wrote unambiguously that "the Spanish business is finished."[10] To the French ministers in the German states word was passed that "the affairs of Spain are no longer worthy of the Emperor's attention."[11]

While it is never safe to take anything that Napoleon said at its face value, the evidence strongly suggests that he seriously believed that the Spanish campaign was over and that all that remained was a mopping-up operation. It is hard to believe that a soldier of his genius could have laid down the plan which Napoleon promulgated from Valladolid unless he was utterly convinced that opposition would be minimal.

On the west side of the Peninsula, Soult, with the strong Second Corps, 23,000 men,* was to march down to Portugal from the north, sweeping up Vigo and Ferrol on his way. According to Napoleon's time schedule, he should enter Oporto 1 February, barely two weeks after the Battle of Coruña, and Lisbon on the tenth. Although these dates were subsequently put back to the fifth and the sixteenth, the rate of marching through difficult country would have taxed fresh men with no enemy before them. Marshal Jourdan remarked that Napoleon "must have supposed that the roads were as freely passable as those from Paris to Lyons."[12] In Soult's rear, Marshal Ney with the Sixth Corps, 16,800 men, was to occupy Galicia as a firm base for Soult and, simultaneously, secure the submission of the Asturias, the long mountainous principality which runs eastward from Galicia between the spine of the Cantabrian Mountains and the Bay of Biscay.

When Soult reached Lisbon, he was to detach one or two divisions to the Spanish-Portuguese border, where they were to join the First Corps, 22,000 men under Marshal Victor,

---

* The strength, on paper, of Soult's corps on 15 January was over 44,000 men (having been reinforced from Junot's corps). Only 23,000 men were with the eagles, since one man in four was sick and 8,000 were detached on various duties.

which was then to march southward into Andalusia, occupying Seville, Cádiz, and Gibraltar. "This operation," wrote Napoleon to Joseph, "will finish the Spanish business. I leave the glory of it to you."[13]

During Soult's promenade through Portugal, Victor was to hold the line of the Tagus around Talavera until he heard that Oporto was occupied. At that point, he was to advance to Mérida on the Guadiana River so as to be ready to receive the reinforcements from Soult at Badajoz, the great frontier fortress, which, it seems to have been assumed, would surrender at his approach. To form a link between Victor and Soult, a single division, 7,700 men under General Lapisse, was stationed at Salamanca. Soult's entry into Oporto was to be the signal for this small force to push its way to Abrantes in central Portugal. It was equipped with six light field guns and had before it the Spanish fortress of Ciudad Rodrigo and its Portuguese opposite number at Almeida.

Meanwhile, in eastern Spain, Marshal Lannes, with two corps, 40,000 men, was to renew the siege of Saragossa and, on its fall, to invade Valencia, joining hands with Victor's men in Murcia. Beyond them, General Gouvion Saint Cyr, with the 41,000 men of Seventh Corps, was to complete the task of subduing Catalonia and securing its communications with France.

Between the two wings, General Horace Sebastiani, who had succeeded Lefebvre in command of Fourth Corps, had 15,000 men to cover the southern approaches to Madrid on the line of the Tagus and, for the time being, to supplement the garrison of the capital, which consisted of a single division (8,500 men), and of Joseph's Spanish Guards.*

The remainder of the 194,000 French troops in Spain had the task of keeping open the lines of communication between Bayonne on the French side of the frontier and Madrid and

---

* Joseph's Spanish Guards, which amounted to around 2,000 infantry and 400 cavalry, formed part, and the only effective part, of the reformed Spanish army. They consisted entirely of Frenchmen, for the most part new conscripts to whom were added some stragglers from the division with which Dupont was defeated at Bailén.

Salamanca. It was a task which they were manifestly too few to perform effectively.

It is clear that Napoleon could not have given such orders to his troops unless he was convinced of three things: that the Spanish armies were irretrievably beaten, that the Spanish people would be content, at least passively, to accept the imposed monarchy, and that the British army had been handled so severely that the cabinet in London would not dare to interfere further in the affairs of the Peninsula.

For all these three assumptions, there was some evidence which could be convincing to one who was anxious to be convinced. Despite their solitary victory at Bailén, the Spanish armies had been defeated at Medina del Río Seco, at Zornoza, at Espinosa, at Gamonal, at Tudela, at the Somosierra, and at Mansilla. Madrid had been recaptured with ease. On scarcely any occasion had the Spanish troops, regular or hastily recruited, shown themselves worthy opponents of the *Grande Armée*. The Spanish generals, with the exception of Castaños and La Romaña, had shown themselves uniformly contemptible. Any other army which the emperor had ever encountered would have capitulated after the beating that the Spaniards had received. The emperor convinced himself that they would do the same. To his trusted ambassador in St. Petersburg he wrote, "You can be assured that there is no longer a Spanish army. If the whole country has not been subjugated, it is because there is so much mud and because there has not been time; everything, however, will be finished."[14]

Equally, he could not believe that the majority of Spaniards, all save the *mauvais sujets*, were not grateful to him for dragging Spain into the nineteenth century. Probably the majority of Spaniards considered Charles IV and Godoy to be personally worthless, and, in Napoleon's view, all he had done was to dismiss their wretched government and replace it by that of his enlightened and liberal-minded brother. There were, indeed, signs that the kingdom was settling down. "The nation," he asserted, "has changed in the past two months; it is weary of all this turmoil and is only anxious to end the whole business."[15] From Madrid, Joseph reported that public opinion was improving. In northwest Spain, too, the attitude of the people seemed acceptable. "The peoples of Galicia seem animated by the best spirit. The bishop and clergy of Lugo have remained in the town, which has been pillaged by the English, who have indulged in every kind of excess."[16] "The barns of the Galician villages are full of English soldiers hanged by the peasantry in revenge for their terrible looting."[17]

Above all, he counted on the traditional Spanish dislike of the British and did his best to heighten this feeling by representing Moore's retreat to Coruña as a cowardly move, a shameful desertion of the Spanish armies in their hour of need. He was, of course, perfectly correct in believing that the Spaniards detested the British. The British were heretics. They had been the champions of the Reformation against the entrenched Catholicism of Spain. They had constantly meddled with the Spanish colonies and with Spanish trade. They had broken the pride of Spanish sea power from the time of the Armada down to St. Vincent and Trafalgar. They were the long-standing ally and most constant support of an independent Portugal. Worst of all, they had seized and continued to hold Gibraltar as a permanent affront to Spanish national pride.

What the emperor failed to realize was that the Spaniards disliked all foreigners, the level of their dislike varying according to the amount Spain had to do with them. Thus, in normal times, the most hated foreigners were the Portuguese, who occupied what could be considered as an enclave of Spanish territory. Spanish relations with France had been cordial as long as the French stayed on their own side of the Pyrenees. Once French armies were marching about on the soil of Spain and interfering with Spanish institutions, the Spanish were as ready to call in the British to assist them against the French as, in 1807, they had welcomed French assistance against the Portuguese. They were even, with reservations, prepared to tolerate Portuguese help against the invaders.

His conviction that the British would abandon their meddling in Spanish affairs was borne of experience. Ever since the French Revolution, the British had been launching small and ill-coordinated expeditions against points on the European coastline only to withdraw them, in varying states of disorder, as soon as the French put serious pressure on them. British war policy had been constant only in its inconstancy and in its persistence. Moore's army had suffered grievously, but not so grievously as Napoleon believed. In writing to his own minister of war, even before the Battle of Coruña had been fought, he considered that "it can be reckoned that, counting the men who are exhausted, sick, prisoners or hanged by the Spaniards, the English army is reduced by one third."[18] Faced with such a loss, it seemed certain that the British cabinet, notoriously weak, would abandon their Peninsular adventure.

Fortified by these illusions, the emperor set out for France, leaving the unfortunate Joseph with titular command of the whole army of Spain.

King Joseph made his formal reentry into Madrid on 22 January. It was a ceremonial occasion. The emperor had enjoined him to "have as many troops as possible, in full dress." "Do it with the greatest possible pomp." "Take care that it is a solemn occasion and that you are well received by the townspeople."[19] The king reported that "the whole population was out, either lining my route or in the church of St. Isidore, where I went for a *Te Deum* to be celebrated. . . . The townspeople seem to hope much of me. I doubt that I shall, in the circumstances, be able to achieve all they hope for; there are so many things over which I have no control."[20] Count Miot took a less hopeful view of the proceedings.

> The procession was altogether a military affair. The King and his suite were on horseback. . . . The streets through which they passed were not deserted, occasional shouts were raised, and, if there was neither warmth nor enthusiasm, there was no positive antipathy. In general there were signs of curiosity,

some of resignation, some of hope, but there were few signs of dislike or contempt. The King dismounted at the Collegiate church of San Isidoro and made a simple, manly speech. One phrase stood out. "The unity of our Holy Religion, the Independence of the Monarchy, the integrity of Spanish territory and the liberty of its subjects. These are the conditions of the oath I took on receiving the Crown. That Crown shall not lose in dignity while I wear it."[21]

Joseph spoke these words in all sincerity. He really believed that he was the legitimate successor to the Bourbons. He believed that he held his throne by virtue of the agreements made at Bayonne between his brother and Kings Charles and Ferdinand. He looked to pick up his reign at the point where he had fled from Madrid after Bailén, as if the whole of Napoleon's campaign had never been. In his conscience he was king of Spain and Spain was France's loyal ally. He ignored his brother's words at Vitoria in November, "Treaties, constitutions and all agreements which have been reached by mutual consent, exist no longer. I am no longer bound by them."[*]

In their attitudes toward the status of Spain were the seeds of much misunderstanding and mutual frustration between the king and the emperor. To Napoleon, Spain was a conquered country, to be laid under tribute and ruled in the interests of France. To Joseph, Spain was, despite some resentment against the change of dynasty, an independent country and a good neighbor to France. "I am convinced," he wrote in March 1809, "that the best thing for both Spain and France will be their close union, their intimate alliance, but *not the enslavement of one to the other*. An enslaved Spain will be an enemy from the start. A free Spain will always be a friend, as her King will always be your brother."[22] He was, perhaps, correct. If the Spaniards could have been convinced that the French had other aims than robbery and enslavement, it is possible that in time they would have accepted Joseph's rule.

[*] See page 58.

It was the arrogance and brutality of the French occupation that made the Spaniards irreconcilable.

Certainly Joseph did all that was in his power to conciliate his subjects. His reformed government included a number of Spaniards of considerable talent, liberal ideas, and breadth of vision. Unfortunately, like so many men of "enlightened" ideas, few of them were competent administrators, and the finance minister, Francisco de Cabarrus, a man of undoubted ability, did much of his best work with a bottle. King and government together sketched out wide schemes for reform and for the improvement of Madrid. Reform, however, is an expensive business, and from the start there was no money. The peacetime economy of Spain had been at best precarious, even when supported by injections of gold and silver from the Indies. Under Joseph the collection of taxes had to be a military operation. The Spaniards had never been enthusiastic taxpayers, and the surreptitious murder of *afrancesado** tax collectors now became a more than usually attractive patriotic duty. Thus, the collectors had to be escorted by troops and this meant French troops. Joseph's experience was that very little money collected by French troops ever reached his treasury.

Nor was the area in which taxes could be raised of any great extent. Looked at in the most favorable light, the French occupation at the beginning of 1809 covered northern Spain down to the line of the Tagus, with the exception of the Asturias and any other tract sufficiently mountainous to shelter guerrillas. Within this area, the greater parts of Galicia, León, Old Castille, the Biscayan provinces, and Aragon were under the control of marshals who needed everything that could be wrung from the country for the support of their own armies and who, as later events showed, would not have handed any surplus to Joseph even had there been such a thing. Joseph's kingdom, in fact, consisted of the city of Madrid and the small wedge of country between the Sierra

---

* *Afrancesado*, "one working in the French interest." The word came to have the same connotation as "quisling" in the war of 1939–1945.

de Guadarrama and the river Tagus. This was not a notably productive region but it was an extremely expensive one to administer. Madrid contained a civil service large enough to administer not only the whole of Spain but the Spanish overseas empire. "There are," wrote Joseph soon after his entry, "10,000 families here, who are receiving no salaries; a year's salaries are outstanding."[23] "They expected to be paid immediately; they expected that all the evils inseparable in a state of war and revolution would end, as if by magic, on my arrival; thus they were prepared to welcome me."[24]

One of Napoleon's last injunctions to his brother was, "Above all, do not be short of money and, if necessary, raise forced loans on the towns, the corporations, the provinces. There is plenty of money in Spain—they found plenty for their rebellion."[25] He did, indeed, leave more than a million francs for the army's pay. To offset this largesse, the last contribution to come from France for many months, all stocks of quinine found in the north had been expropriated to France, as had wool worth three million francs which had been captured at Burgos. Although the emperor had issued stringent orders against looting by his troops, orders which were ignored by generals, officers, and soldiers alike, he sequestered and kept to his own use the estates of the ten principal Spanish families who did not submit to him and ordered Joseph to "seize all the paintings to be found in confiscated houses and suppressed monasteries and make me a present of fifty masterpieces needed by the *Musée de Paris*."[26]

The king sequestered many estates belonging to lesser "rebels" for the public treasury, but they were of little use. They could only be turned into cash if there were buyers, and even the few who could afford the prices held back, since they could not be convinced that, sooner or later, the properties would not have to be handed back to their rightful owners. The only saleable Spanish asset was the wool crop. If that could be sold to France, the Spanish crown could have some ready money. Repeatedly Joseph begged that the fleeces confiscated at Burgos should be released to him. Napoleon's only reply was to forbid the import of Spanish wool into France, choosing the time of shearing to promulgate this ban. In despair Joseph wrote, "This source of income is the last left to the country. It will fail if Your Majesty does not revoke this order, which is as unwise as it is unjust. There will be nothing left but to burn this year's crop."[27] The financial situation was, indeed, desperate. "I have not a *sou* to give anyone. I have been a king* for four years, and my personal bodyguard is still wearing the same uniform I gave him four years ago."[28]

The only success the government could claim was Joseph's personal success in pleasing the people of Madrid. His brother's advice had been draconian. "Arrest thirty of the worst characters and have them shot." "One must be strict with Spaniards. . . . When they are treated gently the rabble think themselves invulnerable; when a few are hanged the game becomes less attractive." "If a hundred incendiaries and brigands are not arrested, you will get nowhere. Of this hundred shoot or hang twelve or fifteen and send the rest to the galleys. I had no peace in France until I arrested two hundred such people whom I sent to the colonies. At that point the mood of Paris changed as if at the blast of a whistle."[29] This form of repression had no attractions for Joseph. From the day after his reentry, he set out to make himself known to his people and went about Madrid with only a small escort and, on occasions, quite alone. He particularly visited hospitals and saw to their well-being, supplying them with wine and bed linen from his own palaces, as well as from the confiscated mansions. According to Miot,

> He was tolerably well received. There were decided symptoms of a favourable change in the feelings of the inhabitants and in the aspect of the town. Aversion was diminishing, hope and confidence seemed about to revive, and, it must be said, that this change was due to the King personally. His natural disposi-

* Including his reign in Naples.

tion was of the greatest service to him; his amiability, his affability and, above all, the preference in all things for Spaniards over Frenchmen were pleasing to the nation. At the same time, the general weariness of strife, the misfortunes of war, the departure of the English, . . . the apparent hopelessness of resistance were concurrent causes which induced the people to lay down their arms and they began to accustom themselves to a yoke which was proving less heavy than they had expected."[30]

So good was the spirit of Madrid that by the end of January the king felt sufficiently settled to reduce the garrison.

Despite his personal success, there were frustrations that made the king's position almost intolerable. The shortage of money to implement his civil projects was a constant source of concern. Repeatedly he begged the emperor for cash, for draft animals, for the proceeds of confiscated wool, for permission to export wool to France. So short was ready cash that the fortifications which Napoleon had ordered to overawe the people of Madrid had to be discontinued as pay could not be found for the laborers. The only answer he got was a cheerful, irresponsible note saying, "If I had any money, I would willingly send you some; but my expenses are enormous."[31] Eventually, when the army was hopelessly in arrears for pay, the emperor allowed money, held by his orders at Bayonne, to be forwarded, saying "I cannot understand how the pay can be in arrears. There is plenty at Bayonne; why does the Paymaster not forward it? He must be an imbecile."[32]

Worse even than his penury was the growing conviction that his kingship was nothing but a matter of form, that he was only a puppet while the French army and imperial officials really ruled the country—and ruled it dishonestly and disastrously. In Aragon, General Junot refused to admit any of Joseph's officials to the province. Wrote Joseph, "He issues decrees daily. . . . He reserves to himself the right to levy taxes. . . . He is raising a guard of young Aragonese. . . . [He] is doing harm to the country, which will rise against him if he persists in treating the people as Helots."[33] Belliard, the governor of Madrid, released a priest who was under a sentence of death for leading a *guerrilla* and imprisoned one of Joseph's Spanish magistrates in a dungeon under the governor's palace. He established an illegal gambling saloon for his own profit. Wrote Joseph to Napoleon, "The brigandage of some of the staff officers continues and I have been forced to take notice of it. . . . Passports and safe conducts are sold. . . . One wretch, condemned to death, was forced to make his will in favour of the scoundrel who imprisoned him. The scoundrel, having watched the man shot, proceeded to sell up his goods."[34] Most infuriating of all was Monsieur de Fréville, the official appointed by the emperor to administer the sequestered estates of the ten families. "He ordered the Intendant for Emigré Property not to obey my orders. This is now the talk of the town. I beg Your Majesty to have him recalled. His staying here, after this occurrence, will be more harmful than all the efforts of the Spanish armies."[35]

Napoleon was not interested. War with Austria was drawing nearer and nearer. "I do not know," he replied, "what to do about Mons. de Fréville. You will readily believe that I am far too busy to think about that kind of thing."[36] His letters became more and more infrequent and increasingly carping in tone. When Joseph sent away the French chief of police whom Napoleon had installed, the emperor was exceedingly angry. "I see with extreme surprise the reason you give—that the constitution forbids a Frenchman holding the post. Let me know if the constitution forbids the King of Spain being at the head of 300,000 French soldiers, if the constitution forbids a Frenchman being Governor of Madrid, with a French garrison? If it lays down that in Saragossa houses should be blown up one after another? It must be admitted that this way of looking at things is small-minded and pitiful."[37]

Joseph was in despair at this outburst. "I can achieve nothing without your complete and exclusive confidence in Spanish affairs. It is you who have given me this crown; if you can find someone more worthy than myself, that man should be king: as for me I can only do what my conscience tells me. . . . The Spaniards would lay down their weapons, they would fall at my feet, if they could know what was in my heart; if they knew that, although I am a French prince, I desire what I must, and what I must do is to govern them as a free, independent nation. . . . At my age I cannot change my principles. *If you cannot agree with me, my shaky crown is at your disposal.*"[38] It was another in Joseph's long series of attempts to abdicate. All he received in return was an acknowledgment.

On the military side, Joseph was more hopeful, at least until the end of May. His scope for actually commanding the French army in Spain was limited. Napoleon had told him to reserve himself for the time being. From Valladolid he had written, "Since you naturally want to be present on a campaign, you should go with the expedition to Andalusia; but it cannot start in less than three weeks from now [11 January]. Then, by taking an unguarded road with 40,000 men you will surprise the enemy and crush them."[39] It was to be twelve months before Andalusia saw a French soldier.

Meanwhile, the corps commanders were working, as best they could, to Napoleon's master plan for the occupation of southern Spain and Portugal, and Joseph, however he might disagree with his brother on civil matters, had an absolute trust in his military judgment. When Marshal Victor raised doubts about the feasibility of his junction with Soult, the king passed his letter on to Paris with a covering note saying that "I do not share the fears of Marshal Victor; I am convinced that everything Your Majesty has planned can be carried out by the forces allocated."[40]

Marshal Jourdan, his chief of staff, had little of the king's confidence. The emperor, in his opinion, must have thought that "only a few marches were needed to make himself master of two kingdoms. He kept repeating that the whole armed force of Spain could not resist 10,000 Frenchmen. He hoped, also, that . . . the British Cabinet would not dare to send another army to the Peninsula, or at least that they would not be able to do so until the country was conquered and quiet. To have indulged these windy hopes, the Emperor must have underestimated the character, energy and patriotism of the people of the two kingdoms. . . . If he had opened his eyes before he left he would have seen that the Spanish armies were reforming as soon as they were dispersed, that armed bands infested the roads, that the inhabitants took flight at the approach of the French and that our armies controlled nothing beyond the reach of their bayonets.

"Quite independent of the difficulties inherent in a war of two nations against one army, the Emperor created additional problems by his organization of the army. The Marshals, accustomed to obeying no one but the Emperor himself, would have felt slighted at having to serve under his brother had they not assumed that his appointment as commander in chief was no more than a formality and that they were at liberty to question the orders he sent to them."[41]

Joseph's military experience consisted of no more than a few weeks in command of a regiment of infantry at Boulogne, and it is scarcely surprising that the very experienced marshals thought little of his military talent and this was made worse by Napoleon's engaging habit of telling his entourage "that Joseph was no soldier and that he knew nothing of war."[42] This would scarcely have mattered if his chief of staff had been a man they respected. Jourdan was one of the heroes of the Revolutionary War. He had lifted the fear of invasion from France in June 1794 by his great victory over the Austrians at Fleurus. It was, however, common knowledge in the army that that victory had only been won by the fortunate appearance of Lazare Carnot, the minister of war, who overruled all Jourdan's plans and led the victorious advance himself. Moreover, when, on the strength of the victory at Fleurus, Jourdan had succeeded to the command of the famous army of *Sambre-et-Meuse* he had, left to his own devices, been thrashed by the Austrians at Stockach. Having been born in 1762, he was, by the standards of the marshals of the empire, a worn-out old man. Soult, Victor, and Ney, all with much more battle experience and far less strategic insight, refused to take him seriously. His position was hopeless—and he knew it. "A commander," he complained to Paris, "must have under his orders officers of lower rank who will obey him rather than colleagues who believe they have more ability than he."[43]

To make Jourdan's position even more difficult, it was known that the emperor disliked him since, as a sincere republican, he had passively opposed Napoleon's assumption of the crown of France. Alone among the marshals he had no dukedom or title of any kind.* In 1809 he was deliberately slighted by having his name omitted from the list of marshals in the Imperial Almanack.

Early in 1809, however these disadvantages had not fully shown themselves. The very fact that all operations were controlled by a prearranged plan meant that the king had little scope to give orders to the marshals so that they had few opportunities of disobeying him. There was, nevertheless, much more military activity than had been anticipated. Before Napoleon had even left Valladolid, the duke of Infantado had threatened Madrid from the southeast with 20,000 men. His advanced guard was smashed at Ucles by Victor (13 January) and Infantado was relieved of his command, but in February two more Spanish armies threatened the capital from the south and the southwest. At Ciudad Real, Sebastiani dispersed the army of Andalusia on 27 March and proceeded to extend the French occupation over La Mancha. On Sebastiani's right, the Spanish army of Estremadura, 22,000 men under Gregorio Cuesta, drove up to the Tagus and destroyed the vital bridge at Almaraz. Victor, with the First Corps, counterattacked and pursued the Estremadurans to the Guadiana and routed them at Medellín (28 March) whereupon they fled into Sierra Morena. It was not the last the French were to hear of the

---

* Ironically, Jourdan, whose republicanism prevented him from being given an imperial title, was eventually made a count by the restored Louis XVIII.

elderly Cuesta, to whom Napoleon had offered the viceroyalty of Mexico. He continued to be a pest to the French and to his British allies alike.

Joseph did his best to consolidate the advantages of the victories at Ciudad Real and Medellín. He sent Joaquín María Solano, an aged and respected counselor, to offer the Seville junta an armistice with a view to ending the war. The junta replied that they would open negotiations when Ferdinand VII returned to Spain and Joseph Bonaparte returned to France. On the defeated Cuesta they showed honors. Every survivor of Medellín was given a medal and a week's pay.

Saragossa finally fell to the French on 20 February, having cost them ten thousand casualties. The devotion of the defenders should have shown both Napoleon and Joseph how deep and fanatical was the pride and determination of the Spaniards. Six thousand had been killed in the fighting. Forty-eight thousand had died of disease and starvation. Even Marshal Lannes, not a sentimental man, reported that the remains of the town were horrifying to look upon. Yet there was a powerful and vociferous minority among the fifteen thousand remaining townspeople, who wished to continue resistance although all hope of relief was long since gone. The lesson was lost on both emperor and king. Joseph Palafox, the gallant commander, was treated as a traitor rather than as a prisoner of war and spent more than four years in a dungeon at Vincennes. A tribute to the courage of the defenders in one of Joseph's Madrid newspapers brought down a blistering rebuke from Napoleon.

The troops who had conducted the siege were not launched into Valencia as had been planned. Marshall Lannes left Spain to rejoin the emperor in Austria and the Third Corps, now under Louis Gabriel Suchet, was required to pacify Aragon. Mortier's Fifth Corps was put into suspended animation, lest it be needed for the imminent Austrian war. More than a month after Saragossa fell, the minister of war in Paris was writing to Jourdan that "the Emperor has given no new orders for the troops who took Saragossa."[44]

In northwestern Spain the situation was chaotic. Ney, operating with insufficient troops in mountainous country, had no chance of pacifying the Galicians, who had the support of the reconstructed remains of La Romaña's army. He based himself on Coruña and Ferrol, judging, most reasonably, that these ports might be used by the British to land arms and, possibly, troops. He endeavored to control the rest of the province with mobile columns which moved about the countryside scattering guerrillas, burning villages, and hanging alcaldes and priests by way of reprisals. He lost touch with Soult almost as soon as the latter marched towards the Portuguese frontier. His communications with the rest of Spain were at best intermittant. He must have wished that they were completely broken when from time to time he received Napoleon's orders and advice. The emperor told him to leave the maintenance of law and order to the Spaniards, to abandon the coast and base himself at Lugo. "If you cannot man the batteries which stop the English getting in touch with the land, you can entrust them to the inhabitants."[45] Nothing illustrates better than this order the extent of Napoleon's illusions about the state of Spain. There was not a single Galician who could be trusted to act as a guide to Ney's troops.

Not content with this, the emperor, who believed that "Ney has more troops than he needs,"[46] kept nagging the unfortunate marshal to occupy the Asturias. Eventually, in early May, Ney managed to concert an operation with François Christophe de Kellermann, in charge of León, and Bonnet, from Santander, to invade the principality. He took 7,500 men, almost half the effectives in Galicia, and marched on Oviedo. He defeated La Romaña, seized the capital and its seaport, Grijón. At this stage he heard that Galicia was all but lost, while Bonnet heard that the Spaniards had actually recaptured Santander during his absence. At once the two commanders turned back and set about restoring order in their base areas, leaving Kellermann to hold down the Asturias. That general soon realized the hopelessness of his task and returned to León.

Above all, the success of Napoleon's dream of subduing the whole Peninsula depended on Soult's invasion of Portugal. News from him was scanty. On 4 February, King Joseph heard that he had entered Ferrol, "of which the inhabitants showed good sense in refusing to allow the English to take over the fortifications.*"[47] Five weeks later, the news came through that Soult had been foiled in an attempt to cross the estuary of the Minho, the river marking the Portuguese frontier, and had retired to Orense, forty miles inside Spain, on 24 February, eight days after his scheduled time of arrival in Lisbon. Joseph estimated that he should reach the Portuguese capital on 15 March.[48] After that there was a long silence. Soult was out of touch.

There were only two ways of getting news of the Second Corps' progress: through Ney in Galicia or through Lapisse at Salamanca. As has been said, communications with Ney were, at best, intermittent and Ney had almost no means of getting in touch with Soult. Lapisse, whose division had been given the task of linking Soult and Victor, was even less successful than Ney. He was held back from even Ciudad Rodrigo on the Spanish side of the frontier by sheer effrontary. Sir Robert Wilson had raised a British paid and officered unit of Portuguese known as the Loyal Lusitanian Legion. Wilson, a man of great talent but an intolerable subordinate, with 1,500 hastily raised Portuguese stretched in a thin chain across Lapisse's front, so imposed himself upon the Frenchman, who had five times his strength, that Lapisse felt himself unable to advance and, for a time, was cut off from Madrid. It was a superb example of military bluff and it worked. Mistaking the Loyal Legion, in their green uniforms, for British riflemen, Lapisse believed himself faced with a powerful army, and after many pleas to Madrid, obtained permission to seek safety from it by marching south to join Victor on the south bank of the Tagus.

* This kind of report helped to confirm the wishful thinking of both Napoleon and Joseph about public opinion in Spain. There had been no question of handing over the forts to the British as there were no British in the vicinity.

Apart from Lapisse's imaginary British greenjackets, the British did not much enter into the calculations of either Napoleon or Joseph between January and May. On 21 March Napoleon considered it faintly possible that there might be some English troops in Andalusia but added, for reasons best known to himself, that if they "have some infantry there, they cannot have any cavalry.*"[49] Three weeks later, Joseph reported to his brother, "All reports agree in stating that the English have effected a landing at . . . Cádiz."[50] On the same day, Napoleon was writing to Joseph that "it seems that the English have not been able to land at Cádiz. Since 15th March they have re-occupied Lisbon with 10 or 12,000 men."[51]

This letter of 12 April was the last that the emperor was to write to his brother for many weeks. Three days earlier the Austrian army had invaded Bavaria and there was war between the Austrian and French empires. Napoleon left Paris on 13 April and rode into Vienna at the head of his troops on 12 May. The eastern war was, however, by no means over. On 20–23 May the French, under the emperor's personal charge, were fought to a standstill while trying to cross the Danube at Aspern and Essling. Until July the Austrians still had everything to play for. Meanwhile Napoleon, established in the palace of Schönbrunn, further alienated his brother's Spanish subjects by arresting the pope. He communicated with Joseph through the intermediary of the French minister of war, General Henri Jacques Guillaume Clarke, whom he considered to be "a man of no talent—he is only conceited,"[52] "and so addicted to flattery that one can never tell how much reliance to place on any opinion he may express."[53]

While the emperor was advancing into Austria, Joseph at last heard rumors about Soult's progress. On 22 April he was able to report that "it is given out that he had to take Oporto by storm (*la torche à la main*), the townspeople having put

* The assumption that the British could have no cavalry in Spain presumably stemmed from the assumption that any troops in the area must be Moore's army, who had slaughtered their horses before embarking. There was, in fact, a single British battalion (1/40th) in Spain. It had been sent to Seville by mistake.

up a strong resistance. Six days later, a report from Kellermann confirmed this news but added rumors gave rise to fears that "Soult's [siege] artillery, which was left at Tuy under guard of the 70th Regiment, had been taken by the rebels, who took 1,500 prisoners."[54]

Notwithstanding this minor setback, Joseph was in an optimistic mood. At the end of March, despite the paucity of news from Soult, he wrote, "Everything leads me to expect a happy outcome from all the military operations. I hope this all the more so that I can send 50,000 men back to Your Majesty, which I shall be able to do as soon as Seville and Cádiz have surrendered."[55] To speed this happy day, he sent "trustworthy envoys, who are thought well of by the Junta at Seville, to arrange to finish the war by the voluntary surrender of Andalusia. We must secure Cádiz and the fleet before despair throws them into the hands of the English. . . . I am pressing General Junot to march into Valencia so as to finish with the south of Spain before the hot weather."[56] He eagerly retailed a rumor that La Romaña, his most inveterate opponent, was prepared to surrender if he could be assured of a pardon. It is hard not to feel sorry for Joseph, with his alternating waves of despair and elation.

Nothing more from Portugal was heard until the fourth week of May. Then news came to hand from Galicia, where a brigade of Ney's troops had succeeded in getting into touch with some of Soult's at Tuy on the Portuguese-Galician border. Soult "is on the right bank of the Douro; 4,000 men of his corps are in occupation of Oporto, which the English are bombarding. Lord [sic] Wellesley and 20,000 English are on the south bank, deployed so as to defend the country." Even this news did not dim Joseph's optimism. "We are," he added, "busy with preparations for the siege of Ciudad Rodrigo."[57] Every effort was to be made to open up communication with Soult across Portugal's eastern border, although Victor raised every possible objection to diverting his strength in that direction. All, in Joseph's euphoric view, was now going well. "The submission of the Asturias," he wrote triumphantly on 30 May, "will allow me to get together the troops which have been employed there, to ensure the success of Your Majesty's plans, which have been delayed by the obstacles experienced by Marshal Soult's corps."[58] Undismayed by the reported presence of 20,000 British troops in Lisbon, Joseph, his belief in his brother's military sagacity undimmed, looked forward to a quick march to Cádiz against token opposition. Thirteen days before he wrote, Soult had been hunted out of Portugal, having lost his artillery, his military chest, his baggage, his transport, his sick, and more than a sixth of his men.

It was not until 10 June that even a muted version of the disaster reached him. Even then it came by way of Paris, since Soult had not seen fit to report to Joseph in Madrid. "Your Majesty's Minister of War," wrote Joseph to the emperor, "informs me by his letter of 1st June that Marshal Soult has had to retreat from Oporto, and that the English army crossed the Douro in his presence on 12th May. I have, therefore, decided to suspend Marshal Victor's advance [on Andalusia] and to draw him back to the Tagus."[59]

King Joseph's bubble had burst. There would be no easy conquest, no "voluntary surrender" of Andalusia, no finishing with southern Spain before the hot weather. Napoleon's master plan had collapsed. The dream of Valladolid had met reality, and any further gains would have to be achieved by fighting. Nor was this the only illusion of Joseph's that was shattered—in the future it would be hard for him to believe, as he had managed to do since the emperor left Spain, that he was the commander in chief of the French army in Spain. Soult had not bothered to tell him of his repulse. Joseph had bravely told the emperor that he had ordered Victor back to the Tagus. This was not true. Victor had refused to obey orders and claiming, not without justice, that his troops could find no food between the Tagus and the Guadiana, had fallen back of his own accord. The king's "orders" were no more than a ratification of Victor's disobedience. Joseph was king of Madrid, but no more.

109

While the king was waiting patiently and with confidence for Soult and Victor to meet triumphantly at Badajoz, the outside world had been pursuing courses which Napoleon's plan had left wholly out of account. The Central Junta, which Napoleon had driven from Madrid in December, had settled itself at Seville. It continued to be a body both fractious and factious, subject to pressure from the mob and to unreasoning bouts of fury against honest if unsuccessful generals, who were doing their best with inadequate means and, sometimes, inadequate talents. At one time even Castaños, the victor of Bailén, was accused of being an *afrancesado*. Nevertheless, for all its follies and perversities, the Central Junta was consistently and bitterly anti-French. They had their moods of being anti-British and they were constantly anti-Portuguese, but their determination to oust Joseph and the French army never wavered. The Spanish colonies rallied to their support and vast sums were sent across the Atlantic to their support, both in the form of the normal "*flota*" carrying the annual "tribute of the Indies" and voluntary contributions from Spaniards in the colonies. They were thus able to equip and, for the time being, pay the remaining Spanish armies, especially with the help of Britain, which supplied vast stores of muskets and ammunition. In the few months that Moore's campaign and the gallantry of the northern Portugese peasantry bought them, these armies could not be trained sufficiently to enable them to meet the French on equal terms, but as long as there was a Spanish army in being, it must tie down vast quantities of French troops.

Quite as effective as their refitting of their armies, was the Junta's proclamation to the people at large. This called upon them to do everything they could to make the lives of the occupation forces intolerable. "All the inhabitants of the occupied provinces able to bear arms are authorized to take up arms, and to attack and despoil French soldiers, individually or in groups, on every occasion that offers, to stop food and supplies that are destined for them; in short to do them as much harm and to cause them as much distress as may be possible.

Such actions will be considered as services to the state, which will reward them according to their merits."[60] Never was an appeal better received. No Frenchman was, henceforward, safe from a knife in the back on a dark night, no French detachment was safe in a mountain pass, all French couriers had to travel under heavy escort. The people of Spain, of all classes, responded with a will, and their contribution to the eventual ejection of the enemy was at least equal to that of the Spanish armies.

Nor were the Portuguese backward in organizing their strength, although the Portuguese regency vied with the Spanish junta in its factiousness and incompetence. Portugal did not have the wealth of the Indies to support its tottering economy, but instead she had a long-standing and close alliance with the richest country in the world, Britain. She had also a deep sense of national shame at her feeble performance against the French invasion of 1807 and a thirst for revenge for the indignities and brutalities inflicted upon her pride and people by Junot's army. It was, therefore, to Britain that Portugal turned for her regeneration. It was obvious that the first need was to recreate the Portuguese army, which had been a useless force in 1807 and which had subsequently lost its best men to forced service in the French army. The regency first asked Britain for a commander in chief for the new army, and on 25 March 1809 there arrived in Lisbon Maj. Gen. (local Lt. Gen.) William Carr Beresford. He was tough, plainspoken, and one-eyed, an above average field commander and an organizer of genius. He took rank as a marshal of the Portugese army and working with a small team of British officers and NCOs set to work without delay to make the Portugese army fit to meet the French in the field. In this he was successful beyond all expectations. It was the Portugese troops, trained by Beresford, who made up the numbers of the small British army and gave it the strength to beat French armies in battle.

For the time being, however, little was forthcoming from Britain apart from Beresford, his cadre of officers, and a supply of arms and money. Contrary to Napoleon's information, the

British did not reoccupy Lisbon in March. They had never withdrawn. Since Moore's army had marched into Spain there had never been less than 10,000 British troops in Portugal. They were, however, under a commander who was timorous by nature and acting under vague orders from London. Sir John Craddock, as far as he understood his instructions, expected to have to reembark his army at an early date. He therefore concentrated his force close to the sea near St. Julian, where he had the city of Lisbon between himself and any possible French advance.

Thus, when Soult began to advance into the north of Portugal, he had nothing to oppose him but Portuguese. Soult had 22,000 veteran troops. The Portuguese could oppose him with two incomplete regular infantry regiments, four militia regiments, ill armed and without discipline, 200 regular cavalry, and a mass of peasants armed with fowling pieces and billhooks. With this motley collection the Portuguese fought a remarkably successful delaying action. Soult's first atempt to cross into Portugal by crossing the mouth of the river Minho in fishing boats was reduced to tragicomedy. Soult returned to Orense and tried again, marching inland by way of Monterey on 10 March. He was opposed and harassed every inch of the way, while behind his columns the Portugese closed in as the ocean does behind a ship. It was not until 27 March that he arrived before Oporto to find the surrounding heights fortified and the city held by 30,000 men, of whom, however, only about 5,000 were regular troops. He stormed the place on 29 March without much difficulty, and a ghastly panic resulted when the townspeople attempted to fly to the south bank of the Douro by a bridge of boats which had been taken up in the center to prevent a French pursuit. "The entrance to the bridge was choked with people . . . and the crowd became shortly a heap of dead bodies of men, women and children. Many were drowned in the river, some crossed by swimming. It is impossible to picture to you the horrid and moving spectacle that this ill-fated town presented. Females of all ranks, half clad, rushing to and fro in frantic despair and attempting the crossing under the fire of the [Portuguese] guns placed on the opposite heights."[61]

Soult had reached Oporto at last, but, apart from pushing an advance guard across the Douro, he could go no further. His men desperately needed rest, having been marching and fighting through the mountains since mid-December. Moreover, it was vital to reestablish his communications with Ney in Galicia, to rescue the garrisons he had left at strong points behind him, and to try to make a link eastwards, along the course of the Douro, with Lapisse's division, which he expected still to be at Salamanca and Ciudad Rodrigo. He did, for a brief moment, contact Ney's men when bringing off the garrisons of Tuy and Valenza, but after that he was again cut off from all news from Spain and France. His attempt to cut a way through to Spain along the Douro was frustrated by the Portugese General Silveira's defense of the crossing of the river Tamega at Amarante. Some of his troops were rested but their morale was not improved by the ill-kept secret that their commander was attempting to build up a party of Portugese traitors who would petition him to assume the crown of Portugal.

All this was soon to become irrelevant. The British had, at last, made up their minds to give large-scale support to Portugal. It had been an unwilling decision. Most of the cabinet wished to make their base at Cádiz and to fight alongside the armies of the Supreme Junta. This they were unable to do. The junta refused to let British troops land at Cádiz. There was little enthusiasm for supporting Portugal. Moore had said that Portugal could not be defended. However, with Cádiz closed to them, Lisbon was the only all-weather port in the Peninsula open to them. Sir Arthur Wellesley, cleared from the stigma of the Convention of Cintra, said that while the frontiers of Portugal were indefensible, Lisbon and its harbor were not. "Even if Spain should have been conquered, the French would not be able to overrun Portugal with a smaller force than 100,000 men."[62] Wellesley rightly forecast that as long as the Spaniards continued fighting, the French would be unable to spare 100,000 men for Portugal, and that even if they did, they would be unable to feed them. A British force in Portugal might, he declared, "eventually decide the contest."[63]

The government had agreed and had appointed Wellesley to the command. They were not enthusiastic. They sent reinforcements to Lisbon, but not very many. The king, George III, agreed to Wellesley's appointment on the unenthusiastic grounds that he was "so young a lieutenant general . . . that this consideration would operate with others against any considerable augmentation of that army."[64]

Wellesley landed in Lisbon on 22 April, assuming as he did so the rank of marshal general of Portugal, thus being recognized as Beresford's senior and commander of all British and Portuguese troops. There were 23,200 British troops in Portugal, and the Portuguese soldiery did not impress him; he considered "the body of men very bad, the officers worse than anything I have ever seen."[65] Setting aside a flank guard to watch Victor's corps between the Tagus and the Guadiana and sending a small British force to support Silveira at Amarante, he had less than 17,000 British to deal with Soult at Oporto. To them he added 5,000 of the least bad Portuguese and set out to do the business. His first plan, to cut off Soult's advance guard south of the Douro, misfired, but by 11 May the British and French faced each other across the Douro. Next morning, while Soult was asleep, the British crossed the broad river in daylight. Although he had only three clumsy wine barges to transport his troops, Wellesley established a strong bridgehead within a mile of Soult's headquarters before the French realized that the British were on the move. Soon after noon, the French army was streaming away to the northwest in complete disorganization. As one of their pursuers wrote, "Every man seemed running for his life, throwing away their knapsacks and arms, so we had only the trouble of making many prisoners, all begging for quarter and surrendering with great good humor."[66]

Since two of Wellesley's subordinates did not act as intelligently as they might have been expected to do, Soult was able to escape over the mountains to Orense in Spain. He lost 4,000 men and all his guns. Wellesley pursued him up to the frontier but then turned back, realizing that an army which abandoned all its impediments could never be caught by one burdened by artillery and baggage. He had, in any case, other plans.

Chapter 5

BATTLE ROYAL

Never was there so murderous a battle.
SIR ARTHUR WELLESLEY

In Madrid, King Joseph was getting what pleasure he could from his crown. His court

was not and could not be as brilliant as that of the Emperor Napoleon, but it was conducted on the same lines and with the same etiquette. Since the palace in Madrid is one of the finest in Europe, it was not surprising to find that the King was better housed than the Emperor himself at the Tuileries. All the walls were dressed with the most beautiful and rare marble, and the mirrors and clocks alone were valued at five million francs.

When the King was not with the army, he normally rose at six or seven in the morning; at nine he received the members of his household and at half past made his breakfast from two boiled eggs or a piece of fish; at ten o'clock he gave audience to his ministers, received Marshal Jourdan and the generals, French or Spanish, who wished to speak to him. At one o'clock he attended the Privy Council and at four he would go up to the Casa del Campo where he would dine with Marshal Jourdan, Count Melito and General Belliard. Sometimes the ladies of the court and some of the officers of the Household would attend. After dinner he would go out on horseback or in his coach, would play *vingt-et-un*, and, before going to bed, would send off the courier to France.

Every French general and colonel who passed through Madrid was always bidden to dinner either with the King or in the household dining room, where, presided over by one of the major-domos, the officers of the household dined every day. They were often joined by the ministers and generals, although there were seldom more than twelve at dinner.

When ladies were invited to dinner, together with the ministers, generals and household officers, there were always sixty or eighty at table, the ladies in court dress, the men in uniform with silk stockings. The King himself wore the uniform of a colonel in his own Guard or a frock coat with epaulettes."[1]

Apart from the beauty of his palaces, the king had little to comfort him in his official life. The emperor bombarded him with complaints. Long before the news of Soult's debacle in Portugal had reached Paris, he had commented, "Things are going badly in Spain. I see nothing but misfortune. . . . The losses I suffer in putting down these minor risings cost me as much as the loss of a major battle." The armies, he said, were directed with "such slowness and such indolence that they achieve less than could be done with a quarter of the number of men. . . . It is hard to imagine such ineptitude. . . . An army is nothing without a head and in Spain there is none." On 3 June, when the wreck of Soult's corps had already been back on Spanish soil for more than two weeks, it was Napoleon's view that "if Soult suffers a setback, the ruin of Spain will follow."[2]

"They must not try to do things at all points of the compass," he scolded,[3] yet his own orders enjoined just that kind of dispersion. On 11 June he declared that "only the English are important."[4] Next day, "The situation in Aragon needs all your attention."[5] Nine days later, "The situation in the north is all important."[6] Four weeks later, "The first task should be to take Gerona, Hostalrich and Lerida," all of which fortresses are in Catalonia.[7]

None of this distracting and contradictory advice was made any more palatable or more relevant by being relayed second-hand. The emperor left Paris on 13 April to conduct the Austrian campaign and his subsequent orders were sent to Clarke, the minister for war in Paris. Clarke rephrased them in more deferential terms and forwarded them to Madrid. Apart from the wounding discourtesy of refusing to reply directly to Joseph's letters, a lot of time was wasted by this roundabout method of communication. The time taken for an order leaving imperial headquarters at Vienna, where they were established on 11 May, to reach Paris, be rewritten, and be forwarded to Madrid was about eighteen days. Since the information on which the orders were based had traveled the same route in reverse, instructions reaching Joseph were based on a situation not less than seven weeks out of date.

Faced with this situation, the king, despite his inexperience and underlying dislike of the military life, resolved to prove to his brother that he too was a great general. Napoleon sensed this and speaking to a mutual friend who was being sent on a mission to Madrid remarked, "I am not happy about the King. He longs to be a soldier although . . . he has told me that the art of war is charlatanism. He will never make a soldier—he has not got it in him. Even his health is not good enough."[8]

Joseph's first attempt to join in the fighting miscarried. In mid-June, hearing that Sebastiani to the south of Madrid was being threatened by a Spanish corps which lurked in the mountains south of Ciudad Real, he marched out with his guard and two French regiments only to find that Sebastiani had driven off the enemy unaided. Undeterred, he determined on a forward policy. "My aim is to put Marshal Soult in a state to beat the English and to prepare an expedition into Portugal, if the English stay there."[9]

Nevertheless, before any large-scale operations could be undertaken there must be supplies of money and rations. "All the resources of the country have been used up by the armies. There is not a *sou* in the Treasury. Up to now I have only been able to manage by minting coins from the palace silverware."[10] To make matters worse, a successful Spanish raid on Santander not only "ruined" two French regiments in garrison there but made away with 300,000 francs in the military chest. In these circumstances, it is greatly to the credit of both Joseph and Jourdan that they were able to collect and transport to Zamora enough guns, ammunition, clothing, and equipment to meet all the material needs of Soult's corps.

Once the emperor's grand design for the submission of the whole Peninsula had crumbled at Oporto, Joseph tried to assert his position as overall commander. The marshals, who were not unaware of the emperor's opinion of the military capabilities of his brother, refused to take either Joseph or Jourdan seriously. Victor grew steadily more insubordinate. Although constantly complaining that he could not feed his troops where he was, he refused to obey an order to send a division to assist Sebastiani. He made every kind of difficulty over obeying an order to probe up to the Portuguese border to seek news of Wellesley's army, alleging that he was threatened by 10,000 Portuguese. The actual force opposed to him was a single battalion of the Lusitanian Legion and some militia. Mortier for long delayed obeying an order to support Soult and Ney, pleading that the emperor's orders forbade him to move west of Burgos.

Most troublesome of all were Soult and Ney. They and their respective headquarters established themselves in Lugo at the end of May. They immediately fell to quarreling. Ney demanded Soult's help in putting down Galicia. Soult, intent on revenging his defeat, had eyes for nothing but Portugal. At one stormy interview, Ney drew his sword on his colleague and had to be restrained by General Maurice Mathieu. The two staffs fell to dueling and the soldiers of the two corps to street brawls. Both marshals poured out their complaints to the king, who commented that "I can scarcely conceive of anything so extraordinary. I do not think that it will be possible for them to act together."[11] He ordered Ney to Madrid, intending to give him command of the Fourth Corps. Ney ignored the letter.

Meanwhile the two marshals temporarily patched up their quarrel and agreed on a plan for a joint operation in Galicia. Ney set out on his part of the campaign, but Soult, as soon as he was out of touch with Ney, marched in the opposite direction and quartered his troops in the plains of León. He did not think fit to mention his intention to Ney, who was so angered that, in defiance of direct orders from both Napoleon and Joseph, he evacuated Galicia, burning twenty-six towns and villages on his route out of irrational spite. The French never reoccupied Galicia.

Apart from Suchet, whose operations in Aragon brought him into scant touch with Madrid, only Sebastiani remained loyal to the king. Joseph wrote of him, "I cannot praise him too highly; the people of La Mancha are orderly; they willingly supply the army and Madrid. Once the English and Cuesta are beaten, it is only by men of Honour like Sebastiani that Spain will be subdued. He has secured these important provinces by his wise and vigorous administration, having first captured them. His troops behave well and, consequently, the inhabitants return to their homes."[12] Jourdan, the chief of staff, was as always loyal but he was sick, tired, and discouraged and wrote seeking the emperor's leave to resign his post.

In despair, Joseph sought Napoleon's permission to send from Spain "all marshals, generals and officers whose services here I do not feel to be necessary. Marshal Ney would serve you well in Germany or under your direct orders. The same might be the case with Marshals Victor and Mortier. Your Majesty will have seen, from the good services rendered by

Generals Suchet and Sebastiani, how advantageous it would be if I had fewer marshals here and more generals like those two, who take notice of my orders and who can pacify their provinces by their good conduct and by the discipline they impose on their troops."[13] The emperor did not reply to this letter.

Another factor inhibiting Joseph's forward policy was the French ignorance of their enemy's movements. Two Spanish armies threatened Madrid. To the south was Venegas with 21,000 men, the Army of the Center. This was watched by Sebastiani, who estimated his opponent's strength at 40,000. To the southwest was the Army of Estremadura, 37,000 men under Cuesta. Victor kept this force in check and estimated its strength at 40,000. Victor and Sebastiani each had about 20,000 available and, as a reserve, 6,000 men could be spared from Madrid. With these 46,000 men available on the line of the Tagus, there was nothing to be feared from Venegas and Cuesta. They were incapable of acting in concert, and although each of them made occasional sallies from their fastnesses in the Sierra Morena, they were driven back each time with contemptuous ease and considerable loss.

The problem was the whereabouts of the British army. Nothing had been seen or heard of them since Wellesley broke off the pursuit of Soult on the northern frontier of Portugal on 17 May. "The English," wrote Joseph on 9 July, "have not yet shown their hand. Will they advance into Galicia? into Castille? or will they stay in Lisbon? If the last is their plan, should we advance by way of Ciudad Rodrigo to search them out? This plan is the one most favored by those who know the country best."[14] The emperor, preoccupied with Austrian affairs, offered no answer to these queries. His view seems to have been that if they did anything beyond holding Lisbon, the British would make a seaborne landing.*

He did, however, give orders to dispose of them. "The

---

* In his only reference to likely British moves in his letters of June and July 1809, Napoleon gives instructions as to what should be done "if the English disembark in Spain" (NC, xix, 15,552. N to Clarke, 18 July 09).

corps of Ney, Mortier and Soult should be formed into a single army under the orders of Marshal Soult. These three corps must maneuver as a single body, march against the English, pursue them relentlessly, defeat them and throw them into the sea. If they concentrate quickly the English must be destroyed and the whole Spanish business finished. They must not march in penny packets. I cannot say where their concentration should take place, as I do not know the situation."[15]

This order reached Joseph on 1 July and Soult on the following day. There could be no question of an immediate advance into Portugal since both Joseph and Soult were agreed that the border fortresses of Ciudad Rodrigo and Almeida must first be taken by formal sieges, as they effectively commanded the most convenient road into Portugal. For this a siege train had to be formed and transported to the frontier. Moreover, the troops of Soult and Ney, who had been continually on the march since the previous November, were not fully fit to undertake yet another major campaign.

Soult had set his heart on conquering Portugal. Ney and Mortier, who both detested him, were less than pleased to have to act under his orders. Nor was King Joseph pleased. He agreed that the arrangement was necessary and undertook to do all in his power to ensure its success, but he was unhappy that of the five corps under his direct command,* three were now allocated to Soult. This left the king with only the corps of Victor and Sebastiani under his immediate control. While they were sufficient to protect Madrid against a Spanish attack from the south, they were barely adequate to give complete security and far from enough to leave him with a striking force with which he could prove himself as an able commander. He began to try to nibble away at the force under Soult. "I do not think," he wrote to Napoleon, "that the corps of Marshals Ney, Soult and Mortier can all go into

---

* The troops in Catalonia and Aragon were, even at this stage, not effectively under the king's control.

Portugal without risking the safety of the north of Spain and the communications with France."[16]

Learning by this time that the emperor would probably not reply to such a comment, the king began to build up an impression of a threat from the south. Venegas and Cuesta were reported as showing signs of renewed activity. This the king blamed on Victor, who had needlessly destroyed the bridges over the Tagus at Talavera and Almaraz. "This, without doubt, will give courage to a timid enemy."[17] Twice, fearing a major Spanish assault, the king marched out of the capital at the head of the reserve. Once he went to Talavera to support Victor, once to Toledo to assist Sebastiani. In neither case was his help wanted.

On the plea of the southern front's being in need of further support, he ordered Mortier to move his corps to Villacastín, sixty miles northwest of Madrid. This would give him a striking force if a favorable opportunity arose for winning some glory in the field. This diversion of Mortier was contrary to the emperor's orders and Soult immediately ordered the junior marshal to disregard the king's orders and move back northward to be closer to the corps of Soult and Ney.

One of the outstanding characteristics of the summer campaign of 1809 was the extent to which the two sides misinterpreted or were misinformed about each other's intentions. The view of King Joseph was that should the British not confine themselves to the defense of Portugal, they would move against Soult's group of corps. This was probably due to the fact that the French knew that Soult's force was the one intended to be used against Portugal and the one which, therefore, represented Portugal's greatest danger. On the other hand, the British believed that their greatest danger was of Marshal Victor's striking into Alentejo between the Tagus and Badajoz. Wellesley's thoughts, therefore, were running on striking against Victor in association with the armies of Cuesta and Venegas, the only allied forces with which he could cooperate while the British army was built up in strength and the Portuguese army was being forged into a usable weapon. His blow against Soult at Oporto he had considered as a welcome bonus. On landing in Lisbon he had written, "I should prefer an attack upon Victor in concert with Cuesta, if Soult was not in possession of a fertile province of this kingdom and of the favorite town of Oporto, of which it is most desirable to deprive him; and if any operation upon Victor, connected with Cuesta's movements, would not require time to concert it, which may as well be employed in dislodging Soult from Northern Portugal."[18]

Joseph and Jourdan, basing themselves on Victor's reports, believed that that marshal's right flank was watched only by a Portuguese force of 10,000 men. French memories of the Portuguese performance in 1807 convinced them that no offensive action was likely in this sector. In fact, from 8 June onwards, the whole movable British force, 21,000 men, was concentrated around Abrantes, ready to march on Madrid along the line of the Tagus. It was Wellesley's intention to make an immediate move eastward, but he was frustrated by the failure of vital supplies to arrive from England and, above all, by a total lack of money, without which he refused to move, since, unlike the French commanders, Wellesley would not feed his troops by requisition.

Had Wellesley known the full picture of the French dispositions, his attempt to reach Madrid would have struck him as foolhardy. As it was, he was optimistic. On 11 June he wrote, "The ball is at my foot, and I hope I shall have strength enough to give it a good kick."[19] He even wrote of the enemy's being forced back to the Ebro. This uncharacteristic optimism was based on false estimates of the operations of both his enemy and his allies. Guerrillas had captured near Toro a French general carrying a dispatch from Soult to the king outlining the operations that he and Ney had agreed for the reconquest of Galicia. Accepting this at its face value, Wellesley assumed that these operations would keep these two corps occupied in northwestern Spain, leaving only Mortier available to support Victor and Sebastiani in the defense of Madrid. He believed, moreover, that Mortier's corps was still at Valladolid. The numerical odds in favor of the allies would, therefore, be very favorable. The British commander can hardly be blamed for not anticipating that Soult would desert his colleague and that Ney would consequently abandon Galicia in flaming pique. His misappreciation of the Spaniards was almost more unfortunate. Both Cuesta and the junta at Seville had promised that food would be made available to Wellesley's commissariat. He had trusted these promises and was bitterly deceived. Nor did cooperation with Cuesta prove satisfactory. "I find Cuesta more and more impractical every day. It is impossible to do business, and very uncertain that any operation will succeed in which he has any concern."[20] "It is evident to me that [he] is too old and has not the talents to conduct in due order the great and confused affairs of a battle."[21]

Thus, by reasoning from false premises, the British army arrived in Spain in a position where it had never occurred to any French commander to expect it. The British crossed the frontier near Zarza la Mayor on 3 July. On the eighth, headquarters were at Plasencia, about 130 miles from Madrid. They were in touch on their right with Cuesta's army, with some 36,000 effectives, which was lying around Almaraz on the Tagus. Thus the allies had 57,000 men, exclusive of Venegas's 23,000 men. Wellesley reckoned that provided that Venegas, who was technically under Cuesta's orders, could keep Sebastiani occupied, they would be able to destroy Victor's corps before help could reach him.

Cuesta was not above refusing to execute a plan of his own devising if his ally accepted it, and the difficulty of concerting an operation with him and the time taken to send detailed orders to Venegas, 240 miles away around Valdepeñas, delayed a further immediate advance. It was not, therefore, until 18 July that the British advanced from Plasencia and three days later that they joined up with Cuesta's army at Oropesa. The two armies marched parallel to each other on the twenty-second. At noon on that day, the Spaniards came in touch with the French cavalry screen which, backed by two battalions of infantry, covered the town of Talavera de la Reina.

All this time Joseph and Jourdan had been living in a fool's paradise. They had busied themselves with getting supplies through to Soult and with organizing a siege train for the projected attack on Ciudad Rodrigo. On the political side, the situation showed some signs of improvement. On the day the British marched from Plasencia, the king had written that "I am content with feeling in Madrid. The appointment of forty Councillors of State, forty magistrates chosen from the most respectable families of the country, has been enough to create a favorable party and to counteract the bad spirit which previously existed. These forty men have stoutly declared themselves as being on my side."[22]

The first sign of trouble came on 22 July, when General Maximilien Sébastien Foy rode into Madrid with letters from Marshal Soult. That marshal had heard, on 19 July, that the British were about to advance up the Tagus. He, therefore, proposed that as soon as this move was confirmed, he should march with his three corps south from Salamanca through the Pass of Baños to Plasencia and the north bank of the Tagus, thus cutting the British off from Portugal with a force of 50,000 men, more than twice Wellesley's strength. To this end he had ordered Mortier to move towards Salamanca, leaving the defense of Madrid to the troops immediately available to Joseph. The king, knowing that Napoleon himself had put Mortier under Soult's command, "thought it his duty to give way" to Soult.[23] While Foy was talking to the king Victor's report that the allies had reached Talavera arrived. Immediately Foy was despatched back to Soult with orders "to concentrate the three corps under your command, and march as rapidly as possible to Plasencia. General Foy assured His Majesty that . . . you will be able to reach Plasencia in four or five marches."[24] If all went well, the British would be cut off.

The plan of an encircling move by Soult was a bold and sound one with the large numbers available. The only foreseeable drawback was that the Pass of Baños was an excellent defensive position where a fairly small number of determined men could impose a considerable delay, even on a force as large as Soult's, which would be unable to deploy. This thought had occurred to Wellesley, who had recognized the potential threat to his rear posed by the road Salamanca-Plasencia. He had therefore asked Cuesta to detail an adequate force to hold the pass. Cuesta assured him that this had been done but in fact sent no more than two weak battalions.

King Joseph, deprived of the support of Mortier's corps, decided to concentrate all his available force against Wellesley and Cuesta. He ordered Sebastiani to leave only the smallest garrisons on the crossings of the Tagus and to march with as many men as possible to join Victor. This Sebastiani was able to do with 15,500 men, since Venegas, who hated Cuesta, had neglected his orders to engage the French attention and was moving forward only small, slow-moving detachments. As a further reinforcement, Joseph formed his guard and a brigade from the Madrid garrison into a division under General Dessolles amounting to 5,700 men. Therefore, when the French army concentrated at Bargas on 25 July, there were in hand 46,000 men, of whom 7,500 were cavalry. No British troops were in the vicinity, but Spanish troops had followed Victor in strength when he had retreated from Talavera.

This division of the allied strength resulted from a quarrel between Wellesley and Cuesta. When the allies reached Talavera, Victor had taken up a strong position on the east bank of the river Alberche, a few miles east of the town. Wellesley, knowing that the allies outnumbered the marshal's 22,000 men by more than two to one, proposed to attack. Cuesta, "owing," said Wellesley, "to the whimsical perversity of his disposition," refused to move. Nevertheless, when on the following day (24 July) it was found that Victor had retired, Cuesta insisted that the French were flying to Madrid and insisted on advancing. Wellesley refused to accompany him, remarking that "Cuesta will get himself into a scrape, but any movement by me to his assistance is quite out of the question."[25] The British were already on half rations and "no man can see his army perish by want."[26]

Cuesta did get into a scrape. His advanced guard found the French in unexpected strength at Torrijos on 26 July. His cavalry suffered a sharp rebuff and he beat a hasty retreat in some disorder, reaching the Alberche at nightfall. Despite Wellesley's pleas, he insisted on encamping his army on the eastern, French, side of the river. Had Victor pursued him with anything resembling zeal, the whole Spanish army must have been destroyed. On the following morning, he consented to cross the river and took up a position, chosen for him by his ally, in the town of Talavera.

King Joseph was determined to prove to his brother that he, too, could win victories. From 25 July, he was at the head of 46,000 men and had an enemy within easy reach. All he needed was to turn his titular command into effective leadership. In fact, he was no more than the chairman of a committee. It was true that three of the four members of the committee would give him sound advice and, under all normal circumstances, their support. Marshal Jourdan, his chief of staff, General Sebastiani, commander of the Fourth Corps, and General Dessolles, commanding the reserve division, were all his friends and mutual trust existed between them. It was the fourth member who was the dominant figure. Claude Victor Perrin, duke of Belluno, marshal of the empire, commander of the First Corps, was an old friend of the emperor from the desperate days at Toulon in 1793. He was a hero of Marengo, Ulm, and Friedland. His corps and its attendant cavalry made up half of Joseph's army. Despite his jovial face, he was hot-headed; his judgment in the heat of battle was suspect, and, over the last six months, he had formed a poor opinion of the abilities of both Joseph and Jourdan which he scarcely bothered to conceal. No one in the French headquarters had any doubt that if there was any credit to be gained, Victor was going to seize it, but that if things went wrong, it was going to be King Joseph's fault.

On 26 July, when Cuesta had blundered up to the French outposts at Torrijos, the committee had been unanimous. Cuesta's army was alone and must be pursued and hammered. Victor led the pursuit but moved cautiously. He did not know where the British were, and although he had every intention of routing them, he was unwilling to meet them unexpectedly. By the evening of that day he had lost touch with the Spanish rear guard.

He started cautiously again on the twenty-seventh. When the heat of the midday sun grew oppressive, he halted his leading infantry while the rear of the army closed up. He sent forward cavalry patrols to try to find where the allies were. It was a very sensible proceeding, but King Joseph was anxious to press forward. He believed that the enemy might slip away. It would be fatal to all his plans if the British retired so that Soult's advance could not cut in behind them. They must be found and fought. Only a battle would pin them down long enough for Soult to arrive from Salamanca. The king sent forward peremptory orders to advance. Victor ignored them. The orders were repeated. Victor stayed where he was. When he received these orders for the third time, the marshal lost his temper. "He mounted his horse and rode back to the King. Instead," wrote an aide-de-camp who was present, "of putting forward a reasoned case, he made a violent scene in front of the whole staff and seemed particularly angry with Marshal Jourdan. Jourdan, although not mentioned by name, thought it his duty to reply. He told Marshal Victor that this was not the time for explanations, but that he could have all that he could wish for later. After this quarrel, which took place before more than a hundred witnesses, the Marshal rode to the head of his divisions and led them rapidly towards the river Alberche."[27]

The First Corps reached the east bank of the river, brushing away some skirmishers whom Victor, wrongly, thought to be Portuguese. From the high ground on that side they could see, three to four miles ahead, the allied army taking up its positions, its right on the Tagus in the town of Talavera, its left on a dominating hill, the Cerro de Medellín. On the cerro could be seen the red coats of the British infantry. Undisturbed by the allies, staff officers went to left and right of the unbroken bridge and found fords. Almost immediately the corps started to cross on a wide front. They were unopposed. Lapisse's division pushed forward through woodland until suddenly it came under a lively fire of musketry. They had, they thought, been ambushed. At once Lapisse deployed his leading regiment and attacked. "The enemy, disconcerted by the vivacity of our attack, retired precipitately on their main position. We took some prisoners."[28]

No ambush had been intended. The British rear guard had had been withdrawing to the main position and had halted in the middle of the wood believing that they were still covered by the light cavalry, who had, in fact, retired to the flanks. Carelessly, they had not established a proper picket line and in consequence some battalions were surprised. The medical officer of one of them wrote,

> The bloody business commenced much sooner than we expected. I myself sat eating under a tree without an idea that the enemy could be less than three miles distant, when the most tremendous firing immediately came driving towards us. In an instant musket as well as cannon balls were flying about in every direction. The soldiers were surprised; some regiments had not yet loaded their firelocks. The [skirmishers] retreated upon us with the enemy after them. One British regiment fired into another. A slight confusion took place which gave advantage to the French and caused much bloodshed. We, in that short space, lost a great part of our regiment. The

enemy followed up their momentary success. We retreated from the wood until we took up a position
on a hill."[29]

It was an auspicious opening of the campaign against the
British. They lost some 400 men, including 80 prisoners. The
French losses were small, less than 100. Believing that they
had defeated an ambush rather than surprising two carelessly
led brigades, the French, and Victor in particular, came to
believe that the British were as easy to beat as the Spaniards.
Joseph believed that he had won a victory.

As the French emerged from the woods, they got a clear
view of the allied position. It was about two and a half miles
long with its southern end secured on the Tagus and the town
of Talavera. For a mile north of the town walls the country
was very blind, being covered with vineyards interspersed
with sunken roads and solid stone walls. North of this stretch
was a mile of open rolling country, rising gently from the
Portina Brook, a largely dry watercourse to the east and
towards the Cerro de Medellín to the north. The cerro itself
was a formidable hill, rising nearly three hundred feet from
the level of the river, with a particularly steep face to the east,
where it fell away to the Portina Brook. To the north of it,
the ground fell away to a plain about a mile wide which was
bordered by the foothills of the Sierra de Segurilla, broken
country unsuitable for fighting. Behind the cerro ran a ridge
shading away to the west.

Both sides recognized that the cerro was the key to the
position. Wellesley had put the main strength of the British
troops as its garrison. The remainder held the open stretch
between the cerro and the broken ground north of Talavera,
where the Spaniards took up the front. Thus 20,000 British
held rather more than half the line, and that the most exposed
part, while 32,000 Spaniards were packed into the southern
half, where their inability to maneuver under fire would prove
less of a liability.

Victor's first move was to find where the Spaniards were. He sent a brigade of light cavalry in the direction of Talavera. Before the horsemen were within range, the Spaniards greeted them with a resounding volley,* while some two thousand of them, with no French in front of them, took to their heels and fled, being, in Wellesley's opinion "only frightened by the noise of their own fire."[30] It was another good augury for the French attack. Victor, indeed, was so confident that without consulting the king, he ordered Ruffin's division to attack the cerro by night. Aided by the carelessness of a Hanoverian brigadier who had failed to post sentries, some French troops reached the crest and inflicted severe losses on one of Wellesley's German battalions, but many more lost their way in the difficult, dark ascent, and, after some anxious moments, the British drove Ruffin's men back down the slope. For the rest of the night neither army moved, but, particularly on the allied side, there were constant outbreaks of musketry due to false alarms.

Victor reported his failure to the king, adding that he would renew the attack at dawn unless he was ordered not to do so. "Perhaps," wrote Jourdan, "we should have told him to wait until we had reconnoitred the enemy position and until we had everything ready for a general action; but the Marshal, who had spent a long time around Talavera and knew the ground perfectly, seemed so certain of success, that the King felt that he ought to let him have his head."[31] There was another consideration. The king knew that if he held Victor back, that marshal "would not omit writing to the Emperor saying that he had been prevented from scoring a brilliant victory over the English."[32]

Thus, at five o'clock in the morning, fifty-four French guns opened fire against the Cerro de Medellín and the open ground to the south. The British reply was weak. Wellesley had only twenty-four guns on that part of the front. Moreover, there

* Wellesley, who was nearby, remarked to a British officer in the Spanish service, "If they will but fire as well tomorrow, the day is our own; but as there seems to be nobody to fire at just now, I wish you would stop it" (Whittingham, 88).

was a strong east wind blowing, which blew the smoke across the Portina and hid the French advance from the British. For some reason Victor again entrusted the attack to Ruffin's division, which had suffered 300 or 400 casualties in its abortive night attack. The early part of its advance was bloodless, as it was covered by the artillery smoke. Driving in the British skirmishers, who put up an obstinate resistance, the whole division came in sight of the defenders, who were lining the crest of the cerro. Ruffin had almost 5,000 men, nine battalions in three close columns. Opposed to them were six British battalions under Rowland Hill. There were only 4,000 of them, but, unlike their opponents, they were drawn out in two deep lines so that every musket could bear on the packed French ranks. For a few minutes there was a blazing exchange of fire. Then, finding that the British were moving against the left flank of their column, the French broke and fled down the hill, pursued by the bayonets of Hill's men, who halted on the line of the Portina, reformed, and marched back to their old position on the crest. Ruffin's division had suffered another 1,500 casualties, twice as many as their opponents.

This second attack was over by eight o'clock, and there followed a lull during which the soldiers of both sides fraternized while drinking from the muddy pools of the Portina, and stretcher parties crossed the lines to collect their wounded. The French cooked and ate their morning meal and those of the British who had any rations did the same.

About ten o'clock, King Joseph rode up the hill opposite the Cerro de Medellín on the French side of the Portina, escorted by his staff and most of the generals. His appearance drew some fire from the British batteries. It was observed that "although it was the first time that he had been on a field of battle, he was constantly in good countenance."[33] He then held a council of war. It was now clear that the British were not fighting a rear-guard action as some French officers had imagined. That day, 28 July, was the one on which Joseph and Jourdan, encouraged by Foy's optimism, had calculated that Soult would reach Plasencia. The news from Madrid was grave. Venegas had at last appeared on the Tagus and was threatening the crossings at Toledo and Aranjuez. The garrisons of these places were small and could not be expected to hold out for more than two or three days, after which Venegas could march to the capital unopposed.

When the king asked Jourdan for his opinion as to whether to renew the attack or not, he replied that "the position was a very strong one, defended by an enemy in superior numbers, and one which to him seemed not to be seizable by frontal attack." He added that Victor might have achieved something if, instead of launching frontal attacks on it, he had moved troops into the plain during the night and had attempted to outflank it at dawn. Now it could be seen that the enemy were moving troops into the plain. This was true. Wellesley, anticipating the next French move, had sent his cavalry into the plain and was supporting them with a division of Spanish infantry, some Spanish cavalry, and a battery of heavy Spanish guns. Jourdan summed up by saying that he was of the opinion that the French "should wait and watch the enemy either in the position which they now occupied or on the line of the Alberche, until the English were forced to separate from the Spaniards by the advance of Soult."[34] He had the warm support of General Dessolles. Victor, determined to revenge himself for his two repulses, insisted that if the whole of First and Fourth corps were committed against the cerro and against its two flanks, a great victory must be won. The Spanish army in and near Talavera could be watched, as they had been so far, by a division of dragoons twenty-three hundred strong. "If," he concluded, "we cannot take that hill, we had better give up soldiering."[35]

The choice, therefore, lay with Joseph. Wisdom dictated that they should wait. Sooner or later Soult's advance must make the British retreat from their formidable position. The chances of victory were less than even. The cerro was a most formidable position. On the other hand, Joseph was afraid for his capital and felt that he could only detach troops to save it if the British were defeated. He was afraid of what Victor would tell the emperor if he were not allowed to attack; above all, he was desperately anxious to win a victory, to prove to his brother that he, too, was a great commander. He authorized an attack by Victor and Sebastiani, supported on the extreme right by a cavalry division, against the whole length of the British line. It failed. There were times, especially on Sebastiani's part of the front, where a breakthrough seemed probable. In the plain to the north an overambitious attack by two British light cavalry regiments was heavily punished, losing 240 men out of less than 900, but the French attack failed utterly. Not a foot of ground could be taken and held.

Just as the French were recoiling, a report was received from General Milhaud, the cavalry commander who was watching the Spaniards, that a strong column was emerging from Talavera and making for the bridge over the Alberche in the French rear. Immediately orders were sent for the whole French army to retire to the river line. The aide-de-camp who took these orders to Victor found him "calm and full of confidence. He told me that General Milhaud's report was not true, that from his position he could see the main road and that not a man had left Talavera."[36] He added that it was his belief that the enemy was retiring and that if the king would put Dessolles's reserve division under his orders, he could take the cerro. Meantime he would wait in his position.

The king refused to commit Dessolles's division but agreed to suspend the order to retreat, and at nightfall the French army held its ground on the east of the Portina Brook. Before midnight, however, Victor lost his nerve and started to march his corps back across the Alberche. When this movement was under way, he told the king and Sebastiani what he was doing. Sebastiani never forgave him, but in the morning the whole French army was on the far side of the river.

King Joseph had gambled and lost. The allies were still firmly in their position. By refusing Victor's demand to be allowed to make a final attempt on the cerro with Dessolles's division, he had not even covered himself against that marshal's reproach to the emperor that he had not had the king's whole-hearted support. No one, not even Victor himself, believed that Dessolles would have turned the scale, but no one believed that Victor would not use the king's refusal as an excuse to cover his own inept handling of the battle.

The only claim that could reasonably be advanced was that the allied advance had been checked, that the British had been fought to a standstill. This was all but true. The British casualties amounted to 5,363 killed, wounded, or missing—almost one in four of the troops present. The French loss totaled 7,268—one in six—but they were much more able to bear the loss of this number, and had they succeeded in defeating Wellesley, it would have been a cheap price to pay. Cuesta returned a loss of 1,200 men, but since the Spaniards had scarcely been engaged, this figure, if true, must have been made up largely of deserters.* This was largely irrelevent, since after their performance on 26 and 27 July, neither French nor British reckoned the Army of Estremadura as an effective force for offensive operations.

Joseph, however, was determined to have a victory, and if he could not have one in the field, he set out to win one on paper. On the morning after the battle he wrote to his brother, from the east side of the Alberche River, mendaciously heading the letter "*Du bivouac de Talavera.*" Grandiloquently he started his report, "Yesterday the English army was driven back into its positions. . . . Apart from 25,000 to 30,000 English commanded by Wellesley, we also had an affair with Cuesta's army which amounted to 35–40,000 men. The battle was very hot, we have suffered losses, the enemy defended his position with the greatest obstinacy. . . . the battlefield, on which we are camped, is heaped with the English dead. . . . The 30th regiment of English dragoons was taken prisoner.**

* Cuesta had 25 men shot for cowardice on 29 July. He would have shot 200 had Wellesley not interceded for their lives.
** There was no regiment called the Thirtieth Dragoons on the British Army List (the Twenty-fifth being the last). This presumably refers to the Twenty-third Light Dragoons, who lost 49 killed, 50 wounded, and 108 missing out of 535 all ranks present.

. . . I had got together 45,000 men, who beat Cuesta on the 26th, the English on the 27th and both together on the 28th. . . . I regret that we did not capture the whole British army. We would have done so if we had had two hours more daylight on the 27th."[37] "Never," he wrote in a supplementary farrago, "have the English made such efforts on the continent. . . . Officer prisoners say that in the battles of the 27th and 28th the flower of the English nobility perished."*

Jourdan, although his advice had been disregarded throughout, loyally backed his master and, unlike Victor, made his reports in accordance with the line taken by the king. He added, "His Majesty preferred to risk a battle as the more honorable of the alternatives open to him."[39]

Even if Joseph could not defeat Wellesley, he should have had the intelligence to know that he could not hope to deceive his brother over such a public event as a major battle. The emperor, moreover, had won the Battle of Wagram early in July and had more time to think about Spanish affairs. "He could not for several days dissemble his regret at the battle of Talavera. . . . and openly said that, although his best troops were in Spain, the movements in that country were a series of blunders."[40] It was the unfortunate and guiltless Jourdan who bore the brunt of his displeasure. "Let Marshal Jourdan know of my extreme displeasure at the inexactitudes and falsities to be found in his report; that his dispatches do not tell me what has occurred. . . . He says that on the 28th the English army was swept from the battlefield. . . . while subsequent reports say the opposite and that we were repulsed throughout the day. . . . It was my army that was beaten. Tell him he can put what he likes in the Madrid newspapers, but that he has no right to disguise the truth from the Government. . . . Tell him that when one attacks good troops, like the English, in good positions without reconnaissance and

---

* The "flower" of the English nobility lost at Talavera consisted of Ensign the Hon. Edward Irby, adjutant, Third Guards, killed; Captain the Hon. William Russell, Twenty-third Light Dragoons; Captain the Hon. Alex Gordon, Third Guards wounded.

without the certainty of success one condemns men to death for no purpose."[41]

Fuel was added to the emperor's rage by Wellesley's dispatch, which was printed in the English newspapers. Wellesley reported that the French left in British hands "twenty pieces of cannon, ammunition, tumbrils and some prisoners."[42] "You will see," wrote Napoleon to the minister of war, "that, according to the dispatches of Wellesley, the English general, we lost twenty guns and three flags.* Inform the King of my surprise, and General Jourdan of my displeasure, that, instead of being told the real state of affairs, I am sent republican romances, the kind of history they write for schoolboys. Tell them I want to know what gunners abandoned their pieces. . . . Allow the King to infer from your letter that I regret to see from his Order of the Day that he told the troops that they had won the battle."[43]

In fact, the allies had only seventeen French guns in their possession at the end of the day, the British having thirteen and the Spaniards four, although Wellesley understood them to hold seven. Jourdan, on 15 September, was still prepared to assert that no guns had been lost, although four days later he reported that, after all, two guns had been lost. Even this reluctant admission was stretching the truth past breaking point. In the interim the British, having no draft animals available, had handed their share of the captured artillery over to the Spaniards, who proceeded to abandon them. Thus, by 19 September, the French had recovered all but two guns. Jourdan, in his memoirs,[44] freely admits that three whole batteries had been captured by the allies, but to let this be known would not have fitted Joseph's attempt to prove a victory.

---

* There is no mention in Wellesley's dispatch of having captured any flags. This may have been a piece of embroidery added by the government or newspapers in London. Some kind of French flag, possibly a camp color, was captured by the Twenty-ninth Regiment. It was, however, not significant enough to be sent to London as a trophy and Wellesley returned it to the Twenty-ninth as "a testimonial of their gallant conduct" (SD, xiii, 348).

It was not only Joseph's victory that failed to materialize. The master plan, concerted with Soult, damaged the British even less than the Battle of Talavera. On the evening of the battle, the king learned that Soult had not started his march from Salamanca on the twenty-sixth, two days before. It had been Joseph's hope that Soult would have left Salamanca on the twenty-fourth and that, with good fortune, his leading troops would have been at Almaraz on the Tagus by the twenty-ninth. This was overly optimistic since the orders for the move did not leave Madrid until late at night on the twenty-second, and however fast General Foy had ridden, he could not have reached Soult at Salamanca before the twenty-fourth. It seems, however, that Foy, in his anxiety to persuade the king to adopt Soult's plan for an advance to Plasencia and the Tagus, had exaggerated the state of readiness of the three northern corps. Mortier's troops were still marching north from Villacastín. Ney's were as far north as the area of Astorga-León-Benavente, while although Soult had some troops around Salamanca, the bulk of his infantry was at Zamora and Toro. It was, in consequence, not until 27 July that Mortier's corps was able to lead the march south from Salamanca. Soult's corps followed on 30 July and Ney's on 1 August.

Mortier reached the Pass of Baños on 30 July and brushed aside the tiny garrison which Cuesta had allocated to guard this vital post. The following day he reached Plasencia, where he captured five hundred British sick and halted for Soult's corps to come up with him.

Even with Soult's belated start there was still a chance that the British might be cut off. Wellesley had remained at Talavera after the battle, burying his dead and tending his wounded. On the twenty-ninth he had been joined with a strong brigade, 3,000 troops from Lisbon, which had made good some of his losses, but although he knew that only Victor's corps was in front of him (Sebastiani and Joseph having marched for Toledo to drive off Venegas), he refused to advance as he could not feed the army. On the twenty-ninth, also, he heard that Cuesta had failed to block the Pass of Baños and that a French force was marching in that direction against his communications. He was not greatly perturbed since, believing that Soult and Ney were still entangled in Galicia, he estimated the strength of this new French force as not being above 12,000 men. There were some more tiresome negotiations with Cuesta, and it was agreed that the Spaniards would continue to face Victor, while the British marched away against the new threat. Wellesley marched west out of Talavera on 2 August with his 18,000 remaining fit men, leaving his wounded in Cuesta's care.

The following day, at Oropesa, Wellesley learned from a captured dispatch that Soult was coming down on his rear with at least 30,000 men. There was just time to avert the catastrophe which Joseph and Soult had planned for the British army. By the evening of 4 August, all Wellesley's men had crossed to the south bank of the Tagus at Arzobispo, while his newly joined light brigade was racing over hills to the southeast to secure the ford at Almaraz. They reached it twenty-four hours before Ney's men appeared on the north bank. Finding the crossing firmly held, Ney decided not to attempt to force his way across. The British were safe, and although Soult defeated Cuesta at Arzobispo and captured 2,000 British wounded, the French plan had failed to achieve its purpose—the British had neither been defeated nor driven into the sea. Wellesley, who on 4 September was created Viscount Wellington of Talavera, withdrew his men to the area Badajoz-Elvas, where he could feed them from Portugal.

Joseph had not gained his victory, but on 11 August he managed to reach Almonacid before Sebastiani had completely finished defeating Venegas and ensuring the safety of Madrid. The king returned to his capital in time to celebrate Napoleon's birthday, a date which the emperor had succeeded in elevating into a major church festival. Joseph did his best to give the impression that the *Te Deum* for Napoleon's fête was, in fact, in celebration of his own victories. He entered the city to the sound of a hundred-gun salute and rode along streets lined by troops whose coats were still covered with the dust of their marches. After Joseph attended the cathedral, there was a reception at court over which he presided in the formal dress of a French prince. Fireworks followed and to round off the evening there was a gala performance at the opera. Throughout the day it was noticed that the king paid marked attention to La Forest, the French ambassador, who rode to the opera in the royal coach and to whom he gave a cross of the Legion of Honor, mounted in diamonds, as "a momento of the feast of Napoleon, celebrated in the palace of the King of Spain." The following day, La Forest gave a gala dinner at the embassy, and on the seventeenth it was the turn of General Belliard, the French governor of Madrid, to play host to the king, the court, and, such as it was, the diplomatic corps.

The French army took up defensive positions with the five corps disposed in a great arc around Madrid, from Salamanca in the northwest to Cuenca in the southeast. Soult continued to agitate for an immediate invasion of Portugal and had to be restrained by an order from the emperor. There was an acrimonious exchange of letters between the king and Marshal Victor arising from the aftermath of Talavera. Joseph pointedly gave Victor permission to go to France on leave and offered command of his corps to Ney, whom he was anxious to please by removing him from Soult's command. Victor, however, did not reply to the offer of leave and Ney declined to take over the First Corps without an order from the emperor. In the end it was Ney who received imperial permission to go on leave, and he rode off to France, returning to Spain and the command of his old corps, the Sixth, early in 1810.

Marshal Jourdan, the only marshal Joseph would have wished to keep, also left Spain. At the end of August he was confined to bed "tortured with nervous troubles, stomach colic and backache."[45] Four weeks later Napoleon wrote from Vienna, "Give Marshal Jourdan the authority he requests to return to France, and let the King know that I have appointed Marshal Soult as Chief of Staff. . . . It is my intention that he should have command of all the Marshals employed in the Army of Spain and that, if necessary, he will take command of one or two corps and lead them against the enemy."[46]

It was the end of Joseph's dreams of military glory. No one was less likely to share any glory that might be won than Marshal Soult. In the future, the king would have to be content with no more than the titular command of the army. Napoleon wrote to Soult, "Since the King has no experience of war, it is my intention that you should be answerable to me until I return to Spain. I wish to enter Lisbon myself as soon as possible."[47]

There was one crumb of comfort for Joseph. On 2 September, the emperor wrote him a short note thanking him for his good wishes on the occasion of his fête. It was the first time he had written to his brother since 12 April.

Chapter 6

CONQUERING KING

The barriers placed by nature between northern and southern Spain have fallen.

JOSEPH'S ORDER OF THE DAY TO HIS TROOPS
AT SEVILLE, 1 FEBRUARY 1810.

PEACE between France and Austria, a peace triumphant for Napoleon, was signed on 14 October 1809. By that time, the British expedition to Walcheren on the Dutch coast was clearly failing, defeated not by the French but, as Napoleon had known that it must be, by "fever and bad air." Moreover, on 21 September, Castlereagh and Canning, the only talented members of the British cabinet, had fought a duel and, as a result, the government had collapsed. "The English ministers," wrote Napoleon to the czar, "are fighting amongst themselves, there is absolute anarchy in the Cabinet. Their folly and inconsequence are beyond belief."[1] It seemed that, with his eastern frontier secured, there was nothing to stop the whole weight of the French army from being turned once more against Spain. It was generally supposed that the emperor would command in person.

143

King Joseph had believed since August that his brother
would return to Spain. Napoleon, as has been seen, wrote to
Soult on 26 September of his intention to lead the French
army into Lisbon. Two weeks later the emperor ordered the
minister of war to prepare one hundred thousand reinforcements for Spain and said that he would lead them himself.
Joseph was so convinced of his arrival that in mid-October he
sent his principal chamberlain and principal equerry to the
frontier "to receive Your Majesty's orders for the arrangements concerned with your arrival."[2] At the end of November,
orders were given for the imperial carriages and riding horses
to be sent to Bayonne, and on 5 December the Old Guard was
ordered to march to the same place. Two days earlier, in a
speech to the Legislative Assembly, the emperor had declared, "When I show myself beyond the Pyrenees, the
terrified leopard will seek safety in the ocean, from shame,
defeat and destruction."[3] Twelve days later he promulgated
his divorce of the Empress Josephine and his intention to
marry the Austrian archduchess Marie Louise.

No one can tell whether it was ever Napoleon's real intention to return to the Peninsula or whether it was all an elaborate fanfarronade designed to frighten the British government.
One thing is certain. He managed to convince his brother that
he was returning, and Joseph knew that once Napoleon returned there would be no further hope of military glory for
him.

For more than three months after the Talavera campaign
fizzled out there was little military activity in western Spain.
Wellington's army was recuperating around Badajoz. The
Spaniards were planning an elaborate campaign designed to
drive the whole French army over the Pyrenees, and the
French were in serious need of time to rest and refit. King
Joseph's government was, as was now usual, on or beyond
the verge of bankruptcy. His household and government were
four months in arrears of salary. His tax collectors were edged
out of the conquered provinces by the French generals, who
were collecting on behalf of their troops and, in some cases,

of themselves. In desperation, he confiscated the goods of all the families who supported the Seville junta and of all the religious orders. The value of these confiscations was enormous; the cash he received from their sale was derisory in amount. Even his most devoted adherent was unlikely to offer a high price for an estate haunted by guerrillas. His action against the monks and nuns merely resulted in confirming the Spanish opinion that since the Revolution all Frenchmen had been heathen. In the king's opinion, however, the confiscation "was generally received better than I had hoped."[4] He may, too, have been somewhat gratified to find that when he established the Royal and Military Order of Spain the prince of the Asturias solicited for membership.

At the beginning of November, Joseph was in the depths of one of his periodic depressions. He wrote to his wife, "The Emperor seems to be displeased with me; he no longer writes to me. . . . If his feelings for me have changed, I must seek a position where I do not continuously require his full confidence. . . . If his aim has been to make me sick of Spain, he has succeeded. Anything else would suit me better. If it is agreeable to him, I will retire to the depths of the country, far from the main roads, with my family. I promise him I will never visit Paris; books and trees will be my diversions; my children will be my amusement. . . . I must have frankness and friendship from the Emperor if I am to remain King of Spain."[5]

Part of the cause of the king's dissatisfaction was his new chief of staff, who took up his post at the beginning of November. Nicholas Jean de Dieu Soult, marshal duke of Dalmatia, was not a pleasant man. He was, said one of his aides-de-camp, "a hard man and supremely selfish."[6] Ambitious, avaricious, and suspicious, Soult had few friends, even amongst his own staff. Nevertheless, he was a supremely competent professional soldier. Napoleon, remembering his part in the victory of Austerlitz, could forgive him almost anything, even his intrigues to secure the Portuguese throne. As a military planner, he had few equals. Tactically, he had his failings. One officer who served under him wrote, "Proud of his reputation, he was full of assurance on the day before a battle: he recovered that assurance on the day after a defeat. But in action he seemed unable to issue good orders, to choose good positions, or to move his troops freely. It seemed as if any scheme which he had once conceived and written down at his desk was an immutable decree from heaven, which he had not the power to vary by subsequent change."[7] This view of Soult is confirmed by Wellington, who remarked that "he is unrivalled as a strategist but timid in action."[8] Timid was not quite the word which some of his French detractors would have used about him. To quote his aide-de-camp, "If I say that he loved vigorous enterprises, I must add that he loved them only if they did not involve too much personal danger to himself, for he was far from possessing the brillant courage of Ney or Lannes. It might even be said that he was the reverse of rash—that he looked after his skin a little too carefully."[9]

Joseph realized that his relations with Soult would be very different to those he had enjoyed with Jourdan. The old marshal had been his loyal adviser and confidant. Soult saw himself in the light of a Prussian chief of staff, the effective head of the army, leaving to the king only the titular command and the faint reflection of any glory that Soult himself won. Nor was Soult the kind of companion whom Joseph would have chosen for himself. Nevertheless, if the king was to win the military glory which he craved, he would have to cooperate with Soult, and he set himself, successfully, to treat the marshal with respect, flattery, and courtesy.

When Soult took over the effective command, his main problems seemed to be in the north of Spain. He reported to Paris that "communications with Bayonne are becoming increasingly difficult; only detachments of two or three hundred men can get through; there are daily skirmishes and several couriers have been seized."[10] There was even more serious trouble in the northwest. In mid-October, General Marchand, commanding Sixth Corps at Salamanca in Ney's absence, heard that a Spanish force was on the move to the south of the main road from Ciudad Rodrigo to Salamanca. He immediately marched against it, taking all his available strength, 12,000 infantry, 1,200 cavalry, and 14 guns. At Tamanes he found the duke del Parque with 20,000 passable infantry, 1,500 horse, and 18 guns drawn up in a very strong position. Rashly, Marchand attacked (18 October) and was repulsed with 1,500 casualties. Forced to retreat, he fell back through Salamanca and on northwards towards the Douro. On 25 October, del Parque, who had won the first Spanish victory since Bailén, marched his troops triumphantly into Salamanca.

The setback did not cause overmuch concern in Madrid. Plenty of troops were available to deal with del Parque. Eight thousand men were sent off from the troops in and around the capital, and Marchand was superceded by General Kellermann. del Parque's occupation of Salamanca lasted less than a fortnight. Thus, when Soult took over, the situation in León was, at least, contained and there seemed no reason for worry, especially as Soult could report, on 6 November, that "the troops on the Tagus and in La Mancha are quiet and, from all I hear, the enemy is not intending any offensive move."[11]

Soult was wrong. As he wrote that report, a large Spanish army was completing its concentration on the northern slopes of Sierra Morena. Even before the final moves of the Talavera campaign had been made, the Supreme Junta at Seville had started making plans for a vast encircling movement which would liberate Madrid and drive the French behind the Ebro. Even given the blind and unreasoning Spanish faith in the invincibility of their armies, this was a foolhardy plan, but the junta was falling into such disrepute that a victory was desperately needed to restore their credit with the Spanish people. They had used every means to inviegle Wellington into cooperating, but believing the Junta's plan to be "rank nonsense,"[12] he firmly and consistently declined to be involved. Wellington was sick of cooperating with the Spaniards. After the Talavera campaign, he had remarked that "the fault I committed consisted in trusting at all to the Spaniards, who I have since found were entirely unworthy of confidence."[13] He was convinced that if he allowed himself to be sucked into the junta's new scheme, he would be fortunate if he could extricate the British army from the debacle that must inevitably follow.

The Spaniards, undismayed, went on alone. del Parque's army, the victors of Tamanes, were in fact the northern arm of the junta's pincer movement. The southern arm consisted of the army that Venegas had commanded so ineffectively during the Talavera campaign, strengthened with large drafts of untrained recruits and three divisions from the army that had been Cuesta's*. Venegas had been displaced by an elderly general, Carlos Areizaga, a man of proven courage but no experience of high command. His force consisted of almost 60,-000 men, including 5,700 cavalry, with 60 guns. On paper it was a formidable force; in fact, much of it was little better than an armed mob. "I wish," wrote the British liaison officer with Areizaga, "I had anything agreeable to communicate to you from this army. . . . but nothing can exceed the general discontent, dissatisfaction, and demoralization of the people and of the army. . . . There is not a man of the least reflection who, as things now stand, has the least hope of success."[14]

With more than three French corps available to oppose him, Areizaga had only one chance of success—surprise. This he realized. Having concentrated his force at Santa Cruz de Mudela at the southern end of the Pass of La Carolina, he advanced on 3 November, moving fast and keeping the troops well closed up. The French were utterly unready for him. On the 8th his main body was at La Guardia, eighty miles from Santa Cruz, and his advanced cavalry, having driven in the French videttes, was threatening Aranjuez on the Tagus, only thirty-five miles from Madrid. Between Areizaga and the capital there were only 5,000 Polish infantry and 1,800 dragoons.

* Fortunately for the Spanish cause, Cuesta had been disabled by a stroke in mid-August and had resigned his command. The remainder of the Army of Estremadura was, in November 1809, commanded by the duke of Albuquerque, a general of modest competence distrusted by the junta for his pro-English sympathies.

Madrid was within his grasp. Then the Spanish general lost his nerve. For three days his infantry waited at La Guardia. Then he made a series of short marches, changing his direction almost every day. Meanwhile, Soult was concentrating the French corps. On 19 November, Areizaga stood for battle at Ocaña. Joseph and Soult came up to him with 33,500 men, the Fourth and Fifth corps supported by the Royal Guards and a strong force of cavalry. Soult, according to King Joseph, was in favor of waiting until Victor, who was some twenty miles away, pressed in on the Spanish rear, but Joseph insisted on attacking at once. He was amply justified. Areizaga had drawn up his men with one flank in the air. The French cavalry, backed by infantry, crashed in on this vulnerable flank while the Spanish attention was held by infantry attacks on their front. Areizaga's great host broke and fled. They left in French hands 14,000 prisoners and 50 guns. In addition, some 4,000 men were killed or wounded. The wreck of the army streamed back over the Sierra Morena as fast as their legs could carry them. The French casualties were less than 2,000. Nine days later, Kellermann routed del Parque, whom he had surprised bivouacked astride the river at Alba de Tormes. The junta's much vaunted concentric offensive had ended, as it deserved to do, in disaster.

Aside from Aragon and Catalonia, over which the king had, day by day, less control or even interest, there was now no effective Spanish army in the field except Albuquerque's 10,-000 men of the Army of Estremadura, which was stationed around Almaraz. There remained only the British. Since early September, Wellington had quartered his army around Badajoz. On 20 November, before the news of Ocaña could have reached him, he made up his mind that his first task must be to defend Portugal. The news of the Spanish defeats only confirmed him in his opinion. "I declare that if they had preserved their two armies, or even one of them, the cause was safe. . . . But no! Nothing will answer excepting to fight great battles in the plains, in which their defeat is as certain as is the commencement of the battle."[15] On 8 December his army started to retreat across the frontier and, except for a single division which halted at Abrantes, moved to a position west of Ciudad Rodrigo covering the road which any full-scale attack on Lisbon must take. The rear of the army, Wellington's headquarters, left Spain on Christmas Eve.

Joseph had anticipated this move. Five days before the first British troops left Spain, the king reported that the "English army has retired into Portugal since 24th November."[16] A month later, Soult was encouraging himself with the thought that they might be leaving Portugal also.[17] In Madrid it seemed that attention could now be turned to completing "the submission of the kingdom."

December was a quiet month from a military point of view. The French troops were moved forward to cover the exits from the main passes of the Sierra Morena, but there was no fighting. In the capital there was even an attempt at gaiety. Major Comte de Saint Chamans wrote that "I found Madrid an amusing town; all the pleasures of a great city were there and I had been without them for a long time. The Spanish ladies said, with great charm, that although they hated the French government and the French nation as a whole, they liked individual Frenchmen, particularly when they got to know them. King Joseph's court was no more boring than any other and there was quite a good Italian opera and a passable ballet. I would happily have spent the winter there."[18]

General Foy, who visited the capital at the New Year, was not so enthusiastic.

> On 1st January the King held a reception to which I went. The salons were filled with Frenchmen but there were only a few Spaniards. Amongst these only one wore the Order of the Golden Fleece—the Duke of Branciforte, brother-in-law of the Prince of the Peace. The grandees are all at Seville. I would be there too if I were in their place; I could not bear the humiliation of seeing my country given a king by fraud and force. King Joseph is a very amiable man, but he has

not been sufficiently lucky and he has not done enough to help his luck. He is fond of pleasure but does not value military glory enough; he is generous but gives carelessly. He does not work hard enough; he is half philosopher, half king. . . . It has now been decided to invade Andalusia; the troops are already moving into position. Many weighty objections have been raised to this expedition; it is said to be unwise since the English, who are still on the borders of Portugal, can, by making a few safe marches, force the army back from Seville and Cordoba to the north bank of the Tagus; it is said that to march the army into Andalusia might prejudice the Emperor's plans if he should come to Spain; it is said that the Emperor would be displeased whether the expedition succeeded or whether it failed. To this Marshal Soult replies that the invasion of Andalusia is the natural sequel to the victory at Ocaña; that the English will not move on Madrid and that, even if they did, he would not be greatly alarmed; that it was uncertain whether the Emperor would come to Spain or not and that he was too great a man to find fault with success. Privately Soult added to me that the King is strongly in favour of the Andalusian expedition; that he would accompany it, bringing his government with him; that, by giving an active turn to events in Spain, he will stop the Emperor from coming to Spain; that the King had, in brief, given him a formal order in his own handwriting to prepare the advance.[19]

Discouraging Napoleon's coming to Spain was not the king's only motive for determining to invade Andalusia. He was, at that time, acutely conscious of being king of only half a country. South of the Sierra Morena lay the richest, most fertile, and most populous province of Spain. In Andalusia were to be found silver mines, mercury mines, and the great mercantile riches of Cádiz. With these under his control, he could pay the expenses of his government; he could even pay the expenses of the French army as his brother kept hounding him to do. With Andalusia conquered, it might be possible to reduce the number of French troops in Spain; he hoped to be able to send 50,000 into Portugal, where they could forage and plunder at Portuguese expense rather than at Spanish. Even if all these dreams were not to be realized, it would put the front line far away from Madrid and New Castille and the only fully pacified part of his existing kingdom would be spared the troubles of supporting 60,000 French troops. Above all, Joseph wanted to make a conquest, to force his brother to admit that he had at least the makings of a great general. Two targets were open to him—Andalusia and Portugal. In Portugal was the formidable Wellington with the British who had fought so staunchly at Talavera. In Andalusia there was only the wreck of the army routed at Ocaña. The emperor had ordered that Portugal should not be invaded before February. There would be plenty of time for that.

While it is easy to see why the king was so determined to occupy Andalusia, it is difficult to understand how he was allowed to undertake an expedition which had such doleful results, all of which were foreseeable. It is remarkable that Soult should have abetted such a blunder and that Napoleon did not forbid it. Soult had for months past been urging an invasion of Portugal and had only been restrained from undertaking it by the emperor's order postponing it until February. It was more than probable that he would have commanded the Portuguese expedition. He and Joseph had been agreed as early as June that "the destruction of the English army is the only important concern."[20] In the early weeks of the year there was more than enough work to be done in putting down the guerrillas and clearing communications with France. Soult, however, begged Berthier* to be allowed to use the new

---

* Louis Alexandre Berthier, marshal prince of Neufchatel and Wagram, was appointed chief of staff of the Army of Spain from 1 December 1809. As such, he was, in Paris, the channel of communication between the emperor and the army in Spain. Soult was chief of staff to the king.

troops which were now beginning to cross the Pyrenees as part of Napoleon's massive program of reinforcement for the unglamorous business of clearing the roads, while he, himself, sought an elusive glory in the south. Since, unlike Joseph, Soult had no need to go in search of military reputation, it can only be assumed that he believed that the campaign would be a short and easy one and that it would give him ample opportunities for enriching himself. In this last belief he was certainly correct. One thing is beyond all reasonable doubt— Soult did not undertake the expedition under protest, as a result of Joseph's written orders. It is certain that he would have had no hesitation about appealing to the emperor over the king's head if he had disapproved of the order, even supposing that that he would not directly have disobeyed such a command. He was, however, careful both in conversation and in writing, at the time and in later life, to give the impression that he was no more than a loyal soldier executing his royal master's design.

Soult's motive in supporting the Andalusian expedition was almost certainly avarice. Napoleon's motive in failing to forbid an operation which he believed to be wrongly conceived cannot be guessed. He knew of Joseph's intentions by Christmas 1809 but he made no comment. It was not until the last day of January, the day that Seville surrendered, that he deigned to notice the plan at all. At that time it can only be inferred that he approved of it. He confined his comments to insisting that the expedition should take with it a siege train, since, "if the enemy know that the means of bombardment and mining are absent, it might stiffen his resistance." He also insisted that strong and properly coordinated forces should be left on the Portuguese frontier to guard against British diversions aimed at Madrid or Salamanca, "as these will encourage resistance at Cádiz." These stipulations were far from forbidding an expedition which he knew was already launched, yet at the end of his letter is a sentence which shows that he correctly assessed the priorities in the Peninsula. "The English are the only danger in Spain; the rest are only a rable who can never stand and fight."[21] Could Napoleon also have been looking to the wealth of Andalusia?

It is sure that, possibly unintentionally, the emperor encouraged his brother to fresh military adventures. On 11 November, in one of his rare personal letters, he wrote to Joseph, "How can it be that, with an army so large and good and with so inconsiderable an enemy before you, things are no further forward?"[22] To Joseph, always sensitive to imputations of military backwardness, this was decisive. Having mulled it over for some days, he replied, "I am concerned that Your Majesty should feel that the army should be further forward; not a day has been wasted since the actions at Ocaña and Alba; I have been pressing the preliminary movements on as fast as possible. . . . The government at Seville is at its last gasp; the moment is at hand, and I shall take advantage of it. All the orders are given; it will not be my fault if things are not settled in Andalusia; everything is ready."[23] The emperor could not claim that he had not been warned.

Five days before Joseph wrote this definite statement of his intentions, Soult had pressed the same plan on Berthier. "At no time since the start of the war in Spain have circumstances been so favourable for the invasion of Andalusia, and advantageous results could probably be obtained. I have already told Your Excellency of the preparations that are being made while we wait for the Emperor to make his intentions known."[24] No comment returned from Paris, and on New Year's Day, when the king was expressing to the emperor his hope that the aide-de-camp would bring back with him "Your Majesty's observations on the orders I have given for the expedition to Andalusia,"[25] Soult was being rather more definite. "According to all the reports reaching him, the King is convinced that the greatest anarchy reigns in Andalusia and that the inhabitants of that unhappy province wait only for an opportunity to declare for him; he further believes that, to profit by these circumstances and to prepare for more important movements, now is the time to cross the Sierra Morena and to establish the Imperial troops on the southern slopes of these mountains. His Majesty has instructed me to give orders accordingly."[26] There was no answer.

By 11 January, when the royal headquarters were at Almagro near Ciudad Real, making last minute arrangements with Marshal Victor, Soult showed himself wholly committed to the enterprise. "It is to be hoped," he wrote to Berthier, "that the war in Spain will be over in a single day. It seems that the enemy is intending to rally the Army of Castille, led by the Duke del Parque, on the wreck of the Army of La Mancha. His Majesty the Emperor can count on his troops gaining another victory and, in consequence, on all the results that must naturally flow from it."[27]

Areizaga, despite his poor showing at Ocaña, was still in charge of the Spanish defense line on the Sierra Morena. He was faced with an insoluble military problem. His political masters, the Supreme Junta at Seville, were wholly discredited by the November disasters and were on the point of disintegration. Contrary to the French fears, del Parque's army did not leave León to join him, and he was left with less than 25,000 men to cover a front of 160 miles. Even the troops he had were, except for the cadres of some regular regiments, peasants hastily dressed in uniforms and with British muskets thrust into their hands.

Against him Joseph and Soult brought 68,000, all, save a few skeletal Spanish regiments composed of *afrancesados*, first-class, war-hardened veterans. Having such a superiority in numbers, the French were able to advance in four disconnected columns and still outnumber their enemy at every point. On 20 January, the main passes over the Sierra were forced. Two days later, Sebastiani on the French left captured Jaén and forty-six guns with little more than a skirmish. The day before, Joseph had marched triumphantly into Bailén, where the bishop had handed over to him two Eagles captured from Dupont's men in the disaster of 1808. The king was able to report to his brother that "Your Majesty's troops are behaving well and bringing the inhabitants back to their natural loyalty. The troops want for nothing."[28]

On 24 January, Victor marched the First Corps into Cordoba unopposed, leading the vast bulk of the invading army, now reunited into a mass 50,000 strong. The king was filled with a confidence he had never known before. "Cordoba and Jaén have opened their gates and have sent deputations to me. Granada will do the same. . . . In a few days I shall be in Seville. . . . the people are overwhelmed with joy; the troops are behaving well. The general pacification will be achieved."[29] To the Spaniards he issued a proclamation. "The new war on the continent* and English help have prolonged an unequal struggle, the horrors of which have been felt by the whole nation. The outcome has never been in doubt; today's force of arms has demonstrated the fact. It is in the interest of France to maintain the independence of Spain. . . . No longer let yourself be swayed by the passions stirred up by our common enemy. There is still time. Rally around me so that from this day there will dawn a new era of glory and happiness for Spain."[30]

Leaving Sebastiani to secure Granada with 10,000 men, while Dessolles with 8,000 more secured the communications back to the Sierra Morena, the main army swept on to the southwest. By 29 January, Victor's outposts faced Seville across the Guadalquivir River. In the city the Supreme Junta took to its heels and fled. Joseph reported, "Andalusia will soon be pacified. All the towns are sending delegations to me; Seville is following suit. The Junta has retreated. I am hoping to enter Cádiz without firing a shot. Public feeling is good."[31]

On 30 January, headquarters were at Carmona, twenty miles from the Andalusian capital. At King Joseph's dinner table the next moves were being debated. Some voices were raised in favor of sending a strong detachment of the army to march immediately on the south bank of the Guadalquivir to seize Cádiz before the shattered Spaniards had time to rally for its defense. It was known that Seville would offer only token resistance and more than two corps were available for opera-

---

* That is, the French war against Austria.

tions. Soult swept all such talk aside. "Give me Seville," he declared, "and I will answer for Cádiz."[32] The decision was taken accordingly. Next day the municipality of Seville sent out a deputation to negotiate. They would surrender on condition that security was guaranteed for life and property and that no extraordinary tax be wrung from the city. King Joseph at once agreed.

The first of February saw the greatest triumph of Joseph's career. He entered the city at the head of his guards and moved in procession to the ancient royal palace. "He was received by an immense crowd of people who filled the streets and squares as far as the Alcazar, where he dismounted and took up residence. Cries of '*Viva el Rey*' arose on every side. No doubt curiosity and fear had a greater share in this triumphant reception than any other sentiment but, whatever the cause, it seemed at the time to justify the expedition to Seville."[33] The king was delighted. He wrote to his brother, "I entered this city yesterday to the cheers of the whole populace. The First Corps [Victor] passed the night here; tomorrow it marches on Cádiz; the Fifth corps [Mortier] marches on Badajoz. Andalusia has been pacified; order is restored; the Junta has dissolved itself; some of its members have embarked for America, some have gone into hiding, some have fled to Gibraltar, some to Cádiz."[34]

Twenty-three members of the junta reached Cádiz, where they needed troops to protect them from the fury of the mob. Their first act on arrival was to abdicate, nominating in their place a regency (29 January) of five members, of whom the principal figure was General Castaños, the victor of Bailén. Fortunately, however, the rump of the despicable junta were not the only Spaniards moving on Cádiz. The duke of Albuquerque, commanding the small Army of Estremadura, had been given the duty of covering Badajoz. The right wing of the French advance into Andalusia had passed across his front far beyond his reach, and finding himself unable to assist Areizaga, he had, after detaching enough infantry to bring the garrison of Badajoz up to a secure strength, marched south hoping to be able to assist in the defense of Seville. The junta, with its customary perversity, repeatedly ordered him to march on Cordoba, but Albuquerque, realizing that it must be in French hands, declined to obey and continued to move south. By intelligent use of his cavalry, he assessed the strength and direction of the French move on Seville. He assessed, too, the anarchy that reigned in the city when the junta fled and realized that, in the existing state of affairs, Seville could not be defended. He determined, therefore, to march to Cádiz, which was all but ungarrisoned. Having picked up a number of isolated detachments along the road, he reached the fortress city on 3 February with 12,000 men. Next day an aide-de-camp of Marshal Victor, riding ahead of the advance guard of First Corps, summoned Cádiz to surrender. He received an angry answer. On the fifth, Victor's men started to come within reach of the fortifications. A further messenger between the lines carried to Cádiz a message calling the city to its allegiance and received the proud answer, "Cádiz, faithful to its word, recognizes no king but Ferdinand VII." Soult had been wrong, disastrously wrong. When he had said on 30 January, "Give me Seville and I will answer for Cádiz," he made the mistake which finally made it impossible for the French to complete the conquest of Spain. If on the following day he had sent Victor marching on Cádiz, no opposition would have been found but a dispirited town guard. The delay allowed Albuquerque, by a stroke of inspired disobedience, to put a regular garrison into the town and, thereby, to save the soul of the Spanish resistance.

With even a moderate garrison, Cádiz is impregnable to a land-based enemy. To approaches by land it is protected first by the river Santi Petri, nowhere less than three hundred yards wide, and running through salt marshes. Once across the Santi Petri, the invader finds himself on the triangular Isle of León, which was liberally endowed with batteries and emplacements, all giving good defensive positions. Even if the Isle of León could be seized, the attacker's difficulties had only begun. The city of Cádiz lies at the seaward end of a sandy spit four miles long. At its narrowest part, where it is no more than two hundred yards wide, this spit was traversed by the stone-built battery of San Fernando, covered across its front by a wet ditch which ran from the sea on one side to the inner harbor on the other. There were other fortifications on and across the spit and, at its furthest end, where it is four hundred yards across, progress is absolutely blocked by the ramparts of the city of Cádiz itself. To protect the seaward approaches, there were twelve Spanish battleships, four British, and a swarm of gunboats of both nations.

As late as 8 February, Joseph was still writing to the emperor that "things are going well and I hope Cádiz will open its gates to me."[35] Ten days later he was less sanguine. "It seems that Cádiz is going to be defended; we must wait for a few days and see what they will do when we have a few batteries mounted against them. It would be opportune if Your Majesty could send the Toulon squadron."[36] Euphoric as Joseph may have been about his triumph in Seville, he should have remembered that between Toulon and Cádiz there lay Admiral Lord Collingwood, Nelson's worthy successor, and the British Mediterranean fleet. One other fact had escaped his notice. The new regency really believed in their British alliance. They rejected the suspicious attitude towards their allies which had characterized the junta. As soon as Cádiz was threatened, they applied to Wellington for help. On 10 February, an Anglo-Portuguese brigade, 3,500 strong, started to land on the isle. "You could not say," wrote a Scottish sergeant who landed with them, "that our reception by the inhabitants was very flattering. Here and there, amongst the crowd, you could hear a '*Viva Inglese*'; but the greater number received us with a gloomy suspicious silence."[37] It was, he pointed out, only five years since the Spanish fleet had put out from Cádiz to be shattered at Trafalgar.

Marshal Victor set about establishing batteries and building landing craft in a commendably industrious fashion. The First Corps, however, continued the hopeless siege until 25 August 1812. Then they retired to the center of Spain. In the meanwhile, the efforts necessary to sustain them in the southwestern corner of the country fatally distorted all French strategy.

February 1810 was the happiest month that Joseph spent in Spain. The Andalusians, partly because they were a naturally hospitable, insouciant people, partly because they had suffered longer than the rest of Spain under the corrupt incompetence of the Supreme Junta, welcomed King Joseph as a savior. At last the king was able to display his very real talent for benevolence. At last he was able to feel that he was among subjects who appreciated him and who believed, as he passionately did, his reiterated promises to work for the good of Spain and for the welfare of the Spanish people. In the rest of Spain, "Public feeling was inexorable; it rejected everything to do with us, even benefits."[38] In Andalusia, the atmosphere was different. Not only were the people willing to accept the benefits which the king, as far as he was able, showered upon them, they even showed themselves prepared to pledge themselves to Joseph's service. Seville was outstanding among the occupied cities for the number of *juramentados*, men willing to take the oath of allegiance to the French king, and in Andalusia it was possible to raise Spanish troops who could actually be used on service and did not, as in the rest of occupied Spain, desert at the first convenient opportunity.

To match this outburst of popular enthusiasm, there were vast material rewards, which, if properly applied, could have gone far to restore the shattered finances of the kingdom. On the military side, there was the capture of the greatest arsenal of the kingdom, filled with cannon of all calibers and with a foundry for making more. The powder and shot found was sufficient to supply the French southern armies for the next two years. Even more useful for the depleted treasury was a great store of tobacco, a royal monopoly, valued at more than a million sterling, a lesser store of quinine, and quantities of silver, copper, and mercury, all of which are mined in Andalusia. Moreover, all the great cities of the province were rich, not only in coin but in pictures, plate, and other art treasures.

It was unfortunate that before the king returned to Madrid, Cabarrus, the minister of finance, died at Seville, worn out by expedients and alcohol. He was given a state funeral and an elaborate monument in the cathedral.

Money was certainly needed. The emperor was again demanding and threatening. "Tell the King of Spain," he wrote to Berthier, while Joseph was receiving the plaudits of the crowd in Cordoba, "that my finances are in confusion; that I cannot afford the vast cost of the operations in Spain; that he must find money in Spain for the engineers, for the artillery, for the commissariat, for the hospitals, the surgeons and for every kind of administration. Tell him that nothing is impossible; that he must provide food for the Army of Spain; that all that I can provide is 2,000,000 each month as a contribution towards the army's pay. Tell him that if he finds that this cannot be done there will be no alternative to my administering the provinces for the benefit of the French Treasury."[39] He had, as he mentioned to his ambassador in Madrid, already spent more than three hundred million francs on the Spanish war.[40]

For once Joseph did not reply with an agonized complaint to the emperor's demands. Almost meekly he replied, "Your Majesty places on this country a burden it is unable to bear. More loans will be needed from France until the pacification of Spain has gone far enough for me to pay them all back."[41] The king was not in a worrying mood. He was devoting his attention to visiting the magnificent archaeological sites of the Guadalquivir Valley, to attending bullfights, where he encouraged the French members of his entourage to take their chance in the ring, and generally to endearing himself to his friendly, cheering subjects.

Nor did he confine himself to Seville. He first moved his court towards Cádiz, to see for himself the siege works which Victor was preparing. Even within the sound of the guns he had an enthusiastic reception. At Xeres de la Frontera, the home of sherry, "although we were within four leagues of Cádiz, the King was greeted with acclamations by the townspeople, and the welcome we received might have made us believe that we were in the midst of a friendly people."[42] At Ronda, southeast of Seville and less than fifty miles from the British-held fortress of Gilbraltar, the town was attacked by guerrillas who had swarmed down from their stronghold in the Sierra de Nevada. They were driven off by the Royal Guards and again there was a warm welcome. It was in Rhonda that he met a descendant of Montezuma, the last king of Mexico, who attached himself to the king's personal following and was rewarded with a key, the badge of a vice-chamberlain.

Next his progress was extended to eastern Andalusia, and everywhere the story was the same. At every town and village the mayors and priests came forward to present their allegiance, girls spread flowers in front of his horse, and the people cried *"Viva el Rey!"* Of his entry into Málaga, Count Miot recorded that he was received "with a welcome far surpassing anything that could have been expected from a loyal and submissive populace. The streets were strewn with flowers, and hung with tapestries; at the windows elegantly dressed ladies waved their handkerchiefs; shouts of joy, cries of '*Viva el Rey*', were to be heard on all sides. A ball and a bullfight were given in his honour; nothing that adulation could offer was omitted. If ever Joseph Napoleon could have felt that he really was the King of Spain, it was at that moment."[43]

At Granada his reception equaled that in Málaga. There was no doubt that in both cities he was regarded as a savior, but whereas in Seville and Cordoba he had been hailed as a deliverance from the excesses of the Supreme Junta, in eastern Andalusia he was looked to as a bulwark against French oppression. Having found his march obstructed by some half-armed bands of peasants, General Sebastiani had taken the opportunity to levy a contribution of five million reals on Granada and twelve million on Málaga. To supplement this, Sebastiani and his subordinate commanders embarked on a systematic pillage, for their own benefit. By confiscation and extortion, money and works of art were constantly looted and sent back to France by the wagon load. The enthusiastic acclaim that greeted King Joseph owed less to any ephemeral regard the inhabitants had to their smiling, courtly, uninvited monarch than to their pathetic belief that he could control the French generals.

Meanwhile military operations were languishing. The remnants of Areizaga's benighted army was beginning to reform itself in Murcia under General Blake, a Spanish officer of Irish ancestry who acquired a certain esteem amongst the Spaniards since "he had won one battle and only lost seventeen." In Cádiz, the regular troops—Spanish, British and Portuguese—in the garrison substantially outnumbered their besiegers. Guerrilla bands, nourished from Gibraltar, were building up their strength in the Sierra de Nevada. To the north, Mortier tried to secure the crucial fortress of Badajoz by threatening it with 9,000 men, but Badajoz was secure and adequately garrisoned. The marshal's summons was rejected with scorn (12 February) and since he had neither a siege train nor sufficient men there was nothing that he could do but retire to the south of the Guadiana.

In February and March 1810, King Joseph was interested in none of these things. He was issuing administrative decrees to liberalize public institutions, founding museums, planning schools for orphans, and declaring amnesties. Between times he attended bullfights and banquets and translated the inscriptions on the Roman ruins at Italica, the birthplace of three Roman emperors, Trajan, Hadrian, and Theodosius. Joseph at last was happy, and the generals could look after the war. He even went so far as to write to his wife, still at Mortefontaine, to join him with their two daughters, "as soon as possible, before the hot weather starts."[44] It was not that he wanted Queen Julie with him—he found her insufferably dull and he was not short of feminine company, least of all in hospitable Andalusia—but he was afraid that she might not be invited to attend the wedding on 2 April of the emperor to the Austrian archduchess Marie Louise. "If you cannot leave as soon as I wish [i.e., before the wedding] I hope that you will permit no one to take your place. The effect here would be deplorable. This nation, which is now giving me a fine reception, is so proud that it would be humiliated if we did not receive our due. You must pretend to be sick and avoid all formal occasions."[45] The king must indeed have been taking his duties conscientiously if he was prepared to give up the delights of his Spainish mistresses to save his other Spanish subjects from the humiliation of having their unwelcome monarch humiliated by proxy at their oppressor's second wedding.

It was a wasted gesture. Queen Julie declined the long journey to Madrid on grounds of health, but she got her invitation to the celebrations and took her rightful place at the ceremony. It was Joseph who was to be humiliated.

Joseph Bonaparte, King of Spain
From the portrait by François Pascal Simon, Baron Gérard

Napoleon Bonaparte, Emperor of the French, in 1810.
From an engraving after Vigneux.

Jean Baptiste Jourdan, Marshal of the Empire.
From an engraving by H. R. Cooke.

King Joseph's Entry into Madrid, 1808
From a wash drawing by J. L. Rugendas.
BY PERMISSION OF THE BRAUN COLLECTION, PROVIDENCE, R.I.

Nicholas Jean-de-Dieu Soult, Marshal Duke of Dalmatia.
From a portrait by G. P. A. Healey.

André Massena, Marshal Prince of Essling.
From a lithograph by F-S Delpech.

Auguste Frédéric Louis Viesse de Marmont, Marshal Duke of Ragusa.
From an engraving by J. N. Joly, after a drawing by Meyer.

Arthur Wellesley, Marquess (later Duke) of Wellington in 1812.
From the portrait by Juan Bauzit.

BY PERMISSION OF THE NATIONAL PORTRAIT GALLERY, LONDON

The Battle of Vitoria, 21st June 1813.
From an engraving by H. Moses and F. C. Lewis after a drawing by J. M. Wright.

King Joseph's Sèvres Breakfast Service, captured at Vitoria.

Jourdan's baton as a Marshal of the Empire, captured at Vitoria. The gold eagles at either end were broken off and "lost" by a sergeant of the 87th (Prince of Wales's Irish) Regiment.

King Joseph's Silver Chamber Pot, captured at Vitoria by the Fourteenth Light Dragoons. It is now used as a loving cup in the Officers' Mess of the Fourteenth/Twentieth King's Hussars.

Chapter 7

THE SHRINKING
REALM

*Never forget that, in whatever position my policy
and the interests of my Empire may place you, your
first duty is to me, your second is to France and
that any other duties, even those to the peoples
whom I may entrust to you, come only after these.*

NAPOLEON

KING Joseph's first objective was to make his rule acceptable,
even welcome, to his Spanish subjects. He believed in all
honesty that he was the legitimate successor to the Bourbons
and intended to uphold all the ancient glories of the Spanish
monarchy. He realized that the intrusion of a foreign sovereign
supported by foreign bayonets was an affront to the national
pride but counted on the necessity for French troops being
short-lived, hoping that Spanish resentment could be over-
come by giving the country the benefits of good and enlightened government.

Being essentially a man of the moderate and liberal phase
of the French Revolution, the new king struck first at feudal-

ism and the entrenched position of the Catholic church. By a single decree (18 August 1809), all the old councils through which Spain had been governed were abolished. Each title of nobility was canceled, although their holders could retain them by taking an oath of allegiance to Joseph. Feudal dues and internal customs duties were swept away. All the smaller religious houses were suppressed. Their inmates were compulsorily reallocated to larger houses and their possessions sequestered to the state. The mendicant orders of friars were prohibited. Even the royal prerogatives were diminished. Some of the royal lands were divided amongst small proprietors and many of the king's hunting rights were surrendered. Nothing better illustrates Joseph's determination to govern Spain fairly and for the benefit of his subjects than his decision, at a time when his government was desperate for money, to end the profitable royal monopolies in the sale of tobacco and liquor and to close the royal cloth factories. These last had, in fact, shortly to be reopened, since alternative work could not be found for the employees.

It is possible that had it not been for the oppression inevitable from the presence of a huge French army and the encouragement given to the patriot cause by the presence in Portugal and Cádiz of a substantial British army, Joseph might have succeeded in reconciling the Spaniards to his presence on the throne. Certainly his own affability and easy manner recommended him to all the Spaniards he met, and he made himself available to all comers, frequently walking in the public gardens of Madrid, almost without escort, and dealing with petitioners in person as generously as his means allowed. His reception in Andalusia went far, at least in his own mind, to create the impression that he was welcome, even if only as an alternative to the blunderings and requisitions of the junta. An English colonel remarked, "The French appear to have reduced the Spanish armies to the exact state they wish, that they are so hardly prest, not merely for provisions but for actual sustenance that they have recourse to exactions more severe than the French themselves enforce, consequently the peasantry will be more inimical to *their own* than to foreign troops."[1] With the acquisition of the wealth and resources of Andalusia, it seemed in February 1810 that King Joseph would be able to finance an enlightened policy, as well as to announce one.

There was, however the other side to the coin. Under pressure from Joseph's Spanish adherents, who were increasingly coming to realize that no compromise with the patriot party was possible and that if the patriots and the British were eventually to succeed, the life of an *afrancesado*, even if spared, would not be worth living, draconian measures were taken against the "rebels" at Cádiz and in the other parts of unoccupied Spain. All civil servants not prepared to renew their oath to Joseph were dismissed from their positions and pensions. State bonds held by those who had not submitted were canceled, and all "rebel" property not already seized by the emperor was sequestered. Any man who had a son serving in the armies of the regency was made liable to provide a soldier for Joseph's levies, failing which he could be mulcted according to his wealth or, if he had no wealth, sent as a hostage to France. These decrees were, probably, disagreeable to the king, who continued to believe that he was the father of a great nation only temporarily divided. Nevertheless, they did something to fill the constant void in the treasury. It is truer to say that they would have helped to fill the void had it not been for the king's good-hearted but irresponsible desire to reward his adherents, both French and Spanish. To Gonzales O'Farrill, his minister of war, he made a grant of four million reals.* The duke of Campo-Alange, his foreign minister, received two million. Each of his twelve aides-de-camp received one million reals.

It may be doubted that Joseph ever had any serious chance of reconciling the Spaniards to his rule by the benevolence and good intentions of his government. Any chance he may

* O'Farrill refused the grant for himself but requested that it be given to his niece, the Countess Jaruco. All such grants made by Joseph were not in cash but in state bonds, which were only cashable at a very considerable discount.

have had was destroyed at a blow by his brother. The emperor was short of money. He had been unable to extract as much as he had hoped from Austria. Prussia was falling behind in the payment of her indemnity for the war of 1807. France and the immediate vassal states were proving incapable of paying the price of empire. Spain was soaking up French money like a sponge. By Napoleon's calculation, it had cost France three hundred million francs by the beginning of 1810. As has already been seen, Napoleon had instructed Joseph that if he could not provide for all the expenses of the French army in Spain, other than two million francs a month for pay, "there would be no alternative to my administering the provinces for the benefit of the French Treasury."[2]

This threat was written on 28 January. Eleven days later, before Joseph in Andalusia could even have received the letter, the emperor set about putting his threat into action. By a decree dated 8 February, four military governments were set up comprising Catalonia, Aragon, Navarre, and Biscay. "It is my intention that administration of the conquered lands should be in the hands of the generals commanding each province, so that the entire resources of each should be employed for the army's expenses."[3] Joseph was ordered to give no instructions to the forces in the new governments, and to the commanders on the spot, the position was spelled out with, to the king, humiliating clarity. For example, Marshal Pierre François Charles Augereau, commanding in Catalonia, was told "that, if communications are open, he should concert his operations with Madrid, but he must not become a part of the army of Spain; that he commands the Army of Catalonia and, as such, will receive orders only from me. He should establish a provisional administration and, instead of the Spanish ensign, should fly the French and Catalan flags. He will forbid any communication between the inhabitants and the king. Neither the king nor his ministers have anything to do with Catalonia."[4]

The king heard of this decision when he was at Ronda, between Seville and Gibraltar. In practical terms, it was not a disastrous blow. None of the forces taken from his nominal command had been effectively under his orders and none of the four provinces had ever contributed a single real to his treasury. In terms of his long-term aim of reconciling the Spaniards to him, it was fatal. Miot de Melito, who was with him when the news came, "saw what a deadly blow had been inflicted on him. None of the Spaniards who had rallied to his cause in good faith could support him further without openly betraying their country. The change of dynasty had so often been defended as securing the independence and integrity of the country. Now these promises were seen to be hollow. There was nothing that the King could do to resist this open violation of promises made to him and of the pledges which he had given in every speech he had made. In my opinion his only course compatible with honour would be to lay down the crown. He could no longer wear it without conniving in the Emperor's decisions and giving the impression that he would be content to reign over whatever was left of Spain so long as he could retain the title of king."[5]

Unfortunately for his honor, Joseph could not bring himself to take this step. Partly for the sheer love of a throne, partly from a sense of duty to those Spaniards who had compromised themselves by serving him, he decided to temporize. He wrote to his wife, asking her to intercede for him with Napoleon.

> I must know what the Emperor really feels about me. If I am to judge by the facts, he can only feel badly though I can not imagine why. What is it that he wants from me and from Spain? Would that he would let me know so that I would no longer be suspended between what I appear to be and what I really am, king in a country where provinces are given over to generals who tax them as they see fit and are ordered to pay no attention to me. If the Emperor's intention is to disgust me with Spain, I must abdicate immediately. If that is what he wants, my wish is only to retire. I have tried two

kingdoms and I have no desire to attempt a third.
My only wish is to live quietly on a French estate,
far from Paris. . . . If you cannot make my brother
see the truth, I can only repeat that I must abdicate.[6]

Simultaneously he sent to Paris a special ambassador whose
official function was to congratulate the emperor on his
marriage to the Austrian archduchess Marie Louise. The
man chosen was Don Miguel José de Azanza, who had
served the Bourbons as viceroy of Mexico. To mark the importance of his mission, Joseph created him duke of Santa Fé
and invested him with the Order of the Golden Fleece.

Santa Fé, an honest but guileless man, had little chance of
persuading the emperor to change his policy, but any chance
he may have had was blighted by a futile gesture of defiance
which the king made before his ambassador left Madrid. On
17 April, Joseph published a decree dividing Spain into thirty-
eight perfectures, with subprefectures and cantons, on the
French model. Since this new organization covered the whole
of Spain and blithely ignored the emperor's new military
governments, it was a move ill-calculated to persuade
Napoleon of his brother's obedience.

On arrival, Santa Fé sought an interview with Napoleon.
Had he, asked Champagny, the minister of foreign affairs,
much to say to the emperor? "No," replied Santa Fé, "but
I have much to hear. All we ask is to know his intentions."
Four weeks elapsed before, on a Sunday afternoon, the ambassador was summoned to see not the emperor but, once
again, Champagny. Saying that he was speaking "by the
emperor's orders," he proceeded to reproach the Spanish
government. France, he asserted, had already provided 400,000
men and 300,000,000 francs for the conquest of Spain, and
she could provide nothing further. If King Joseph wanted
money, he must tax his subjects, sell the property of the
church, and stop giving vast presents to his entourage. He
should also stop spending large sums on raising Spanish troops
who immediately deserted. Santa Fé defended his master as
best he could, particularly complaining that it was of little

use if King Joseph imposed taxes, since any money collected was immediately seized by the French generals. Champagny was unimpressed and cold in his manner.

Again the wretched Santa Fé was kept waiting for a month. On 19 July, he was summoned for the third time to the Ministry of Foreign Affairs. This time Champagny's reproaches were sharper. The king was not following the instructions the emperor had given him. He was being too indulgent to the rebels and not doing enough to support the French army. If King Joseph could not bring himself to obey his imperial brother's orders, there would be no difficulty in bringing Ferdinand, prince of the Asturias, back to the throne. Ferdinand would do what he was told.

While Santa Fé was waiting for an audience in Paris, the emperor was going steadily forward with the partitioning of Spain and with reducing the forces under Joseph's control. In mid-April he ordered that the Second and Sixth corps, those formerly commanded by Soult and Ney, should be put under the command of Marshal André Masséna, prince of Essling and, with the newly arrived Eighth Corps, should form the Army of Portugal. To give the new army an administrative base in Spain, the districts of Salamanca and León were put under Masséna's direct control. A month later, in order to secure Masséna's communications with France, two more military governments were established covering Burgos and the districts of Valladolid, Plasencia, and Toro. Shortly afterwards, Santander and the Asturias were put under the exclusive command of General Bonnet. Thus, by midsummer, Joseph's kingdom stretched only from the Sierra de Guadarrama to the defenses of Cádiz. Nor was this reduction in size the whole of the emperor's long-term scheme. In February, the ambassador in Madrid was told in confidence that "it is my intention to annex the left bank of the Ebro, possibly even going as far as the Douro."[7]

Despite all his efforts to keep the news that their country was being dismembered from his people, Joseph realized that it was a hopeless task. Three months after his first triumphant entry into the city, Joseph returned to Seville on 11 April. "He was somewhat coolly received. The resistance of Cádiz and the rumours circulating about the Emperor's designs on Spain had opened the eyes of the people. In vain the King took part in all the striking and theatrical Easter ceremonies. It did not bring him a warmer welcome."[8]

Meanwhile, the generals were asserting the independence of their military governments. Marshal Augereau in Catalonia had Barcelona placarded with a verbose proclamation which read, "Catalans, who in ancient history were the conquerors of Athens, your former trade with the east is to be re-established! Napoleon the Great offers you a new life; his eyes are fixed upon you. He holds you in his guarding arms. Your sacrifices have only benefitted those vile pirates, the English. What have you to hope for from them, those persecutors of our religion, who have never given freedom to Catholics, who every year burn the Holy Father in effigy? My worthy Catalans! Close your ears to the siren song, which flatters only to deceive."[9]

More humiliating than the windy proclamations of French generals was the king's inability to protect his subjects from the rapacity of the occupying army. It was no secret that huge flocks of Merino sheep were being driven over the Pyrenees by French soldiers to graze on the estates of French generals. In Valladolid, General Kellermann forbade all communication with Madrid, despite the fact that the supreme court of Spain sat in Valladolid and was thus prevented from exercising its functions. In the same city there was publicly displayed a table of ransom rates, graded according to rank, by which Spanish prisoners of war on their march to France could purchase their freedom. On his way to take up the command of the Army of Portugal, Marshal Masséna, not a man overly concerned with financial niceties, was horrified by the robbery and plunder in which he saw French officers and soldiers indulging and which he "lamented having neither the means nor the hope of being able to end."[10]

The king's authority was not safe from insult even in the

shrinking area which he could still claim to control. Ney, back in command of the Sixth Corps, sent troops into the province of Ávila, "the only province that has always been peaceable and which has always been invaluable in supplying the corps in its neighbourhood. He even went so far as to seize the cashboxes of my tax collector in the town of Ávila itself under the noses of my garrison who, fortunately, did not resist. . . . Your Majesty cannot wish that his brother, however unworthy, should be humiliated and abused in this way.*"[11]

At Toledo, less than fifty miles from Madrid, an officer of the French intendant general tried forcibly to seize the local revenue. The Spanish treasurer resisted him and was upheld by the king. Next morning, at his *levée*, Joseph confronted Deniée, the intendant general, and ordered him to send his "blackguard" subordinate back to France. Then, "his voice rising and speaking in jerks," he launched into a tirade to those present. "I am determined to make an example of those who are working against the interests of my brother. . . . I am as good a Frenchman as anyone, yes, as anyone. The French troops have seen me sharing their trials. . . . France is my country and Spain is my religion. . . . One knows one's duty when one reaches my age, and no Spaniard should doubt that their concerns are nearest to my heart."[12] He went on, speaking directly to the French ambassador to say that if his brother wished to treat him as if he were a *préfet*, he was ready to lay down the crown which the emperor had given him rather than see Spain devoured and dismembered. He even went so far as to talk about resisting oppression by force of arms. With a vehemence which surprised both the ambassador and the French generals who were present, he added that he would either be an independent king or a private citizen in France."[13] That evening, it being the fête of the emperor (15 August), he duly attended a gala performance at the opera. Before leaving his palace, he called in General Bigarré, one of his aides-

---

* Napoleon confirmed that Ávila was in Joseph's area of responsibility but did not reprimand Ney. Nor did he order him to return the stolen cash.

de-camp, to give him some orders. Dressed in his most brilliant clothes, bespangled with diamonds, which Bigarré valued at eight million francs, he walked up and down talking until suddenly he stopped and turned to his companion. "You see all this splendour? Well, I would gladly give them all up —this fine palace and all the treasures it contains. I would rather give them all up and live at Mortefontaine as a French prince with my wife and children, than live as a vassal king in Spain."[14]

It was not only the impertinent behavior of a junior official at Toledo that raised this public storm. On 14 July, Napoleon had taken the final step in reducing the king to the level of a provincial governor. He had given Soult control over everything south of the Sierra Morena, creating the corps of Victor (First), Sebastiani (Fourth), and Mortier (Fifth), together with Dessolles's division (formerly part of the Madrid garrison) into the Army of the South (*Armée du Midi*). Joseph was thus deprived of the command of all the French troops in Spain apart from his own guard and a few detached battalions. Worse than that, by taking Andalusia with its rich revenues from Joseph's domains, the emperor had condemned his brother to perpetual, hopeless bankruptcy. Soult was indeed told that he must hold the king in due deference "and work in concert with his ministers although you are the actual commander in chief." Any faint glimpse of hope that this guarded instruction may have given to the king was immediately nullified by another sentence in the same instructions which enjoined Soult to hold to "the principle that war must support itself (*La guerre doit nourir la guerre*)."[15]

It would seem that at this juncture the emperor was intent on humiliating his brother. Not only did he give to Soult permission to sell the English merchandise captured in the ports of Andalusia, a resource he had specifically forbidden to Joseph, but on the same day that the orders creating the Army of the South were issued, he had Berthier write to Joseph a peculiarly ungenerous letter. "The Emperor learns with the greatest distress that the troops besieging Cádiz are in rags; that their pay is nine months in arrears. His Majesty cannot send more than 2,000,000 francs a month into Spain, since France is drained of money. The war in Spain should be self-supporting; the whole resources of the country ought to be devoted to feeding, paying and clothing the troops who have made the conquest. Recruiting and paying Spanish troops is only feeding and paying the enemy. The needs of the army must come before all civil needs and first priority must be given to supplying the French troops who alone keep Your Majesty on your throne."[16] To make the pill the harder to swallow, Napoleon dispatched, five days later, "a convoy, under heavy escort, containing 3,000,000 francs. It must go straight through to Seville and be used only to pay the Army of the South."[17]

This was the nadir of Joseph's relationship with his brother. Now, if ever, was the time when he should have resigned the throne. He had the title of king of Spain and the Indies. He was referred to in the old Hapsburg and Bourbon style as "His Most Catholic Majesty." His actual realm consisted of the province of New Castille, and even in that small kingdom, he was not secure against the raids of the guerrillas, whose incursions threatened the bridge at Aranjuez and who, on more than one occasion, rode up to the gates of Madrid. The troops under his orders would hardly have made up a fit command for a *général de division*,* and even these Soult was trying to draw away, claiming to control all the troops in La Mancha and on the Tagus,** and appealing to Paris for them over the king's head.[18] "If," counterclaimed the king, "orders from Marshal Soult can rob me of the troops around Madrid, how can I be sure that one morning I shall not wake up to find myself a prisoner of the armed bands from Estremadura or Valencia. . . . The Marshal maintains that our defence is

---

* A *général de division* was the equivalent of a lieutenant general, but in both the French and British armies a division was normally commanded by a lieutenant general, rather than, as now, a major general.

** Soult also tried to bring into his sphere the Second Corps, his old command now under Reynier, which had been assigned to the Army of Portugal.

at his discertion, that it should be carried on by detachments that he may be good enough to lend us—unless he prefers to hand us over to the rebels."[19] The king, Soult riposted, "is advised by people who are over-influential and who lead him into false courses. They embitter him and make him pay too much attention to the fears which arise from reports from all parts of Spain, especially from Madrid. . . . In my view, it is essential that the headquarters of the army and of the administrative services, parts of which remain in the capital, should join me in Seville as soon as possible. Madrid should form no more than the government of an administrative district. If this were done there would be more action and less vexation."[20] It is small wonder that relations between the king and Soult deteriorated sharply from that time onwards.

Joseph had every encouragement to abdicate. His brother Lucien had recently taken ship for America to escape from the emperor's dictation about his choice of a wife. He was intercepted by the Royal Navy and spent the rest of the war living the life of an English country gentleman in Worcestershire, composing an epic poem about Charlemagne. Although brother Jerome was busy accumulating debts, mistresses, and the imperial displeasure as king of Westphalia, brother Louis, the morose king of Holland, had secretly quitted The Hague by night and, leaving his instrument of abdication behind him, crept away to live in Austria.

Joseph learned of Louis's defection in July. He learned, too, that Holland had immediately been annexed to France, and it is charitable to suppose that he did not follow his brother's example in order to save his Spanish subjects from a similar fate. "Spain," he wrote, "is a lion which justice can lead by a silken thread, but which a million soldiers will not be able to subdue."[21] Perhaps he saw himself as the only man who could hold the silken thread. Perhaps, as others have maintained, he could not bear to tear himself away from his palaces, from his Royal Guard (even if unpaid), from his eight million francs worth of diamonds, and from the enchanting Donna Amalia, marquise de Montehermosa, wife of one of his chamberlains. Perhaps both factors weighed with him. Probably he was merely incapable of taking decisive action in defiance of his imperial and overwhelming younger brother.

Although "my determination not to remain in a position unworthy of me remains unshakeable,"[22] all he did was to send another special ambassador to join the luckless Santa Fé. This time he chose José Martínez Hervas, marquess of Almenara, who had succeeded Carrabus as minister of finance. With him went a long letter from the king which opened by saying, "My position in this country, which has always been difficult and frequently deplorable, is now such that it cannot long continue." If the emperor could not find it possible to reverse his decision to break Spain up into military governments, the king would be abandoned by his guards, by his household, and by "everything which goes to make a government." "I shall have no alternative to returning to France and putting myself at Your Majesty's disposition, requesting permission to rejoin my family from whom I have been separated for six years, that I may find in domestic obscurity the love and peace that I have lost for a throne without having gained anything in exchange, since to me the throne has been a place of torment, from which I have watched helplessly the devastation of a country which I had hoped to make happy." If the army in Andalusia was to be taken from his command, what was left to him? He was "the watchman for the Madrid hospitals, the guardian of the army's stores, the commandant of a prisoner-of-war camp." It was impossible for the revenues of Spain to meet the cost of the French army. Almenara knew all the "deplorable details" of the Ministry of Finance and would be able to make this clear. Spain could only be saved on four conditions. "First, if the army is put under my command; second, if I have the right to send home officers whose conduct is conspicuously bad; third, if I am authorised to reassure the nation about the changes in government and the dismemberments which are threatened; fourth, if Your Majesty has the confidence in me which he ought to have and lets me speak and write to the Spaniards as I think best about their situation and mine, and if Your Majesty ceases to believe stories put about by envenomed and mediocre grumblers. Given these conditions I undertake, first, that the French army will not cost a *sou* more than the two million francs allocated to it, and shortly to relieve Your Majesty even of that burden, although the subsidy will be essential to me in the early months; second, that Spain will be pacified as well as Naples was; third, that Spain will soon be as useful to France as she is now baneful."[23]

Almenara's mission got off to a bad start. His first action was to pass to Champagny the confidential instructions given him in Madrid. On Napoleon's instructions, Champagny replied, "I have been unable to place this document before the Emperor. Each word in it is so soaked in rancour that it would be more suitable in an English pamphlet than in the files of my ministry. I therefore return it to you."[24]

In fact, no diplomatic finesse could have made Almenara's mission any more successful than Santa Fé's. Napoleon's instructions to Champagny were explicit. "It seems important to me that these negotiations should be conducted in a leisurely fashion. You should start by explaining my feelings about the Convention of Bayonne; after that explain the importance of the Portuguese campaign and stress how much the whole Spanish affair is costing me. Give them time to reflect about that. Not until after about four days should you let them know that I require the left bank of the Ebro as an indemnity against everything that Spain has so far cost me. I am sure that, as in all negotiations, we should not seem to be in a hurry."[25]

To make a bad bargaining position worse, it became known at this time that one of Santa Fe's reports to Madrid had been captured by guerrillas and was published in the Cádiz newspapers. All Champagny's reproaches about the expenses of Joseph's court, the king's gifts to his ministers and staff, the cost and uselessness of raising Spanish troops, and the king's failure to give enough assistance to the French army immediately became public property. "It almost seems," wrote

Miot in his diary, "that fate is playing games with us by making our situation more difficult. . . . It is easy to see the sensation the publication of these letters will cause in Spain. It will ruin the King's party."[26]

By the beginning of October, it was known in Madrid that Napoleon was demanding the left bank of the Ebro together with Biscay, Navarre, and Saragossa. Santa Fé, himself a Navarrese, firmly refused, pleading that he had no instructions and that he was convinced that the king would never consent to parting with Spanish territory. Champagny produced draft treaties by which, in exchange for the country across the Ebro, Spain should receive the whole of Portugal "after the conclusion of a general peace."

Joseph awaited the outcome of the negotiations with unconcealed impatience. On 12 October, he wrote to his wife, "I am impatient to know the Emperor's decision, being convinced that the affairs of this country, spoiled though they may have been, could be re-established by me, and by no one else. There is not a moment to lose."[27] One crumb of comfort was thrown to him from Paris. On 28 September, his command was constituted the Army of the Center. It consisted of the Royal Guard and the Spanish troops, of 4,000 French cavalry, and of two divisions of French infantry with some artillery. The whole amounted to little more than 20,000 men, including the Spaniards, and was notably smaller than the armies of Portugal, the South, Catalonia, and Aragon, but at least it put the king on a footing no lower than the army commanders and, by defining the troops under his command, saved him from the encroachments of Soult.

But to be an army commander was not enough. "The Spanish business can only end favourably to us on two conditions:

"1st. Absolute fidelity to the promise of Spain's integrity and independence which I made with the Emperor's guarantee.

"2nd. The absolute and effective command of the French troops being placed in my hands."[28]

Joseph was crying for the moon. Napoleon had long since

abandoned the idea of maintaining Spain as anything other than an appanage of France, even supposing that he had ever, in his innermost heart, seriously entertained any other notion. His real ideas were communicated to his ambassador in Madrid early in November. "At Bayonne the Emperor reunited the Spanish nation and gave to it one of his brothers as King. Through its deputies, the Spanish nation swore obedience to him. Believing in consequence that he had reconciled the majority of the nation, His Majesty treated with the King of Spain.

"Thereupon the whole Spanish nation took up arms. The King, hunted from his capital, had every Spaniard against him; he became nothing but the commander of the French armies. Thereupon the Emperor entered Madrid by force.

"Many battles have been fought since then. Andalusia and Seville have been conquered by the French army. No Spaniard has rallied to the King; no Spanish forces have fought against the rebellion. 400,000 Frenchmen alone have had to conquer all the provinces, to capture all the fortresses, all the towns, all the villages. Spain belongs to the Emperor by right of conquest."[29]

In Paris the negotiations dragged on into November, and meanwhile a new hazard appeared for Joseph's throne. At Cádiz there opened the first sitting of the "rebel" Cortes, a parliament for the patriot cause. It was a tiresome body. Conditions in Spain, particularly in the occupied provinces, did not permit of anything approaching democratic elections, and the body that met in September had a liberal majority which, whatever its merits, was totally unrepresentative of the reactionary views of both the mass of the Spanish people or of Ferdinand VII, whom it formally acknowledged as king. Like most inexperienced liberal bodies, it devoted the bulk of its time to nonessentials. Its first action was to dismiss the regents, who, since their appointment at the time of the flight from Seville, had done a reasonably competent job of organizing the war effort and appoint others more to their taste. Then they settled to such delights as constitution making and decreeing liberty of conscience and the press, although there they had sharply to go back on their tracks, at least as far as concerned religion. Nevertheless, for all its faults and follies, the Cortes did represent a rallying point to the Spanish people, and as such constituted a real threat to the alternative, French imposed, government.

Santa Fé left Paris at the end of October after a final interview with Napoleon at which "Napoleon poured forth complaints against the king, entered into long recriminations and found it strange that the king should complain of his situation, although other sovereigns were worse treated than he was and did not complain."[30] Held up interminably by the operations of the guerrillas who plagued the road from the Pyrenees to Madrid, Santa Fé brought this discouraging news to the capital on 5 December. At the same time came the news that Almenara had been summoned to a final interview with the emperor, that it had lasted two and a half hours, and that at the end of it the ambassador had been ordered to return to Spain immediately. He reached Madrid late on the evening of 9 December.

On 10 December, Miot wrote in his diary,

> The king called the ministers together to hear the result of M. d'Almenara's mission. I was present.
>
> The negotiations had been taken up with useless demands and recriminations which did nothing to advance things. We are to get no help with money, no change in the system of military governments, no real satisfaction about our just complaints against the conduct of French generals. All the hopes we had about these negotiations have proved vain.
>
> The only opening, which arose from the final interview, is that the king has permission to open negotiations with the Cortes on the Isle of León in the following terms.
>
> He may propose to the Cortes that they recognize him as King of Spain, according to the Bayonne

constitution. On his side the king would recognize them as the true representatives of the nation. After such an agreement Cádiz would return to its allegiance to the king and the integrity of Spanish territory would be maintained. If this approach failed the Emperor would consider himself released from his agreements with the Spanish nation and the king should call a Cortes of his own, in opposition to that at Cádiz. He would rule Spain through his Cortes but he must not call to it any deputies from the provinces across the Ebro. They would not be permitted to attend.

This sad conference lasted until an hour after midnight.[31]

Joseph, by his obstinacy and through Santa Fé's Navarrese pride, had at least bought some time, but he was in despair. Next day, speaking to Miot, he "admitted the uselessness of the approaches he has been authorized to make and turned his mind once more to leaving Spain altogether."[32]

Napoleon may have been misguided in his dealings with King Joseph, but he did keep one essential fact constantly to the front of his mind. Spain could never be pacified while there was a British army in Portugal. French troops could rout their Spanish opposite numbers at almost any odds, but so long as there were British soldiers in the Peninsula, there would always be, at the back of every Spanish mind, a glimmer of hope. Joseph could never be more than a puppet at the head of an army of occupation until the redcoats had been driven back into the sea. As the emperor kept reiterating, "The English are the only danger in Spain; the rest are no more than a rabble who can never stand and fight."[33]

To make sure of finishing the job, the emperor should have gone back to the Peninsula himself. Only he could have coordinated the whole French military effort sufficiently to have had a chance of clearing Portugal. He did not wish to go. He underrated the British army and especially its commander. His new wife was expecting a baby which might turn out to be the longed-for heir to the imperial throne. More than anything, Lisbon was so far from Paris. "It is too far," he said, regretfully. "In Poland I am in the centre of Europe; in Lisbon I would be at the edge of the world."[34]

He might as well have been in Moscow. Instead he sent his most trusted marshal, André Massena, duke of Rivoli, prince of Essling.

Massena, whom Napoleon described as the "spoiled child of victory," was fifty-two in 1810, eleven years older than Napoleon, Wellington, and Soult. Before the Revolution he had been a grocer and if not, as some have asserted, a smuggler, he was certainly a corsair. The lure of a quick profit was never far from his mind. Nevertheless, as a commander he had few equals. He had commanded a corps in Napoleon's brilliant Italian campaign of 1796. His defense of Switzerland three years later was an epic of determination and skill, as was his defense of Genoa, which, although he was eventually forced to surrender, made possible Napoleon's victory at Marengo. His principality of Essling is the best testimony to the emperor's appreciation of his services in the Austrian war of 1809. His face, never handsome, had been marred when Napoleon had destroyed one of his eyes in a shooting accident.*

By 1810, Massena was past his best. His skill and determination were unabated, but physically he was going downhill. General Foy, who saw him when he arrived at Salamanca in May to take up his command, was shocked by his appearance. "Good God! How he has changed. This is not the old Massena. The man with the flashing eyes, the expressive face, the alert figure. This is not the Massena I knew in 1799 whose head reminded me of the head of Marius. He is only fifty two,

---

* Apart from their military genius, one of the few things that Napoleon and Wellington had in common was that they were both bad shots. Some years after Waterloo, Wellington accidentally peppered an old woman with buckshot. The difference between them is shown by the fact that whereas Napoleon put the blame on Berthier, Wellington gave his victim a sovereign.

yet he looks as if he was sixty. He is thin, stooping and his eye . . . has lost its brilliance. Only the voice retains its vividness."[35] What he had to say was scarcely encouraging. On assembling his new staff, he said, "Gentlemen, I am here against my wishes. I feel too old and too tired to go to war again. The Emperor has ordered me here and when I told him why I wished to decline he replied that my reputation alone would be sufficient to end the war. That was gratifying to me but no man has two lives to live, least of all a soldier."[36]

Great as was Massena's reputation, much more was needed to drive Wellington out of Portugal. Wellington himself reckoned that he was safe unless the French could bring more than 100,000 men against him. Massena set out on his task with 65,000, with a promise of 20,000 more to follow. Napoleon maintained that since "it appears from the returns of the English army, extracted from the English papers, that their army consists of 23,000 English and Germans and of 22,000 Portuguese, he should have more troops than he needs."[37] The emperor had deceived himself. The returns on which he had calculated were those of a period when the British were much beset by sickness, due to their long stay in the unhealthy Guadiana Valley after Talavera, and in any case, as he must have known, British returns showed only "rank and file," excluding officers, sergeants, and drummers, who added an eighth to the strength. It is also probable that he overlooked the numbers of artillerymen, engineers, and members of the wagon train, who, owing to the chaotic organization of the British army, were returned separately. In fact, by the summer of 1810, the Anglo-Portuguese army exceeded 60,000 in strength, and, with the assistance of a Spanish division lying near the Portuguese border, was at least equal in numbers to Massena's. The French advantage, such as it was, lay in quality. The Spanish troops were known to be unfit to stand in the field. The Portuguese were an unknown quantity. Both Napoleon and Massena had low opinions of their potential.

Two other factors weighed against Massena. His corps

commanders, Ney, Junot, and Reynier, though brave and capable leaders of troops in battle, were neither tacticians or strategists. Ney, moreover, detested Massena and had no hesitation in saying so amongst his own officers. Junot was jealous of Massena, feeling that he should have been allowed to command the Army of Portugal himself in order to revenge his Portuguese humiliations of 1808. To make the atmosphere at headquarters worse, Madame Junot, who accompanied her husband as far as Salamanca, made public scenes whenever she met Massena's mistress, the sister of one of his aides, who accompanied him everywhere dressed as a Hussar. It was an unfortunate chance that two of the three corps commanders were among the very select number of French generals who had been defeated by the British—Junot at Vimeiro and Reynier at Alexandria (1801) and Maida (1806).

In addition, Napoleon had done nothing to coordinate Massena's operations with those of the other armies in Spain. No orders were given to Soult to use part of his army to invade southern Portugal, a move which would have forced Wellington to divert some of his strength away from the Army of Portugal. As late as the end of July, when Massena was already over the Portuguese border, it was Napoleon's view that "it is not necessary to take Badajoz as this would involve us in a great siege and then in another, that of Elvas, an even stronger fortress. Once the English have been beaten and have re-embarked, Badajoz and Elvas will fall automatically."[38] Without the possession of Badajoz and Elvas, Soult could not invade southern Portugal. It is clear that Napoleon did not consider that the eviction of Wellington's army would be an operation of any great difficulty.

Massena's orders prescribed a deliberate advance rather than a dashing stroke. "Tell the Prince of Essling. . . . that I do not wish an immediate entry into Lisbon, as I could not feed the city with its immense population which lives on imported food. He should employ the summer months taking Ciudad Rodrigo and Almeida. There is no need to hurry. He should proceed methodically."[39] Accordingly, Ciudad

Rodrigo, the fortress which commanded the road into Portugal on the Spanish side of the frontier, was invested in the first week of June by Ney's corps.

The town surrendered on 9 July. The Spanish governor, Andrès Herrasti, with his garrison of 5,500 men including only one regular battalion, put up a brave defense, but against Ney's augmented corps, 30,000 strong and well equipped with siege guns, he had no chance unless the British intervened. This Wellington refused to do. Napoleon had forecast that, having less than 3,000 cavalry against Massena's 8,000, Wellington "will never offer battle in open country."[40] Although his outposts were within sight of Ciudad Rodrigo, the British commander refused to move. A large detachment of his army was still away to the south in case Soult should move, and even counting on the support of 3,000 Spaniards, his force scarcely outnumbered Ney's. "I must leave the mountains and cross the plains, as well as two rivers, to raise the siege. To do this I have about 33,000 men, of which 3,000 are cavalry. Included are 14 or 15,000 Spaniards and Portuguese, which troops, to say the best of them, are of doubtful quality. Is it right, under these circumstances, to risk a general action to raise the siege of Ciudad Rodrigo? I should think not."[41]

With Ciudad Rodrigo in his hands, Massena pressed on slowly into Portugal. On 24 July, Ney drove the British light division back over the river Côa and cleared the way for the siege of Almeida, the Portuguese equivalent of Ciudad Rodrigo. This should have stood a siege at least as long as its sister fortress, but when, on 26 August, the French bombardment opened, Massena had one of his rare strokes of good luck. That evening a spark from an exploding shell fired a train of powder from a leaking barrel. The train led straight to the main magazine, which exploded. One of Ney's staff who was watching wrote, "The earth trembled and we saw an immense whirlwind of fire and smoke arise from the middle of the town. It was like a volcano erupting. Enormous blocks of stone were hurled into the trenches, killing and wounding some of our men. Heavy guns were blown off the ramparts and hurled far outside them. When, at last, the smoke cleared, much of Almeida had disappeared, the rest was in ruins."[42] The governor surrendered the next day.

By the time that Massena had completed the concentration of his whole army and arranged for it to be issued with fifteen days' bread, it was mid-September, but when they advanced, the French found that they had no opposition. Wellington had broken contact and fallen back. His plan was to draw the French deeply into Portugal, relying on the ancient laws of that kingdom to defeat the enemy. Under these laws, the countryside could be evacuated and swept bare of provisions while every able-bodied man between sixteen and sixty was liable to serve in either the militia or the Ordenanza, a guerrilla organization of medieval origin. As the French pushed on, they began to realize what they were up against. Massena reported, "Our marches are through a desert; there is not a soul to be seen anywhere; everything is deserted. The women, the children, the old men have all gone. We can find no guides."[43] The absence of guides was serious, for the maps on which the French staff relied were far from accurate. These came from a Spanish atlas, published by Tomás López in 1778. The French had found them reliable in Spain but had failed to realize that López's delineation of Portugal was based more on fancy than topography. Nor was the advice of the handful of Portuguese traitors who accompanied the French of any practical use. The result was that the army advanced by a road that was not only circuitous but, in Wellington's gleeful words, "the worst in Portugal." Behind the French army there closed a cordon of militia and Ordenanza. The army was like a ship forcing its way through an angry sea. It advanced but left no lasting trace behind it. Madrid and Paris heard nothing from it.

Massena's ill-chosen road from the frontier to Coimbra and Lisbon had yet another drawback. It led straight to the Serra do Busaco, a ridge ten miles long and rising, steep-faced, as much as a thousand feet. It was God's gift to a defensive commander, and Wellington resolved to stand there for a delaying action. On 27 September, Massena, after inadequate reconnaissance and believing that he was faced only with a rear guard, hurled the corps of Ney and Reynier at the whole of Wellington's army. They were bloodily repulsed, losing 4,600 men killed, wounded, and taken prisoners. The allied loss was 1,250.

Knowing that there was a road which, if, Massena had bothered to look for it, would have enabled the French to circumvent the Busaco ridge, Wellington again broke contact and fell back south, leaving Coimbra to the mercies of the French.

The French entered Coimbra on 1 October and set about an orgy of plunder. It is said that the earlier plunderers were new conscripts, but it is certain that many officers joined in. Massena himself set a bad example. He removed all the scientific instruments from the university for his own use. One large telescope he sent as a present to Ney. Personal relations at the head of the army were not improved when, according to common report amongst the troops, Ney returned it, remarking that he was not a receiver of stolen property.

It was not until 4 October that the French moved on again. It was clearly impossible to catch up with the main body of the British, even though they were encumbered by a vast flock of refugees. Nevertheless, Massena expected Wellington to stand and fight once more before he embarked and determined to take his whole army in pursuit, leaving in Coimbra 4,000 sick and wounded under the guard of only a single company of marines and a few convalescents. Hardly had the rear of the Army of Portugal left the city before Colonel Nicholas Trant, with a few Portuguese dragoons and six battalions of militia, swept into it, capturing the garrison and the invalids and releasing 400 allied wounded who had had to be left there, being too sick to be transported. It was a serious blow to the army's confidence in Massena. There was much murmuring against his callousness in leaving the wounded to their fate, and "it must be admitted that Marshal Ney, General Reynier and General Junot did nothing to stop the dissatisfaction."[44]

It was a week before Massena realized that while Wellington was determined to stand, the decision to fight was left to the French, and that they could only exercise their option under the most disadvantageous terms imaginable. On 11 October, he saw for the first time the foremost of the lines of Tôrres Vedras. The British had stopped retreating. Wellington had deliberately led the French as deeply as possible into the devastated countryside of Portugal. Now he had brought them up sharply against a series of fortifications, based on naturally rugged country, on which, quite unknown to the French, thousands of Portuguese had labored for a full year and which stretched from the estuary of the Tagus, swarming with British gunboats, to the Atlantic, where the Royal Navy reigned unchallenged. Three options faced Massena. He could retreat whence he had come. He could assault the lines. He could stay where he was, hope that something would turn up, and try to find something for the army to eat.

His pride would not allow him to retreat. To assault the lines seemed suicidal; even Ney, "the bravest of the brave," considered them impregnable. He decided to wait. He reported that he believed "that he would compromise His Majesty's army if he were to attack lines so formidable and defended by thirty thousand English and thirty thousand Portuguese, supported by fifty thousand armed peasants and the vast population of Lisbon. He believes that the English cannot long hold out in the straitened position in which they find themselves."[45] He was doing what he could to make it appear that he was besieging Lisbon. The reverse was true. It was the allies who were behind the fortifications, but behind them, sea power brought them food, munitions, and reinforcements. It was the Army of Portugal which was under siege. In front of them stretched the lines. On either flank were British sailors. Behind them was an invisible net of Portuguese, the ends secured at the fortresses of Peniche and Abrantes.

Nothing but a substantial detachment could force its way through. Within the French enclave, foraging parties grubbed in the fields to glean a few potatoes and tore up the floorboards of deserted cottages in the hopes of finding concealed grain.

Even to send back a report to Paris it was necessary to escort the bearer with a battalion of infantry and a squadron of dragoons and to cover his departure with a deception operation requiring a brigade of cavalry and a strong force of infantry. The officer chosen, General Foy, set out on 29 October and after great difficulties and dangers reached Ciudad Rodrigo in eleven days. From there he rode post and was in Paris on 22 November. Two days later, he was sent for by the emperor, who was impatient for news. A fortnight earlier he had scrawled a note to Marshal Berthier saying, "Send a staff officer from Paris with orders not to come back without news from Portugal."[46] He received Foy

striding up and down the room, picking up the map, throwing it down, going back to it, pressing his visitor with questions and not always waiting for an answer. "You were wounded at Busaco? What the devil was Massena doing getting into that mess? What was he thinking of? Attacking a position like that frontally? . . . And letting his sick be taken by fifteen hundred peasants, when a thousand men could have defended them! It is the height of folly. It is as bad for an army to lose its hospitals as it is to lose its colours. In any other country, in England for example, Massena would lose his head on the scaffold for that. Did you ever hear of an army plunging into a country without securing its communications? Would any commander cross a river, even a stream, without leaving the crossing secure? Has any one ever known me to do such a thing? Just because I have always been victorious, do you think it is all luck? The English are brave and honourable; they are good in defence. Massena and Ney do not know them but Reynier has been beaten by them two or three times. He should have known. Lord Wellington has behaved like a clever man. The total desolation of a kingdom could only be done by clever measures cleverly co-ordinated. I could not have done that—not even me, with all my power. Massena is a stubborn fellow but throughout this campaign he has carried on like a tyro. After the setback at Busaco, he should have consolidated his position at Coimbra."

"Sire, he was afraid that you would have reproached him saying, 'If you had pushed on to Lisbon, the English would have taken to their boats.' " The Emperor smiled, "Very probably I would," he replied. . . . "If I had gone to Portugal this year the English would have re-embarked. . . . I wanted to go to Spain at the end of last year. If I had been there Cádiz would have been taken; but they started without me and they lost Cádiz. When I am there, I can get things done which no one else can. I always expected a Spanish revolution. A great nation that has never been conquered will not go under without a struggle; but that damnable business of Dupont's set the rebellion off. I thought it would be easy to change things in Spain; still, I do not regret what I have done there; that nation had to be destroyed. The Spaniards are proud. . . . sooner or later they would have done us a bad turn. If it was not they who attacked us first, it was only because of their corrupt minister, their feeble king, their shameless queen. The Spaniards fight badly; they have nothing like the courage of our rebels in La Vendée. They have never stood against our troops."[47]

The emperor still had a lot to learn about Spain.

Chapter 8

THE FAMILY

REUNION

A clap of thunder will put an end to the Peninsula business.

NAPOLEON, 16 JUNE 1811

Two days after Joseph and his ministers had heard Napoleon's message, Joseph wrote to his wife, "I shall leave Spain as soon as I can do so honourably. First, however, I must have news of Marshal Massena, of whom I have heard nothing since what was gleaned from General Foy when he passed through Valladolid on 3rd November."[1] It is scarcely remarkable that no one had bothered to tell the king about the position of the Army of Portugal. He knew of it only several days after Foy had had his first interview with the emperor in Paris. He seemed almost resigned to ineffectiveness. He wrote to Berthier that "one of Marshal Soult's aides-de-camp and General Kellermann [Governor of Valladolid] have told me all they have learned from General Foy. I have written to Marshal Soult telling him to move against Badajoz. I do not know whether he will see fit to pay attention to anything I tell him."[2]

The king was right in pressing for Soult's Army of the South to make some movement to help the Army of Portugal. As has been seen, the emperor had assumed that Massena's force would be strong enough to drive Wellington into the sea without assistance. Soult, whose sphere of responsibility stretched only as far north as the Sierra de Morena, was unlikely to do anything of his own accord to help a colleague. On 29 September, two days after Massena had been checked at Busaco, Napoleon had sent vague orders to Soult to use one of his corps, Mortier's Fifth, in the Badajoz area to stop the Spanish Army of Estremadura under La Romaña from sending support to Wellington.[3] He sent a stronger note on 14 November after hearing that part of La Romaña's army had joined Wellington inside the lines of Tôrres Vedras. Mortier's corps, he said "should have followed La Romaña and threatened Lisbon from the left bank of the Tagus."[4] He added, quite falsely, that the British part of the garrison had left Cádiz and complained that no assault on Cádiz had been made. "It cannot be well defended since there are only Spaniards there."[5]

Soult refused to send Mortier careering off to the mouth of the Tagus. "It is quite impossible to do so without compromising both them and the whole Army of the South. There are six fortresses on this frontier—Badajoz, Olivenza, Juramenho, Elvas, Campo Mayor and Albuquerque—which together contain more than 20,000 infantry and 2,500 cavalry.* I am certain that if I sent a corps of 10,000 men to the Tagus as was the Emperor's intention this corps could never reach its destination and would be surrounded before I could come to its aid."[6] He decided that he would march northward with the largest field force that he could safely collect and lay siege to Badajoz. At the New Year he set out from Seville with 20,000 men. On 23 January, he took the dilapidated fortress of Olivenza and three days later invested Badajoz.

---

* Soult underestimated the opposition. The allied force in Estremadura, including the garrisons, totalled 42,300 men, including 6,000 British. Mortier's corps he also understated, but only by 3,000 men.

Meanwhile, the Army of Portugal was in dire straits. Deciding that it was impossible to feed his troops in face of the impregnable lines. Massena had made a short retreat (14–18 November) to a strong position, with his left flank secured on the Tagus at Santarém. There he hung on grimly, astonishing the British by his ability to feed his army. "It is," wrote General Rowland Hill, "a difficult matter to starve a Frenchman."[7] Nevertheless, the strain was showing on his army. On 1 January, only 46,000 of his original 65,000 were still with the Eagles. Losses from sickness, disease, and desertion rose steadily. Three batches of reinforcements, totaling 10,000 men, fought their way through to join him, but his situation became increasingly hopeless. Only massive support from Soult or from the direction of Ciudad Rodrigo could enable Massena to stay in Portugal unless, as both Napoleon and Massena hoped, the British political situation induced the London government to withdraw their army.

On 5 February 1811, General Foy, with an escort of 1,800 men, cut his way through to the headquarters of the Army of Portugal with orders from the emperor. They were not encouraging. Napoleon ordered Massena to hold on to his position until help arrived. Soult, he asserted, was coming to his assistance from south of the Tagus and a column from the Army of the Center was pushing toward him from the east. "The Emperor," said Foy, "called on the army of Portugal for a struggle of attrition [*une lutte de fatigue et de persévérance*]."[8] It was too late. Massena waited another month and then retreated. His intention was to take up a new position behind the Mondego with new, unravaged foraging grounds behind him, but he was thwarted. Colonel Trant at Coimbra, having no more than a handful of Portuguese militia, presented such an imposing front to the French advance guard that Massena convinced himself that he could only cross the Mondego in a set-piece attack. With Wellington's men pressing his rear, there was no time to mount such an operation. To the ill-concealed joy of every man in the Army of Portugal from Marshal Ney downward, Massena gave orders for a retreat to Spain. By 4 April, there was not a French soldier in Portugal except for the beleaguered garrison of Almeida. Massena's army had lost in Portugal 25,000 men and every piece of transport save 36 wagons.

A week after Massena evacuated Santarém, Soult accepted the surrender of Badajoz at the hands of a traitorous deputy governor. It would in any case have been too late to help the Army of Portugal, and, as it happened, Soult had immediately to take the bulk of his strength back to Cádiz, where in his absence an Anglo-Spanish force from the garrison had made a seaborne landing in rear of Victor's lines of investment, inflicting on the besiegers a sharp tactical defeat at Barossa (5 March).

While the last of the three French attempts to conquer Portugal was ending in failure and recrimination, King Joseph, whose information of events in Portugal came largely from extracts from the English press edited by the emperor, published in *Le Moniteur*, and forwarded from Paris, was conducting his own campaign, not against the Spaniards but against his imperial brother and La Forest, the French ambassador in Madrid. Having decided that Napoleon's proposal to obtain recognition from the Cortes at Cádiz was wholly impracticable, he opened his campaign by two petulant acts of defiance. First, he sent one of his senior advisers into Andalusia "to gather up the scattered strands of civil government."[9] This, apart from irritating Soult, achieved nothing. Then, he dismissed General Belliard, Napoleon's appointee, from his post of governor of Madrid on the grounds that it was incompatible with his job as chief of staff of the Army of the Center. In Belliard's place he appointed General Blaniac, a French officer in the Spanish service, so that "at least in the town where I live, I have a governor who is responsible to my own ministers."[10] This move was equally futile. As soon as the emperor heard of the change, he ordered Belliard's reinstatement, since "no French troops should ever be under the command of a Spanish officer."[11]

Four days after Almenara's return, the king gave audience

to La Forest. The ambassador had a cold reception. The king said that Almenara had been sent back from Paris "as if he had been an inconvenient witness, an importunate beggar." He went on to say that, in his opinion, an approach to Cádiz was premature, that it would have no chance of success as long as the English had a strong position in Portugal. La Forest bowed and made no comment. He was anxious to break off the interview. The king would not let him go. He talked of the Treaty of Bayonne and of how his success in governing Naples had given him the right to be considered as a king in his own right rather than merely as the emperor's appointee. He said that "when he subscribed to the Treaty of Bayonne he had known that rebellion had broken out in Spain but he believed that things would have settled down if he had been allowed to control events in Spain. He did not, in consequence, consider it just that he should be held responsible for the results of policies of which he had disapproved." At this point, La Forest declined to pursue a conversation which was implicitly a criticism of the emperor, his master. Joseph, however, insisted on continuing, and before the ambassador could make his adieux, asserted that he would never agree to ceding the line of the Ebro to France. He added that a few days previously he had been on the point of leaving for France and that it was still his wish to retire into private life.[12]

Having met a blank wall of defiance with the king, La Forest proceeded by an indirect approach, seeking to influence the Spanish ministers. It was not until mid-January that he sought another audience with the king. Meanwhile, the king had other, more pressing concerns. Above all was the shortage of money. His government had been on the verge of bankruptcy ever since it was first established, but things had never been so bad as they were in the early months of 1811. "Things cannot go on as they are," he wrote on 21 February. "The troops are quite without pay, my government has none to give them. My Guard is eight months in arrears; the civil service 13 months."[13] "Does the Emperor realise," he asked in March, "that I have been forced to sell the sacred vessels from my private chapel to buy bread for the troops in Madrid? What shall we do for bread tomorrow?"[14] To his wife he wrote, "If, as the reports have it, we are going to war with Russia,* the Emperor must send me financial aid and show more confidence in me. Perhaps if he does I shall be able to support him better than he expects and possibly even send some troops to assist him. But, as things stand, the lack of money, the means of putting down chaos, is making the war endless by exasperating the people."[15] The fact of the matter was, as he showed in detail in a letter to Berthier, that "my total income is not more than four million *reals* a month. My outgoings, cut to the bone, are twelve million *reals*. My senior ministers have asked me for rations for their families and I have had to refuse them lest all my civil servants ask for the same. My ambassador to Russia is bankrupt; my ambassador in Paris has died in poverty."[16] Almost desperately, he pleaded for orders from Paris to the armies of the North** and South to give him a monthly subvention of four million reals. He received no reply.

There were occasional moments of optimism to brighten the prevailing gloom. At the beginning of March, he was able to persuade himself that "brigand chiefs [i.e., guerrilla leaders] are every day going back to their homes and many rebels are turning from Cádiz to Madrid."[17] Six weeks earlier he had put to the emperor a grandiose scheme for solving all their difficulties. "A considerable party in Valencia, led by the archbishop, has offered to receive me in that city and to acknowledge my authority. I would already have gone there had I not feared that it might be contrary to Your Majesty's arrangements. The example of Valencia, of my presence there, of the exercise of mercy and oblivion for past misdeeds, would have great influence in Cádiz. I am sure that sooner or later a similar

---

* The war with Russia did not break out until June 1812, but its inevitability was the talk of Paris early in 1811.

** The Army of the North was formed on 8 January 1811 and covered the provinces of Navarre, Biscay, Burgos, Valladolid, Salamanca, the Asturias, and Santander. The commander, until June 1811, was Marshal Bessières, duke of Istria.

movement would open the gates of Cádiz to us. I beg you to let me have your orders and I will obey them, but I am ashamed of staying here uselessly, when I am certain that I could sway the balance in Valencia, Murcia, and Andalusia."[18] On receipt of this letter, Napoleon glanced at it, stuffed it in his pocket, and showed it to no one.

On 8 February, the king had a three-hour interview with La Forest. Although dinner was announced, Joseph would not take his place at table, but led the ambassador into an adjoining room and harangued him. "The first hour was a cruel trial for me," wrote La Forest. "I saw that the King was not master of himself or of his words. He had wholly forgotten that he was speaking to the Emperor's representative. His imagination played over his imagined grievances. He reviewed with prolonged indignation the humiliations inflicted on him by the generals. He asserted that he would be forced to agree to the Emperor's demands through sheer starvation. . . . I do not go into the details since the King was not speaking within the bounds of reason, thinking that I had been sent to him to dictate his instrument of abdication."[19] He strode up and down the room, hurling sentences at the ambassador, who was standing respectfully by the table. " 'The Emperor,' he declared, 'does he realise how he is treating me? His hate pursues me; he is afraid ever to see me again.' 'Sire,' put in the ambassador, 'you will throw yourself in his arms.' "[20]

The king stopped in his pacing and fell silent. La Forest seized his opportunity to expatiate on the emperor's merits, on his virtues, on his kindness. The king turned to him and asked, "You are not deceiving me? Even if politics come between my brother and myself, at least I would like to think that we are at heart united. Yes, you are quite right. I would throw myself in his arms—if he opens them to me."[21]

By the end of that interview, La Forest was convinced that the king would agree to all Napoleon's demands, that he would submit to the cession of the Ebro provinces, that, despite his kingly title, he would act as no more than the least important of the army commanders. He sought frequent audiences with him. On 10, 12, and 26 of February, on 3, 7, and 29 March he hammered away at the king's determination to preserve the territorial integrity of Spain as he had sworn to do at Bayonne. Sometimes the king disputed the ambassador's arguments, more often he meekly agreed. La Forest believed he had won a great diplomatic triumph.

In fact, he had defeated his own ends. While verbally the king agreed with him, Joseph, as his letters to the queen show, was harboring strong mental reservations. The ambassador's suggestion that he should throw himself into his brother's arms had determined him to do just that. He would go to Paris and, confident as always in his own charm, would persuade the emperor to let him be a real king of a united Spain.

The problem was how to go. Napoleon had recently sent to Joseph, through the intermediaries of the minister of foreign affairs and Queen Julie, a message to the effect that, although consent might be given to his formal abdication should he be determined to quit Spain, he would be treated as a deserter if he left the country without the emperor's leave. It was more than unlikely that permission to return to Paris for consultation would be granted. For a time, he had to consider how to evade this prohibition. One chance appeared in March. The king fell ill with "a feverish cold and inflammation of the chest."[22] He wrote to the emperor claiming, "My health, which has broken down in the last ten days, forces me to leave this country to recuperate in the bosom of my family. Perhaps the gentler air of Mortefontaine will give me back my former vigour."[23] As usual, the emperor, who at this time had more vital family affairs on his mind, did not reply. La Forest, who believed the king's illness to be more imaginary than real, counseled him not to travel without positive permission from Paris.

Then, on 13 April, General Defrance arrived from Paris with notification of the birth of Napoleon's son, the king of Rome. He brought with him two letters. One was a formal notification as from one monarch to another. The other was a friendly, brotherly letter, describing the difficulties of the empress's delivery. This letter ended, "Since I do not intend to arrange the baptism for six weeks I am instructing General Count Defrance, my equerry, who brings you this letter, to bring you another inviting you to be godfather to your nephew."[24]

By accident or design, the letter of invitation was not enclosed. Joseph decided not to await it. He had told the emperor on 24 March that he must return to France for his health. He wrote to Queen Julie, "General Defrance brought me a letter from the Emperor announcing the birth of the King of Rome and saying that he wished me to be godfather. However the letter of invitation has not reached me. I believe I need not wait for it. . . . The Emperor has sanctioned my journey by his silence."[25]

He waited a few days until Defrance had left the city on his way back to Paris. Then he handed over the government to the duke of Santa Fé and gave a fifteen-minute audience to La Forest. Meanwhile, he threw himself into the celebrations to mark the birth of Napoleon's long-awaited heir. These, owing to the poverty of the Spanish court, were chiefly at the expense of the French ambassador, culminating, on 22 April, in a grand ball at the embassy, and not only within the embassy, since the square outside was illuminated with lanterns and torches, an orchestra played for public dancing, and wine was distributed free to all comers. "This," reported La Forest, "gave singular pleasure to the populace." Miot de Melito, who considered La Forest a verbose nonentity, reported that "the people of Madrid took little interest in the celebrations."[26]

Within the embassy, where the splendidly dressed throng was entirely French or *afrancesado*, there was undoubtedly enthusiasm and "everybody was agreeably surprised when the King arrived at half past ten and was good enough to stay until half past eleven, walking through the salons and twice going into the ballroom. After he had left, the dancing continued until two o'clock."[27] Hardly had the dancers gone home when, at dawn on 23 April, King Joseph, with eight members of his council and a small mounted escort, drove out of Madrid. At the cities along his route, he received the homage of the municipal authorities and reaffirmed his promise to maintain at all costs the integrity of Spanish territory. No one believed him. Few Spaniards believed that he would ever return. He crossed the border on 10 May, skirting Bayonne where he feared that there might be orders to turn him back or even arrest him. He stayed at Dax and it was there that he was found by an aide-de-camp from Berthier bearing orders forbidding him to leave Spain. These, however, Joseph considered to be out of date, since he had already left the country. He continued his journey and reached Paris on 15 May.

The emperor was far from pleased to hear that the king of Spain was in Paris. Whatever his opinion of Joseph's effectiveness as a public figure, Napoleon had a genuine fondness for him. In public matters and on paper, he could deal with him ruthlessly, inconsiderately; privately and face to face, he found it impossible to maintain the hectoring tone which he believed policy to demand. It is easier to be abusive to a friend when he is a long way away. Faced with the alternative of creating a public scandal by arresting his brother or deporting him to his kingdom, Napoleon decided to put a good face on the king's unauthorized arrival.

The brothers met at Rambouillet on 16 May, the day after Joseph's arrival and the day on which, by coincidence, Marshal Soult was being repulsed at Albuera, near Badajoz, by Beresford, at the head of the southern corps of Wellington's army. Joseph took the opportunity to present a memorandum setting out his conditions for retaining the Spanish throne. It was a modest document, far from the more grandiose claims he had so frequently made in his earlier letters. There was no mention of the cession of the Ebro provinces but, when discussing Catalonia, Joseph acknowledged that "until pacification is complete, this army and the territory it occupies will be governed by orders from Paris."[28] All he stipulated was that he should receive reports of the doings of the Army of Catalonia and that justice should be administered in his name. Nor did he call for the abolition of the military governments. Instead, he asked that in the districts of the armies of Aragon and the North the governors should carry on the civil government through Spaniards appointed from Madrid. He also asked that estimates should be submitted to Madrid for the military costs, which were a charge to the Spanish treasury. In Andalusia, perhaps because of his growing mistrust and dislike of Soult, his demands were somewhat higher. Apart from requiring estimates of costs for Spanish expenditure, he asked for the right to appoint all Spanish officials—military, civil, ecclesiastical, and legal.

His underlying principle was that the pay of all French troops should be a charge to France, while their rations, hospital expenses, and specifically local charges should be paid by Spain.* In return, he insisted that, except in Catalonia, all taxes raised should be paid into the Spanish treasury and that the treasury should only make payments with his authorization and against estimates previously submitted. In this way the bankruptcy of his government could be averted and a limit put to the peculations of the French generals.

As lieutenant of the emperor, a title he still held, Joseph claimed supreme command of all the armies in Spain (except that of Catalonia), but he asked for a senior marshal to act as his chief of staff and to coordinate the operations of all the army commanders. In particular, he asked that "in special circumstances the King may give the command of [the Armies of Portugal and the South] or parts of each to one or other of the marshals, or better still to the marshal who will be acting as his Chief of Staff."[29] This proposal was eminently sensible. The events of the past nine months had shown how much it was necessary. The next eighteen months were to prove that the French domination of Spain could not continue without it.

---

* For the armies of Aragon and the North he offered to pay for the artillery and engineer services. He also agreed to supply rations and hospital services to the Army of Portugal "until Portugal can support them."

The emperor and the king met alone and neither left a record of the conversation. It is, however, possible from subsequent events to reconstruct much of what transpired. The first decision was that Joseph's visit was to be considered to be official, and a fulsome letter of invitation, bearing all the marks of being written for publication, was concocted for him. Joseph's memorandum does not seem to have been discussed, but there seems little doubt that the king launched into a diatribe against the French generals in Spain, against their misconduct and the humiliations they had heaped upon him. Napoleon then set about the task of persuading him to return to Spain. The occasion of the baptism was to be a high point in the empire's history, and the abdication of the king of Spain would be a most damaging indication that behind the glitter and the glory, the empire was not as stable and immutable as it appeared to be. Napoleon, therefore, told his credulous brother a fairy tale. The obnoxious military governments were only a temporary measure. They had, nevertheless, been remarkably effective. So much so that the English, realizing that Spain was being brought back to order, had offered to evacuate Portugal if the French troops would leave Spain. Moreover, they would recognize Joseph as king provided that the French would agree to the House of Braganza in Portugal. Meanwhile, the Cortes should be called and French troops should be recalled as the king found that he no longer needed them. Some financial assistance should be given to the king for the essential expenses of his court, for his government, and for the pay of the Army of the Center. The English peace offer was, of course, a figment of the imperial imagination. The nearest that it came to reality was that the terms outlined were those offered by Napoleon to the British almost a year later.[30] Joseph, however, believed in it and saw hope for the future. He agreed to return.

After the brothers parted, Joseph withdrew to his family at Mortefontaine, while, a few days later, the emperor went off on a tour of northern France. From Caen he wrote to Berthier instructing him to visit the king and tell him the reply to his memorandum. It was clear that Napoleon was still irked by Joseph's presence in France. "He may leave when he sees fit. If he does not wish to wait for my return, he need not do so."[31] He made a few minor concessions to Joseph's wishes. In the military governments justice was to be done in the king's name and Spanish officials should be attached to the army commanders, who would make known to Madrid the needs of each army. They were also to remit to the royal treasury one quarter of the revenue of every province. "As soon as provinces have sufficient strength to protect themselves against *guerilla* raids, they should be returned to wholly Spanish administration, only providing what is necessary [to the occupation forces]."[32] General Belliard was to be called chief of staff of the Army of the Center rather than chief of staff to the king of Spain, and the king might send him or any other officer óf the Army of the Center back to France if he was dissatisfied with their conduct. Permission was also given for the withdrawal of Marshal Bessières, commanding the Army of the North, who "is not agreeable to the King."[33] To judge by Joseph's correspondence, Bessières had given less offense to him than any of the other marshals. His fault lay in his inability to hold northern Spain in subjection with insufficient troops and a number of penetrating analyses of imperial strategy in Spair When the Russian campaign began, Bessières would be needed to command the Imperial Guard, and he would work more easily if he believed that it was Joseph rather than Napoleon who had insisted on his recall. As a further emollient Marshal Jourdan, the king's friend, was to be reinstated and, provisionally, to be assigned to the Army of the North.

"I have thus," went on the emperor,

> satisfied the wishes the King expressed to me save in the matter of the supreme command of my troops. I cannot give supreme command of my armies in Spain as I cannot see any man capable of leading them, although the command ought to be unified. It is in the nature of things that a marshal stationed in

Madrid and directing operations would expect to have the glory to go with his responsibility. The commanders of the Armies of the South and of Portugal would think themselves under the command of the King's Chief of Staff rather than of the King himself. Consequently they would not obey orders.

Apart from the command of the Army of the Centre, the King will command any troops which enter its area. If the Army of the South retreats on to the Army of the Centre, it would come under the King's orders; the same would apply to the Army of Portugal. The King would command both armies if they came into his area of command.

If the King goes into the area of another army, he would be received with the honours due to a supreme commander. Nevertheless, I do not intend to alter the system of command, . . . except as far as it is necessary to ensure that the King receives reports of everything that happens, that he knows everything and can act centrally to keep the other commanders fully informed of events. This exchange of information, of comment and of advice may even be carried out through the Spanish Ministry of War.

You should let the King know that 500,000 francs will be sent to him each month; but that from 1st July he can count on receiving one million each month.

I want to do everything to send the King back to Spain with renewed splendour, but nothing that will disorganize the Army of Andalusia and the other armies.[34]

These concessions were announced to the king by Berthier at Mortefontaine on 1 June. Joseph raised some points of detail, but he did not withdraw his agreement to return to Madrid. Why he did not do so is a matter for conjecture. The scraps which the emperor had tossed to him were far from meeting any of the basic objections to his situation which he had raised so often before. There was to be no overall commander, instead he was to have the formal pomp of a supreme commander but no one was to have the essential power to coordinate the armies against the Anglo-Portuguese army. He may have believed that his brother would send him a million francs each month, but after his experience, he can scarcely have believed that the army commanders would part with a quarter of the revenue of the provinces they occupied. Nevertheless he agreed. His admirers have maintained that he went out of a sense of loyalty to his brother. His minister of state thought that he could not bear to part with his crown. His friend Count Miot thought that the deciding factor was his longing to return to the marquise de Montehermosa. It is possible that a month with the cloying Queen Julie may have made the marquise even more attractive.

Before he could return, however, he had to fulfil the ostensible object of his visit. On 9 June, the king of Rome was baptised at Notre Dame. That morning both the emperor and the empress gave receptions to the distinguished foreigners attending the ceremony. King Joseph was present, attended by the party that had traveled with him from Madrid, both Spaniards and Frenchmen. "The Emperor received the former very graciously, the latter rudely."[35] Hardly was the baptism over when the emperor ordered a letter to be sent to Joseph about "the impropriety of several Frenchmen present wearing the Spanish cockade. Tell him it is contrary to my orders. He knows full well that I do not receive Frenchmen in foreign service. Happily I did not see them at the audience or I should have turned them out. It is my wish that they should leave for Bayonne tomorrow."[36] They were at least more fortunate than a Westphalian aide-de-camp incautiously included in his entourage by King Jerome. He was ordered off parade by the emperor in person as the procession crossed the Place de la Concorde.[37]

It was not until seven o'clock in the evening that the emperor arrived at Notre Dame for the baptism. He entered in a great procession headed by heralds, pages, masters of ceremonies, chamberlains, aides-de-camp, equerries, ministers, and generals. Then followed Berthier's wife, the princess of Neuchatel and Wagram, with a candle, Princess Aldobrandini with a cloth for the consecrated oil, the countess of Beauvau with the ceremonial salt cellar; next, the alms dish carried by the duchess of Dalberg, the ewer, the borne by the countess Villain, and the napkin in the hands of the duchess of Dalmatia, wife to Marshal Soult. Behind them came the senior godparents, the grand duke of Wurtzburg, representing the emperor of Austria, grandfather and godfather, with Madame Mère, grandmother and godmother, who was attended by Queen Hortense, Louis of Holland's deserted wife and daughter of the emperor's divorced wife. Immediately behind them, the king of Rome was carried in the arms of his governess, who was supported by two noble subgovernesses, the child's nurse, and Marshal the duke of Valmy. Next came the empress under a canopy supported by the canons of the cathedral, her train carried by Prince Aldobrandini and flanked by maids of honor. The beautiful Princess Pauline Borghese, the only one of Napoleon's sisters to be present, led the ladies of the household behind Marie Louise. Then came the highest dignitaries of state, Eugène de Beauharnais, viceroy of Italy, Borghese, governor general of the departments beyond the Alps, Jean Jacques Régis de Cambacérès, archchancellor, and Berthier, chief of staff. Finally, immediately before the emperor, came the princes of the blood, Prince Joseph, king of Spain, and Prince Jerome, king of Westphalia, dressed in the uniform of white satin, embroidered with gold, which only members of the immediate imperial family could wear.

As the emperor held up the newly baptized child to the acclamations of the crowd in the great church, it seemed that the future of the empire was assured for ever. There were some, however, who were not happy. One of them was King Joseph. He was having a bad day. Queen Julie had refused to attend the ceremony, pleading illness, and the king, although a godfather, was not even allowed to approach the font, since precedence gave all the ceremonial functions to the grand duke of

Wurtzburg. The king absented himself from as many as possible of the subsequent celebratory functions. Napoleon, too, was pondering an insoluble problem. The emperor of Austria had sent, as a christening present, the Order of St. Stephen, mounted in diamonds and estimated to be worth one and a half million francs. Napoleon was determined that the child should not receive any foreign order, already he had the Grand Cordons of the Legion of Honor and of the order of the Iron Crown of Italy, but could see no way of returning the unwanted gift without offending the feelings of his father-in-law and, he hoped, faithful ally.

King Joseph set out to return to Spain on 16 June, after a final interview with the emperor. As he was riding south from Paris, Napoleon was opening the *Corps Legislatif*, the body that passed for a parliament under the imperial system. He likened the war in Spain to the Punic War between Rome (represented by France) and Carthage (Britain) and prophesied an early, successful end to it.

> Since 1809 most of the fortified towns in Spain have been taken by memorable sieges; the rebels have been beaten in battle after battle. England understands that this war is coming to its final phase, that intrigue and money will be insufficient to prolong it. She has found that her position has changed. At first she was no more than an auxiliary; now she has to play a leading role. All her regular troops are in the Peninsula; England, Scotland and Ireland are stripped of troops.* Rivers of English blood have been spilled in battles which have proved glorious to the French armies. This struggle against Carthage, which seemed that it could be concluded on the sea or beyond it, will now be decided on the plains of Spain. A clap of thunder will put an end to the Peninsula business,

* In 1811 the British army had a strength of 211,250 regular troops. Of these, 63,500 were in the British Isles, as were 84,620 militia. In the Peninsula (Portugal, Cádiz, and Gibraltar) there were 58,600 (including those on passage).

will finish the English army and will avenge Europe
and Asia by ending this second Punic war.[38]

In his less public thoughts, the emperor had less confidence
in his putative clap of thunder. Three days after his speech,
he reverted to his schemes for invading England. "The way
the war is going in Spain makes the implementation of these
plans even more necessary. . . . 80,000 men will be available
to threaten England on this front; these, together with the
steps I am taking to raise a party in Ireland, should bring satisfactory results."[39] Ten days later more realistic ideas came to
the fore. He decided to concentrate his planning on an expedition of 8,000 men against the Channel Islands of Jersey
and Guernsey.[40] Even this modest scheme came to nothing.
Instead he poured more men into Spain.

While the emperor toyed with the invasion of England and
built up his army in Germany for the campaign in Russia he
knew to be inevitable, Joseph slowly made his way back to
Madrid. After spending three days near Bayonne, he crossed
the Bidassoa into Spain on 27 June. He was pleasantly surprised by his reception. From Vitoria on 2 July he wrote,
"My return seems to have improved the spirit of the people."
A week later he was in Burgos, from where he reported that
"the news of my return has done much good; my actual
presence has done a little." He added, more cautiously, "that
there have never been so many guerrilla bands as there now
are in northern Spain. . . . The further I go into Spain the more
I am convinced of the need to lower the level of taxation imposed on the provinces." On 11 July, at Valladolid, he was
"well pleased with the reception which the inhabitants here
have given me." He reentered the capital on the sixteenth
and was "quite satisfied with the welcome I received."[41] Even
the more gloomy Miot recorded, "A large concourse of
people was waiting for him on the road. A kind of triumphal
arch had been erected a short distance from the town and
the magistrates of Madrid were assembled there to greet him.

A large number of carriages containing the principal inhabitants of the capital were drawn up on each side of the road. The satisfaction which was visible on the faces of the people, and their frequent acclamations made this a happy day for the king."[42]

His happiness could not last long. The government was as penurious as ever and, to make matters worse, the harvest was bad. It had been a bad year for the crops all over western Europe, and nowhere was the effect felt worse than in Madrid, with its large population dependent for food on the surrounding provinces. These were squeezed dry by the foraging parties of the Army of the Center and by intruders from the Army of Portugal. Worse still were the guerrillas who would descend on the farms and carry off the crops in order to sell them to the English, who paid for their supplies in gold. It was particularly humiliating to feel that the small part of Spain which was, at least in theory, under the king's direct control was acting as a source of supply to the enemy. In Madrid the food situation became increasingly serious. One of the king's aides-de-camp wrote, "By November bread had become so scarce and expensive that many families faced actual famine. Hearing this the King allocated half his civil list to buy grain at any price to assist the wretched people whose sufferings were becoming so serious that every night many died of starvation. He had bread baked at the palace and taken to the homes of the needy by servants who were forbidden to say from where it came.* . . . More than 1,500 people died of hunger that winter."[43]

The promises made to the king in Paris were disregarded almost entirely. No money was forthcoming from the army commanders and the promised million francs monthly from France arrived sparsely and irregularly. For months after Joseph's return, the only financial assistance that reached Madrid was half a million francs which had been promised before his departure. It was not until 28 November that a

---

* Soup kitchens were set up at the gates of the French barracks but many defiant patriots refused to accept food from their oppressors.

further half million was received, although convoys carrying coin for the armies of Portugal and the South on several occasions passed through Madrid. By the end of October the Spanish treasury had a deficit of "two million francs apart from being a year in arrears."[44]

Most of the army commanders refused to accept the Spanish commissaries whom the king had been told to send to them to safeguard his share of the provincial revenue. Dorsenne, who succeeded Bessières in command of the Army of the North, was one of the few who did and promptly received orders from Paris not to employ him since "Spaniards cannot be employed in the commissariat, there being no guarantee of their faithfulness or their loyalty."[45] Nor was attention paid to the agreement that any troops entering the area of the Army of the Center should come under the king's command. The campaign on the Portuguese frontier having necessitated the stationing of most of the Army of Portugal in the Tagus Valley, the king made over the provinces of Estremadura and Ávila and the Talavera district to them. This was insufficient for them, and although Joseph sent large quantities of supplies to them, their foraging parties ranged widely over the central district. They even imposed a tax of a million reals on the province of Toledo, and Toledo was the king's only source for his own supplies. "This," the King complained, "is an impossible state of affairs. Madrid has nothing to depend on but Toledo, as all the other provinces [of the Center] are either barren or occupied by *guerillas*. I cannot have my authority ignored in this area. This is the only place where things go well and they will be destroyed."[46] The question of who should command the troops of the Army of Portugal during their stay in the Center was not even raised.

"How long," the king asked, "can public opinion go on supporting a man who has no money, no territory, no troops and no authority? I have only one consolation—that I have not deserved my fate. But I cannot be consoled for the fact that the Emperor is wasting his forces in Spain while, with a little support, the whole business could be ended."[47] Despondent he might be, but he gave up his constant threats to abdicate. Instead, he seemed to become resigned to being forced out of Spain by factors over which he had no control. "If Your Majesty does not send me more than half a million francs, I think that, despite the desires of myself and of Your Majesty, I shall not be here for long."[48]

He was allowed one crumb of comfort. On 17 July, Napoleon finally sanctioned Marshal Jourdan's return to Spain. He reached Madrid on 29 September, appointed initially as governor of the city but becoming the king's chief of staff on 28 October.

The king and his chief of staff were supposed to have an overview of all the French armies in Spain, even if they had no power to coordinate their movements. It cannot have been a comforting survey that they made together on Jourdan's arrival. During the summer of 1811, the French strength in Spain reached its numerical apogee. There were, apart from 8,000 men in reserve at Bayonne, 354,461[49] men on the rolls of the six armies. Of these, 291,414 were "present under arms," the remaining 63,000 being sick, missing, or detached. Nevertheless, there was scarcely an inch in Spain on which an isolated French soldier could walk in safety. French power extended no further than the range of their guns. At night it scarcely extended beyond the lunge of their bayonets. Matters were worst in Catalonia, where Marshal Alexandre Macdonald* commanded the 23,590 men of the Seventh Corps. It was more than his force could manage to keep open the road to France and to keep Barcelona supplied. On 9 April, the fortress of Figueras, which commanded the only good road from the frontier to Barcelona and was less than twenty miles from France, was surprised by the guerrilla leader Rovira, a doctor by profession. He took 700 prisoners and captured 16,000 muskets, many pieces of artillery, and the military chest containing 400,000 francs. It was 19 August before Mac-

---

* Macdonald was relieved of his command in October 1811 and was succeeded by General Decaen.

donald could recapture the place, at a cost, from fighting and disease, of more than 5,000 men.

Also concerned with the communications with France was the Army of the North, whose responsibilities stretched from the French frontier to Ciudad Rodrigo on the Portuguese frontier. For this vast area there were 88,442 effectives. Most of these troops were tied down in garrison duty. Many others were engaged in keeping open communications with the Army of Aragon and with reinforcing that army. One division, 8,000 men under Bonnet, was assigned to holding down the Asturias, a hopeless task for such a small body of men in mountianous country. For the most part it had to restrict itself to holding Oviedo and Grijón. On occasion, even these had to be evacuated. Against the guerrillas which the king had remarked as being so rife, Dorsenne, the army commander, had little to use as a mobile force beyond two divisions of the Imperial Guard with supporting cavalry, 17,500 men. Fine soldiers as these were, they were wholly inadequate to cope with their task.

In Andalusia Soult could field, including garrisons, 68,827 men. Of these, one corps, 27,201 strong, was permanantly engaged in the abortive siege of Cádiz. Another corps of 20,830 held the eastern parts of the province and bickered with the Spanish forces in Murcia. From the remainder he had to provide garrisons for Seville and Cordova and provide divisions to support his earlier capture, Badajoz, far to the north of the Sierra Morena, the northern boundary of his army's sphere of responsibility.

In the front line against the menace from Portugal were the 38,633 effectives of the army of Portugal. Massena had made one last effort against Wellington on 3–5 May when he attacked at Fuentes de Oñoro with 48,500 men and 38 guns.* Wellington, not without difficulty, repulsed him with 37,000 British and Portuguese and 48 guns. A few days later Massena

---

* Later the army had to send some 10,000 men under D'Erlon to join the Army of the South.

was relieved of his command by Marshal Auguste Marmont, the thirty-seven-year-old duke of Ragusa, one of Napoleon's oldest friends and, like him, a gunner. His first concern was the reorganization of his army, which had suffered much in morale and discipline during the hardships of the Portuguese campaign.

His adversary, Wellington, had under his command 63,000 effectives all of ranks, of which 37,000 were British and 26,000 Portuguese.[50] Until Massena's threat had been disposed of at Fuentes de Oñoro, he had kept the bulk of his army, some 39,000 men, on the northern part of the front, facing Ciudad Rodrigo. He had, however, detached nearly 20,000 men under William Beresford to try to recapture Badajoz. Beresford laid siege to the place at the beginning of May, but had to raise it when Soult marched to its relief with 24,000 men from the Army of the South. Reinforced by 14,000 ill-trained Spaniards, the allies gave battle at Albuera, one of the bloodiest engagements of the war.* Soult was defeated and retired to the south of the Sierra Morena. The siege was renewed under Wellington's direction but was again inconclusive, although almost the whole of the allied northern corps was brought south to support it. Marmont, who showed a willingness rare amongst the marshals to assist his colleagues, brought the whole Army of Portugal to Soult's assistance. For a week in late June, 50,000 of the allies, in a strong position between Elvas and the river Gevora, faced 60,000 Frenchmen. Soult and Marmont, having relieved and restocked Badajoz, parted, Soult to deal with a threat to Seville from a Spanish force, Marmont to find food for his men in the valley of the Tagus. A corps of 15,000 men under D'Erlon was left to support the fortress. Wellington, on his side, was glad to be able to remove his troops from the Guadiana Valley, which in summer was notoriously unhealthy. He left Row'and Hill with 13,000

* Out of 10,499 British troops present, 4,689 were casualties. The 1/3rd (Buffs) lost 643 out of 755 present. Soult had some 7,000 casualties out of 24,000.

British and Portuguese to watch D'Erlon and took the rest of his army back to the Ciudad Rodrigo front.

The fact was that the situation on the Portuguese frontier was deadlocked. The British could not take Badajoz or Ciudad Rodrigo, which were the only doors through which they could invade Spain. Wellington admitted that all he could do was to "watch for opportunities of undertaking important operations of short duration."[51] The French were equally incapable of advancing into Portugal and driving out the British. But while Wellington could afford to wait, the French did not have time on their side. Despite their great strength, their armies were badly overstretched. One of Bessière's more perceptive appreciations of the situation before he was recalled was that "we are occupying too much ground and wasting our resources. We are grasping at dreams. Cádiz and Badajoz swallow up everything we have; Cádiz because we cannot take it; Badajoz because it needs an army to support it. We should destroy the second and, for the moment, give up hope of taking the first."[52]

The only part of Spain where things were going well was in the area of General Suchet's Army of Aragon, which could field 44,000 men. He laid siege to Tarragona at the beginning of May and took it on 28 June, thereby winning his marshal's baton. Encouraged by this success, Napoleon gave orders for Suchet to invade Valencia, the only one of the great provinces of Spain which had never been occupied by the French. Valencia was a rich province where many of the grandees who had embraced the patriot cause had their estates, but its occupation at this time was an irrelevance. The French army was already occupying too much ground for its strength. To include Valencia in its zone of occupation could only make matters worse unless, as was hoped, its subjection would so demoralize the Spaniards that they would abandon their resistance all over the country.

Nor were the resources of the Army of Aragon sufficient to the task, although Napoleon somewhat exaggerated the opposition that might be expected from the Spanish Army of Valencia, which in October 1811 totaled 36,000 troops, with only one-sixth well-trained regulars. Against these Suchet could make available 26,000 men while still leaving behind sufficient men to secure his communications. In reserve there were allocated to him two divisions, 15,000 men from the Army of the North. In addition, once the campaign was under way, the king was ordered to send a force, hopefully estimated at 6,000 men, to advance on the Valencians' flank by way of Cuenca. By devotedly paring his garrisons, Joseph managed to send a strong brigade, 3,000 men under General D'Armangnac, which managed at least to prevent the Spaniards at Murcia from going to the assistance of Valencia.

Having detached D'Armangnac, the Army of the Center was absurdly thin on the ground, and it became necessary for Napoleon to order Marmont to station one of his divisions in La Mancha. Nor was this all the subtraction from the troops facing Wellington. The Army of Portugal was ordered to find a corps of 9,000 to support D'Armagnac, while Marmont was told to move his own headquarters back from Plasencia to Valladolid and to station the bulk of the remainder of his army in Old Castille. Marmont was assured, from Paris, that "the English army has 20,000 sick and barely 20,000 men with the colours, so that it is impossible for them to undertake any offensive operations."[53]

Suchet crossed into Valencia in mid-September. He was detained for a time by the fortress of Saguntum, which he took on 25 October, having defeated a relieving army under the unfortunate, incompetent, but always resilient Joachim Blake. On 9 January 1812, the city of Valencia, which contained Blake and the remnants of his army, surrendered to him. He treated the city with the greatest harshness, shot many civilians for their part in its defense, and sent 500 monks and 350 university students to France. Of the prisoners, two hundred were shot on the road back to France since they were incapable of keeping up with the column. He also imposed on Valencia a fine of fifty-three million francs. Almost the only pleasant thing to record about the capture of Valencia is that Suchet sent three million of these francs to King Joseph in Madrid.

Valencia had been captured. The French army had become even more extended, but that was not the worst immediate result of the invasion. In obedience to his orders, Marmont had sent General Montbrun, with two weak infantry divisions, all the light cavalry of his army, and 36 guns, altogether 10,000 men, to operate against the Valencian flank and rear. Montbrun was at Almanza, southwest of Valencia, when he heard on 13 January that Suchet had taken the city and the Valencian army. Suchet urged him to return to the Tagus, but being a young and ambitious commander, anxious to win an independent success, he ignored this advice and marched on Alicante, a fortified town with a garrison of 6,000 men. Having nothing more powerful than field guns, he could do no more harm to Alicante than to summon it to surrender. This he did on 16 January. Not unnaturally, his summons was refused. He thus had no recourse but to return to Toledo, which his advanced guard reached on the twenty-ninth, the main body coming in two days later. By that time the Portuguese frontier had flared into life. Wellington had seen the opportunity which Napoleon had offered him and had struck at Ciudad Rodrigo.*

---

* It is fair to Montburn to add that even if he had not made his promenade to Alicante but had turned back from Almanza on 13 January he could still not have affected the issue at Rodrigo. The blame for his absence must rest entirely with Napoleon, who ordered detachments to be made from the Army of Portugal on wishful thinking about the effective strength of Wellington's army.

Chapter 9

SUPREME

COMMANDER

They all with one consent began to make excuse.

LUKE 14:18

IF the French kingdom of Spain gained the province of Valencia, it lost Catalonia. Although the formal proclamation was delayed for some months, the province was divided into four departments,* on the French style, and French prefects and other administrators appointed to each. Since less than a quarter of Catalonia was effectively occupied by the French army, the influence of the new regime was very limited, the more since the French troops, from generals down to private soldiers, treated the new officials with scant attention. While the conscription was not applied to this new accession to the empire, an attempt was made, with a predictable lack of success, to raise three Catalan battalions in the French service.[1]

The New Year of 1812 was not a happy one for King

* The four departments were Monserrat (capital at Barcelona), Segre (capital at Puigcerda), Bouches de l'Ebre (captial at Lérida), and Ter (capital at Gerona).

218

Joseph. He celebrated it by writing a despairing letter to La Forest.

> You were a witness, *Monsieur l'ambassadeur*, six months ago to the eagerness with which the people of this capital welcomed my return from Paris. At that time I shared their hopes. Now I share their despondency and like them I am anxious that things should change. I have written directly to the Emperor, I have written to Marshal Berthier. I have had no reply. . . . None of the promises made to me in Paris have been kept. . . . I do not wish to complain, only to make my present position clear. I have nothing but the province of Madrid. . . . I was promised the loan of a million a month; this would have sufficed for the expenses of my household, of my guard and for the upkeep of my embassies abroad. . . . My household has been kept going by pawning the few diamonds left to me and by being in debt everywhere for my day to day costs. Such is the poverty of my civil servants that many of my principal officials have not a fire on their hearths; some others have no bread. To some to whom the state owes 10,000 francs in salary, I have been able to give no more than one hundred francs.[2]

He bombarded the emperor with letters, begging that his promised monthly million should be paid to him. More in hope than expectation, he suggested that Valencia should be made over to him, that he should be allowed to visit the newly won province. Napoleon had other things on his mind. Nothing but force could make the Russians submit to his orders to exclude British trade. He had determined on war as soon as summer came. A vast army would be needed. There were more than 350,000 on the rolls of the armies in Spain. They must make their contribution. He withdrew the two divisions of the guard, the only striking force of the Army of the North, and all the Polish troops, a total of 27,000 experienced men. They were to be replaced in time by an equivalent number of newly drilled conscripts. As for the needs of Spain for money and supplies, he wrote to his chief of staff, "In the 'Reveries' of Marshal Saxe* there are, amongst many mediocre things, some ideas on methods of making conquered countries pay contributions without exhausting one's own troops. I think these ideas are good. Read them yourself and put them in the form of an instruction to be sent to my generals in Spain."[3]

More practically, a little money was sent. Three hundred and eighty thousand francs reached Madrid on 24 January, but it was far from enough. "Discontent is raising its head among the French troops of my own Guard at the moment when I need them most," complained Joseph to Berthier. "The officers have not been paid for nine months; the men are no better off. Many are asking to be allowed to return to France. Several have deserted."[4] Nevertheless, for the rest of his reign, money was to be the least of the king's worries.

As was to be expected, the army commanders were, at best, lax in sending reports to Madrid. On 21 January, the king was complaining that he had heard nothing from Suchet in Valencia and that he had no idea where Montbrun and his detachment from the Army of Portugal could be found. He heard from Suchet on the twenty-fifth but he had no news of Soult since the fifth of the month. Nothing had been heard from Marmont and the Army of Portugal, but "a civil official coming from Talavera has told me that General Brennier's division [of the Army of Portugal] left that town on the 19th January marching to Ciudad Rodrigo. For the last five days heavy gunfire has been heard from Ciudad Rodrigo."[5] The following day he wrote to Suchet that "the English are making a show** of besieging Ciudad Rodrigo and have heavy

---

* Maurice comte de Saxe (1696–1750). Son of the elector of Saxony. One of the greatest soldiers in the French army in the eighteenth century. Victor of Fontenoy, Roucoux, and Laufield.

** The emperor also seems to have believed that the English move on Rodrigo was a feint "to divert attention from the siege of Valencia" (NC, xxiii, 18,455. N. to Berthier, 27 Jan 12).

artillery there. Marshal Marmont has been apprised of this and is marching against them with 50,000 men."[6] There is no clearer proof of the justice of Joseph's complaint that the generals told him nothing of their doings than that Rodrigo had fallen to a British assault on 19 January. The fortress is less than a 160 miles from Madrid.

Wellington had known since Christmas Day that the Army of Portugal had made detachments towards the east and that large bodies of French troops were leaving Spain. By New Year's Day he had learned that the bulk of Marmont's army was moving from the Tagus Valley. The larger part of his army was stationed on the Portuguese border within reach of Rodrigo. His siege train was stored within the walls of Almeida. He saw his opportunity and took it. On 8 January, the fortress was invested and on the evening of the nineteenth his Third and Light divisions surged over the breach. "As soon as the French suspected we were coming, they threw a quantity of light balls which enabled them to see completely the whole of our troops. Our troops then pushed on and the whole business was finished in less than a quarter of an hour."[7] The French governor did not distinguish himself, and his garrison, less than 2,000 men, was very inadequate in numbers for its task. But if the town was badly under-garrisoned, it was heavily over-gunned. The British captured in it 153 heavy guns, including the entire siege train of the Army of Portugal, the only siege equipment in northern Spain. Wellington, for the loss of 1,100 killed and wounded, had secured the northern of the two gateways from Portugal into Spain. He lost no time in setting his own siege train on its toilsome way to the southern gateway, Badajoz.

From Marmont's point of view, Wellington could not have struck at a more embarrassing time. Not only were two of his infantry divisions and most of his cavalry out of touch on Montbrun's wild goose chase to Alicante, but he was in process of moving his headquarters and the bulk of his army, on Napoleon's orders, from the Tagus Valley to the neighborhood of Valladolid, where he was to take over responsibility for the defense of León and for Bonnet's division, which was stationed in the Asturias, both of which had previously been in the charge of Dorsenne and the Army of the North. In making these new dispositions, the emperor assured him that "the English, having suffered heavily, are finding it difficult to fill the ranks of their army. All considerations, in consequence, tend to the belief that they will confine themselves to the defense of Portugal. . . . They know that if they press in upon Ciudad Rodrigo they run the risk of being brought to battle. That is the last thing they want."[8] The same letter assured him, "The conquest of Portugal and the immortal glory of defeating the English are reserved for you."

On about 7 January, Marmont received a letter from Dorsenne, who was awaiting him at Valladolid, enclosing a report from the governor of Salamanca to the effect that the British were crossing the frontier. Dorsenne commented, "I give no credence to this news since, for the last six months, I have perpetually been receiving reports of a similar nature."[9] When Marmont reached Valladolid on the twelfth, he agreed with his colleague and, the next day, he reported to Paris, "It is not improbable that the English may make a move at the end of February."[10] It was, therefore, a most unwelcome shock for the two army commanders on 14 January, after they had dined, to receive definite news from Salamanca that Wellington, with five divisions,* had opened the siege six days earlier. Not more than 20,000 men were immediately available to march to the relief of the town. This was clearly an insufficient force, and aides-de-camp were immediately sent galloping in all directions to achieve a larger concentration. Bonnet, in defiance of the emperor's instuctions, was ordered to evacuate the Asturias. The guard divisions, on the march to France, were ordered to retrace their steps. Montbrun's detachment was urgently recalled, and another Army of Portugal division, which was in La Mancha, was also called in. By these means Marmont reckoned that he would be able to put 32,000 men into the field by 27 January and 40,000 by the start of Febru-

---

* Wellington, in fact, had seven divisions in hand.

ary. Salamanca was given as the point of concentration. The
marshal was within twenty-five miles of that place on 21
January, still with no more than 20,000 men, when he heard
that Ciudad Rodrigo had been stormed two days earlier. There
was nothing he could do about it. Even when his whole force
was gathered together, he could achieve nothing without lay-
ing siege to Rodrigo himself. For that he must have heavy
guns, and all his heavy guns were in Wellington's hands. He
sent Bonnet back to the Asturias and put his remaining divisions into cantonments, almost equally divided between the
south bank of the Douro and the north bank of the Tagus.
He reported to Paris that "everything seems to show that Lord
Wellington intends to besieze Badajoz and I need to be able
to go to its help."[11]

Joseph was still ignorant of the fate of Rodrigo on 1 February, almost a fortnight after it had fallen. His chief concern
was that the return of the Army of Portugal to the valley of
the Tagus meant that once again it would have to live at the
expense of the area properly belonging to his own Army of
the Center. He was, nevertheless, glad to have its protection
on the western side of Madrid, believing that his own troops,
many of whom were now necessary to guard the communications with Suchet in Valencia, were insufficient to keep the
capital safe. Moreover, he agreed with Marmont about Wellington's intentions. "Reports reaching me from all sides speak
of the enemy's march towards Badajoz."[12]

Marmont and the king might be unanimous in believing
Badajoz to be in imminent danger, but they were not in Paris.
In Napoleon's view, Badajoz was the responsibility of Soult,
and the Army of the South "is very strong and now has its
flank covered by the Army of Valencia."[13] Marmont's only
task was to keep the British away from Badajoz by keeping
the bulk of their strength tied down around Ciudad Rodrigo.
"Your best way of helping the Army of the South is to establish your headquarters at Salamanca and concentrate your
army there. Re-occupy the Asturias but do not detach more
than one division to the Tagus valley. You will thus oblige

the enemy to stay around Almeida for fear of an invasion. You can drive in his outposts. You could even march on Ciudad Rodrigo, if you have the necessary siege artillery and, since your honour is involved, you could take that fortress. If, on the other hand, you are short of supplies and artillery, you can at least make a raid into Portugal. Go to the Douro and threaten Almeida. This will contain the enemy. . . . You must suppose that the English are mad if you believe them capable of marching on Badajoz while you remain at Salamanca so that you could reach Lisbon before they could."[14]

It was useless for Marmont to point out that it was impossible to concentrate the army at Salamanca. "It could not subsist there for a fortnight. . . . When I transferred to the north in January, I found not a grain of wheat in the depots, not a *sou* in the military chests, unpaid debts everywhere. As a result of the ridiculous system of administration here, there was a famine—real or artificial—of a severity which has not been recognized. . . . We have not four days' food in any of our depôts, we have no transport, we cannot requisition from the poorest village without sending to it a foraging party two hundred strong."[15] All the satisfaction he received from Paris was to be told that he had no responsibility for defending Badajoz and that he worried "too much about things that do not concern you. Your mission was to protect Almeida and Ciudad Rodrigo—and you allowed them to fall. . . . You are becoming alarmed because Lord Wellington has sent a division or two towards Badajoz. Badajoz is a very strong fortress, and Marshal Soult has 80,000 and can draw help from Marshal Suchet. If Wellington were to march on Badajoz you can bring him back promptly and triumphantly by marching on Ciudad Rodrigo and Almeida."[16] The emperor, remarked Marmont, "believes to be true whatever is most convenient."[17] By 16 March, every one of Wellington's divisions was concentrated around Elvas, within a single march of Badajoz. All that remained on the Rodrigo front was a regiment of German Hussars, backed by a few brigades of Portuguese militia.

Marmont duly made his raid into Portugal. It achieved nothing, as he knew must be the case. He had no guns to batter Rodrigo and Almeida. There was no food in the district over the Portuguese frontier and he could reach none of Wellington's own supply dumps. He penetrated as far as Guarda where, on 14 April, he routed two brigades of Portuguese militia. Next day his advanced guard pushed on along the road to Celorico, only to be pulled up short by the news that Badajoz had fallen and that the leading troops of Wellington's army were already back on the north bank of the Tagus. Within a few days, the Army of Portugal would be cut off from Spain. By 23 April, the whole army was back in Spain. Marmont had carried out his orders, losing fifteen hundred horses in doing so, but, as both he and Wellington had foreseen, the results had been negligible.

The British had stormed Badajoz on the night of 6–7 April. The town was a fortress of a very much higher quality than Ciudad Rodrigo. Its governor, Armand Philippon, and garrison of 4,700 men put up a magnificent defense. They defended the two breaches successfully to the end, and it was only because so many men had been sucked in to secure these vital points that the British were able to break in by escalade at two other points. In the matter of bravery it is hard to know whether to admire more the French defenders or their British assailants. The whole siege cost Wellington 4,670 casualties, 3,713 in the assault alone.* Nevertheless, he had secured the southern gateway to Spain, and with all four frontier fortresses in his hands, the initiative had passed irrevocably from the French to the Anglo-Portuguese army. For the rest of the war, Wellington made the moves and the French countered them as best they could.

Soult had been at Cádiz when news reached him, on 20 March, that Badajoz had been invested. He was not greatly disturbed by the news. "The garrison lacked for nothing. There were rations for more than two months; an abundant provision of ammunition. The strength of the garrison was 5,000 men all told. They had beaten off three assaults in the

---

* In the assault there were 2,983 British casualties and 730 Portuguese.

past and were quite convinced that whatever force the enemy brought up to the breach they would never be able to break through."[18] Moreover, Soult was counting on Marmont's putting into operation his plan to keep half his army in the Tagus Valley and to go to the help of Badajoz as soon as it was attacked. Unfortunately, neither Berthier nor Marmont had thought to explain to him that the emperor had explicitly forbidden any such move. Working on these two false assumptions, Soult collected 13,000 men from Andalusia and marched over the Sierra Morena to join up with D'Erlon's corps of 12,000, which was already in Estremadura. The two forces met at Llerena on 5 April. Between this combined force of 25,000 French troops lay Wellington's covering force, 31,000 men under Thomas Graham, drawn up on the old battlefield of Albuera. Soult was resolved to give battle whatever the odds[19] but, on 8 April, when he was at Villa Franca, "I learned that the fortress of Badajoz had fallen, by surprise, into the hands of the enemy. In consequence I determined, in view of the greatly inferior forces which I could oppose to the whole English army, to return to Seville."[20] Soult was in no doubt that the fall of Badajoz was due solely to the fact that Marmont had failed to come to its aid. Henceforward, it became increasingly difficult to interest him in anything beyond the borders of Andalusia. This obsession with his own territory was to have the gravest consequence for King Joseph in the following summer.

On 2 March, Joseph's aide-de-camp, General Bigarré, delivered dispatches to Napoleon in Paris. "On seeing me the Emperor said in a friendly manner, 'Ah, here you are, Bigarré, how is Joseph?' While he opened the two packets I had brought, he asked me what Marmont had been doing while Wellington took Ciudad Rodrigo. He thundered against General Montbrun who, he said, had done nothing during his promenade to Alicante except levy contributions. 'There is,' he said, smiling, 'only Suchet who understands his business.

If I had two more generals like him to lead my troops in Spain, the war would be over.' "[21]

The question of supreme command in Spain was becoming increasingly pressing. As long as he was in France or no further east than Vienna, Napoleon had been content to try to exercise a minute supervision over the movements of each of his armies in Spain, but even he, with his passion for centralization, could not disguise from himself that he could not continue to do so from the depths of Russia. As early as 2 February, Joseph had been informed that "if the political situation obliges the Emperor to go to Poland, it is his intention to give you the overall command of all the armies in Spain."[22] It was not a satisfactory solution. Napoleon had himself spelled out the objections to it the previous May (see page 204). He had come to the conclusion that the army commanders would not obey the king. Nevertheless, when faced with the necessity of appointing a supreme commander, it was impossible to see an alternative. Of the marshals still active and not, like Massena, in disgrace, Berthier was indispensable for the Russian campaign and Murat, even if he was capable of doing the job, was king of Naples and could hardly be made commander in chief in his brother-in-law's kingdom. The same objection could well be raised to Charles Jean Bernadotte, who, quite apart from being Joseph's wife's brother-in-law, was prince royal of Sweden. Next in seniority was Soult, who was on the worst of terms with King Joseph. Soult could not be asked to serve under a man junior to himself, and the emperor was far from willing to remove him from Spain. There was, therefore, no alternative to appointing Joseph to the place he had always solicited and to allow Jourdan, who was senior to Soult but not of the caliber to make a commander in chief, to continue to act as chief of staff.

He finally came to a decision on 16 March. "Inform the King of Spain, by special messenger who must leave this evening, that I confide to him the command of all my armies in Spain, and that Marshal Jourdan will act as his Chief of Staff.

Tell the King that, in political matters, I will communicate with him through my ambassador in Madrid. You will also write to Marshal Suchet, to Marshal Soult and to Marshal Marmont telling them that I have given the command of all my armies in that kingdom to the King of Spain . . . and that they will conform to all orders which they shall receive from the King, so that the movements of all the armies may be co-ordinated [*pour faire marcher les armées dans une même direction*]."[23] More than two weeks later, in a letter proving how impossible it was that Wellington could take Badajoz, he reiterated that he had confided to the king "the military and political direction of all matters in Spain."[24]

Even with the assumption that Catalonia was no longer a part of Spain, it is clear that the military command given to Joseph was far from complete. No instructions had been given to Dorsenne, commanding the Army of the North, or to General Reille, who commanded a temporary Army of the Ebro, which was responsible for upper Aragon. Both these officers declined to acknowledge the king's supremacy, as did Marshal Suchet. Suchet, in fact, held two commands, those of the Army of Aragon and the Army of Valencia. In the first of these capacities he had earlier been forbidden to take orders from the king. Now he claimed exemption from the king's orders in both capacities, despite the new orders.

This left Joseph's new command comprising the armies of the South, of Portugal, and of the Center, his old command. Madrid had no information about the state of Soult's army except that its theoretical strength was about 54,000 men. "We do not know what this army has in munitions, in food or in means of transport. All we do know is that they are far in arrears of pay."[25] To make matters worse, Soult had withdrawn all the detachments which guarded the road between Seville and Madrid. "He can only be communicated with with the greatest difficulties. We do not even know whether he has received the news that the Emperor has put him under the King's command."[26]

There was more information about the Army of Portugal,

but it brought little comfort. There were 52,000 men on the rolls, but after deducting 6,000 men in the Asturias, from whence the emperor had forbidden their removal, and the garrisons of all the important towns in the area of Salamanca, Benavente, León, and Valladolid, "it can not be reckoned that Marshal Marmont could dispose of more than 25,000 men in any operation which takes it out of its own area. This army is without supply depôts and transport. Its pay is far in arrears and it is in such a parlous state that a dangerous inclination to pillage is showing itself. . . . It will be seen from this report that the Army of Portugal is in no state to fight alone against the English army on the Tormes,* and far less able to go to seek out the enemy either in Portugal or in Estremadura."27

The Army of the Center comprised 9,500 French troops, 5,800 enrolled Spaniards with, at the beginning of April, a fortuitous addition of 3,200 French drafts, who were on their way to join Soult but could not get through to him. With no more than 18,500 men, wrote Jourdan, "it is easy to believe that this army is not in a position to give help to others. The garrison of Madrid is so weak that, if the Royal Guard left the city, Madrid would not be safe."28

Summing up his view of the situation, Jourdan wrote, "One can see that the Imperial Armies can undertake nothing beyond the occupation of the conquered provinces. It is also clear that if Lord Wellington, who can move with 60,000 men, apart from the Spanish armies and the *guerillas,* moves against either the Army of the South or that of Portugal, whichever he attacks will not be able to resist him. . . . If things stay as they are and Lord Wellington marches against either army, only a catastrophe can be expected."29

The only thing that could put the situation on a sound footing was the establishment of a reserve of 15,000-20,000 men who would be available to the king, who could march with them to any place where danger threatened. Since the army

---

* The Tormes is the river which runs down to the Douro from Salamanca and is the first even partially practicable defensive position which Marmont could take up against troops advancing from Ciudad Rodrigo.

commanders would not, and could not, part with any of their own troops to form this reserve, the emperor should be asked to provide fresh troops for this task. "If the Emperor cannot send the 15-20,000 men who are considered indispensable, then His Imperial Majesty must give orders for the evacuation of Andalusia."[30] This would enable 15,000 men to strengthen the Army of Portugal and 30,000 men to reinforce the Army of the Center and form the reserve.

Jourdan agreed with Bessières's comments on the situation when he said that "we are occupying too much ground and wasting our resources," but he had no real hope of achieving anything. The emperor was far too occupied with his preparations for the Russian war to spare another large body of troops for Spain. Nor would he consent to give up the richest and most peaceable province in occupied Spain. All that Joseph could do was to give orders to Soult and Marmont that if one was attacked, the other should immediately march to his assistance with all his available forces by the shortest possible route. Even this simple operation was made much more difficult when on 19 May General Rowland Hill, in a brilliantly executed raid, cut the bridge across the Tagus at Almaraz. This greatly lengthened the communications between Soult and Marmont since, in the future, couriers between them had to go by way of Toledo and the outskirts of Madrid.

Napoleon left Paris for the east on 9 May. Before leaving, he ordered Clarke, the minister of war,* to write to King Joseph his final instructions about Spain. The king was enjoined to "keep the conquests already made and extend them successively. Do not take the offensive against Portugal unless circumstances are wholly favorable. Above all keep communications with France open. It will not escape Your Majesty that he should pay particular attention to the north of Spain for that is the part in which it is most essential that the enemy do not establish themselves. To ensure this the most active opera-

---

* On 4 May, Berthier ceased to be chief of staff to the Army of Spain and Clarke became the channel of communications on military matters between the emperor and the king.

tions must be undertaken against the brigands. These should not be limited to short pursuits of them which leave them the ability to reunite and make more trouble later. In the present state of affairs you should maintain the defensive against them, but assuming an imposing aspect so that they can take no advantage of our position. The forces which His Majesty has put under your orders will permit you to do what is necessary in that direction."[31]

Few more infuriating documents can ever have been sent to a commander in the field. From Madrid it was obvious that the most vital danger lay in Portugal, where Wellington, at the head of 66,000 British and Portuguese troops, could choose whether he struck at Soult or Marmont, who were incapable of supporting each other by reason of the distance between their cantonments. Yet on this front the emperor merely ordered an attitude defensive yet imposing and did not even deign to consider what the enemy might do. Neither Joseph nor Jourdan doubted the importance of keeping safe the northern part of Spain, but the Army of the North was manifestly too weak to put down the guerrillas in that area. Dorsenne, at this time, followed Bessières back to France, having failed in an impossible task, and was succeeded by General Louis Marc Caffarelli. Baron Thiebault, who served under both of them, considered the first to be "an incompetent mountebank," the second, "a brainless peacock,"[32] but this was beside the point. No one could successfully command the Army of the North without many more troops than were allocated to it. Since the emperor would provide no more troops, that army could only be reinforced from the forces of either Soult or Marmont, and these were already dangerously weak. To add that the forces allocated to the king were sufficient for whatever was necessary was either insulting or merely showed that the emperor had no conception of how events in Spain stood.

The problems facing the new supreme commander would have taxed the skill and ingenuity of the most capable of

Napoleon's marshals. It cannot be wondered at that King Joseph, whose military experience was minimal, failed to solve them. Jourdan could tender the right advice—that it was vital to collect a central reserve—but neither Joseph nor Jourdan could impose their will on Soult, Suchet, Marmont, and Caffarelli. No one but the emperor could do that, and the emperor was steadily moving away from Spain.

There were more than 250,000 French troops under arms in Spain. Wellington's army was, all told, less than one-fourth of that strength, but he could outnumber either of the two armies facing him, and unless they could be persuaded to support each other, they would be defeated in detail. All the army commanders adopted a *non possumus* attitude. Suchet resolutely refused to part with a single man—indeed, he asked to be reinforced. Caffarelli in the north agreed with the greatest reluctance to support Marmont but, in the event, failed to keep his promise. Of the two commanders immediately concerned, Marmont was the more forthcoming, perhaps because he thought it improbable that Wellington would march into Andalusia. Soult was resolute in having nothing to do with helping Marmont. In an endeavour to persuade him to permit D'Erlon's corps, now reduced to 12,000 men and stationed on the northern slopes of the Sierra Morena, to march north across the Tagus should Marmont be attacked, the king sent his aide-de-camp, Colonel Deprez, to see Soult at Seville.

Deprez's report made uncomfortable reading in Madrid. Soult, he said, was extremely dissatisfied at not having been appointed chief of staff in Jourdan's place and "I should warn you that the order appointing Your Majesty as supreme commander of the army has not yet been published to the troops."[33] Joseph's orders for the march of D'Erlon should Marmont be attacked gave rise to a long discussion, "and the Marshal seemed little disposed to obey. . . . I suggested that that Army of the South should be considered as a part of the whole French army in Spain and that, as such, it was under an obligation to go to the assistance of the other corps. . . . Finally I asked the Marshal whether, if the English advanced in the north, Count D'Erlon would be ordered to cross the Tagus. The answer was a positive 'no.' "[34] "The Army of the South," asserted Soult, "cannot send Count D'Erlon to the valley of the Tagus without being obliged to evacuate Andalusia within a fortnight."[35]

Even making allowances for Soult's contempt for the king and his anger at Marmont's failure to rescue Badajoz, it is hard to avoid the conclusion that, at this stage, he was behaving like a spoiled child. Even the most pessimistic French estimates of Wellington's strength did not credit him with sufficient troops to undertake two major offensives at the same time. It followed, therefore, that if the allies struck at Marmont, Soult could afford to detach D'Erlon to his aid since, *ex hypothesi*, Wellington would have no force available to endanger Andalusia. The fact is that Soult's two years as an independent ruler in Seville had inflated his sense of his own importance. A French officer who visited him in his capital wrote, "He seemed to be King of Andalusia rather than the Emperor's representative there. No monarch ever surrounded himself with more majesty; no court was ever so deferential. Like Homer's Jupiter, Olympus trembled at his nod. General Godinot, a most worthy officer, shot himself on returning from an unsuccessful expedition, being unable to endure the tone in which Soult reprimanded him. The Marshal was always surrounded by a glittering guard. Every Sunday picked troops lined the route between his palace and the cathedral. Soult would go to Mass in procession, followed by the municipal authorities and a resplendent staff."[36] Power had gone to Soult's head.

Some color was lent to Soult's fears for his beloved viceroyalty when, at the beginning of June, General Hill, commanding Wellington's right wing, made a short foray with 18,000 men toward the Sierra Morena. The only incident of note was a cavalry action at Maguilla (11 June) which reflected scant credit to the contestants on either side, but it was enough to convince Soult that Andalusia was in mortal danger. He reinforced D'Erlon with 8,000 men and cried to Madrid for help. It is, perhaps, remarkable that although

D'Erlon reported Hill's strength as 30,000 men, Soult reduced this estimate to 20,000 in his report.

In Madrid, Joseph's position was intolerable. It was obvious that Wellington was about to strike, but impossible to tell which way he would move. On 14 June, Jourdan wrote to Marmont, "In your letter of 6 June you say that Wellington is about to attack you. However, we receive letters from Marshal Soult asserting that the blow will fall on him. He declares that 60,000 of the allies are about to invade Andalusia. We are too far away to know which of you is being deceived."[37] Jourdan went on the reiterate that if it were to turn out that Soult was being attacked, Marmont was immediately to send three divisions to his aid. This was small comfort to Marmont, who, in order to find food, had been obliged to scatter seven of his divisions in the area of Salamanca, Benavente, Valladolid, and Ávila. His eighth division, Bonnet's, was far away in the Asturias. When he could concentrate all these divisions, he would, after deducting sick and essential garrisons, muster about 50,000 men. He had, however, Caffarelli's promise that he would come to his aid with 8,000 men and 22 guns from the Army of the North.

It was not until late at night on 18 June that news reached Madrid that Wellington had advanced in strength from Ciudad Rodrigo five days earlier. Immediately Joseph sent instructions to Soult and Caffaraelli to march the detachments ordered earlier to Marmont's support. Another order went to Suchet requiring him to march in person to Cuenca with a corps large enough to cover the center and act as events might dictate.

One immediate problem was to determine whether the whole Anglo-Portuguese army was marching on Salamanca or whether Hill's corps was still around Badajoz. There was no immediate way of discovering this fact, and Joseph's orders to Marmont had to take this into account. "In my opinion, if General Hill with his 18,000 men have stayed on the left bank of the Tagus, you will be strong enough to beat the English, especially if you receive help from the Army of the North.

You should choose for yourself a position on which to fight and make your dispositions accordingly. On the other hand, if General Hill has joined the main the body of the English, I imagine you will not be strong enough to be certain of victory. In this case you must manuever to avoid a battle until you have been joined by the troops I have ordered to your support from Count D'Erlon and Marshal Suchet."[38]

Thus Marmont had permission to fight, provided that, as was the case, Hill had not joined Wellington. Before he did so, however, his army had to be concentrated. To delay the British, 800 men had been left in three fortified convents commanding the bridge over the Tormes at Salamanca. The concentration point for all the divisions was given as Fuentesauco, twenty miles north of Salamanca on the Toro road. By evening on 19 June, 40,000 men were assembled there—the whole army except for some detachments and Bonnet's division, which could not be looked for until the end of the month. Wellington, in the meantime, laid siege to the three convents and disposed the bulk of his army to cover the siege on a strong position, the heights of San Cristóbal, to the north of the city. The allied army had a total strength of 48,000 men, including 18,000 Portuguese and 3,000 Spaniards.

In Madrid there was nothing but bad news. Suchet had flatly refused to send any troops to cover Madrid. Caffarelli claimed that he was unable to detach anything from the north, and Soult, who could claim that since Hill had not joined Wellington he was not enjoined to send D'Erlon across the Tagus, predictably did nothing. Both Suchet and Caffarelli had some reason for their inaction. Wellington had done his best to arrange diversions against the coasts of occupied Spain which would tie down as many French troops as possible. An Anglo-Sicilian expedition was assembling to land on the east coast of Spain. The whole operation was delayed owing to the vacillations of Lord William Bentinck, the British commander in Sicily, and did not in fact land until the end of July, but Suchet had been warned of its intention and was not unaturally unwilling to part with troops while it was imminent. A far flimsier threat detained Caffarelli. Commodore Sir Home Popham, with a small naval squadron and two battalions of Royal Marines, made a series of descents on the coast between Santander and the mouth of the Bidassoa. Working in the closest cooperation with the guerrillas of Biscay, he made June and July hideous for Caffarelli's army, who were constantly moving along the rugged coast in a vain attempt to march as fast as a battleship could sail. For a time, Popham was able to make Santander a fleet base for the British, and for two weeks the Spaniards were able to seize and hold Bilbao. Faced with this constantly moving menace, Caffarelli declined to send any infantry to assist Marmont, although he eventually agreed to send a trifling force of cavalry and artillery.

On 27 June, the Salamanca convents surrendered and Marmont, who had been hovering about the north of the city, not daring to attack, unwilling to retire, fell back to the line of the Douro, taking up a position based on fortified bridgeheads at Zamora, Toro, and Tordesillas. Bonnet joined him there on 7 July and, by various shifts, he was able to increase his cavalry force by 1,000 men. He now had 43,000 infantry, 3,200 cavalry, and 78 guns. This was a force so nearly equal in numbers to Wellington's as to make no difference, the more so since Wellington's army was made up of Spaniards and Portuguese. From 2 to 15 July, the two armies faced each other, peacefully, across the broad but by no means unfordable Douro.

While the first stage of the summer campaign was going on in Spain, the future of Europe was being settled fifteen hundred miles away to the east. While Wellington was besieging the Salamanca convents, Napoleon was at Danzig. One evening Colonel Rapp, one of his aides-de-camp, dined with him together with Murat and Berthier. The emperor "was silent for a long time; then suddenly he asked me how far it was from Danzig to Cádiz. 'Too far, Sire.' 'It will be much further in a few months.' 'So much the worse!' "[39] On 24 June, the French advanced guard crossed the Niemen into Russia. As he watched them go forward, the emperor remarked, "In less than two months the Russians will be suing for peace."[40] Behind the cavalry screen marched 510,000 men. Less than half of them were French. The remainder were made up of contingents of various sizes from Anhalt, Austria, Baden, Bavaria, Berg, Croatia, Dalmatia, Denmark, Hesse-Darmstadt, Holland, Illyria, Italy, Lippe, Mecklenburg, Poland, Portugal, Prussia, Saxony, Spain, Switzerland, Westphalia, and Württemberg. If there had not been 250,000 French troops in Spain, the *Grande Armée* might have been a more reliable force.

The distance from Madrid to Marmont's position on the north bank of the Douro is, even allowing for detours, less than 150 miles. It might well have been six hundred. Correspondence between the king and Marmont became all but impossible. Madrid knew that Marmont had fallen back on the Douro but little more. No report from the Army of Portugal reached the king's headquarters between that of 14 June and the end of the month. Marmont received his last letter from Madrid on 12 July. It was dated 30 June, having taken twelve days to cover the short distance. This letter claimed that Wellington had 50,000 men but that, as far as could be calculated in Madrid, only 18,000 of them were British. "This being so, the King believes that you are strong enough to win a victory and wishes to know why you have not taken the offensive. I am requested to invite you to explain your reasons by express messenger." Hill, he was told, was still in the south and, if he moved north, would be shadowed by D'Erlon. It might be, however, that D'Erlon might be slow in following. Therefore, the king "wishes you to take advantage of the present opportunity to fight Wellington while he has not all his forces with him."[41]

To a man like Marmont, who still had his reputation as an independent army commander to win, this was as good as an order to attack at all costs. His position behind the Douro was becoming daily more difficult. There were reports that the Spanish Army of Galicia was moving against his rear.* There

---

* Santocildes, who commanded this army of 15,000 men, had agreed to harass Marmont's rear but in fact settled down to besiege Astorga.

was actual pressure on his rear and eastern flank from a brigade of Portuguese cavalry and a force of militia which was making foraging difficult and dangerous. Bonnet had already joined him, so that his own army was as strong as it would ever be. His last information from Caffarelli told him that no help could be looked for from the Army of the North. He knew Soult and Suchet too well to hope for assistance from them. Although he could not know it, his letters to the king and the king's letters to him were being captured and taken straight to Wellington's headquarters, where they were deciphered by the ingenious Captain George Scovell. If he was to attack, the sooner he did so the better the chance of success. He gave orders to recross the Douro on 15 July.

In Madrid, King Joseph was in despair. Soult had flatly forbidden D'Erlon to move north, irrespective of Hill's movement, and continued to claim that Hill was attacking with a corps of 30,000 men. Nothing that Joseph could say could make him change his attitude. "You may have deceived yourself," he wrote to the marshal on 30 June, "but if you have formally forbidden Count D'Erlon to cross the Tagus . . . you have given him orders which contradict those I have given you. You have set your authority above mine and you do not recognize me as commander in chief of the armies in Spain."[42] The king went on to say that if Soult persisted in refusing to obey his orders, he was to hand over command of his army to the senior divisional commander. Soult took no notice. Nor did Suchet or Caffarelli agree to send Marmont any help.

There seemed to be only one course which the king could take, for, if no commander, he was not without courage. On 9 July, he called in all the outlying troops of the Army of the Center and concentrated every available man in Madrid. He left on 21 July, sending ahead a letter to Marmont. "Having given up hope of finding help for you from the Armies of Aragon and the South, I have evacuated all the provinces in the district of the Army of the Center. I have left garrisons only in Madrid, Toledo and Guadalajara, and I am leaving this evening with a corps of 13–14,000 men. I will march towards

Villacastin and Arevalo . . . I do not know where you are;
nor have I any accurate idea of the enemy's position or
strength. I do not, therefore, know what you ought to do,
nor can I send you orders."[43] Before leaving he had sent definite orders to Soult to send 10,000 men to Toledo immediately, evacuating such parts of Andalusia as this step made
necessary.

The king's little army marched briskly over the Sierra de
Guadarrama and reached Espinar on the evening of 22 July.
Rumors from the country people there reported that Marmont had crossed the Douro and was in contact with Wellington near Salamanca. This decided Joseph to change his route
westward. On the night of the twenty-fourth, the main body
bivouacked at Blascosánchez, and orders were issued to march
for Peñaranda on the following day. That evening a peasant
brought news. The Army of Portugal had been in action with
the British at Salamanca two days earlier. It had been seriously
beaten and was at that time at Arévalo. The Army of the
Center was exposed to the whole strength of the allied army.

The next day a letter reached the king from Marmont, who
had been wounded by grape shot "breaking my right arm and
giving me two large wounds in my side." The French loss, he
estimated, "is about 5,000 men. That of the English infinitely
greater. It is difficult to express the damage done by our
artillery."[44] A more realistic letter from Gen. Clausel, who had
succeeded Marmont in command, hoped that, in time, he
would be able to get 20,000 men together but stated that
meantime no useful purpose would be served by joining with
the Army of the Center, as even together they would not be
able to resist Wellington. Clausel's intention was "to get as
far away as possible [from Wellington] to avoid engagements
and risk of another useless battle."[45]

Marmont had, as he intended, taken the offensive on 15
July. Brilliantly he had feinted with his right and struck with
his left. On the morning of 18 July, the allied right was
almost overwhelmed. Riding to the point of danger, Welling-

ton was all but captured, and the commander of the light division's outlying picket was astonished to see

> Lord Wellington with his staff and a cloud of English and French dragoons and horse artillery intermixed, come over the hill at full cry, and all hammering at each other's heads in one confused mass. . . . Lord Wellington and his staff with two guns took shelter for the moment behind us, while the cavalry went sweeping along our front where, I suppose, they picked up some reinforcements, for they returned almost instantly; but the French were now the fliers; and, I must do them the justice to say that they got themselves off in a manner most creditable to themselves. Marshal Beresford and the greater part of the staff remained with their swords drawn, and the Duke* himself did not look more than half pleased.[46]

The British army, caught off balance, rapidly regained its poise, but Marmont continued to threaten its right flank. Wellington therefore fell back towards Salamanca, and for several days the two armies marched parallel to each other, frequently within canon shot. At nightfall on 21 July, the allied army was astride the Tormes River covering Salamanca. Wellington knew, from intercepted dispatches, that the king was on his way to join Marmont with a force that would give the French a definite superiority in numbers. Marmont was ignorant of this fact but had heard that a thousand cavalry and a battery would join him from the Army of the North in two or three days' time. He did not consider it worthwhile delaying his operations to wait for so small a reinforcement.

Wellington did not intend risking his army unless he could count on an overwhelming victory. This was unlikely when the king joined forces with Marmont. "I have therefore determined to cross the Tormes, if the enemy should; to cover

---

* Wellington was made a British earl after the taking of Ciudad Rodrigo and at the same time the Spaniards created him duke of Ciudad Rodrigo and a grandee of Spain. He was not made a British duke until 1814.

Salamanca as long as I can; and above all, not to give up our communication with Ciudad Rodrigo; and not to fight an action, unless under very advantageous circumstances, or if it should become absolutely necessary."[47] Marmont realized that Wellington, whom he considered an unenterprising general, would fall back on Portugal if he saw his communications with Rodrigo threatened. He was, however, anxious not to allow the allies to slip away unmolested. He wanted some sort of victory to his own credit. He wanted not a battle but "an advantageous rearguard action in which, using my full force late in the day when only a part of the English army remained in front of me, I should probably score a point."[48]

During the morning, Marmont could see the clouds of dust raised as the supply column of the allied armies took the road to Rodrigo. He calculated that the bulk of Wellington's army would be marching with it. Only two or three allied divisions were visible, the remainder being concealed behind the two low ridges meeting at right angles where the allied position was. The morning was passed in fruitless maneuvering, and it was well into the afternoon when Marmont, reckoning that Wellington would have thinned out his rear guard, began to push out his advance guard, three divisions, along a parallel ridge, aiming to turn the allied right. With his imperfect knowledge of the allied strength, it was a rash operation. To make matters worse, the divisions advanced carelessly. They became separated and there was straggling within them. They were passing along the strongest part of Wellington's front. There were 14,000 French infantry with, on their safe, southerly flank, 1,700 cavalry. Parallel to them were 32,000 allied infantry and 2,000 cavalry.

Wellington, high on the ridge, was having a late lunch. "The whole French army was in sight, moving. I got up and was looking over a wall round the farm yard and I saw the movements of the French left through my glass. 'By God!' said I, 'that will do.' "[49] He launched his right against the disordered French columns, rolling them up from the flank. "There was no mistake. Everything went as it ought; and there never was an army beaten in so short a time."[50] Marmont was wounded soon after Wellington's attack was launched. Bonnet, the next senior general, fell a few minutes later, so that it was Clausel's task to extricate the French army. He did all that a man could, but there was no hope of turning defeat into victory. Covered by its only intact division, the Army of Portugal streamed away southeast to Alba de Tormes. Here they had their only piece of good fortune of the day. The Spanish general commanding the place had evacuated the fortress which dominated the bridge. Had he not done so, the whole of Marmont's army must have been lost. Next day fortune turned against them once more. At García Hernández, the rear-guard division was attacked by the heavy dragoons of the King's German Legion. In an unprecedented charge against steady infantry formed in square, ready to receive them, the Germans broke two squares, inflicting 1,100 casualties and destroying three battalions. The rear-guard duty was handed over to the cavalry of the Army of the North, which had at last arrived, and on the evening of 23 July, the wreck of the Army of Portugal reached Peñaranda. Of the 49,646 men who had fought at Salamanca, 14,000 were casualties and another 12,000 were dispersed and only rejoined the army after some days or weeks. Wellington, who had brought 51,930 men to the battle, suffered 4,762 casualties. Twenty guns and more than 7,000 prisoners were left in allied hands. It was a high price to pay for the lesson that Wellington was not, after all, an unenterprising general.

The emperor received news of the disaster at Salamanca on 1 September at Ghjatsk. A week later he was to fight the battle of Borodino. In two weeks he was to enter Moscow. "Affairs in Russia were too serious at that moment for him to pay much attention to Marshal Marmont's reverses in the Peninsula. 'The English,' he remarked, 'have their hands full there. They cannot leave Spain to go and make trouble for me in France or Germany. That is all that matters.' "[51]

Nevertheless, he found time next day to make Marmont the scapegoat. He wrote to Clarke at the War Ministry,

I have received Marshal Marmont's report of the battle on the 22nd July. If it was not so important it would be laughable. It is all nonsense and as complicated as the inside of a clock. Nor is there one word to tell what actually happened.

Wait until the Marshal returns to France and has recovered from his wounds. Then ask him for categorical answers to the following questions.

Why did he give battle without orders from his commander in chief?

Why did he not seek orders as to what he should do, as as subordinate part to the whole system of my armies in Spain?

How could he change from the defensive to the offensive without waiting for a corps of 15–17,000 to join and assist him? . . . One is led to the conclusion that Marshal Marmont was anxious that the King should not share in a victory and that he sacrified the honor of France and the good of my service to his own vanity.[52]

It was an unjust verdict. Marmont had the king's permission to fight a general action. He had, indeed, been urged to fight. He could have no idea that the king was marching to his help. He had been told that no other reinforcements would be available to help him. It was only on the evening of the day before the battle that he heard that a brigade of light cavalry was nearing him from the Army of the North. Believing that he could inflict heavy loss on Wellington's army on 22 July and that if he waited Wellington would slip back to Portugal unharmed, he could see little point in waiting for a triffling addition to his strength. Marmont can be censured for mishandling the battle, but not for engaging in it. Had he succeeded in mauling two or three allied divisions, which was what he tried to do, the war in the Peninsula might have taken a very different course in 1812 and 1813. Napoleon's sweeping attack on the marshal only showed that he still had no conception of conditions in Spain.

Chapter 10

ON HIS
TRAVELS AGAIN

*Being so far away, there is nothing I can do for
the armies in Spain.*

NAPOLEON, 19 OCTOBER 1812

WELLINGTON, being always anxious to husband the strength
of his troops, did not press his pursuit of the Army of Portugal,
and Clausel reported that it might be possible to cooperate
with the king and his 15,000 men. Joseph, in consequence, did
not immediately retreat behind the Guadarrama Mountains to
protect his army and his capital. Instead he marched eastwards
to Segovia, which he reached on 28 July. There he waited for
three days, hoping for more and better news from Clausel.
While there, he received a letter from Soult explaining why he
had refused to allow D'Erlon to march to the assistance of
Marmont. He justified his disobedience by claiming that if he
released any troops across the Tagus he would have to evacuate
the whole of Andalusia and that the loss of the whole of Spain
must follow. "We could not find food either in the Tagus or
in Estremadura and, falling back from one position to another,

we should have to go back as far as the Ebro."[1] As an alternative, Soult put forward the proposal that the king and the Army of the Center should join him in Andalusia so that heavy pressure could be put on the southern borders of Portugal.

Joseph had already sent orders which made this argument out of date. On 29 July, he had written to Soult, telling him briefly of the disaster that had overtaken Marmont and adding "you will see how mistaken you have been about Lord Wellington's intentions." As for future plans, "it is my firm intention not to risk my communications with Madrid and with Valencia and . . . I give you the formal order to evacuate Andalusia and to march to Toledo with all your forces. This is the only way to restore the situation and I am sure that the details I give you will leave you in no doubt that no other course is open to us."[2]

There was no further news from Clausel. Having taken stock of the state of his army, he decided that the best thing for him to do was to put as many miles between it and the allies as possible. He therefore crossed the Douro on 27–28 July, paused to evacuate as many stores and wounded from Valladolid as could be transported, and fell back behind Palencia. Finding that he was no longer being pursued, he halted. No word of this movement reached the king, but to Paris Clausel reported that although "armies usually suffer in morâle after a setback, it is hard to understand the extent of the discouragement which exists in this one. I cannot, nor should I, conceal that a very bad spirit prevails, as it has done for some time. Disorders and the most revolting excesses marked every stage of our retreat. I will use every means in my power to put an end to deplorable outrages which every day are committed under the very eyes of the officers, who do nothing to check them."[3]

It was to be many weeks before the king again heard directly from Clausel, and meanwhile his danger was growing daily. After his triumphant entry in Valladolid on 30 July, Wellington decided that to pursue Clausel further would overextend his army. Instead, he turned his main strength against Madrid.

On 29 July, there had been a skirmish between the cavalry of the Army of the Center and some Portuguese horse within ten miles of Segovia. Taking the hint, Joseph started to withdraw over the sierra on 1 August, leaving a strong rear guard. It was not until 7 August that the allies started to march up the mountains, and on the eleventh their advanced guard, D'Urban's brigade of Portuguese dragoons, reached Galapagar unopposed. Pushing forward from there, they found Treillard's light cavalry at Las Rosas and Majalahonda. The French fell back, under the fire of the British horse artillery, but Joseph was not prepared to yield his capital without at least a token struggle.

He ordered Treillard to counterattack and this was done with striking success. Two thousand Frenchmen charged in on 700 Portuguese and routed them. The allied supports, two German dragoon regiments, were caught unprepared and had great difficulty in holding Treillard's men. Three British guns were captured, but the French were forced to leave them behind when they withdrew. Treillard inflicted nearly 200 casualties (he claimed 710) and carried away the commander of one Portuguese regiment who was wounded.

Meanwhile, in Madrid there was confusion. "Everyone is packing up his valuables and making ready to run. Apart from the many Spaniards of birth and wealth who are committed to the king, there are a vast number of minor officials and hangers-on around the palace who, by choice or habit, have stayed in their old jobs. None of these poor wretches dare stay behind when the King leaves—theirs would be a dreadful fate, left to the savage patriotism of their compatriots. Since the orders for departure were given, everyone has been hunting for vehicles and carriages at any price. . . . All night long I am kept awake by an endless procession of carriages, carts and wagons passing my window."[4] Escorted by 5,000 infantry, the huge convoy, accompanied by thousands of Spaniards on foot, wound out of the city, crossed the Toledo bridge, and took the road to Aranjuez. On 11 August, Joseph wrote to Paris, "More than 2,000 vehicles left Madrid yesterday, making for the Tagus. I am leaving tomorrow for the south bank of the Tagus. I have only 8,000 men in hand. If Marshal Soult started as soon as he received my letter from Segovia, or when he first heard of the affair on 22nd July [Salamanca], I hope to join him where the Andalusian road debouches into La Mancha."[5]

On 12 August, Wellington's army marched into Madrid. "Nothing," wrote an infantry officer, "could exceed the frantic joy expressed by the people of all classes on Lord Wellington's entering Madrid. Ladies threw down their most valuable veils and shawls for his horse to pass over; they got hold of his legs as he sat on horseback and kissed them."[6] The object of all this adulation reported, "It is impossible to describe the joy of the inhabitants on our arrival. I hope that the prevalence of the same sentiment of detestation of the French yoke . . . will again induce them to make exertions in the cause of their country, which, being more wisely directed, will be more efficacious than those they formerly made."[7] The following day, the constitution devised at Cádiz was proclaimed in the streets amidst acclamations.

While Madrid rejoiced, the king and his army were making a painful two-week march into Valencia. In the districts through which they passed, "the inhabitants had flown, taking their animals with them, destroying their ovens and their mills. Wheat could be found, but no corn. The heat was dreadful, the streams had dried up and the wells in the villages through which we passed were exhausted."[8] "Many of the troops died of thirst. They could be seen lying beside the road, stretched on their backs, dying in terrible convulsions under the eyes of their comrades. Their thirst was made worse by the cloud of dust raised by the convoy. This cloud was several leagues long, half a league wide and quite high. This formless corrosive dust penetrated everywhere, whatever was done to prevent it. It blinded cavalry and infantry alike, clogging the palate, drying the tongue, attacking the lungs and causing a violent, racking cough."[9] "It was impossible to maintain order and discipline amongst the troops who received no rations. . . .

Many stragglers and great numbers of servants attached to the convoy committed great disorders and many crimes. Anyone who fell behind or turned aside for water or food fell into the hands of the *guerillas* who followed the column or harried its flanks."[10] The guerrillas commanded by Bartholomeo Muños seized seven carriages belonging to the French ambassador, sending one of the coachmen back to his master with a polite note addressed to "The Ambassador of the Wandering King."[11]

On 31 August, the weary procession reached the city of Valencia. "The King," wrote Miot,

> made his entry amid the cheers of the people. The archbishop and clergy received him at the gates and the magistrates offered him the keys of the city. He was conducted to the cathedral where a *Te Deum* was sung. Thus Joseph, though conquered and a fugitive, was a king once more in Valencia. But although he was showered with honors, Marshal Suchet handed over to him no part of the administration. The King and those in his service, French and Spanish, were looked upon merely as refugees, and few pains were taken to conceal how far from welcome they were. After a few days' rest the families of all the King's French adherents, civil and military were, without exception, sent back to France. The Spaniards, except for those belonging to the royal household, were dispersed in neighbouring villages and forbidden to set foot in the city.[12]

Joseph had a few things to console him. His health had stood up to the strain of the journey and some letters from Queen Julie, captured by the guerrillas, were courteously forwarded to him under a flag of truce by Lord Wellington. He even allowed himself a measure of optimism. "If Marshal Soult comes over the mountains from Andalusia, and if we receive 20 or 30,000 reinforcements and several million francs from France, I am quite certain that Spanish affairs can soon be restored."[13] It was disturbing that he had heard nothing from France or from the *Grande Armée* since 2 June and that he was out of touch with the armies of the North and of Portugal.

This optimistic phase did not last. When the king had been in Valencia a week, Colonel Deprez returned from Soult's headquarters with a reply to Joseph's letter from Segovia ordering the evacuation of Andalusia. Soult admitted that he had heard of the defeat at Salamanca from the Cádiz newspapers but had assumed that the news was exaggerated. He did not seem to be much more impressed by Joseph's account of the event. While deploring the losses suffered by the Army of Portugal, he remarked that, with affairs in the Peninsula in their present state, pitched battles should only be fought as a last resort. Joseph's order to evacuate Andalusia struck him as being

> very extraordinary. I am far from believing that Your Majesty had really determined to carry it out. Is the fate of Spain already settled? Is it Your Majesty's wish to sacrifice Spain for the sake of the capital? Is the march of the Army of the South the only course open? Is it realised that once I start such a retreat, I shall be followed by 60,000 enemies, who will give me no rest and may well not give me the opportunity to march in the direction which Your Majesty wishes? There is only one way to re-establish the situation: let Your Majesty come to Andalusia, bringing all the troops of the Army of the Center and such of the Armies of Portugal and of Aragon within the reach of orders. What good will it do if Your Majesty keeps Madrid and loses the whole kingdom? . . . As soon as we have 70 or 80,000 men concentrated in the south, the theatre of operations will change. The Army of Portugal will find that it is disengaged. . . . The loss of a battle by the

Army of Portugal is something that can easily be put
right; but the loss of Andalusia and the raising of
the siege of Cádiz are events that will resound all
over Europe and even in the new world.[14]

Taken together with Soult's earlier refusal to allow D'Erlon
to go to Marmont's assistance, this new letter, with its veneer of
deference and undercurrent of defiance and disobedience, was
little short of mutiny. The king had done everything he could
to avoid an open conflict with Soult. While he was on his
march from Madrid he had appealed to the marshal to "put
aside the past; let us keep our minds on the present. Let us
agree that your duty is to obey me and not to send me instructions."[15] There could be no doubt that Soult was declining to
accept the king's authority, and in Joseph's view, the marshal
was directly responsible for the loss of the battle of Salamanca.
The time had come to appeal directly to the emperor. Joseph
wrote a memorandum setting out his complaints against Soult
and on 8 September ordered Colonel Deprez to set out for
imperial headquarters.

That night a small French ship was driven by the British
coastal forces into Grao, the port of Valencia. The captain
was carrying a letter, entrusted to him by Soult, addressed to
the minister of war in Paris. Unaware of its contents, he
handed it over, for onward transmission, to Marshal Suchet.
Suchet took it straight to the king. It was in cipher, but only
the cipher normally used between army commanders, and
there was no difficulty in discovering its meaning. As soon as
its content was known, messengers were sent galloping after
Deprez to recall him. Soult had added *lèse majesté* to mutiny.

The marshal started his letter by making his excuses for
having refused to comply with the king's orders. "I must
assume that the losses we have suffered in Castille have been
much exaggerated, and from that I conclude that the Emperor's affairs in Spain are not as desperate as the King appears
to imagine." He went on to say that "I fear the object of all
these false dispositions [i.e., the evacuation of Andalusia] is to

oblige the French armies to retire at least behind the Ebro and later to claim that this was, to use the King's own expression, the only course available, in the hope of making some profitable arrangement." The implication was that the "profitable arrangement" was to be between the king and the Cortes at Cádiz. His evidence for such a conspiracy was slender and confused. He had read in the Cádiz newspapers that the king's ambassador to St. Petersburg had joined the Russian army. Prince Bernadotte* had established diplomatic relations between Stockholm and Cádiz and had recruited 250 Spaniards for the Royal Swedish Guards. The only solid piece of evidence which Soult could produce was that emissaries from the king had, from time to time, passed through the Cádiz lines to try to open negotiations with the Cortes. This negotiation was, as Soult well knew, carried on not only with the emperor's knowledge but on his orders.

"I draw no conclusions from these facts but I am all the more watchful. However, I have thought myself obliged to reveal my fears to six generals in this army, having put them on oath never to disclose what I have told them except to the Emperor himself, or to persons specially authorized by the Emperor to receive this testimony if, meantime, I am no longer able to give evidence myself."[16]

Joseph was, not unnaturally, furious at this accusation against his loyalty and good faith. Colonel Deprez was sent off once more with desperate plea to the emperor. "I demand justice from Your Majesty. Let Marshal Soult be recalled, tried and punished. I can stay here no longer with such a man."[17]

Deprez reached Paris on 21 September. He was kindly received by Clarke, the minister of war, who agreed that Soult was behaving intolerably but said that while there was no doubt that Joseph had the right to deprive him of his command, "he acknowledged that such a step could not be taken except on the express orders of the Emperor."[18] Clarke had,

---

* Marshal Bernadotte had, with Napoleon's permission, accepted the rank of prince royal of Sweden, with the reversion of the Swedish throne. He had married Desirée Clary, the sister of Queen Julie.

in fact, already made up his mind that Soult was culpable and three weeks earlier had written a strongly worded order to the marshal reaffirming and explaining Napoleon's order giving Joseph supreme command. He urged him to obey orders that he might receive from the king and, without equivocation, blamed the marshal for the Salamanca disaster. "If you had reinforced Count D'Erlon's corps so that it was strong enough to have attacked General Hill, Lord Wellington would not have been able to concentrate the bulk of his army so far from Ciudad Rodrigo and to have brought such a superiority of numbers against the Army of Portugal, which led to the taking of the Salamanca forts, the battle of 22 July and all the consequences from these events which we still have to fear."[19] By the time this letter reached Soult, the whole situation had changed.

Deprez rode on eastwards and reached Moscow on the evening of 18 October. He could scarcely have arrived at a worse time. Napoleon had been in the city for a month waiting for the czar to put forward a peace offer. On that day, he finally knew that none would come. When Deprez arrived, "the Emperor had just learned that his advanced guard had been attacked and forced to retreat. Already the departure of the army had been determined upon and they were beginning to march. When my arrival was announced to His Majesty he did not respond in a favorable manner. However, in the middle of the night, I was called. I gave the Emperor the despatches which I carried and, without opening them, he questioned me on their contents."[20] Napoleon's first concern was to discuss what had happened. He blamed Marmont for engaging the English unsupported. He agreed that the king had been right in leading the Army of the Center to Marmont's support but complained that he had taken this step too late. He then proceeded to find fault with some other details of Joseph's maneuvers.

"At last he turned to Marshal Soult's letter to which he attached no importance. The Marshal was mistaken but he, the Emperor, could not bother with such trifles at a moment when he was at the head of 500,000 men and was undertaking vast operations. These were his very words. He went on to say that Soult's suspicions did not greatly surprise him. These views were shared by many of the generals in Spain, who feel that Your Majesty prefers Spain to France. While the Emperor knows that you are French at heart, it was easy to be misled by hearing Your Majesty's conversation. He added that Marshal Soult was the only military brain in Spain and that he could not withdraw him without risking the safety of the army."[21]

The next morning, before leaving Moscow, Napoleon dashed off a note to the minister of war. "Being so far away there is nothing that I can do for the Armies in Spain. Tell the King and Marshal Soult . . . how necessary it is that, in their present situation, they should unite and, as far as is possible, minimize the effects of a bad system."[22] While he dictated this note, the French army was leaving Moscow. "It was not only the number of fighting troops who made up the endless procession, but the innumerable wagons, carts, droshkys and chaises, often laden with booty. The number of guns, limbers, transports and the like, moving in ten parallel columns, took up an interminable stretch of road. . . . Whereas most officers owned a cart, the generals had half a dozen. Supply officers and actors, women and children, cripples, wounded men and the sick drove in and out of the throng; countless servants and maids, sutlers and that sort of person accompanied the march. . . . The great congestion of wagons and troops poured through the fields in three wide columns. Inexhaustibly they seemed to press out from the ruins of Moscow, and the heads of these columns vanished far away on the horizon."[23] The *Grande Armée* was marching to its doom. It was small wonder that the emperor could find no time to concern himself with petty wrangles in Spain. He had never given the Peninsula sufficient attention even when he had time to spare.

When Soult wrote his accusatory letter on 12 August, he had already given orders to prepare for the evacuation of

Andalusia. The troops in garrison at the castle of Niebla, the most westerly of the permanent strong points in Andalusia, withdrew on the same day on which the letter was written. Three days later the most southerly garrisons, those of Ronda and Medina Sidonia, blew up their works and retired. Within the week a particularly heavy bombardment of Cádiz was launched, under cover of which the stores and fortifications, built up over more than thirty months of siege, were destroyed by fire and demolition. By 24 August, the siege was at last raised, and from all directions French columns were converging on Seville. Soult himself left that city on the night of 26–27 August with his main body escorting a vast and miserable convoy of *afrancesado* Spaniards who dared not stay to meet their loyal compatriots. He left a small rear guard in Seville to cover the retreat of a few outlying columns, but this was overwhelmed the following night by an allied column from Cádiz, spearheaded by British guards and British riflemen. They took two field guns and 200 prisoners.

Meanwhile, D'Erlon was withdrawing from Estremadura, covering his retreat with a series of cavalry forays. Hill lost contact with him on 26 August and on the thirtieth the French corps joined Soult at Cordoba. He was not pursued since Hill had contingent orders to move to Madrid as soon as he was disengaged. Four days later, with 45,000 men in hand, Soult set out for Granada, where he stayed until 16 September. He was not much disturbed in his march. The bulk of the garrison of Cádiz was untrained in field operations and quite devoid of transport. Hill's Anglo-Portuguese corps was in full march for the Tagus. Thus, instead of the 60,000 enemies whom he had claimed would follow him, he was actually molested only by the irrepressible Ballasteros, whose division of less than 6,000 men could do him no serious harm. His vast convoy pursued its way, almost in peace, by way of Baza, Huescar, and Hellin towards Valencia. It was a barren route by bad roads over the mountains. Food was short, the difficulties of transporting 6,000 French sick were enormous, and, as might be expected, the wretched Spanish refugees suffered most of all. His advanced cavalry was in touch with Suchet's outposts before the end of September, and the marshal himself reached Almansa on 2 October.

Next day, 3 October, a council of war was held at Fuente la Higuera, fifty miles from Valencia. The meeting between the king and Soult was an awkward one. If it had happened a few weeks earlier, it is probable that Joseph would have ordered the marshal into arrest for insubordination, if for nothing more serious. Such a move might well have led to fighting between the men of the Army of the South and those of the king and Marshal Suchet. Realizing that the future of the occupation, and of his own throne, depended on cooperation, Joseph behaved generously. "One can imagine," wrote Jourdan, "that their first interview brought out some sharp words: they were alone. However, Joseph, always a generous man, controlled himself and showed that he was prepared to forget the past. He called Marshals Jourdan and Suchet into the room and they settled down to immediate business."[24]

The military situation had, to some extent, changed in their favor. Wellington, in following up his victory, had overextended his army and divided it into two parts. His army had suffered much from its exertions, and he had only 27,412 British rank and file under arms compared to 35,284 when the campaign had opened in June. Owing to wounds and disease, he was also even more short than usual of capable generals. In an attempt to secure his northern flank against the armies of the North and of Portugal, he was endeavoring, with less than his usual determination and skill, to take the castle of Burgos. He had with him 24,000 Anglo-Portuguese troops and 11,000 Spaniards. The two French armies on that side could put into the field 53,000 men. His southern flank was on the Tagus, south of Madrid. Here Rowland Hill commanded 31,000 British and Portuguese and 12,000 Spaniards. These were exposed to attack by the combined forces of the French armies of the South and the Center, together with anything that Suchet could be induced to spare. One factor was acting to help him. On 7 August the Anglo-Sicilian force which had been expected since June had landed at Alicante, eighty miles south of Valencia. Unfortunately, it had a nervous and inactive commander, or rather series of commanders, so that it remained a potential nuisance rather than an active threat to Suchet's army. To offset this putative advantage, the news that war had broken out between Britain and the United States warned him that he could look to few reinforcements from home and that supplies of corn coming into Lisbon might be seriously interrupted. He knew that he was taking a gamble by thus extending his army and that he risked being overwhelmed in detail. He was, however, least worried about the southern Tagus front since he counted on the autumn rains making that river unfordable, as it usually was by October, and had, moreover, the promise of a force of 15,000 Spaniards under Ballasteros to operate against the flank of any French column advancing from Valencia to Madrid. In both of these hopes he was disappointed. The rains, although they fell heavily and distressfully on his siege works around Burgos, failed to fall on the upper Tagus, and the river remained fordable at many places. Ballasteros, hearing that the Cortes had offered Wellington supreme command of all the Spanish armies, refused to obey orders and was exiled to Ceuta in Africa. It was a sad end to the career of a general who by his persistence had done so much to disturb Soult's sojourn in Andalusia.

Thus, although Joseph's council of war could not know all the details, there was every hope of regaining Madrid and a chance of cutting Wellington off from Portugal. At the council, "the King invited each of the Marshals to give his opinion on what operations should be undertaken. All were unanimous on one point, that contact should be re-established with the Army of Portugal. There were, however, differences on how to proceed."[25] Suchet was anxious to get the armies of the South and the Center out of his territory as soon as possible. They were proving a great strain on the resources of Valencia and the plundering habits of Soult's men was not helping the system of pacification by justice which he was pursuing with a fair measure of success. He asked to be reinforced by 5,000 men from Soult's army. Jourdan believed that the combined armies of the king and Soult could seize Madrid without help from Suchet but that it was vital to establish communication with the Army of Portugal, to keep open communications with Valencia, and to give over to Suchet's care all the sick of Soult's army.

Soult refused to give any opinion verbally. He offered to give a written opinion but meanwhile asked for the king's orders.* Joseph, keeping his indignation under control, decided that all three marshals should make written submissions. Meanwhile, he required that the troops should be ready to move in six days' time. Suchet having undertaken to provision them, Soult agreed to be ready.

Having considered the three written opinions, Joseph, on 7 October, gave out his orders. Suchet's army was to remain at its existing strength but should undertake the care of Soult's 6,000 sick. The other two armies would advance on Madrid in two columns but, to make their strengths more equal, Soult was to make over to the Army of the Center one infantry division and a brigade of cavalry. D'Erlon was to have the command of the Army of the Center. Even before he received these orders, Soult had asked for a further six days before starting. When he received them, he flatly refused to hand over any of his troops, claiming that the Army of the South had been entrusted to his care by the emperor and that the king had not the power to detach any of them.

Joseph replied firmly. "I repeat the order to execute exactly the moves I prescribed on 7th October. If you should not do this, it is my order that you hand over command of the Army of the South to Count D'Erlon and proceed to Paris to account for your actions."[26]

The advance therefore started on 15 October, with Soult's army, 40,000 strong, marching north from Albacete towards Taracon. Two days later the Army of the Center left Valen-

---

* According to Jourdan's account (p. 437) Soult did give a verbal opinion. A reading of Joseph's letter to him of 9 October (JN, ix, 92) makes it clear that he refused to do so.

cia. On 23 October, they reached Cuenca, where the army
came under D'Erlon's command and joined the detachment
from the Army of the South, making their strength up to
21,000. Thus the two prongs of the advance northward comprised 61,000 men with 84 guns. There was still no close
communication with the Army of Portugal. The last letter
from the king which General Souham (who now commanded
that army) had received was dated 1 October, having taken
seventeen days to travel from Valencia to his headquarters at
Pancorbo near the Ebro. This had been written before Soult
had joined the king and while foreshadowing a mass advance
from the south had given no definite plan. It urged him to
advance with caution, to pursue the allies if they began to
retreat from Burgos, and to send troops in the direction of
Cuenca to contact the king's advance. It so happened that
Souham was ready for something more enterprising. The
Army of Portugal had been recruited up to 41,500 by a strong
draft from the Bayonne reserve and had, in close support,
more than 11,000 men of the Army of the North. Thus, there
were available to oppose Wellington's northern corps of
35,000 British, Portuguese, and Spaniards, not less than 52,000
Frenchmen. In the whole picture, therefore, 112,000 French
troops were closing in on 78,000 allies, of whom 23,000 were
Spaniards of very dubious reliability. By a coincidence most
fortunate to the French, Souham started to press in seriously
on the troops covering the siege of Burgos on 18 October,
just at the time that the southern advance was thoroughly
under way. As Wellington remarked, it was "the worst
military situation I was even in."[27]

The autumn campaign of 1812 turned out to be an anti-
climax. By evacuating Andalusia and by denuding the northern
and central provinces of garrisons, the French had accumulated a substantial numerical and qualitative superiority over
any force that Wellington could collect to oppose them. Both
French forces struck at a time when all Wellington's calculated risks had miscarried. He had failed to take Burgos; the

Tagus was still fordable in many places and Ballasteros had mutinied. Yet, by 10 November, he had his army reunited around Salamanca. His northern corps had fought some dangerous rear-guard actions; Hill's corps from Madrid escaped with no more than a few skirmishes. Joseph reentered Madrid, after an absence of twelve weeks, on 2 November. "A new and hastily formed municipal body received him and, in a greatly embarrassed speech, endeavored to excuse the inhabitants by pleading the disasters of the times, and entreated the royal clemency. Nor was the appeal made in vain; there were no recriminations and no informers were listened to."[28] The capital was again abandoned on 4 November, only four days after the king's return, as the army pressed on to the northwest. Behind it trudged a crowd of refugees who dared not stay in the city if there was no French garrison.

There was a final chance of attacking and beating Wellington's army on 15 November. Wellington, with 65,000 men, offered battle, standing on the defensive in the position from which he had attacked Marmont on 22 July. The French had available about 85,000.* Every senior officer on the French side was in favor of attacking. On the previous days there had been discussions and disagreements as to how best to carry out the operation but, in the end, Soult's opinion was agreed. He was given command of the combined armies of the South and the Center. The Army of Portugal was ordered to conform to his movements and loyally did so. But so dilatory was the marshal in his movements, so concerned was he with protecting his young brother from his own incapacity as the commander of a brigade of light cavalry, so indecisive was he in his movements, that the British general decided that there was no chance of fighting an advantageous defensive action and in the early afternoon gave orders for his army to take the road to Portugal. By this time, "rain was falling in torrents and the sky was so overcast that at four o'clock it was as

---

* Both sides had many sick due to hard marching. On the French side, Caffarelli's contingent from the Army of the North had returned to its own district to endeavor to reconquer it.

dark as night."[29] Joseph had no hesitation in attributing the lost opportunity to Soult's "extreme circumspection."[30] "Thus," wrote Jourdan, "Lord Wellington effected his retreat unmolested, without even being harassed, in the presence of 80,000 of France's best troops, and the opportunity was lost of putting right in a single day all the misfortunes of the campaign."[31] The next day troops were sent off in pursuit, but they could do no more than engage the rear guard and collect stragglers. "Was this," asked Miot, "all that could have resulted from all our gathering of forces? Our army was numerous, the enemy inferior in strength; our leaders were able and experienced, our soldiers willing. How could victory have been doubtful, if the will to conquer had equalled the means available?"[32]

The allied army fell back to Ciudad Rodrigo. Its retreat was miserable. The supply services misrouted the rations; the weather was abominable; three divisions lost their way owing to the mule-headedness of their commanders; the second in command of the army was captured; discipline broke down in some regiments; some 3,000 stragglers and drunkards fell into French hands, dead or alive. Nevertheless, the army survived with its fighting strength almost unimpaired. Wellington admitted that the year's campaigning had not yielded the fruits that at one time seemed possible but claimed, "In the months elapsed since January this army has sent to England little short of 20,000 prisoners and have taken and destroyed, or taken to themselves, the use of the enemy's arsenals in Ciudad Rodrigo, Badajoz, Salamanca, Valladolid, Madrid, Astorga, Seville, the lines before Cádiz, etc.; and upon the whole we have taken or destroyed, or we now possess, little short of 3,000 pieces of cannon. The siege of Cádiz has been raised, and all the countries south of the Tagus have been cleared of the enemy."[33]

On the evening of 2 December, the king returned to Madrid. He had regained his capital but could not be said to have recovered his kingdom. Andalusia was lost forever. The northern provinces, except for isolated French garrisons, were in the hands of the guerrillas, and Mina, the greatest of the guerrilla leaders, was financing his operations by collecting customs duty on goods imported from France. Communications between Paris and Madrid ran, when they ran at all, through Valencia. The king and Soult were scarcely on speaking terms. It could be claimed that the British had been driven back inside Portugal, but the outlook could scarcely be gloomier.

The only consolation that could be found was that the evacuation of Andalusia had allowed the armies of Portugal, the Center, and the South to concentrate their attentions against the most dangerous enemy, the Anglo-Portuguese army. After one division was sent to the Army of the North, there were more than 95,000 men available under arms, and they were, by the New Year, spread out in cantonments between the southern foothills of the Cantabrian Mountains on the right and the river Guadiana on the left, the most northerly division being stationed at León, the most southerly at Daimiel, near Ciudad Real. While small flank guards had to be assigned to watch the Spanish armies of Andalusia and the Asturias, neither of these opponents showed many signs of enterprise or even organization, and the main body of the army could keep its attention fixed on Wellington, whose 60,000 Anglo-Portuguese effectives were in winter quarters between the Douro and the Tagus, the most part of them being stationed well inside Portugal. At least on this side there was no immediate cause for alarm.

Back in Madrid, Joseph tried to return to the pretense that he was king of Spain. He attended the opera, he walked unescorted in the public parks, he opened hospitals and attended a masked ball in the costume of a Parisian water carrier. He also attempted to collect the taxes that had fallen due during his absence. The citizens of Madrid were unimpressed. They did not believe that the uninvited king would be with them for long. They did not even feel grateful to him for taking no reprisals against those who had enthusiastically embraced the patriot cause during his two absences. The only people in Madrid who showed any animation were the fairly small number of *afrancesados* who had returned with the army from

Valencia. They, realizing that the future held nothing for them but death, exile, and disgrace, were remarked to indulge in a frenetic gaiety. The social life of Madrid was never so lively as it was in the early months of 1813 while Joseph's Spanish supporters made the best of the time that was left to them. From Paris there was silence. The road between Burgos and Vitoria was in the hands of the guerrillas.

The day after Joseph reentered Madrid, Napoleon, having seen Marshal Ney's magnificent rear guard ensure that the remnant of the *Grande Armée* could retreat across the river Berezina, dictated and dispatched to Paris the Twenty-ninth Bulletin. This document admitted that the Russian expedition had failed, that the army had suffered severe losses and was in full retreat. It ended, "Our cavalry was so short of horses that all the officers who still had one horse were formed into four companies of 150 each. Generals served as captains, colonels as sergeants. This sacred squadron, commanded by General Grouchy, never let the Emperor out of its sight in all the movements of the army. His Majesty's health has never been better." Two days later at Smorgón, thirty miles east of Vilna, the emperor called one of his aides to his room. "He carefully shut the door and said to me, 'Well Rapp, I am leaving this evening for Paris. My presence there is necessary for the good of France and even for this unfortunate army. I am handing over command to the Marshal Murat.' I was much taken aback by this news and replied, 'Sire, your leaving will create a grievous impression amongst the troops—they are not expecting it.' 'I must go. I must watch what Austria does and keep Prussia loyal. . . . When they know I am in Paris, leading the nation and at the head of the two hundred thousand men I shall raise, they will think twice before making war against me.' "[34]

That night he set out in a sleigh, accompanied by his master of the horse, General de Caulaincourt. In the two weeks before he reached Paris, he spoke frequently of his troubles in Spain. "Doubtless," he said, it would have been better to have wound up the war in Spain before embarking on this Russian operation—though there is room for discussion on that point. As for the war in Spain itself, it is now little more than a matter of *guerilla* contests. On the day the English are driven out of the Peninsula, there will be nothing left of the war but isolated bodies of rebels. . . . He returned continually to the subject of England, which occupied his mind above everything else. . . . The marshals and generals who have been left in Spain to look after themselves, might have done better but they will not agree amongst themselves. There has never been any unity in their operations. They detest each other to such an extent that any of them would be in despair if he thought he had made a movement which might give credit to another. Therefore there is nothing to be done there except to hold the country and try to pacify it until I can go there myself and put some vigor into operations. Soult has ability: but no one will take orders. Everyone wants to be independent and to play the viceroy in his own province. In Wellington my generals have come up against a general superior to some of them. . . . In the long run, however, our momentary setbacks, although they delight the city of London, have little effect on the general course of affairs—indeed, they cannot have any real importance, as I can change the face of affairs in Spain whenever I please.[35]

He reached Paris at midnight on 18 December, unheralded.

The Empress, who was sad and unwell, had just gone to bed. Frightened at hearing noises in the anteroom opening off her bedroom, she was rising to find out what was going on, when the Emperor entered, rushed up to her and clasped her in his arms. The noise which had frightened her had been the discussion between two men, hooded and wrapped in furs, with the lady-in-waiting who slept in the next room. This lady had, as was her duty, been defending the door of the Empress' bedroom when, to her astonishment, one of the men threw back his cloak and disclosed himself as the Emperor.[36]

For all that he heard of these dramatic affairs, King Joseph might have been on the other side of the Atlantic. It was not until 6 January that a copy of the Twenty-ninth Bulletin reached Madrid, forwarded from Valencia by Suchet. It was clear that the emperor had suffered a major setback in Russia, but the extent of the actual disaster, the loss of more than 250,000 dead, was not apparent. No orders reached Madrid from Paris. The bulletin had reached London on 21 December and Wellington saw a copy in Lisbon on 18 January, despite adverse winds. The fact that Joseph heard nothing from Paris did not mean that the emperor was not thinking of the war in Spain. He was desperately anxious to limit his liabilities there and to use some of the troops from the armies in Spain to form a basis for the new *Grande Armée* which he was using every piece of his energy and organizing ability to build. There were to be no reinforcements, no supplies of money for Spain. Joseph must do the best he could with what he had available. "If," remarked Napoleon, "he has to abandon the capital again, he will just have to defend the ground foot by foot until I can come in person and put an end to the Spanish business."[37]

It was not until 14 February that letters from Paris at last got through to Madrid. It was only then that the king learned that the emperor had returned to Paris on 18 December. Most revealing was a letter dated 3 January from Colonel Deprez, the aide-de-camp whom Joseph had sent to Moscow with his complaints against Soult. The unfortunate Deprez had retreated with the army every step of the way from Moscow to Vilna.

It is impossible to describe the distress of this army. No rations were issued for more than a month; there was nothing to eat but dead horses; often even marshals had no bread. The severity of the weather made the scarcity more deadly; each night we left hundreds of dead in the bivouacs. On can say, without exaggeration, that 100,000 men have been lost in this way alone and one can only say that the truth is that the army is dead. The Young Guard, to which I was attached, was 8,000 strong at Moscow. At Vilna it scarcely mustered 400. All the other corps suffered in the same way and . . . I am convinced that not more than 20,000 men will have reached the Niemen . . . If Your Majesty should ask me where the retreat will stop, I should reply that that depends on the enemy.[38]

Far more welcome to Joseph was an order recalling Soult to Paris* He left Madrid on 2 March, having been received in frigid audience by King Joseph, who, it was remarked, pointedly abstained from asking him to dinner. With the marshal went a long convoy of baggage wagons carrying his Andalusian loot, in particular a priceless collection of Murillos, formerly the property of the churches of Seville. At the same time, the incompetent Caffarelli was recalled and command of the Army of the North was given to General Clausel, with Gazan taking over Soult's Army.

Soult and Caffarelli were not the only soldiers to be recalled from Spain. Nearly 20,000 men were to be removed from Spain to fight on the eastern front, 15,000 of them from the armies facing Wellington. Since, however, the muster rolls of the armies of Spain counted more than 250,000 men, it appeared in Paris, where details of the large numbers of men sick,

---

* Despite Joseph's complaints, Soult was not recalled in disgrace. He was needed at imperial headquarters as alternate chief of staff since Berthier was showing signs of extreme mental strain and it was thought that he might break down at any time.

detached, and missing counted for little, that there were still quite enough troops in the Peninsula to hold down the country and contain Wellington.

Napoleon first gave tactical directions for the new situation in Spain on 3 January. In a minute to the minister of war he wrote, "Let the king know, in cypher, that as things stand I think he would do best to put his headquarters at Valladolid. He will have learned from the 29th Bulletin how things stand in the north and will realise that this state of affairs is absorbing all our attention and effort. He should occupy Madrid with his flank, but headquarters must be at Valladolid and he must make use of the inactivity of the English by pacifying Navarre, Biscay and the province of Santander."[39] Hearing nothing from Spain, he wrote four weeks later, "Repeat the orders to the King of Spain to move his headquarters to Valladolid, to occupy Madrid only as the left extremity of his line and to bring back substantial forces to the North and to Aragon so as to regain control of the north of Spain."[40] Again, a week later, he wrote, "The order to the King of Spain to move to Valladolid must be repeated. General Reille [now commanding the Army of Portugal] must send help to Navarre as the English are in no condition to do anything."[41] It was several weeks before news reached Paris that these orders had been obeyed. At the end of January, the latest letter from Madrid which had reached Paris was dated Christmas Eve. At the end of February, the minister of war had no Spanish news later than 8 January, and as late as 16 March he was complaining that "seventy two days have passed since the courier left with the Emperor's orders [of the 3rd January]. I have as yet received no answer."[42] It was not to be expected that such a state of affairs would dissuade the emperor from attempting to direct the war in Spain from Paris and points east.

Joseph, meanwhile, was obeying his orders. The cantonments of the Army of the South were drawn in. The divisions stationed across the Tagus marched north and established astride the Sierra de Guadarrama, and, on 17 March, riding in the midst of his guard, the king left Madrid for the last time.

He reached Valladolid six days later, accompanied by a huge convoy. As Jourdan remarked, "The arrival of the court in Valladolid brought there the ministers, the civilian officials of the household, numbers of civil servants and a crowd of other personages, as well as their families. It would certainly have been prudent to send them on to Bayonne, but the King could not bear to send into exile those of his subjects who had been faithful to him, and who would find themselves destitute in a foreign country. Moreover, he was afraid that their departure would show only too clearly that there was no longer hope of holding Spain and that this would discourage the army. Therefore the headquarters of the army remained encumbered with all these refugees, with their followers and with their carriages."[43]

Chapter 11

RETREAT

Bearing in mind the circumstances in which the enemy finds himself, there is no reason to suppose that he will take the offensive.

CLARKE, MINISTER OF WAR, 16 MAY 1813.

KING Joseph was not alone in having troubles. In Portugal, Wellington was much beset with problems of a different kind. Most of them stemmed from the fact that Wellington's own British force formed only part of an allied army. Without Portuguese and Spanish support he could not find the strength to take the field with any hope of success. Under Beresford's careful training, the Portuguese army had been raised to a standard at which it was fit to take the field alongside the British and to stand against the French. In 1813 Wellington could say of them that they "are now the fighting cocks of the army."[1] The Portuguese government was quite another matter. It was not a question of disloyalty to the British alliance but the fact that "there exists in the people of Portugal an unconquerable love of their ease, which is superior even to their fear and detestation of the enemy."[2] As soon as the immediate threat to Portugal passed, as it demonstrably did pass with the battle of Salamanca, the Portuguese government, never an energetic body, relapsed into lethargy. They created

268

Wellington, now a British marquess, duke of Vitoria in the peerage of Portugal but became increasingly remiss in providing the pay and rations of their army, even though almost all the money needed for such provisions was supplied to them as a subsidy from the British government.

The Spanish government was even more troublesome. They had never wanted a British alliance. They had reluctantly made Wellington supreme commander of all their armies, but they obstinately declined to give him the power to direct them. They had more than 160,000 men under arms, but few of them were trained and, since they had no transport and little ammunition, very few of them could take the field. "I do not expect much from the exertions of the Spaniards. They cry *viva* and are very fond of us, and hate the French; but they are, in general, the most incapable of useful exertion of all the nations I have known; the most vain, and at the same time the most ignorant, particularly of military affairs, and above all of military affairs in their own country."[3] He admired the soldierly quality of the Spanish peasant and warmly acknowledged his debt to the guerrillas, but as for their governments and generals, "It is impossible for any rational man to talk to any of them. . . . Examine any transaction in which they have been concerned and it will be found characterized by delay, weakness, folly or treachery."[4]

As far as the British government went, Wellington had less cause for complaint than usual. Despite the demands of the American war he was not, as he had feared, left without reinforcements. Although he had to send home seven veteran units, all of which had fallen below their workable strength, he received in return six infantry battalions and two brigades of cavalry, a net gain of some 2,500 bayonets and sabres. In addition, he was sent 5,000 men in drafts. To offset these gains, one of his infantry brigades became so riddled with fever and dysentery that 700 men died and it was incapable of taking the field until August. Moreover, the government had succeeded in securing a quantity of gold coins, "pagodas," in India. These they had reminted into guineas and sent to Lisbon. Although the British army was still beset by debt, at least there was enough cash available to open the campaign. Wellington was optimistic. He wrote to Beresford, "I propose to get in fortune's way . . . and we may make a lucky hit in the commencement of the next campaign."[5] In May 1813, he was able to bring forward an Anglo-Portuguese force of 81,000 all ranks, of whom 52,000 were British. There were 67,000 infantry, 8,000 cavalry, and 102 guns. Of all the troops available to the Spanish government, only 21,000 could be found in a fit state to take the field, and even they had no reserve ammunition. Four thousand more joined before midsummer, by which time the fate of the campaign had been decided.

Napoleon's troubles surpassed even Joseph's in their magnitude. His army in the east was manifestly incapable of resisting the pressure of the Russian armies, even though this lost momentum as soon as the French were cleared from Russian territory. Prussia deserted Napoleon and joined Russia as an ally. Austria, while not abrogating her alliance with France, relapsed into increasingly hostile neutrality. Sweden, under the former marshal Bernadotte, Joseph's brother-in-law, joined the Russians in the hope of acquiring Denmark. Murat, his own brother-in-law, to whom the emperor had resigned the command of the *Grand Armée* for the final stages of the retreat, slunk off to his kingdom of Naples and set about coming to an arrangement with the Austrians which would enable him to keep his crown whatever the fate of Napoleon. The Russians entered Berlin on 4 March, and ten days later, General Lauriston, in an unnecessary panic, evacuated Hamburg. The emperor ordered Marshal Davout to retake it, but in doing so he evacuated Dresden, capital of the king of Saxony, Napoleon's only remaining faithful ally.

By superhuman efforts a new *Grand Armée*, 145,000 strong, was raised and equipped. The emperor left Paris on 14 April. He defeated the eastern allies at Lützen (2 May), reentered Dresden on 8 May, and defeated them again at Bautzen (19 May). These, however, were only tactical victories, bought at a cost of almost 25,000 causalties to the French. Strategically, the advantage and the initiative lay with the allies.

In these circumstances, it is small wonder that the emperor had little time to devote to the problems of Spain. Such thinking as he did was colored by the difficulties of communicating with King Joseph. The problem of clearing the northern provinces of Spain became an obsession with him. His orders for putting down the guerrillas of Biscay and Navarre fatally weakened the forces available for guarding the Portuguese frontier. Joseph was ordered to put the pacification of the northern provinces above every other consideration, and to ensure that the Army of the North had sufficient troops to undertake the task, Clausel was to be reinforced with as many of the six infantry divisions of the Army of Portugal as he should require. Joseph obeyed these orders. By May, five of these divisions were on the north bank of the Ebro. For the rest, it was Napoleon's view that "the English seem to be building up their army in Portugal and they appear to be intending either to advance into Spain or to sail from Lisbon with 25,000 men, part English and part Spanish, to effect a landing on some part of the French coast while we are engaged in the north [of Europe]. To stop this expedition the Army in Spain must always be ready to take the offensive. It must threaten Lisbon and the conquest of Portugal should the enemy weaken their army in the Peninsula."[6]

With much of his infantry detached beyond the Ebro, the idea of advancing on Lisbon seemed to Joseph a fantasy. He had too few troops and too many generals.

> There are four commanders in chief at Valladolid. . . . they divide the command, argue amongst themselves and snatch supplies from each other. I am not obeyed. How should I be obeyed after the example set by Marshall Soult? As far as I can tell no letter has been written to the generals commanding the Armies of Portugal, the South and the North telling them that they must obey me in all things, at

all times. Meanwhile the lack of unified system re-
duces the supplies available. No magazines have been
established while the enemy, who have everything
in plenty, is preparing to start the campaign. . . . I
can only repeat what I have said so often before.
When disaster comes, it will be too late to do anything about it. The Emperor's ambassador keeps repeating to me, "The King must make himself
obeyed". This phrase is nothing but wind. How can
I make myself obeyed by generals who can quote
orders from Paris as an excuse for disobedience?[7]

When the king asked for money to pay the troops, the
minister of war smugly wrote that the emperor

instructs me to reply that the money needed for
the armies in Spain will be found in the rich and
fertile provinces devastated by the *guerillas* and the
rebel juntas; that if enough vigor and activity are
devoted to re-establishing order and tranquillity all
these resources will become available. This will be
a further inducement to Your Majesty to use all the
means at your disposal to put an end to the civil war
which disturbs the peaceable inhabitants, ruins the
countryside, exhausts our armies and deprives them
of all the benefits which they should enjoy from the
peaceful occupation of these districts. Today Aragon
and Navarre are ruled by Mina; their produce and
their revenues go to sustain this disastrous struggle.
It is time to put an end to this disastrous state of
affairs and to restore to the legitimate government
the resources of an area which flourishes in time of
peace.[8]

Joseph manfully forbore to comment that the emperor had
specifically deprived him of the revenues of Aragon and
Navarre three years earlier.

The task of guarding the Portuguese frontier was left to
the armies of the Center and the South, supported by the

cavalry of the Army of Portugal. The total strength available was 33,000 infantry, 9,000 cavalry, and 100 guns. The infantry divisions were widely dispersed between the Douro at Zamora and the Tagus at Toledo. A strong screen of cavalry covered the northern flank to guard against a possible Spanish incursion from the Asturian mountains. Headquarters were at Valladolid and around that city were grouped such reserve formations as could be spared. A single infantry brigade of the Army of Portugal was under the king's command and was stationed at Palencia, thirty miles northeast of headquarters. Another brigade of the same army was at Burgos. The remaining five divisions were north of the Ebro, their whereabouts unknown to the king. Clausel did not report to Valladolid on the progress of his operations in the north.

Whatever the illusions of the emperor and his minister of war, it was obvious to Joseph and Jourdan that the initiative rested with Wellington and that without the Army of Portugal, they had insufficient troops to halt him if he advanced in strength. Jourdan put the essential question to Paris. "Supposing that Lord Wellington starts his campaign before General Clausel has completed his operations, and that the enemy compels the Imperial troops to take up a position on the right bank of the Douro. Should the King, with the Armies of the South and Center, defend the line of the Douro and risk a battle? Should he halt the operations in the north? Should he retire on Burgos and wait until General Clausel has finished his operations and then advance with all the armies united? Your Excellency will understand that the outcome of the campaign may well depend on the answer to these questions."[9]

Jourdan overrated the perspicacity of his correspondent. The minister of war's answer, written long after it had ceased to be of anything but academic interst, did not answer the marshal's questions. It merely stated that the problem did not exist. "Bearing in mind the circumstances in which the enemy finds himself, there is no reason to suppose that he will take the offensive. His remoteness, his dearth of transport, his constant and timid caution in any operation out of the ordinary, all demonstrate to us that we can act as seems most suitable without worry or inconvenience. I will say further that the disagreements which exist between the English and the Spaniards, Lord Wellington's journey to Cádiz, the changes in his army, some regiments of which have been sent back to England, should be further favorable factors towards executing, fearlessly, all the movements called for in the Emperor's orders."[10] On the day that this optimistic letter was written, Wellington's headquarters moved into Palencia, thirty miles nearer France than Valladolid.

In April and May, it seemed to Joseph and Jourdan that three lines of advance were open to Wellington. He could march up the Ciudad Rodrigo–Salamanca road, the route he had used in 1812. He could advance on Madrid by way of Talavera and the north bank of the Tagus, as he had done in 1809. It was also conceivable that he might push forward on the north bank of the Douro. This, however, seemed improbable, as the roads within the Portuguese frontier, through the mountainous Trás-os-Montes province, were well known to be deplorable. Of the three alternatives, French opinion was that Wellington was most likely to choose the Rodrigo–Salamanca route as being the most direct and that which had been used the previous year. Moreover, it was known that Wellington's headquarters were at Freneda, not far from Rodrigo.

Joseph's plan, therefore, was to take up a defensive position on the north bank of the Douro, with his right at Toro and his left at Valladolid. On that line the armies of the South and the Center should be able to defend the limited number of bridges and fords until the missing infantry of the Army of Portugal, supported, it was hoped, by Clausel's two disposable divisions from the Army of the North, could come up into line. This reinforcement of more than 40,000 men would give Joseph a force large enough to drive Wellington back into Portugal, even if he could not be brought to battle and defeated. Everything depended on Clausel's being willing to part with the mass of infantry under his command. Whether he would do so remained an open question. The king heard nothing from him dated later than 10 April.

It was difficult for the French to get information about Wellington's movements and intentions. Almost to a man the Spanish population refused to give information to the French, while risking everything to pass news to Wellington and his admirable system of agents within French-held territory. "Despite the care taken by headquarters to establish a secret service," wrote Jourdan, "despite the money lavished upon it, it was never possible to obtain accurate information about the Anglo-Portuguese army. Such reports as were received were so contradictory that, instead of making things clearer, they increased disquiet."[11] At the end of March, a usually reliable spy reported that Hill was about to march on Madrid with Wellington's southern wing. A few days later General Leval, commanding at Madrid, asserted so vehemently that Hill was actually on the march that Jourdan started reserve divisions moving southwards to his help. At the end of April news came in that the British were handing over the frontier near Ciudad Rodrigo to Spanish forces and were moving south to the Tagus Valley. Hard on the heels of that piece of information came a report that Wellington had set off on another visit to Cádiz to settle his differences with the Spanish government. Color was lent to this story by the fact that some Spanish generals had sent messages to King Joseph offering to bring over to his service 10,000 Spanish troops, formerly under the command of Ballasteros, as a protest against Wellington's appointment as supreme commander.

By the second week of May, all reports suggested that an allied advance was imminent. Some stories gave 15 May as the starting time. Nothing happened, but confusion was increased by a story reaching Valladolid on 20 May that three divisions and eight regiments of cavalry had crossed the Douro at Lamego, deep inside Portugal, and were advancing on Astorga. It was added, however, that Wellington was still at Freneda and that he had been reviewing his troops near Rodrigo on 17 May. On the previous day a report had asserted that Hill, with the southern corps, was advancing towards the Pass of Baños, aiming for Ávila. On the 22 Hill's objective was reported to be Salamanca. At the same time, a message came in from Benavente saying that a cavalry sweep had established that there were no allied troops in Spain on the northern bank of the Douro, saving a few commissaries and ration parties.

It was not until 24 May that definite information came in that Wellington had passed Ciudad Rodrigo in great strength and was marching on Salamanca, while Hill was coming up from the Pass of Baños to join him. General Villatte, who commanded the forward French division at Salamanca, added to the message a statement that Lord Wellington was sick and was moving a day's march behind his columns in a traveling carriage.

Orders were immediately sent out for all the French divisions of the armies of the Center and South to concentrate around Medina del Campo, between Salamanca and Valladolid. Some time was lost because General Gazan, commanding the Army of the South, who already had contingent orders to call Leval in from Madrid as soon as the allied advance was confirmed, rode in from his headquarters at Arévalo to see the king at Valladolid, to ask whether it was now time to give orders to evacuate the capital. The one brigade of the Army of Portugal within reach was ordered to move towards Zamora to strengthen the right flank of the Douro position, which was to be based on the Esla tributary.

Villatte, at Salamanca, had his own division, about 6,000 men and a single cavalry regiment. He decided to hang on as long as possible to judge the size of the force opposing him. By noon on 26 May, he was satisfied that a very sizable force was approaching and evacuated the town, drawing up his force on the heights behind. There, Wellington launched two cavalry brigades, some 1,600 horsemen, at him. The French had to retire in haste before their line of retreat was cut. They had, in fact, stayed too long. The British cavalry could not harm their formed columns, but the horse artillery did some damage and they left 200 prisoners behind, together with some artillery wagons. Wellington did not press their retreat.

Having reached Salamanca, Wellington halted. The French, therefore, had time to continue their concentration around Medina del Campo. It was with heartfelt relief that their head-quarters learned that Leval and the Madrid garrison had reached Segovia on 30 May and was now safely on the northern side of the Sierra de Guadarrama. A long convoy of refugees which accompanied him was sent off towards Burgos under Spanish escort. Joseph's holding force for the line of the Douro was coming together smoothly.

The king, indeed, was remarkably unruffled by the allied advance. As late as 30 May he was still writing letters to the minister of war devoted largely to complaining that Clausel was no better at sending reports to him than Caffarelli had been, that the French treasury was sending only two million francs a month for all the armies in Spain, and that the administration of all the armies would have been better organized if plans he had made in the previous November had been approved by the emperor at an earlier date. In particular, he was in no great apparent hurry to call up the infantry of the Army of Portugal. His first letter about them to Clausel was notably leisurely. "General," he wrote on 27 May, three days after news of Wellington's advance reached him, "I have received none of your letters since 10th April. For a long time the infantry of the Army of Portugal, less three battalions, has been on the territory of the Army of the North. The English have crossed the Agueda and are advancing on the Tormes.* If, when this letter reaches you, your operations are sufficiently advanced to make it possible without compromising the issue, send back the troops from the Army of Portugal. You will understand how important this is."[12] He followed this up with further letters on 30 May and 7 June.

Even allowing that Joseph undervalued the strength of his enemy, believing that there were only 55,000 English and Portuguese, supported by 25,000 Spaniards,[13] he can scarcely

---

* They had crossed the Tormes at Salamanca the previous day.

be acquitted of dilatoriness in calling up the infantry from the north of Spain. There were probably two reasons for this. First, he was uncertain whether he would be right in recalling troops from Clausel in view of the emperor's reiterated orders to give absolutely priority to the pacification of northern Spain. As late as 5 June, he was writing to Paris to ask, "Should I call the Army of Portugal back to me? I wrote to you on this subject on 30th May. If such be the Emperor's wish, I beg you to send orders to this effect to General Clausel, from whom I suppose that you receive reports."[14] The other reason was that, like many Frenchmen at that time and since, he would have agreed with Clarke's estimate of Wellington's "constant and timid caution in any operation out of the ordinary."

It is extraordinary that as late as 5 June the king could have been in any doubts about Wellington's enterprise. On 2 June, the British Hussar brigade had charged in on a French dragoon brigade at Morales, five miles east of Toro, and broken one regiment to fragments. Behind the Hussars were huge marching columns. The allies were across the Douro in great strength. The defensive position Joseph had intended to take up on the north bank of the Douro was turned before it had been occupied.

Wellington had appreciated that the French would expect him to advance up the Ciudad Rodrigo–Salamanca road and was more than ready to do so with a strong force. On this road he took 30,000 men, but of these only five brigades, less than 15,000 men, consisted of British infantry. The rest of his infantry was Portuguese and Spanish. There was, however, a very strong cavalry component, 2,750 British and 1,300 Spanish, which screened the advancing columns and prevented the weak French patrols that lay in their path from discovering the strength and number of the infantry brigades hidden within the inevitable dust cloud. Having seen this column safely into Salamanca, Wellington handed over command to Hill and at dawn on 29 May rode off northward, escorted only by a handful of staff officers. That evening he reached the

Douro near Miranda do Douro, fifty miles from his starting point, and crossed the river in a basket swinging on a rope slung between the cliffs on either bank. Next morning he rode twenty miles to Carvajales, where he was at the headquarters of his real striking force.

Under the command of General Thomas Graham, 42,000 Anglo-Portuguese troops, including six infantry divisions, had struggled through the mountains of Trás-os-Montes. The French had been right in reckoning the roads there as deplorable. A cavalry officer wrote, "The roads were dreadful in places—much easier to march up an English staircase than to ascend them,"[15] but they were passable. By 26 May, the whole of this corps was behind the Portuguese frontier, covered by a screen of Portuguese dragoons whose presence did not alarm the French. On that day, the force moved forward in three columns, with, on their left hand, the Spanish Army of Galicia, 12,000 strong. It was not until they reached the Esla River on 28 May that any sign of their advance was seen by the French cavalry screen. Even then, the reports sent back to French headquarters greatly underestimated their strength.

The Esla near its junction with the Douro is a broad river, with a swift current and high banks. There were no bridges and the few fords were closely watched by French patrols. Fortunately a Portuguese officer was able to point out a difficult ford near Almendra, which was unknown to the enemy and therefore unwatched. At dawn on 31 May, the Hussar brigade rode their horses into the river, accompanied by a battalion and a half of infantry, marching in column. "It was soon evident," wrote a private soldier, "that we had either missed the ford or that the water was risen by the rain. Whichever was the cause, we soon found the water was so deep and the stream so rapid that in a very short time the whole of the infantry was upset. Some sank to the bottom, borne down by the weight of the firelock and knapsack, to say nothing of the pouch containing sixty rounds of ball cartridge. . . . There were three regiments of cavalry and two of infantry plunging about in the river and so dark we could scarcely see each other, besides expecting every moment to receive a volley from the enemy."[16] Finally the advanced guard crossed with an infantryman clinging on to each stirrup of the Hussars. The nearest French picket was captured entire, most of them being asleep.

The nearest heavy body of French troops was far behind their cavalry screen. Daricau's division of the Army of the South, 4,800 strong, had been sent to Zamora as soon as it was known that Wellington was advancing from Ciudad Rodrigo. At Zamora they were joined by Digeon's division of 2,100 dragoons. However, Daricau, as soon as he heard that the allies were in strength on the Esla, considered his position unduly exposed and retired on Toro, whither Digeon followed him as soon as he learned that the Esla had been crossed. The British were, therefore, able to enter Zamora unopposed on 1 June. At that Daricau and Digeon again retired, leaving a cavalry rear guard at Morales, somewhat to the east. Leading the allied advance, the British Hussars charged in on Digeon's two regiments on 2 June and broke the French Sixteenth Dragoons, capturing 2 officers and 208 troopers, for the loss of only 16 men.

That day Wellington established his headquarters in Toro, and work was started on repairing an arch of the bridge over the Douro which the French engineers had demolished. There was need for speed, since the troops of Hill's corps had broken up their bivouacs around Salamanca and were marching north to join the main body. Crossing the bridge "in Indian file by means of planks having been laid over the broken arch, the guns and baggage passing through a deep ford,"[17] all Hill's men were on the north bank of the Douro by the evening of 3 June. The whole of Wellington's Anglo-Portuguese striking force, 80,000 men, was concentrated on the flank of Joseph's delaying position. Its advanced cavalry was approaching Tordesillas, less than twenty miles from the king's headquarters at Valladolid.

The news that the mass of the allied army was moving on the north bank of the Douro demolished Joseph's plan to stand on the line of that river until his distant reserves could join him. It did, however, relieve him of another worry. The fact that Hill had not advanced beyond Salamanca meant that Leval's division from Madrid and the forces that had been covering this move were no longer in danger of being cut off from the main army. Nevertheless, it was clear that Valladolid was untenable. Two courses were open to the king. He could fall back on Burgos, fighting delaying actions wherever the ground was suitable, or he could advance on the south of the Douro. Wellington had put his whole strength in a position where it threatened the French communications and their line of retreat. Joseph could do the same by pushing forward to threaten Salamanca and Rodrigo. This was the plan favored by Jourdan. Wellington was notoriously sensitive about his communications, and a large army on his right rear would certainly, the marshal argued, pull him sharply back to Portugal. If the worst came to the worst, the French could always retreat. "It was," he maintained, "doubtful whether Wellington would have continued his advance eastward, giving up his line of communication with Portugal. It is probable that he would have recrossed the Douro to follow the French, who in any case could have fallen back on Aranda [de Douro], and from there on Burgos or Saragossa. Having thus gained time, General Clausel would certainly have come up, and a battle could have been fought in good cavalry country. This idea was put to the King who was not attracted to it since it contradicted the orders he had received, which had enjoined him above everything to keep the direct communications with France open."[18]

Joseph decided on retreat. On 2 and 3 June, huge convoys of refugees, baggage, and heavy artillery were sent off towards Burgos, with an escort of 4,000 men, mostly Spaniards but including a battalion of the Royal Guard. To the king it was essential that the army should pick up all the infantry from the north so that it would be large enough to fight a battle. Jourdan's plan might delay the allies, it might even maneuver them back to Portugal, but it would not defeat and cripple the Anglo-Portuguese army. This became the overriding strategic idea in the king's mind. As he wrote to Paris on 5 June, "Let us beat the English, the real enemies of the French in Spain. Then the Spaniards will become allies once more and will re-enter the French sphere of influence, where they have been for the last hundred years, and which every day they more regret leaving."[19]

On the evening of 3 June and all day on the fourth, the French pulled back to a position on the Carrión River with their right at Palencia, their left at Dueñas. Headquarters were established at Torquemada, and it was here that Joseph received a letter from the minister of war, dated 10 May, urging him to "take steps to hold the English in check, to threaten Portugal," so that Wellington could not part with troops for operations against the French coasts. He was also urged to send reinforcements to Clausel in the north and to Suchet in Aragon.[20] No irony could have been more bitter, but Joseph answered calmly, pointing out that he had done everything he could to help Clausel but that now he desperately needed Clausel's help in exchange. Only the suggestion that he should send help to Suchet roused him to sharpness. "As for Aragon, I know nothing of what happens in that province. I have never received a report from the commanders there. I do not even know their names."[21] He wrote off at once to Suchet begging him to send what help he could.

There was no future in standing on the Carrión. The British were swinging around the right of the French position. By stages the army had to be pulled back. Jourdan was sent on ahead to reconnoiter the position at Burgos, which had put up such a fine defense the previous year, but Miot noted in his diary for 7 June, "The army is in full retreat."

Headquarters reached Burgos on 9 June with an allied column hard on the heels of the rear guard. Jourdan had no good news for them. Major repairs to the fortifications had been put in hand after the 1812 siege. They were far from complete. The castle was indefensible. Worse than that, the huge convoys of refugees were still in and around the town and had eaten most of the stores of provisions which had been built up there. There was no news from Clausel, none from Paris. It could not even be known whether Clausel had ever received the king's requests for help. It was decided that, at last, a formal order should be sent to him to bring his whole strength to join the king. The order went off under an escort of fifteen hundred men.[22] The refugee convoys went off to Vitoria.

Despite this bad news, the French army took up a defensive position at Burgos and offered battle to the allies. A party was building up in favor of risking a battle. "Some opinions were strongly put forward in favour of such a course as being the most honourable. The King was easily persuaded to such a view, which appealed to him more than any other. Thus we spent three days at Burgos, while reconnaissances were made with the aim of finding a defensive position, whose natural features would offset our inferiority in numbers. But soon we had to return to Marshal Jourdan's view that the enemy was not seeking a battle, that his only object was to manoeuvre us out of our positions, in the hope of getting across our communications with France. The enemy's movements on our right left no doubt that this was indeed his aim."[23]

Jourdan was perfectly correct. Wellington had no intention of fighting a battle for Burgos. His troops were working steadily around the French northern flank so that Burgos would soon cease to be tenable. No one at French headquarters realized the scope of Wellington's plan. While King Joseph was hesitating at Burgos, Wellington was planning to clear the French from the whole of northern Spain. On 10 June, the day after Joseph reached the town, the allied commander was writing to the British officer at Coruña. "There are at Coruña certain ships loaded with biscuit and flour, and certain others loaded with a train of heavy artillery and ammunition. I shall be very obliged if you will request any officer of the navy who may be at Coruña to take under his convoy all these vessels and to proceed with them to Santander. If he should find Santander occupied by the enemy, I beg him to remain off the port till the operations of this army have obliged the enemy to abandon it. If the enemy should not be in Santander, I beg him to enter the port; but to be in readiness to quit it again, if the enemy should approach the place, until I communicate with him."[24] The allied supply base was to be swung forward from Lisbon to the port most suitable for conducting a campaign on the north bank of the Ebro.

Wellington was now aiming for total victory, for the expulsion of the French from Spain. For the past four years, he had pursued what he called his "cautious system." His army had been so small that the most he could hope to do was to isolate one of the French armies and smash it before the others could come to its assistance. Now, in June 1813, he was raising the stakes. By switching his base from Lisbon to Santander, he was counting on making the Pyrenees his front line. The risk was enormous. If Clausel could come to Joseph's help with all the infantry under his command, if Suchet could be persuaded to part with some troops from the armies of Aragon and Catalonia, the Anglo-Portuguese army would be overmatched in numbers and quality. If the allies suffered even a minor check on the north bank of the Ebro, there was little hope of being able to keep even a toehold in the Peninsula. The garrison of Lisbon consisted of one understrength British battalion, a handful of veterans, and some dismounted Portuguese dragoons. There were no transports available to evacuate the Anglo-Portuguese army if it had to fall back on the coast. There could not be another Coruña. Everything depended on the calculation that neither Clausel nor Suchet would be both able and willing to reinforce Joseph's army above 80,000 at a time when the king would be deep inside Clausel's own district. Everything depended on being able to hustle the king so fast that his guerrilla-ridden communications would not be good enough to call up the large numbers of reinforcements that were available within a few days' march.

Perhaps Wellington's greatest ally was his own reputation for caution. At French headquarters it was an article of faith that "the enemy would never dare to operate beyond the Ebro."[25] Even at Wellington's own headquarters, he remarked, "Some of my officers remonstrated with me about the imprudence of crossing the Ebro, and advised me to take up the line of that river. I asked them what they meant by taking up the line of the Ebro, a river three hundred miles long, and what good I was to do along that line? In short, I would not listen to the advice."[26] "I thanked them but said to myself I preferred the Pyrenees."[27]

Thus the French decided to seek their sanctuary behind the Ebro. There had been some cavalry skirmishing north of Burgos on 12 June, which suggested that Wellington was moving around their right in strength, and that evening the whole army set off to the rear. The castle, which had proved such a bulwark to their defense in the previous year, was demolished with such overenthusiasm that more than a hundred Frenchmen and many Spaniards were killed by the explosion.

On 16 June, the royal headquarters were set up at Miranda de Ebro. As Miot confided to his diary, "after five years of war and trouble, here we are in the same place as we were in 1808."[28] All the way back from Burgos the argument had raged. Should we stand and fight or must we fall back and find Clausel? It was assumed that Wellington would not involve himself beyond the Ebro, "in mountainous country; that he would only push a few Spanish units in that direction; that his largest and best forces would come to face us."[29] General Gazan pressed for a battle in the intermediate position at Pancorbo, where the country gave a strong, natural line for defense. He was overruled since it was obvious that the Pancorbo position could be turned and isolated. Most of the troops were stationed on the north bank, although a strong advanced guard of three infantry brigades was left on the south to lead the offensive which Joseph still hoped to start as soon as Clausel joined him. Cavalry probed south to find Wellington's advancing columns. All they saw were a few

Spanish lancers. On the credit side, two divisions of the Army
of Portugal joined, adding more than 10,000 men to the army's
strength.*

The fact that these divisions joined the main army was
fortuitous. They had been stationed close enough to the rear
of King Joseph's force to hear that they were needed. Clausel
did not receive the king's appeals for help until 15 June, the
day before Joseph reached the Ebro. On that day, three letters,
of increasing urgency, reached him. He immediately agreed
to suspend his operations "which have been successful in all
directions," and to bring "the troops of the Army of Portugal
towards Burgos. I shall reinforce them with all the disposable
troops from the Army of the North. Even by leaving Pamplona lightly guarded as well as the main points on the line of
communication, Bilbao, Castro and Santoña, Your Majesty
should not reckon on more than 4,000 men from the Army
of the North."[30]

Clausel was at Pamplona when he received Joseph's letters.
It is about seventy-five miles from Pamplona to Miranda de
Ebro, four days' hard marching for infantry. It took him two
days to collect the forces immediately available—four divisions, two of his own army and two of the Army of Portugal
—and set out on 17 June to join the king. Since his last information told him that the main army was at Burgos, he
directed his march on Miranda de Ebro and took the shortest
route by Estella, Logroño, and the north bank of the Ebro.
He reached Logroño on 20 June. There were no orders awaiting him and no firm news of the king's movement. All he
could discover was that troops of the Army of the Center had
been at Haro, about two-thirds of the way from Logroño and
Miranda, but that they had marched off. The only definite
information was an order dated 18 June from the French governor of Vitoria to the commandant at Logroño telling him
to arrange for 30,000 rations to be sent to Pancorbo, on the

* These two divisions, those of Sarrut and Lamartine, were the second
and third to be gathered in from the Army of Portugal. The other, that of
Maucune, which had been stationed at Palencia and Burgos, had joined the
main army as it retreated.

south side of the Ebro.[31] Clausel devoted the twentieth to send-ing out search parties to find the king's army. They found nothing.

A further substantial detachment of disposable troops was in Biscay. General Foy had under his command, apart from the local garrisons, two marching divisions. With these he had been clearing the ports along the coast and watching over the safety of Bilbao. Although Jourdan had written to him several times previously, the first that Foy knew of the retreat of the main army was a letter from Jourdan dated 18 June which reached him two days later when he was halfway between Bilbao and San Sebastián. This ordered him to bring his troops, about 11,000 men, to Vitoria "if their presence is not necessary where they are at present."[32] Given this option and not appre-ciating the desperate urgency of the king's need for reinforce-ment, Foy did not move immediately. He took time to recall his scattered detachment and to cover the move of a large convoy which was bringing quantities of coin from France for the pay of the army and with which his wife was traveling. Only when these were in safety did he make a move to the king's support.

While Clausel and Foy were gathering their forces and while the main army were scouring the country in front of Miranda de Ebro for signs of the allied army, Wellington was continuing his advance. While the French were retreating from Burgos, almost the whole of the allied army had turned north. For three days they marched through "a dreary region of solid rock, bearing an abundant crop of loose stones, with-out a particle of soil or vegetation visible to the eye in any direction."[33] But on 14 June, the advanced guard came to an "enchanting valley studded with picturesque hamlets and fruitful gardens producing every kind of vegetation."[34] They had reached the Ebro near Medina de Pomar, thirty-five miles upstream from Joseph's headquarters at Miranda de Ebro. There was no opposition and by the sixteenth the whole army was across. Leaving a division of 7,000 men at Medina de Pomar, Wellington turned eastward, driving for Vitoria.

The French, he said, "must either fight, or retire out of Spain altogether."[35]

It was not until the seventeenth that the first news of allied troops on the north bank reached the royal headquarters. Even then, only cavalry was reported. Rightly, Joseph and Jourdan assumed that it was Wellington again aiming to turn their right. They were, however, wrong in assessing the direction he would take. Wellington was aiming at Vitoria. They took him to be marching on Bilbao. Orders were therefore issued for Reille, with the Army of Portugal, to march north so that he could reinforce the garrisons of the coastal towns and block the allied advance.

With two of his divisions, Reille pushed northward on 18 June only to be faced with more than three allied divisions at Osma, where Wellington's advance crossed his own route. There was a brisk skirmish and a considerable cannonade before Reille was able to disengage his forward troops and retire the way he had come. He suffered about a hundred casualties.

Much less fortunate was his third division, Maucune's, which he had ordered to join him by a side road. His leading brigade was resting from the midday sun in the village of San Millan when it was surprised by the Hussars of the King's German Legion with Wellington's light division at their backs. They were driven away in disorder by the British riflemen when, to the astonishment of both sides, the second French brigade marched into the middle of the light division, "out of an opening between two perpendicular rocks."[36] Finding themselves hemmed in between two forces of British light infantry, the French broke and fled over the mountains, leaving their baggage and three hundred prisoners in allied hands. Maucune's division, in King Joseph's opinion, was finished as a fighting formation.

The engagements at Osma and San Millan showed the French the terrible situation they were in. For a moment, on the evening of 18 June, there was something like panic. A captured British officer who was with the Army of the South recorded, "All the confident and matured arrangements of the French army were at once overset; hurry and confusion followed the knowledge of what had happened, and an immediate night march was the consequence. Drums beat in all directions; cavalry filed past in all directions; while the town, crowded with unwieldy ambulances containing plunder, presented a scene of strange confusion."[37]

As the French retreated on Vitoria, the same officer got a glimpse of King Joseph's army on the march.

> As the Franco-Spanish court moved with the troops, there was a great display of uniform; the civil departments of the army, officers attached to the household or the Spanish ministers, were alike loaded with embroidery; the general officers, even in the forenoon, constantly wore their uniforms. Accompanying the Army of the South, numerous ladies, dressed *en militaire,* and on horseback, having forsaken the plains of Andalusia, followed the fortunes of their Gallic lovers. The assemblage was motley in the extreme; nor could it be doubted that habits of luxury, added to the facility of procuring transport in a country where every animal was by them considered the property of the first military person that secured it, had to a great degree encumbered the French armies.[38]

At Miranda there was further debate amongst the generals. Reille was for falling back down the Ebro towards Saragossa, there to join up with Clausel and to be in touch with Suchet's army. The king, according to Jourdan, "did not think he could adopt this plan, for he had been ordered to preserve the main road to France at all hazards. Moreover it would mean leaving in the hands of the enemy an immense convoy of Spaniards who had been faithful to him and all the stores that had been brought away from Madrid, Burgos and other towns. It might also expose General Clausel, whom he had ordered to join him, to the risk of finding the English in Vitoria instead of the French. He ordered a retreat on Vitoria."[39] By the evening of 19 June, the whole French army was in the small plain of Vitoria, Reille having exchanged a few shots with Wellington's advanced guard on the banks of the Bayas River to cover the retreat.

On the afternoon of that day, the king held yet another council of war. Jourdan, unimpressed by the strength of the position at Vitoria, advised a further retreat up the main road to the defiles near Salinas, where they could stand in a strong position until Foy and Clausel could join them. This would be only a short retreat, would immensely strengthen the army's fighting position, and would still be in accordance with the king's orders "to preserve the main road to France at all hazards." The army commanders, Reille, D'Erlon, and Gazan, "anxious to make their marks, gave it as their opinion that the army should stay around Vitoria. Their advice was adopted."[40]

It would, indeed, have been difficult to abandon Vitoria without a struggle. The little city was clogged with refugees, Spanish and French. The streets were jammed with baggage wagons and artillery. All these moved more slowly than the fighting troops and must be given a start so as to have a chance of reaching safety behind the Pyrenees. Even more important was the fact that it would be very much more difficult for Clausel to come up to a position in the rear of Vitoria. Foy, too, had orders to rally on Vitoria. Without these two large forces, the most that could be hoped for was a minor defensive victory. Joseph was still hoping for much more than that. Once all his troops were concentrated, he still looked forward to taking the offensive and driving the wreck of the allied army back to Portugal, even to Lisbon.

The troops had been retreating continually for four weeks. Those who started from Toledo had already covered three hundred miles. During this long withdrawal, there had been scarcely more than half a dozen minor skirmishes. The vast bulk of the army had not fired a shot, had not seen a British soldier. No army can retreat so far and so fast without damage to its discipline and morale. At all ranks the feeling was rife that Spain was to be abandoned without an effort's being made to save it, that all the sacrifice and suffering of the last five years would turn out to have been made in vain. No one felt this more keenly than the king, and his anguish was heightened by the knowledge that his army believed, and scarcely bothered to conceal their belief, that it was all his fault.

Nevertheless, by halting at Vitoria, Joseph was not deliberately offering battle. While his heart told him that he must make a supreme effort to save Spain, even if only to avoid his brother's scorn, his head, and Marshal Jourdan, insisted that it would be madness to do so until his army was complete. Within a few days' march there were six divisions of French infantry, more than 30,000 men, to say nothing of thousands more in garrison. With these to support him, there would be every chance of driving Wellington back, even if he could not be routed. Jourdan was still anxious to maneuver against the enemy flank, to feint against his lines of communication, confident that this would delay the allied advance and give time for Clausel to join. He was, however, resolute in his opposition to risking a full-scale action against superior numbers. Increasingly the subordinate generals were disagreeing with him, saying that the time had come to stand and fight for the honor of the French army. "The army," it was asserted, "would be dishonoured by leaving Spain without having encountered the enemy. The Emperor would never forgive us for abandoning his conquest without having defended it to the last extremity. . . . All our young officers were of the same opinion, and sarcasms and jests were showered on the prudence of those who were opposed to fighting; their prudence was called by another name."[41]

In fact, at the time that the army first took up its position near Vitoria, neither the prudent nor the bellicose expected to have to fight a battle there. Over the past month Wellington had so frequently forced the French to retreat by turning their right flank that they assumed he would do the same again—that he would move the bulk of his army towards the coast, aiming for their communication with Bayonne. They still believed that Wellington was a cautious general, who would never fight a general action if he could achieve his aims by other means.

Vitoria was important as a road junction; it was a valuable rallying point for Clausel and, perhaps, Foy; it could be a good starting point for an offensive operation. As a defensive position, it was far from ideal. If the French army were to stand at bay and fight for its life, far more favorable ground could be found within a day's march. It is impossible to believe that Joseph deliberately chose the banks of the Zadorra as the place at which he would make a supreme effort to save his crown.

The twentieth of June was a day of indecision. The French settled into their positions. News was received that Clausel was, or had been, at Logroño but nothing was known of his intentions. Marshall Jourdan took to his bed with a fever. The great convoy of refugees and stores had reached Vitoria on 18 June but it had not yet set out again for France. Some ascribed the delay to the king's wish to see something of the marquise de Montehermosa, who had traveled with it from Madrid. Another school of thought maintained that the king was sufficiently consoled by the presence of Nancy Derrieux, the wife of a French commissary. Spanish troops were found on the roads to Miranda and, towards evening, on the road leading northwest. Of the Anglo-Portuguese army there was little sign. The king had intended making a reconnaissance of his positions but, on hearing of Jourdan's illness, postponed it until the following day. Wrote Count Miot later,

> The town was crowded with carriages and vehicles of all sorts. A train of siege artillery, useless in field operations, encumbered the outskirts of the town and blocked the road to France, which, if we suffered a reverse, would be necessary for our retreat. No measures were taken to reconnoitre the road to Salvatierra and Pamplona which we should need if the main road was cut. No new dispositions were made,

no orders were issued. This silence and inaction led to the supposition that we were in a state of security. . . . Towards five o'clock the troops posted on the road from Vitoria to Bilbao were attacked. The firing was sharp but ceased at nightfall and a report was spread that we had been engaged only by a party of *guerillas*. Nobody, however, believes this. Retreat was again proposed, but it was now too late . . . the opportunity had been missed. We tried to persuade ourselves that General Clausel would join us before the allied army was upon us; there was nothing else that could be done. The convoy at last set out at 2 A.M. on 21st June. The artillery train had to stay where it was as there were not enough horses to draw it.[42]

With the convoy marched the 3,000 remaining men of Maucune's shaken division. It was a detachment that could ill be afforded.

Chapter 12

THE RECKONING

The whole thing is the king's fault.
NAPOLEON, 11 JULY 1813.

ON the morning of 21 June, King Joseph mounted his horse
at 4 A.M. and, accompanied by Marshal Jourdan, set out to
visit his troops. In Jourdan's opinion, "no report had been
received which led us to believe that an attack was imminent."[1]
The previous evening, recovered from his fever, the marshal
had written a dispatch to Paris explaining the difficulties of
the situation but showing clearly that he did not expect any
immediate trouble. Clausel, he hoped, would join the king on
the twenty-first and, if he did, all should be well. "The King
does not yet know what decision he will have to take: if
General Clausel does not arrive soon, we will have to retreat
westward into Navarre." Wellington, he believed, was undertaking a great encircling movement which might cut the main
road from Vitoria to San Sebastián and France. If that happened and Clausel had still not joined, the army would have
to fall back on the bad road to Salvatierra and Pamplona.[2]
Further strength was given to the belief that Wellington intended to outflank the position in a wide sweep when, during
the night of 20-21 June, a deserter came into the lines of the
Army of the South "and gave information that some hours

earlier Lord Wellington had set out with a large body of troops on the Bilbao road. The deserter was immediately sent to the King's headquarters."[3]

Vitoria lies toward the eastern end of an oval of undulating ground which is some twelve miles from east to west, seven miles from north to south. This plain is surrounded by hills which, though steep and rugged, are almost nowhere impassable to infantry and cavalry. They are also cut by passes through which run the many roads that meet at the city itself. Across the plain runs the river Zadorra, which enters by a defile at the northeastern part of the oval, passes the city about two miles on its northern side, and flows fairly steadily westward until it comes to a sharp knoll, the knoll of Arinez, after which it meanders sharply for some distance before taking a southwesterly course until it leaves the oval at its western end through a defile leading to the village of La Puebla. The main road runs through the same defiles as the river at either end of the oval and, in addition to a number of rough tracks, there were also roads leading south to Logroño, to Salvatierra, and north to Bilbao. The river itself was not very wide, about forty yards, but had steep banks and was fordable in many places if approached with caution. Fortescue describes it as "a merry brawling trout stream."[4] It is crossed by a number of bridges, and it is indicative of how little the French expected to be attacked that none of them had been demolished, although two to the north of the city had been barricaded.

After detaching Maucune's division, the king had about 57,000 combatant troops to defend the city. There were 46,000 infantry, 9,000 cavalry, and 104 field guns. Considering that the French were expecting Wellington to wheel right around Vitoria, behind the encircling hills, it is surprising that the main strength of the army was guarding against an attack from the southwest, through the defile of La Puebla. This was because it was only in this way that the plain could be approached without the enemy's having to force a crossing of the Zadorra. It might have been better to hold the narrow defile itself, but this would have meant extending the army too far—it is ten miles from the defile to Vitoria and the front line was therefore retired about three miles, with its right on the river and its left on the hills. This gap was held by three divisions of the Army of the South. The fourth division of this army was in reserve behind them, near the knoll of Arinez, and an independent brigade held the village of Subijana de Alava in front of the main line. A strong picket was stationed on the Point de Puebla, the end of the heights above the defile. From here could be seen an allied camp further downstream. The whole of this sector was entrusted to General Gazan as commander of the Army of the South. To support his position he had fifty-four guns.

Behind Gazan's army, to the east of the knoll of Arinez, were the two divisions of the Army of the Center, commanded by D'Erlon. To the west of the knoll was a cavalry brigade, which watched the far side of the river and the bridges around the village of Tres Puentes at the sharpest of the Zadorra's bends, where it swirled around a sharp mound topped by an ancient chapel. A third line was originally assigned to the two remaining divisions of the Army of Portugal under Reille. News that Spanish troops were on the Bilbao road, which ran north from the city, had caused a change of plan, and one of Reille's divisions had been thrown forward on to the north bank, supported by a brigade of cavalry. The other was held back on the river line north of Vitoria near the village of Gamarra Mayor. To their right, guarding the defile of Salinas, through which the Zadorra enters the oval plain, there were 2,000 Spanish troops, the remaining remnant of all those Spaniards the king had so trustingly enrolled, stiffened by about a thousand men of the Army of the North who had been collected in and around Vitoria. A cavalry brigade watched the southern road to Logroño and the ultimate reserve was the Royal Guard stationed, with the remaining cavalry, to the west of the city.

The king's reconnaissance on the morning of 21 June was

a leisurely, academic affair. Count Miot, who rode out an hour after Joseph and Jourdan had set off, found him on a ridge two miles from the city near the hamlet of Zuazo de Alava. This was the position held, in the original dispositions, by the Army of Portugal. The command party had not yet viewed the actual positions of any of their forward troops. Even the Army of the Center was still more than a mile ahead of them. The king had, however, decided that the positions which his army had been occupying for thirty-six hours were the wrong ones. Certainly the position was a strange one. Five or six miles separated the armies of the South and of Portugal, and they had their backs to each other. There was in addition a long section of the intermediate flank which was protected by little more than the dubious obstacle represented by the river Zadorra. It struck him that the army would be more concentrated and less vulnerable if Gazan was brought back to the Zuazo position, where it would be close to Reille's left flank and where the Army of the Center could act as a reserve to both, with only a short march to the support of either of them. "The three corps, being more concentrated, would have been able to give mutual support rapidly and the commander in chief would have been able to keep a general oversight over the whole of the more contracted battlefield." Such was Jourdan's view, and he added, "These new dispositions would have been taken up the previous day, had it not been for the Marshal's illness."[5] It was decided to send an aide-de-camp to Gazan so that the redeployment of the Army of the South could be discussed.

Gazan had other concerns on his mind than a move which the king seemed to regard as little more than a staff college exercise. "At 5 A.M. much movement was seen in the enemy camp. Troops could be seen forming up and tents were being struck. I at once warned the King and he immediately came to the right of my line and observed the enemy movements. Shortly afterwards General Maransin [whose brigade held the advanced post in the village of Subijana] reported that a strong column had reached La Puebla and was moving up the main road towards Arinez while a smaller column was moving towards the crest of [the heights of La Puebla]."[6]

Joseph galloped from his position in the rear to a knoll in a bend of the river across the bridge from the village of Nanclares. This was the extreme left of the Army of the South's main line and was held by Leval's division. On his right the king could see large masses of British infantry and cavalry moving up on the opposite bank. Shortly after his arrival, a whole division could be seen drawn up near the village of Nanclares. Meanwhile, Gazan was taking steps to halt the advance from La Puebla. Concerned that Spanish troops could be seen scaling the heights on the east of the road and driving in a picket of *voltigeurs* which was stationed on the crest, he ordered Maransin to evacuate Subijana and march up the heights on his left. Not wishing to leave Subijana undefended, he sent orders to Daricau, commanding the center division of his line, to send forward a brigade to occupy the village. Daricau, however, reacted slowly, and when the brigade he sent forward approached Subijana, they found redcoats in possession. The British were indeed astonished to find the village undefended except by artillery firing from the rear. "The enemy opened on us with fourteen pieces of artillery, from their position, as we moved down, but with little effect. I could never persuade myself that they would resign so important a post as the village without a struggle; and when we got close to it, and began to find the ground difficult and intersected with walls, I expected every moment to be saluted with a murderous discharge of musquetry, and to see them issue forth; and I had prepared my men to look for, and disregard, such an attack. Not a soul, however, was in the village."[7]

Nor was Maransin in time to recapture the heights overlooking the defile. As soon as his battalions were seen to leave Subijana moving towards the Point de Puebla, a British brigade swung off to their right to support the Spaniards already on the heights. There was some bitter fighting on the crest but although the allied advance eastward was checked, Maransin was unable to dispossess them of their commanding position. The battle had begun badly. The allies had secured the defile and established themselves on the heights. It was now open to them to drive eastwards along the crest, outflanking the Army of the Center and reaching Vitoria almost unopposed.

The idea that they might do so, while thrusting another column at the city up the Logroño road, became implanted into the minds of Joseph and Jourdan. The allied troops who had so far appeared on both banks of the Zadorra, those that advanced from La Puebla and those who could be seen around Nanclares, could not be estimated at more than three or four Anglo-Portuguese divisions. Wellington was known to have eight such divisions,* apart from a number of independent Portuguese brigades and an unknown number of Spanish formations. Where was the rest of the British infantry? Could it be that Wellington, who over the last month had so consistently turned the French right, had changed his tactics and was now marching round their left? Jourdan became obsessed with the idea that this was the case.

General Gazan, whose concern was naturally with the enemy who were attacking and threatening his own divisions, did not agree. While the fighting around Subijana and on the heights of La Puebla was going on, he was constantly glancing over his right shoulder at "all the troops massed in rear of the village of Nanclares, from whence a party moved to Villodas [two miles further upstream] but did not attempt anything. This inaction of the enemy force on my right gave me the idea that the attack on my left was not the real threat and that it was made only in order to make us weaken our right by moving forces to meet it. I suggested this to the King but the idea was hardly considered. Marshal Jourdan announced openly and publicly that all these movements were feints to which no attention should be paid and that if we lost the battle it would be because the mountains on the left of the Zadorra remained in enemy hands."[8]

* The French had no way of knowing that Wellington had left the Sixth Division at Medina de Pomar.

With this in mind, Gazan was told to send his reserve division, Villatte's, up to reinforce Maransin on the heights. At the same time, D'Erlon was ordered to send one of his two divisions, that of Cassagne, to the eastern end of the La Puebla heights to watch the road from Logroño.[9] As a result of these moves, the western approach to Vitoria, which had originally been covered by three and a half divisions forward with three divisions in reserve, were left to the care of three forward and one reserve divisions.

Nothing could have suited Wellington better than the French redeployment. He had planned an elaborate encircling movement, aiming to sweep around the French right and cut the road to France northeast of Vitoria. To do this he had available 75,000 men with 75 guns. His cavalry, at 8,000 sabres, was somewhat fewer than the king's, but his infantry was distinctly stronger, 63,000 to 46,000, although some 7,000 of them were Spaniards. In order to hold the main French strength at the western end of the Vitoria plain while the main road was cut at the eastern end, the allied army was divided into four columns. On the right Rowland Hill commanded one Anglo-Portuguese, one Portuguese, and one Spanish infantry division and two cavalry brigades, a total of some 30,000 men. His first objective was the defile of La Puebla and the heights to the east of it. It was his troops who had engaged Gazan's men and taken Subijana early in the morning. On their left, across the Zadorra, was the right center column under Wellington's personal direction. It comprised two Anglo-Portuguese divisions and four cavalry brigades, 13,500 infantry and 4,500 horse. These were the troops whom the French could see advancing to the village of Nanclares, the movement which Jourdan believed to be a feint.

Beyond Wellington's column was that of Lord Dalhousie, 14,000 infantry in two Anglo-Portuguese divisions, whose task was to march over the rocky mass of Monte Arato and come down to the river line east of the village of Tres Puentes, where the river ran almost straight from east to west. On the extreme left was Lt. Gen. Sir Thomas Graham, a sixty-five-

year-old Scot, who led 30,000 men—one British and one
Anglo-Portuguese division, a small Spanish division, two
Portuguese brigades, and two British cavalry brigades. Graham's orders were to march right around Monte Arato and
to advance southwards on Vitoria by the Bilbao road. He was
enjoined to "turn his whole attention to cutting off the retreat
of the enemy by the great road which goes from Vitoria by
Tolosa and Irun to France."[10]

This was a complicated plan, and one which, to have total
success, depended on the exact timing of the movements of
two columns, the left center and left, which were out of contact with each other and with Wellington himself. Both columns were liable to delays due to long marches over bad
roads. In the event both Dalhousie and Graham were later
than Wellington had hoped, and although Hill on the right
had made an excellent start to the day by his advance through
the La Puebla defile, he was ordered to halt after the capture
of Subijana until there was some sign of the arrival of the
two lefthand columns. The ensuing lull, broken only by heavy
firing around the Point de Puebla as Gazan's reinforcements
tried to drive the allies off the heights, helped to convince
Jourdan that the movements of the allied right and right
center columns were merely feints to draw French attention
away from a real attack from the south, up the Logroño–
Vitoria road.

The immobility of Wellington's right center column was
not, in fact, part of his plan. He had intended to pass them
across the river by the bridge of Nanclares. This was found
to be heavily garrisoned by Leval's division on the right of
Gazan's front line, and Wellington did not judge it worthwhile to incur heavy losses by storming it. He next considered
passing a division across at Villodas, the next bridge upstream.
Gazan had remarked that troops had been moved towards it,
but again Wellington had decided that it would cost too much
to force a crossing before the French reserves were drawn
away by the arrival of Dalhousie and Graham.

It was not until after midday that firing broke out to the

north of Vitoria, announcing that Graham was pressing in on Reille. Almost at the same time a peasant reported to Wellington's staff that the bridge at Tres Puentes, near the point of the sharp bend in the river, was intact and unguarded. Wellington immediately ordered Sir James Kempt's brigade of the light division to cross and establish itself on the far bank. They

> moved off by threes at a rapid pace, along a very uneven and circuitous path, (which was concealed from the observation of the French by high rocks), and reached the narrow bridge which crossed the river. The First Rifles led the way, and the whole brigade passed at a run, with firelocks and rifles ready cocked, and ascended a steep road of fifty yards, at the top of which was an old chapel. We had no sooner cleared it than we observed a column of the French on the [knoll of Arinez] and commanding a bird's eye view of us. . . . Two round shot now came among us; the second severed the head of our bold guide, the Spanish peasant. Sir James Kempt expressed much surprise at our critical position and at our not being molested, and sent his a.d.c. at speed across the river for the 15th Hussars, who came forward singly and at a gallop up the steep path, and dismounted behind our centre. Some French dragoons, coolly and at a slow pace, came to within about fifty yards of us to examine our strength but a few shots from the Rifles caused them to decamp.[11]

> Scarcely the sound of a shot from any direction struck the ear, and we were in momentary expectation of being immolated; and, as I looked over the bank, I could see *El Rey* Joseph, surrounded by at least five thousand men, within five hundred yards of us. The reason he did not attack us is inexplicable.[12]

El Rey Joseph was in no position to attack Kempt's 2,500 infantry and Hussars in their exposed position. With Cas-

sagne's division of the Army of the Center marching uselessly
away to counter an imaginary threat from the Logroño road,
the only available reserve was the second division of the same
army, Darmagnac's. It was clear that this could not be spared,
since hardly had Kempt's men appeared at Tres Puentes when
Dalhousie's column started to make its appearance over the
shoulder of Monte Arato and began to take its place along the
river on Kempt's left. From north of Vitoria, the sounds of
battle drew nearer as Graham's men forced the Army of
Portugal back to the river line. Worse still was the news that
northwest of the city, Longa's Spaniards from Graham's column had crossed the river in the face of their *afrancesado*
compatriots and had cut the main road to France. Apart from
this setback, Reille's men were containing all Graham's attacks, but they were under increasing strain as the superior
allied numbers were deployed against them.

The loss of the bridge of Tres Puentes was the turning point
of the battle. It gave Wellington the ability to pass two
columns, his own and Dalhousie's, across the river in the rear
of the Army of the South. It could only be a question of time
before Gazan's position became untenable. In that general's
words,

> Faced with this new situation, the King ordered me
> to break off all attacks on the enemy and to with-
> draw the Army of the South to a position in the rear
> which would be shown to me. Such a movement
> would be very difficult to carry out as two thirds of
> the army was engaged with the enemy and it must
> take a long time to send orders to General Villatte,
> who was up in the mountains and far in advance of
> the line which the other divisions were holding. I
> pointed this out to His Majesty. I told him that, if
> the attacks which the enemy were making across
> the Zadorra could be held, I thought I could be
> answerable for holding my present position. His
> answer was that we must retreat. I therefore set

about rallying the troops and giving orders for the divisions to fall back in succession until they reached a position which Marshal Jourdan would point out to me.[13]

The indefinite goal given for Gazan's retreat was the final error which made a crushing defeat for the French inevitable. The Army of the South fell back in very good order, but it was never possible to bring them into line with the divisions of the Army of the Center which Joseph had intended to take station on Gazan's right. It was scarcely to be wondered at that D'Erlon's men could not stand their ground. Hurriedly formed and already exhausted by useless countermarching, the two divisions of the Army of the Center were faced by three and a half divisions of Wellington's best troops (Third, Fourth, Light and part of Seventh), which poured over the river on either side of Tres Puentes. Behind them rode Wellington's cavalry reserve. Gazan, hard pressed by Hill's three divisions, found that "the right of my line was being continually outflanked. Not receiving the further orders to take up a position of which the King had spoken to me and the enemy being almost at the gates of Vitoria, I was forced to continue falling back."[14]

The retreat of the armies of the South and Center laid open the flank of the Army of Portugal. Reille's men had fought magnificently against Graham's greatly superior strength, and for hours denied the allies the vital bridge at Gamarra Mayor. It was not until their left was exposed that they gave way and, still in good order, formed the rear guard of the whole French force. The infantry of the other two armies, who had suffered more in morale than in casualties, streamed away eastward on the only road open to them, a rough track leading to Salvatierra and Pamplona. As a contemporary Englishman wrote, "The soldiers were not half beaten, yet never was a victory more complete."[15]

In Vitoria, the chaos was indescribable. Some wagons had upset, blocking the streets, and a vast mass of guns, limbers, carts, and carriages was jammed immovably in and around the town. Unable to get his artillery through, Gazan ordered his gunners to cut the traces and get away on the draft horses, leaving their pieces to add to the confusion. Into this scene of chaos rode the British Hussar brigade.

King Joseph and his staff left the field as soon as it became obvious that Vitoria could not be held. Unaccountably, the king elected to travel in his carriage and, with his household, set off up the Salvatierra road. "Not only," wrote Miot, "had the road not been repaired, it had not even been reconnoitred. We knew only that Salvatierra lay to the east of Vitoria, and we could find no better guide than a member of the Household who had been born at Salvatierra, and who offered to lead us. Just as we were setting off, the enemy appeared to the left of the town, which had been left undefended by the retreat of the Army of the South, and a strong body of hussars charged round the plain to the north of Vitoria. This unexpected attack terrified the crowd near our carriages and they fled in all directions. Dreadful confusion reigned. The gunners cut their traces, many of the infantry left their ranks and sought safety in flight."[16]

The appearance of the Hussars brought all movement to a halt, and as Joseph sat in his carriage, two British officers* galloped up and, not recognizing the exalted occupant, fired their pistols through the carriage window. The king hurled himself out of the door on the other side and, scrambling onto a troop horse, took shelter behind the light cavalry of his guard which General Jamin brought up to his rescue. Then he rode off up the Salvatierra road.

Fortunately for the French, the Salvatierra road was narrow and difficult. Two French regiments, the Fifteenth Dragoons and the Third Hussars, were sufficient to hold back the mass of the British cavalry who could not deploy. The ardor of the pursuers was reduced by the prospect of unlimited booty in and around Vitoria. "Such a scene has seldom been witnessed," wrote an eyewitness.

* Capt. Henry Wyndham, Fourteenth Light Dragoons, and Lieutenant Lord Worcester, Tenth Hussars.

Cannon, overturned carriages, broken-down wag-
gons, forsaken tumbrils, wounded soldiers, civilians,
women, children, dead horses and mules, absolutely
covered the face of the country; while the inhabitants
and others had diligently commenced the work of
pillage. Seldom on any previous occasion had so rich
a field presented itself. To the accumulated plunder
of Andalusia were added the collections made by the
other armies; the personal baggage of the King, *four-
gons* having inscribed on them in large characters,
"*Domaine Exterieur de S. M. l'Empereur*"; wagons
of every description, and a military chest containing
a large sum recently received from France for payment of the troops, but which had not yet been
distributed; jewels, pictures, embroidery, silks, everything that was costly and portable, seemed to have
been assiduously transported, adding to the unmili-
tary state of these encumbered armies.[17]

Monsieur Thibault, the king's treasurer, tried to defend
the royal strongboxes containing one hundred thousand
dollars and was shot dead for his pains. Sergeant Costello of
the Ninety-fifth admitted to making away with more than
one thousand pounds and there were many who did better.
Jourdan's marshal's baton was found amongst his baggage.
One soldier broke off the gold eagles at either end; another
kept the staff itself. Eventually both parts were retrieved and
the whole presented to Wellington.* For those who could not
reward themselves with coin or plate, there were dozens of
Spanish ladies who had accompanied their French lovers and
now, afraid to fall into the hands of their compatriots, were
only too anxious to find themselves a British protector. "The
fact is, monseigneur," said a captured French officer to Well-

---

* Wellington sent the baton to the prince regent, who wrote back, "You
have sent me amongst the trophies of your unrivalled fame, the staff of a
French marshal, and I send you in return that of England." This caused
some consternation in the War Office, as no design for a British field
marshal's baton existed.

ington, "that you had an army, while ours was a mobile brothel."[18]

More to the point, the allies captured 151 brass guns on traveling carriages, 415 caissons, 14,249 rounds of ammunition, 1,973,400 musket ball cartridges, 40,688 pounds of gunpowder, 56 forage wagons, and 44 forge carts.

It was eleven o'clock that night before the king reached Salvatierra. He was having supper with O'Farrill, his minister of war, Count D'Erlon, and Count Miot, when Jourdan, who had become separated from the royal party, arrived. "As he entered, he said, 'Well, gentlemen, you would have a battle and it appears that we have lost it.' Then he sat down to share our meagre meal and nothing more was said."[19]

Considered in terms of casualties, Vitoria was not a major action. The cost to the French in dead, wounded, and prisoners was less than 8,500. The allies lost rather more than 5,000. A month earlier at Bautzen in Germany, Napoleon had won a mere tactical victory at a cost of 13,500 casualties against 20,000 inflicted on his Russian and Prussian adversaries. Vitoria was decisive. After it, the French had no alternative but to retreat into France. Apart from a gallant rear guard who held off Wellington's rather unenthusiastic pursuit, the rest of the army was little better than a partially armed mob of fugitives. So little were they under discipline that the French governor of Pamplona shut the gates of the city against them for fear of the outrages they might commit and the inroads they would make into the garrison's stock of food. By the end of the month, the French army was on the line of the Pyrenees and the Bidassoa. There the king's part of the army was joined by Foy, who, with his two divisions, conducted a most skillful retreat, picking up the coastal garrisons on his way. Clausel almost marched to Vitoria twenty-four hours too late. On the afternoon of 22 June, his main body was at Trevino, less than ten miles from the battlefield. There he heard from peasants that there had been a great battle on the previous day which the French had lost. Knowing no further details, he sent forward his cavalry to discover the situation. They found Wellington's rear guard in firm possession and no sign of the French. Clausel therefore retreated hastily and, evading an allied attempt to cut him off, eventually reached safety in France by way of Saragossa and the central Pyrenean pass of Jaca. Thus, at long last, King Joseph had united under his command the whole Army of Spain, about 85,000 men present and under arms. Unfortunately, all that remained of the kingdom of Spain were three beleaguered towns—Pamplona, San Sebastián, and Santona.*

Important as were the effects of the allied victory in Spain, it was almost more significant on France's eastern front. The battles of the early summer had decided nothing. There had been victories which Napoleon's depleted resources of manpower could not afford and which did nothing serious to bring Prussia and Russia to wish for peace. Both sides, however, were in urgent need of a breathing space, and on 4 June Napoleon agreed to a suspension of hostilities, the Armistice of Pleichwitz, originally intended to last until the end of June but later extended. "I decided on it," he wrote, "for two reasons; my lack of cavalry, which stops me from striking effective blows, and the hostile attitude of Austria. . . . It will, I think, last throughout June and July and . . . if I can, I shall wait until September to strike the decisive blow. By then I hope to be able to crush my enemies."[20] The time the emperor had bought with this armistice he used to build up his army in the east and in complicated diplomatic maneuvers intended to keep Austria neutral. His enemies similarly built up their strength and used every endeavor to persuade Austria into the war on their side. On 30 June, the news of Vitoria reached the allied camp, and Prince Metternich, the Austrian chancellor, was violently woken in the middle of the night by a colleague who burst into his bedroom crying, "*Le roi Joseph est f— en Espagne.*" Mobilization was set in hand at once,

---

* Sucher still held Aragon and Catalonia and had indeed just frustrated a very inept Anglo-Sicilian attempt on Tarragona, but these provinces were now part of France, according to the emperor's decree.

under cover of renewed diplomatic activity. On 12 August, with her army fully ready, Austria declared war on France. The united armies of Austria, Prussia, Russia, and Sweden moved forward. The road led to Leipzig and Paris.

Meanwhile, Joseph was making the best of a bad job and was establishing his army for the defense of the French frontier. Personally he was in the situation that had become habitual to him, despairing and penurious. He wrote to his wife,

> I do not think that affairs in Spain can be re-established except by a general peace. I am staying here because the frontier is in danger but as soon as the first terror wears off and the defense is organised I shall be useless here and I want to retire either to Mortefontaine or to the south of France. I cannot see that there is anything for me to do here once the Emperor has taken the appropriate steps. Morover my Household is still costing me 300,000 francs a month and I have not a *sou* to pay them with; since the disastrous events of 21st June they have been living on whatever money my officers and my servants happened to have in their pockets. To give you an idea of the situation, I must tell you that since the murder of Mons. Thibauld, I have had no money except a single gold napoleon. When I retire to Mortefontaine, I shall be able to live on my allowance as a French prince and, if the Emperor wishes to make over to me some hundreds of thousands of francs, I shall be able to make some slight provision for all my dependents.[21]

On the day that the king was writing to Queen Julie, there was nothing further from the emperor's mind than making some hundreds of thousands of francs available to his brother. This was the day, 1 July, that he received the first news of Vitoria. It was only an incomplete account which reached him at his headquarters in Dresden. Jourdan's full report on the battle was delayed in reaching Paris, and the minister of war could only forward a quick note from Joseph saying that 21 June had been an unfortunate day, "on which the French army, attacked in its position by forces double its own, having inflicted casualties on the enemy equal to those it had suffered itself, had had to retreat on Salvatierra. On this day I think that the losses in killed and wounded in the two armies were equal; but we had to leave behind almost all the artillery and equipment of all kinds. Only the gun teams were saved."[22] Incomplete as this information was, it was enough to make Napoleon decide that Joseph must be replaced. Marshal Soult was in Dresden and received orders to set out for Spain before ten o'clock that evening with a commission as the emperor's lieutenant general in Spain and orders to "take all necessary measures to re-establish my affairs in Spain and to preserve Pamplona and San Sebastián."[23] He was to have the command not only of the French troops but of the Royal Guard and the Spanish troops.

At the same time, the emperor wrote tersely to his brother, "I have decided that it would be proper to nominate Marshal Soult, Duke of Dalmatia, as my lieutenant general and commander in chief of all my armies in Spain and in the Pyrenees. You will hand over command to him. It is my wish that you, yourself, should stay at Burgos, San Sebastián, Pamplona or Bayonne, according to circumstances. You will put your Guard and the armed Spaniards under the Marshal's orders. It is my wish that you do not interfere with the affairs of my armies."[24]

Soult was to travel incognito; he was to spend no more than twelve hours in Paris and to see no one but the minister of war and Cambacérès, the archchancellor and effective head of the regency. "I do not," wrote Napoleon, "intend that the Empress* should be told about this. None of this is to appear in the newspapers."[25] The king's whereabouts were also to be kept a secret. "Under no circumstances may he go to Paris. If he is already at Bayonne he should stay there. If by chance he

---

* The empress was titular head of the regency.

has already passed that town he should go secretly to Morte-fontaine and stay there without seeing anyone. No Spaniard and no officer in the King of Spain's service will be permitted to cross the Garonne. All refugees will be kept together in some town to be nominated."[26]

The emperor had cast Joseph for the scapegoat. To the minister of war he wrote, "All the stupidities which have been committed in Spain stem from my misplaced kindness to the king. He not only does not know how to command an army, he does not even know enough to leave it to be commanded by someone else."[27] "I blame him for everything that has happened in Spain for the last five years. He has shown neither military talent nor administrative ability. . . . [He] must not blind himself to my opinion of him."[28] "It is all his fault. One can tell from the English accounts how stupidly our army was commanded. . . . Of course the king is not a soldier, but he must be responsible for his defects and his greatest defect was to follow a profession which he does not understand. If the army was short of one man, it was a general. If it had a man too many, it was the king."[29]

On receiving the first accounts of Vitoria, the minister of war had written to Joseph a letter in which he remarked that "it will be distressing to the Emperor to reflect that the enemy owes nothing of his success to superiority in numbers but rather to the way in which they have been commanded. In the four armies which Your Majesty commands there are, according to the latest returns, 118,828 men under arms. Lord Wellington can hardly put half as many in the field, even if Spanish troops are included. Thus I can find no explanation for the phrase in Your Majesty's letter which says that the battle was fought against forces twice as great as your own, and the Emperor may well feel that he has been misled by people who are either ill-informed or evil-minded."[30]

For this offensive implication, the minister received an imperial rebuke, but not for insolence. "I am not happy with your letter to the king. There are too many compliments in it. When one of my armies has been lost by ineptitude, I do not have to take the public into my confidence, but at least there is no reason to pay compliments. Rather the reverse. The whole thing is the king's fault. He does not know how to command and has not sent a report. . . . His conduct has caused nothing but trouble for my army for the last five years. It is time to make an end."[31] Even if Joseph had successfully counter-attacked, he was not to be forgiven. "If the king has re-taken Vitoria, things can be handled more gently. . . . If he has re-established my affairs in Spain, my intention is unaltered. He must leave the army which he is quite incapable of commanding."[32]

However angry the emperor was with his brother, he had, as well he might, some feelings of guilt. It was, after all, no one's fault but his own that Joseph had gone to Spain, and no one but Napoleon had consistently refused or ignored the king's repeated requests to be allowed to abdicate. It was scarcely Joseph's fault that his total military experience before going to Spain was a few weeks as a colonel of infantry at Boulogne. Napoleon was prepared, even in July 1813, to take a limited share of the blame. "In the final analysis, I do not pretend it is not all my fault. If, as I had considered doing when I left Paris [in April 1813], I had sent Marshal Soult to take command at Valladolid all this would never have happened."[33] From the emperor, it was a generous admission.

He was also prepared, after six weeks had elapsed, to give the French public some idea of what had happened. "It would be advisable to let the public know about affairs in Spain. Nothing must be said about Vitoria or about the king. The first announcement to be put in *Le Moniteur* should read as follows: 'The Emperor has appointed Marshal Soult as his lieutenant general commanding in Spain. The Marshal took command on 12th July and immediately made dispositions to march against the English who are besieging Pamplona and San Sebastián."[34]

The omission of the king's name from this bulletin was less to save him from public obloquy than to protect the reputation of the dynasty. It was, however, a kindness on Napoleon's part to arrange that his old friend and valued adviser, Senator Roederer, break the news of his supercession to Joseph before the arrival of either Soult or the emperor's decree. His mission was to induce the king to hand over the command to the marshal without creating a public scene and to stay "at Pamplona or San Sebastián should the military situation permit and, in any case, to come no further into France than Bayonne."[35]

Roederer reached Bayonne at midday on 11 July and went at once to the royal headquarters at St. Pée, near St. Jean-de-Luz. The king was out visiting his army when Roederer arrived, but he was able to talk to the civil and military officers of the household and headquarters, who already knew of Soult's appointment, news having reached them through an officer of the ordnance service who had received a letter from his chief in Paris. Although they were naturally worried about their own futures, the officials were, in general, pleased at Soult's appointment. "They seemed impressed by his talents and praised his firmness which they hoped would make the generals obey him and put an end to the anarchy which reigned in the army."[36]

At length the king returned to St. Pée, received Roederer with "much benevolence," and took him into his study.

> I told him the object of my mission. He told me that he had known of Soult's appointment to the command since the previous evening. He did not seem greatly upset and even less surprised. It seemed to me that his experience of war had changed many of the ideas he had expressed to me in earlier days. He acknowledged that he lacked much necessary military knowledge and spoke of himself with much modesty. He observed, however, that even if the battle of Vitoria had cost the army its baggage, its artillery and something of its honor, at least it had cost it nothing or almost nothing in men or in horses, even in artillery horses, although the guns themselves were lost.

When we had been talking for about half an hour, an aide-de-camp from the Minister of War was announced bringing the Emperor's orders and a despatch from the Minister. The King had him brought in and told me to stay. The a.d.c. gave His Majesty the despatches which he took and signed to the officer to retire. I stayed alone with him.

The King opened the letter and read it very slowly. Then he re-read it twice, went back several times to different passages and then, for a long time, had his eyes fixed on the paper without reading, reflecting on what he had just said to me and on what he must do next. At least he gave the letter to me to read. Having read it, I observed that, in substance, the letter was the same as the message I had been instructed to give him verbally, with the difference that the Minister's letter was an official one for the King of Spain, while my mission was to the Emperor's brother and was intended to allay anything in the letter which might vex the King in the arrangements which the Emperor thought necessary for the defense of the frontiers of France and for the safety of the army as well as being in the interests of the King and for the retention of his crown.

Then the King burst out. He said that Marshal Soult, who had dared to accuse him of coming to an understanding with the English, had evidently succeeded in getting his lies believed and that he was coming to arrest him. The order to stay at Pamplona, San Sebastián or Bayonne and, in particular, the order to hand over command of his Guard, already made him Soult's prisoner. If all the Emperor wanted him to do was to resign the crown why should he not retire quietly to Mortefontaine. He wished for nothing but to live privately with the Queen and their children. He was disillusioned with grandeur. All he wished was retirement and obscurity. He would even lay aside all the rights and dignities of a French prince if that was the Emperor's wish.

The King added that he certainly did not fear an enquiry into his conduct, even by the most severe judges. He was, indeed, anxious for such an enquiry. What he could not support was the idea of being Soult's prisoner.

I tried, uselessly, to explain that this was not intended. The King merely included me in his suspicions and seemed to read the most odious imaginable motives into my coming. I did not try to continue the conversation and let several intervals of silence elapse. At last calm returned. Gently the King challenged some of the remarks I had made and I replied that the Emperor had not made Soult his Lieutenant in Spain because of his offensive conduct to the King but in spite of it. The appointment had been made because of the Marshal's ability, his experience, his knowledge of Spain and of the authority which his record gave him over the generals. That, on the contrary, the King, by the gentleness of his character, by his very royalty which seemed to put him under an obligation to the French officers who risked their lives for his throne, prevented him from being sufficiently severe to keep the generals under control. I told him that the French troops I had met on the road had all paid tribute to bravery which he had shown at Vitoria but that their opinion, like that in France, in the army and even among his own officers, favored Soult's appointment and that, in consequence, he could not hope to succeed by putting his own distress against an arrangement that had been determined only by a most grave situation and most important considerations. I assured him that the idea that he was to be arrested was only an illusion. The Royal Guard had only been put under the Marshal's orders because it was a unit needed by the army, being élite troops drawn from the French army. Furthermore, I pointed out that there was no evidence that the Emperor wished to deprive him of the Spanish crown. It seemed more probable that the fact that the Emperor did not wish him to leave Spain indicated that he did not wish him to go far from Spain so that it should not be thought that he had abdicated. . . .

As soon as the King turned his mind to the serious considerations which had led to the Marshal's appointment and stopped thinking about the personal slight which he believed himself to have suffered, he came back to reason, to his natural affection for the Emperor and to his confidence in him. He said to me, "I was distressed by the appointment of the Marshal but, by talking so patiently to me you have made me see that the Minister of War's letter was not an indication that my throne is to be taken away. I quite understand that I must hand over command of the army. No one would obey me. There are things about war I do not understand. I have told the Emperor in a recent despatch that the army needs a leader." He talked in this way for some time, reverting occasionally to the idea of being Soult's prisoner. He asked me if I thought he would be allowed to go for a few days to Barèges or Bagnères to take the waters, whether he might buy or rent an estate near Bayonne where he could spend the summer with his family. I left the King about ten o'clock at night.[37]

Next morning the king was anxious to be away. "The night has dissipated his gloomy prognostications. He was calm. He remarked that he was impatient for Marshal Soult to arrive. He had put the appointment of the Marshal in the Orders for the Day, which he showed me. At that moment it was announced that Soult had reached Bayonne."[38]

The meeting between Joseph and Soult was cold and formal. The king handed over his military papers and announced that he intended to establish himself at the chateau of Saint Esprit on the outskirts of Bayonne. That afternoon he reported to the emperor that he had handed over command, adding, "I would wish to return to the bosom of my family. I need repose after so many tribulations. Here I am surrounded by wretched Spaniards for whom I can do nothing; by men I am forced to turn away."[39]

Soult, running true to form, celebrated his triumph over his old enemy, the king, by publishing an order of the day directly critical of the king's conduct of the campaign. Referring to the allied advance, he averred that, from the French point of view,

> With well-stocked fortresses on his front and supporting his rear, an able general, having the confidence of his troops, could by choosing good positions have faced and defeated this motley adversary. Unfortunately at this critical moment timid and vascillating counsels prevailed. The fortresses were abandoned or demolished. Hasty and ill-directed marches gave the enemy confidence and an army of veterans, even though weak in numbers, but great in every military virtue, which had fought, bled and triumphed in every province in Spain, saw with indignation that its laurels were being tarnished and that it was being forced to abandon its conquests, the trophies of many a hard-fought day. When, at last, the indignant voice of the troops brought this dishonorable flight to a halt, their commander, moved with shame, gave way to the general demand to offer battle near Vitoria. Could it be doubted that after this general enthusiasm and this fine display of honor, that a victory would be obtained by any general worthy of his troops?
>
> Soldiers! I share your grief, your sorrow, your indignation. I know that the real blame belongs not to you but to others. It is up to you to put things

right. I have assured the Emperor of your bravery and zeal. It is his intention that the enemy should be driven back from these mountains, from whence he proudly looks out over our fertile valleys, and that he should be pursued to the other side of the Ebro. Let us start our victories at Vitoria. Let us celebrate the Emperor's fête in that city.[40]

On 28 July, five weeks after Vitoria, Soult advanced his reorganized army to within sight of Pamplona. On 1 August, he was back in France, having lost 13,000, 5,000 more than Joseph had lost on 21 June.

EPILOGUE

NAPOLEON wrote that he blamed Joseph for "everything that has happened in Spain for the last five years," and claimed that "he has shown neither military talent nor administrative ability."[1] Undoubtedly Joseph had made mistakes, not least during the Vitoria campaign, but nothing he could have done could have saved his crown. He had been put into an impossible situation and the outcome was inevitable. He was the wrong man for the job, and, although he did his best under intolerable circumstances, he could not be expected to stand against his three adversaries—the obstinate pride of the Spanish nation, the skill and determination of Wellington's army, and the irresponsible and ill-informed meddling of the Emperor Napoleon. In the last analysis, the faults committed in Spain were Napoleon's faults. He put his brother into a situation which would have taxed the talents of a genius and proceeded to thwart every effort he made to make a success of the task he had been given.

Napoleon was not under the illusion that his brother was a genius. After the war, in St. Helena, he remarked that, "Joseph has intelligence but he dislikes work. He knows nothing of soldiering, although he pretends to. He knows nothing and he loves pleasure."[2] This had been his opinion at least since the turn of the century, and it must be asked why, holding such a view, he cast Joseph as king of Spain. The answer must be that he had wholly misunderstood the role Joseph was to play.

The emperor had been under the illusion that the Spaniards were so disgusted by the rule of the Bourbons that they would welcome a gracious, kindly, liberal-minded alternative monarch who could bring them reform without revolution. For such a role Joseph would have been ideal. He had many of the qualifications for a reliable constitutional figurehead and a taste for the ceremonial side of kingship, but the Spaniards wanted nothing of the kind. Much as they disliked the government of Charles IV and the prince of the peace, the overwhelming majority infinitely preferred native Spanish incompetence to any foreign-imposed utopia. They were, moreover, prepared to give their lives and their property to avoid any such imposition. War to the knife was no empty phrase in Spain, and early in his reign Joseph discovered that his own talents were not those which the Spanish people required. Nor had he the mental toughness needed to implement his brother's policy. He was in the age-old dilemma of a liberal faced with the real world.

Although he quickly realized that his ideas were incompatible with the emperor's designs, he remained optimistic about the extent to which the Spaniards would have accepted him had he been able to implement his own enlightened plans. His Spanish adherents included the most talented and competent men of their generation. They shared the king's ideals and gave him the illusion that "the Spaniards would lay down their weapons, they would fall at my feet, if they could know what was in my heart."[3] He would not realize that it was impossible to carry out a liberal reconstruction of the whole fabric of the state in a country which was having to be subdued by a large and increasingly rapacious army of foreign troops. He clung to the belief that it was the depredations of the French armies rather than the irreconcilability of the Spaniards that made his task impossible. His repeated offers of abdication were protests against French policy rather than admission of failure to win Spanish acceptance.

Epilogue

Before 1809 was out, it was clear to Napoleon that his brother could never be a satisfactory king of Spain. His gentle approach could not win over a significant amount of Spanish support, nor was it in his character to apply the harsh measures that Napoleon recommended. Why, therefore, did the emperor not sanction Joseph's abdication? Part of the reason was his concern for the prestige of the dynasty. The Bonaparte family, Napoleon always excepted, did not shine at kingship. Lucien had fled the continent rather than rule as an imperial puppet. Louis had crept away in the night from his Dutch capital and sought asylum in Austria. Jerome kept his Westphalian throne but was a figure of fun to all but his creditors. It would seriously tarnish the imperial image if Joseph, the eldest brother, was publicily admitted to be a failure.

This, however, was only a part of the story. The larger part of the reason was a mixture of imperial indecision and inattention. Napoleon admitted as early as November 1808 that he had made a serious miscalculation over Spain. "I thought that troops would only be required to maintain public order and to garrison the fortresses."[4] He had miscalculated the temper of the Spanish people, the natural resources of the country, the number and quality of the forces needed to subdue it, the constancy, if not the skill, of the Spanish armies, the determination and skill of the British intervention, the amount of military support that Spain and Britain would be able to obtain from Portugal. The fury and ubiquity of the guerrillas never entered his calculations at all. Not later than November 1810, when General Foy brought him the news that Masséna could not take Lisbon and drive Wellington into the sea, it was clear that he had become involved in an adventure that showed every sign of ending in disaster. The more he considered the Spanish imbroglio in terms of troops, money, and prestige, the more horrifying the picture became. And so he put the whole business out of his mind for every moment that he could do so. He frequently refused to read reports. Occasionally he would stuff an important letter from

Spain into his pocket and forget about it. Increasingly, he delayed taking decisions on Spanish affairs, leaving them to Berthier or Clarke. Even when he read reports, his mind rejected the information they contained. Nothing he was told would convince him that food for the troops was not in abundance throughout the country. He refused to understand that if a large body of troops remained concentrated in any one Spanish locality, it must starve. When a commander dispersed his troops to find food, Napoleon attributed it to lack of determination or insubordination. Time and again he asserted that even though cut off from its colonial wealth, Spain was rich enough to support its people, its monarchy, its government, and more than 250,000 French troops. That this was not true he attributed to Joseph's incompetence.

The fact was that knowing that he had disastrously overreached himself, Napoleon refused seriously to consider Spanish problems. He would deal only with points that forced themselves on his attention. Then he dealt with them piecemeal, working on outdated and incomplete information mixed with his own illusions. Therefore, since it required little attention to keep Joseph on the Spanish throne, Joseph stayed king of Spain until Wellington extruded him. The alternative required the finding of a substitute ruler, and even if one could be found, he would require realistic briefing and a whole series of crucial decisions before he could take up his task. This Napoleon was not prepared to attempt. Once the whole basis of his original assessment of the situation crumbled at Bailén, Saragossa, Cádiz, and Tôrres Vedras, he resolutely refused to assess the situation again. He would patch up the crumbling fabric, but he could not summon up the interest to redesign the whole edifice.

It must also be asked why Joseph consented to retain his throne. It was always open to him to put his reiterated abdication into effect and leave the country. The emperor could hardly keep him on his throne with an armed guard. His motives were mixed. First and probably foremost was loyalty to his brother. The king frequently disagreed with the emperor and disapproved of his policies. He could scarcely have suffered more humiliating treatment at his hands. Nevertheless, Joseph was greatly attached to Napoleon. The ties of family were exceedingly strong amongst the Bonapartes. They quarrelled and disputed endlessly when their star was in the ascendant. In times of adversity they closed their ranks and faced the world united.* It was unthinkable for Joseph to desert the post his brother had entrusted to him, however much he might dislike his brother's policies. If Napoleon would not consent to his abdication, he would not abdicate.

Not all Joseph's motives were so lofty. Undeniably he enjoyed being a king. The deference of his courtiers, the acclamations of the crowd, his diamond-encrusted clothes, his splendid palaces with their myriad mirrors and chandeliers, the guards of honor, the solemn *Te Deum*, the civic dignitaries on bended knee, the illusion of planning the betterment of his people were meat and drink to him. Within the palaces of occupied Spain, he could indulge his talent for cultured conversation, his natural idleness, his taste for luxury, his natural charm, his penchant for pretty women. It would be a wrench to give all this up for the rural seclusion of Mortefontaine, the suffocating valetudinarianism of Queen Julie, and his dignified, meangingless functions as grand elector of the empire.

Joseph was an ambitious man. His brother, his younger brother, was the most famous general, the greatest lawgiver, the most powerful ruler of the age. Beneath all his loyalty, his admiration, his genuine affection for his brother, Joseph had a strong streak of jealousy. He, also, wished to be a conqueror, a lawgiver, a sovereign. His ambitions did not match those of his brother. He did not wish to be emperor of Europe. He only aimed to be "His most Catholic Majesty of Spain and the Indies," the enlightened monarch of an ancient,

---

* Only Caroline, who married Murat, can be accused of desertion. Even Lucien, who had fled when Napoleon was at the height of his power, rallied to him when he was in an insecure position in 1815.

proud realm, who would be supported by the love and, particularly, acclaim of his grateful people. He also longed for at least one victory which he could call his own.

Joseph's detention in Bayonne did not last long, and even during it, he managed to slip away for a few unauthorized days at the spa of Bagnères de Bigorre. Then came leave from the emperor to retire to Mortefontaine provided that he stayed there and under no circumstances visited Paris. To make sure that he did not do so, the minister of police was instructed that "if the King comes to Paris or Saint-Cloud you must arrest him. He must be made to realize his situation."[5] This order Joseph regularly disobeyed, finding both Mortefontaine and Queen Julie insupportably dull. Frequently he slipped off to Paris to attend the opera or to visit friends, sometimes alone, sometimes with Count Miot. General Savary, the minister of police, knew all about these visits, but not relishing the idea of arresting his master's brother, contented himself with asking Miot to draw the king's attention to the irregularity of his proceedings. It may be that Savary felt that he owed Joseph something of a favor, since it was he who in July 1808 had advised the king, unnecessarily as it turned out, to quit Madrid after Bailén. For this false move Joseph had readily accepted the blame without implicating Savary in his decision.

Meanwhile, the war was going badly for France on both fronts. Soult showed himself no more capable of holding Wellington in check than Joseph and Jourdan had been. He made two great efforts to relieve Pamplona and San Sebastián. The first cost him 13,000 men, the second 3,800. Neither achieved anything. On 8 October, Wellintgon threw his left across the Bidassoa into France. A month later, at the battle of the Nivelle, the allies surged over the western Pyrenees, took St. Jean-de-Luz, and threatened Bayonne. These defeats, however, were of small moment except inasmuch as they allowed the enemy to establish himself on French soil. At Leipzig on 16-18 October, the eastern allies destroyed the reconstituted *Grande Armée,* inflicting on it 45,000 casualties.

The remainder took up a position to defend France on the line of the river Rhine. The emperor returned to Paris to build yet another army.

In Paris, Napoleon's thoughts turned to the 100,000 veterans who were still engaged under Soult and Suchet on the Pyrenees and in Valencia. If these could be disengaged and employed on the Rhine, many of his troubles would be at an end. He therefore turned to a daydream that had been in his mind for at least two years. In 1811, when the duke of Santa Fé had been sent to Paris as special ambassador, he had been told, on the emperor's orders, that if Joseph continued to complain, there would be no difficulty in restoring Ferdinand, prince of the Asturias, to the throne of his fathers. In April 1813, Napoleon, trying to convince an increasingly hostile Austria that he had plenty of troops to deploy in the east, had told the Austrian ambassador that he had only to return Ferdinand to Madrid to be able to take the French armies from Spain for use in Germany. In November 1813, the emperor decided to turn this fantasy into reality.

Since 1808 Ferdinand, who to the people of Spain was the true king but to the French was no more than prince of the Asturias, had been accommodated at Talleyrand's country house at Valençay. There he had filled in the time between lengthy church services by making himself adept at ecclesiastical embroidery. On 17 November 1813, he was visited by Count La Forest, whose task as Napoleon's ambassador to King Joseph had come to an end. He carried a letter from Napoleon which accused England of "fomenting in Spain anarchy, Jacobinism and the annihilation of both monarchy and nobility, with the object of setting up a republic. I cannot be indifferent to the ruin of a nation so near my own border, and with which I have so many interests in common. I am therefore anxious to remove all pretexts for English intervention, and to re-establish those bonds of friendship and neighborly affection which have long united our two nations."[6]

To implement this bland ignoring of five years bitterness, La Forest put forward a project whereby Ferdinand should return to Spain as king, undertaking to expel all British troops from Spanish soil. In return the French would evacuate those parts of Spain as they still occupied and would return the 100,000 Spanish prisoners of war. Ferdinand was also required to promise a complete pardon to all those who had supported King Joseph, confirming them in their titles and estates, but, as a bait, was offered Joseph's fourteen-year-old daughter Zenaïde as a bride. Ferdinand declined Zenaïde, on the grounds that such a marriage would be offensive to Spanish feeling, but after a few days' haggling accepted the rest, not excluding a clause giving to his parents a pension of 30,000,000 *reals* a year. It was recognized that the agreement of the Cortes, now sitting in Madrid, would be necessary to such an agreement and two highly placed emissaries were passed through the French and Spanish lines in eastern Spain to seek their agreement. The Cortes, as was to be expected, refused its consent. The Emperor sent Ferdinand back to Spain in any case, apparently counting on his honor and his powers as an absolute monarch to enable him to implement the Treaty of Valençay, irrespective of public feeling in his realm.

Aside from the morality of acknowledging Ferdinand as king of Spain when Charles IV and Joseph, both of whom had been recognized as king by the emperor, were alive and unconsulted, it is incredible that Napoleon should have trusted Ferdinand to keep his word and withdraw Spain from the war. The whole of his record showed that Ferdinand was unworthy of any kind of trust and, indeed, as soon as he reached Spanish soil, he repudiated the Treaty of Valençay. To show that his bad faith was not only directed against the enemies of his country, he proceeded, on reaching Madrid, to arrest the members of the regency and the leading liberal members of the Cortes, telling the other members of that body to return to their homes since they formed part of an illegal gathering. It cannot even be argued that Napoleon sent Ferdinand back to Spain knowing that nothing would do more to disorganize that unhappy country. He seems seriously to have believed that his scheme would work. On Christmas Day

1813, he wrote confidentially to his minister in Italy, "I have come to an agreeemnt with the Spaniards which leaves me free to use my troops in Aragon, Catalonia and Bayonne."[7] More practically, on 10 January, when he believed that Ferdinand's emissaries would have reached Madrid and gained the agreement of the Cortes to the treaty, he gave orders for Soult and Suchet to send to the eastern front 14,000 and 10,000 men respectively on the assumption that the Spanish armies would soon cease to oppose them. Spanish troops continued to fight beside their allies, and 10,000 of them were present at Toulouse when, on 10 April 1814, Wellington defeated Soult for the last time. Two days later, news reached Toulouse that the eastern allies were in Paris and that the emperor had abdicated.

Joseph had been loyal to his brother to the end. On hearing of the Treaty of Valençay, he wrote to Napoleon of his wish that the emperor should believe "that my heart is all French. Brought back to France by force of circumstances, I would be happy to be of some use to him. I am ready to undertake anything to prove my devotion. I also know my duty to Spain and wish to perform it. Rights are only held so that they can be sacrificed for the common good of humanity and I would be happy to sacrifice my rights if, by doing so, I can contribute to the pacification of Europe."[8]

Considering the humiliating way in which the emperor had treated his brother, it was a generous letter of abdication and an offer of help. Napoleon needed Joseph's help but could not resist one more chance to humiliate him. "You are no longer King of Spain. I want no part of Spain for myself, nor do I wish to give it to anybody. All I want is to be quit of its affairs, to live in peace with it, and to be free to use the army I have there."[9]

Joseph in 1814 was made lieutenant of the (French) realm, responsible for the safety of the empress and the regency and for the defense of Paris. His performance in this role was uninspiring, and he called down on his head much abuse from his brother before the empire finally collapsed. Then, as the count of Survilliers, he retired to Switzerland and lived quietly for a few months beside the lake of Geneva. He returned to Paris to give Napoleon his support and counsel during the Hundred Days and after the disaster of Waterloo escorted him to Rochefort, where he surrendered to Captain Maitland of H.M.S. *Bellerophon*. The former emperor, now General Bonaparte, was exiled to St. Helena. Joseph took ship to the United States and lived there peaceably until 1832, farming, entertaining his neighbors, and fathering a daughter on a Quaker girl, Annette Savage, whom he later married to another French refugee. He returned to Europe in 1832, living in England for a time and then traveling on the Continent, although France refused to receive him. He died in 1844 in Florence with his wife, the longsuffering Queen Julie, at his bedside. At his request, he was buried with the Golden Fleece, Spain's highest order of chivalry, about his neck. He had awarded it to himself.

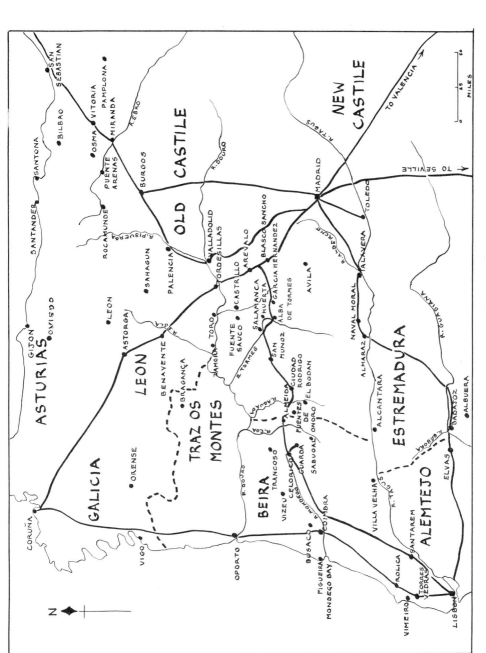

A. Northwestern Spain and Portugal, 1807–1813.

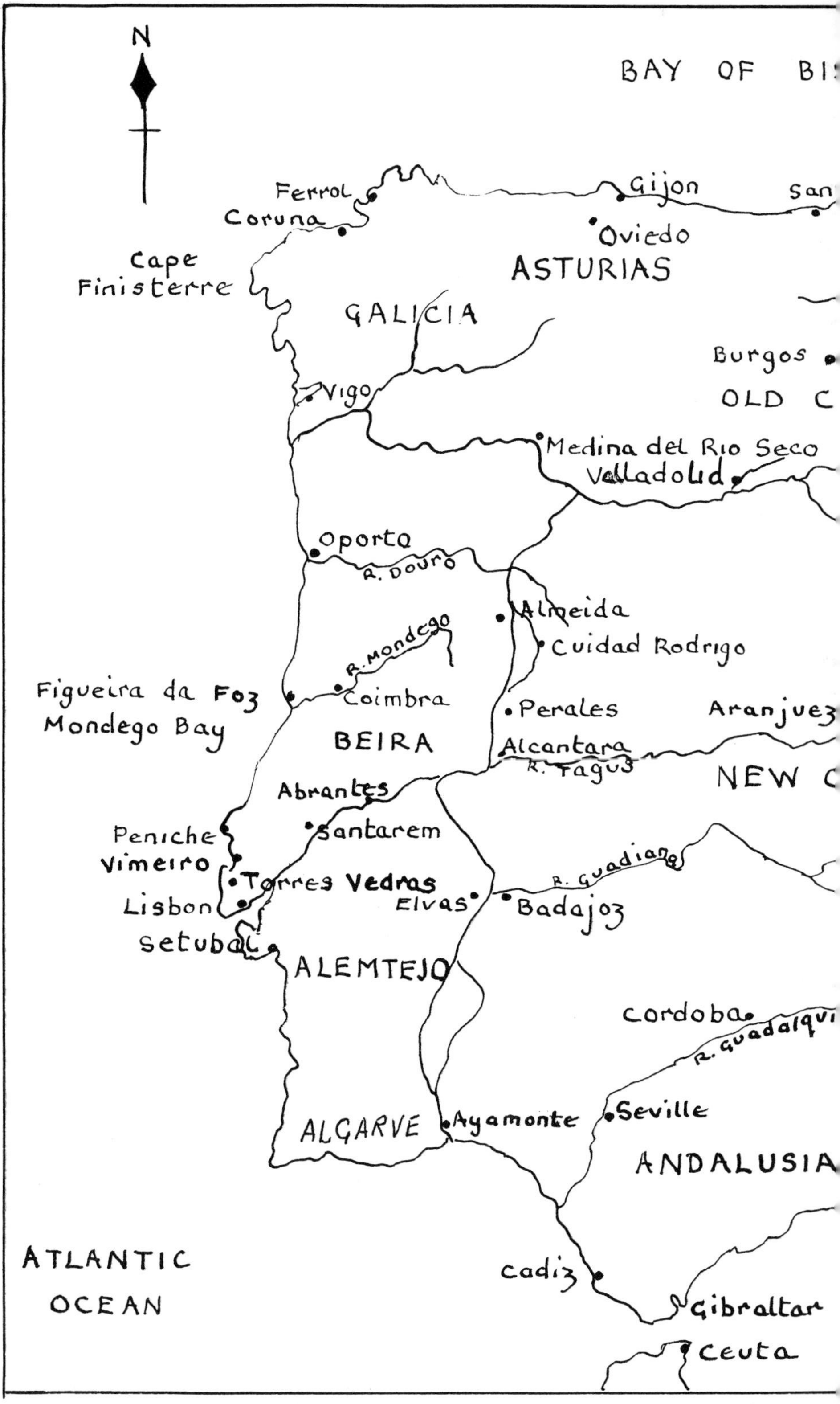

B. Spain and Portugal, 1807–1813.

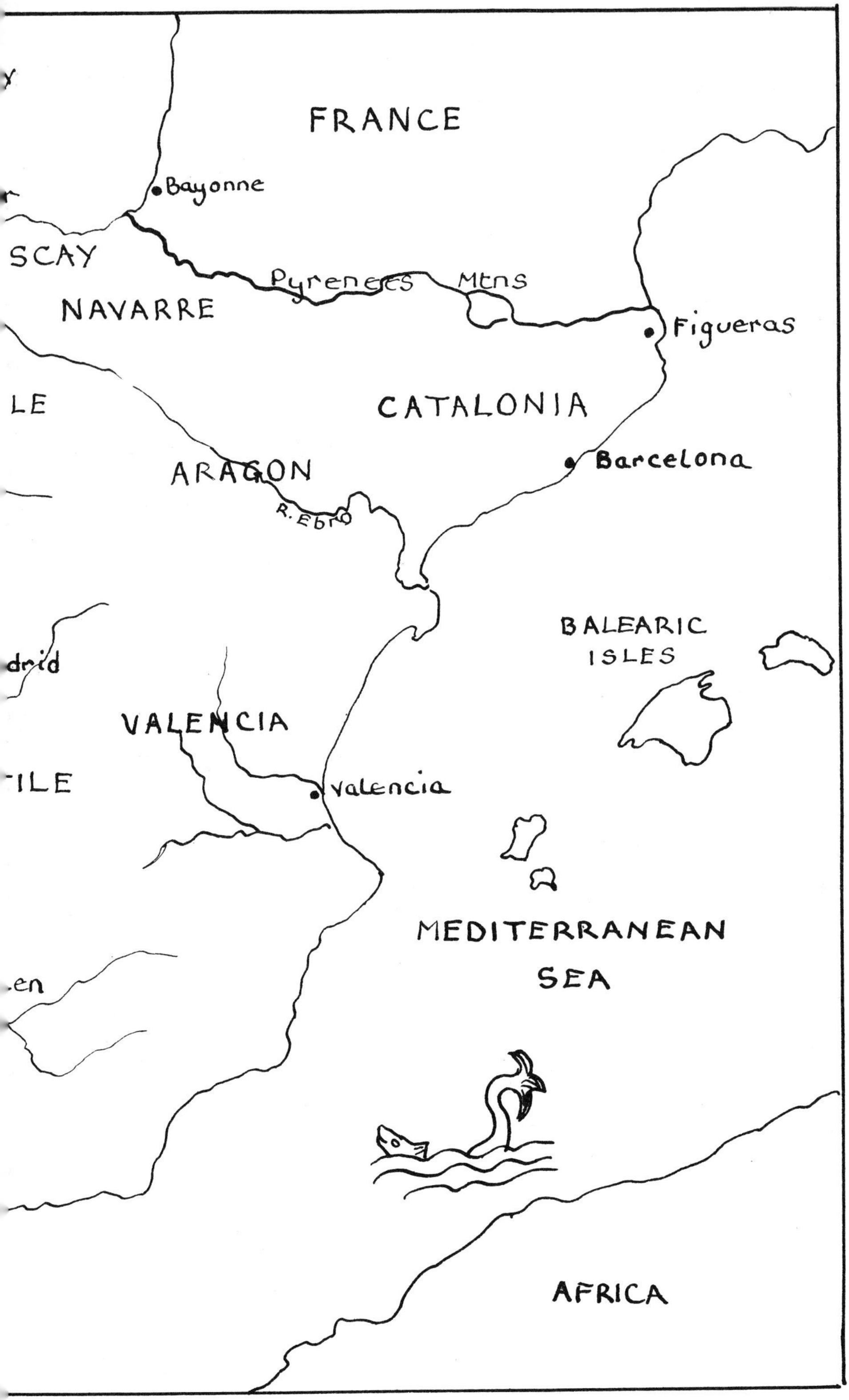
FRANCE
Bayonne
Pyrenees Mtns
NAVARRE
Figueras
CATALONIA
Barcelona
ARAGON
R. Ebro
BALEARIC ISLES
VALENCIA
Valencia
MEDITERRANEAN SEA
AFRICA

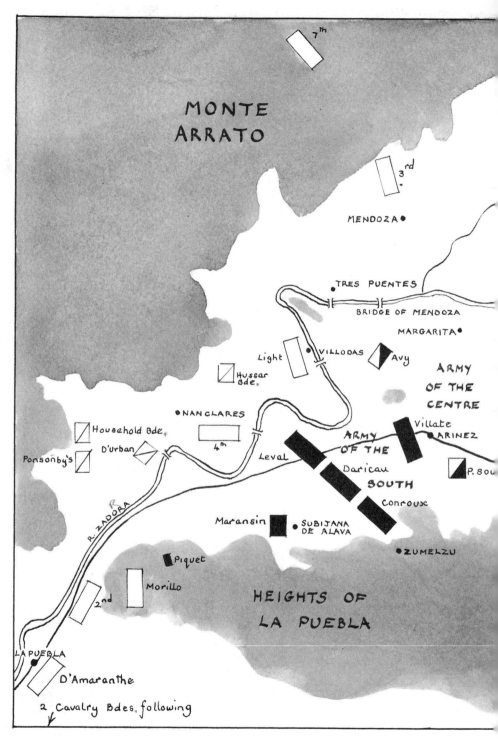

C. Vitoria, 21st June 1813.
Situation at 9 A.M.
Ground more than 100 metres above river level is shaded.

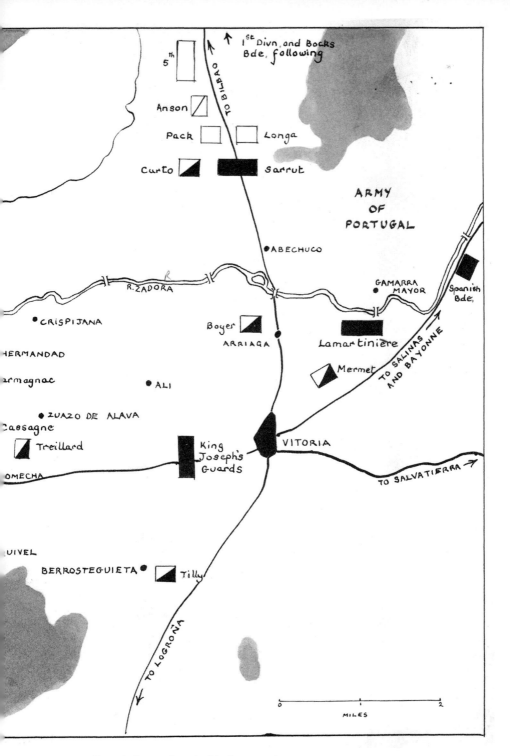

French formations in black.
British, Portuguese and Spanish formations in white.

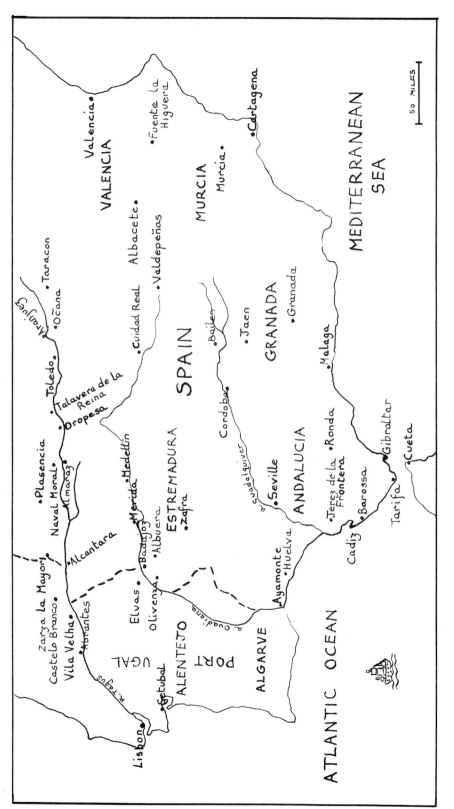

D. Southern Spain, 1810–12.

BIBLIOGRAPHY

With abbreviations used in the References

Bigarré *Memoires du Général Auguste Bigarré, Aide-de-Camp du Roi Joseph (1775–1813)*. n.d.

Brett James *1812. Eyewitness accounts of Napoleon's Defeat in Russia*. Antony Brett James. 1966.

Cammisc *Some Letters of the Duke of Wellington to His Brother, William Wellesley Pole*. Vol. xviii. (Ed. Sir Charles Webster.) Campden Miscellany. 1948.

Cau *Memoires of General de Caulaincourt, Duke of Vicenza*. (Ed. Jean Hanoteau. Tr. Hamish Miles.) 1935.

Cintra Proceedings of the Inquiry relative to the Armistice and Convention &c. made and concluded in Portugal in August 1808. 1809.

Colborne *Life of Sir John Colborne, Lord Seton*. (Ed. C. G. Moore Smith.) 1903.

Cook *Memoir of the Late War*. J. H. Cook. 1831.

Croker *The Croker Papers*. (Ed. L. W. Jennings.) 1884.

DMS. *The Dickson Manuscripts*. (Ed. J. H. Leslie.) 1808–1809.

Donaldson *Recollections of the Eventful Life of a Soldier*. Joseph Donaldson. New ed. 1841.

Ellesmere *Personal Reminiscences of the Duke of Wellington By Francis, 1st Earl of Ellesmere*. (Ed. Alice, Countess of Strafford.) 1904.

Fée *Souvenirs de la Guerre d'Espagne*. A. L. A. Fée. 1856.

Fortescue *A History of the British Army*. Vols. iv–x. Sir John Fortescue. 1915–1920.

Foy *Vie Militaire de General Foy* (Ed. M. Girod de l'Ain.) 1900.

GG *L'Espagne et Napoleon*. 3 vols. Geoffrey de Grandmaison. 1908–1931.

Gordon *A Cavalry Officer in the Corruña Campaign. The Journal of Captain Gordon*. (Ed. H. C. Wyllie.) 1913.

Gourgaud *The St. Helena Journal of General Baron Gougard*. (Tr. Sydney Gillard.) 1932.

Graham *Life of Thomas Graham, Lord Lyndoch*. Alex M. Delavoye. 1880.

Greville *The Greville Memoirs*. (Ed. H. Reeve.) New ed. 1896.

Bibliography

Harris *Recollections of Rifleman Harris.* (Ed. J. Curling.) 1848.

Hill *Life of Lord Hill,* Edwin Sidney.

Hugo *Memoires.* Général J. L. S. Hugo. 1823.

JN *Memoires et Correspondance Politique et Militaire du Roi Joseph.* 10 vols. (Ed. A. Ducasse.) 1854.

Jourdan *Memoires Militaire du Maréchal Jourdan* (Ed. De Grouchy.) 1899.

Kincaid *Adventures in the Rifle Brigade.* John Kincaid. 1830.

Lapène *Campagnes de 1813 et 1814.* Lapène. 1823.

Lefebvre *Napoleon: From 18 Brumaire to Tilsit.* Georges Lefebvre. (Tr. H. F. Stockhold.) 1969.

Leith Hay *A Narrative of the Peninsular War.* Andrew Leith Hay. New ed. 1832.

Leslie *Military Journal of Colonel Leslie of Balguhain.*

LIN *Lettres Inedites de Napoleon Ier.* (Ed. L. Lecestre.) 1897.

Marmont Memoires du Duc de Raguse. 5 vols. 1848–1850.

Marshall-Cornwall *Napoleon as Military Commander.* Sir James Marshall-Cornwall. 1967.

Masson *Napoleon et Son Fils.* Frederic Masson.

Maxwell *Life of Wellington.* Herbert Maxwell.

Méneval *Memoirs to Serve for the History of Napoleon 1st from 1802–15.* Baron Claude Francois Méneval. (Tr. R. H. Sherrard.) 1894.

Moore *Narrative of the Campaigns of the British Army in Spain commanded by Sir John Moore.* James Moore.

MM *Memoirs of Count Miot de Melito.* (Ed. Fleischmann. Tr. Hoey and Lillie.) 1881.

Napier *History of the War in the Peninsula and the South of France.* William Napier. New ed. 1853.

NC *Correspondance de Napoleon Ier.* 32 vols. 1854–1869.

Neal *Letters from Portugal and Spain.* Adam Neale. 1809.

Oman *History of the Peninsular War.* 7 vols. Sir Charles Oman. 1902–1930.

Patterson *Camp and Quarters.* John Patterson. 1840.

Pen Sketches *Peninsular Sketches by Actors on the Scene.* (Ed. W. H. Maxwell.) 1845.

Rapp Memoires du Général Rapp. 1823.

RG "The French Fleet 1807–14." Richard Glover. *Journal of Modern History,* Vol. 39, No. 3, September 1967.

Roederer *Autour de Bonaparte: Journal du Comte P. L. Roederer.* (Ed. M. Vitrac.) 1909.

St. Chamans Memoires du Général Comte de St. Chamans. 1896.

Savary Memoirs of the Duke of Rovigo, written by himself, illustrative of the history of the Emperor Napoleon. 2 vols. 1828.

Bibliography

SD *Supplementary Dispatches and Memoranda of Field Marshal the Duke of Wellington.* 14 vols. (Ed. 2nd Duke.) 1858–72.

Sherer *Recollections of the Peninsula.* G. M. Sherer. 1823.

Simmons *A British Rifleman. Journals and Correspondence of Major George Simmons.* (Ed. W. Verner.) 1899.

Stanhope *Notes on Conversations with the Duke of Wellington.* Earl of Stanhope. 1889.

Thi *Memoirs of Baron Thiebault.* (Tr. A. J. Butler.) 1896.

Tomkinson *Diary of a Cavalry Officer.* William Tomkinson. (Ed. J. Tomkinson.) 1894.

TS Journal of T. S. of the 71st Highland Light Infantry. 1828.

WD *The Dispatches of Field Marshal the Duke of Wellington.* 12 vols. (Ed. J. Gurwood.) 1834–1839.

Wheeler *The Letters of Private Wheeler.* (Ed. B. H. Liddell Hart.) 1951.

WV *History and Campaigns of the Rifle Brigade. Willoughby Verner* 1912–1919.

Wyldmem Memoir annexed to Wyld's Atlas showing the Principal Movements. Battles and Sieges in which the British Troops born a Conspicuous Part.

Manuscript Letters of Assist. Surgeon W. M. Brookes, Maj. John Campbell, Lt. Col. G. H. Duckworth. In the author's possession.

The following abbreviations are also used in the references:

JN = Joseph Napoleon, King of Spain.
N = Napoleon I, Emperor of France.
W = Arthur Wellesley, Lord Wellington.

REFERENCES

Preface
1. Lefebvre, 163.
2. Marshall-Cornwall, 228.

Chapter 1 The Confidence Trick
1. RG, Document of 30 Jun 11.
2. WD, viii, 7. W to Gordon, 12 jun 11.
3. Thi, ii, 196.
4. NC, xvi, 13,327. N to Clarke, 5 Nov 07.
5. Thi, ii, 199.
6. LIN, i, 136. N to Junot, 7 Jan 08.
7. NC, xvi, 13,416. N to Junot, 23 Dec 07.
8. *Ibid.*, 13,409. Decree of 23 Dec 07.
9. *Ibid.*, 13,351. N to Junot, 12 Nov 07.
10. MM, ii, 77.
11. Jourdan, 9.
12. Beauharnais to Talleyrand, 12 Jul 07. Quoted in GG i 89.
13. *Ibid.*
14. JN, iv, 438.
15. MM, ii, 215–16.
16. NC, xvi, 13,652. N to Murat, 14 Mar 08.
17. *Ibid.*
18. *Ibid.*, 13,632. N to Murat, 9 Mar 08.
19. *Ibid.*, 13,652. N to Murat, 14 Mar 08.
20. GG, i, 145.
21. GG, i, 146.
22. Cau, 461.
23. GG, i, 145.
24. Murat to N, 19 Mar 08.
25. NC, xvi, 13,694. N to Murat, 29 Mar 08.
26. *Ibid.*
27. Cau, 27.
28. MM, ii, 231.
29. Cintra, 250.
30. *Morning Chronicle.* 11 Jun 08.
31. Cau, 31.
32. MM, ii, 215–16.
33. NC, xvi, Appendix. N to Louis Napoleon, 27 Mar 08, 7 P.M.
34. MM, ii, 173.

35. *Ibid.,* 170.
36. *Ibid.,* 156.
37. MM, i, 499.
38. *Ibid.,* 570.
39. JN, iv, 334. La Romaña to JN, 14 Jun 08.
40. *Ibid.,* 336. Ferdinand to JN, 22 Jun 08.

Chapter 2 The Crown in His Pocket
1. NC, xvii, 14,099. N to JN, 16 Jun 08.
2. Senftt, Memoires. Quoted in GG, i, 253.
3. JN, iv, 339. JN to N, 10 Jul 08.
4. *Ibid.*
5. *Ibid.*
6. *Ibid.,* 343. JN to N, 12 Jul 08.
7. NC, xvii, 14,184. N to JN, 12 Jul 08.
8. MM, ii, 274.
9. NC, xvii, 14,192. N to Savary, 13 Jul 08.
10. JN, iv, 371. JN to N, 19 Jul 08.
11. *Ibid.,* 375. N to JN, 21 Jul 08.
12. *Ibid.,* 373. JN to N, 19 Jul 08.
13. *Ibid.,* 378. N to JN, 23 Jul 08.
14. La Forest to Champagny, 25 Jul 08. Quoted in GG i 273.
15. MM, ii, 253.
16. JN, iv, 375. JN to N, 20 Jul 08.
17. MM, ii, 253.
18. JN, iv, 381. JN to N, 24 Jul 08.
19. *Ibid.,* 385. JN to N, 26 Jul 08.
20. *Ibid.,* 386. Jn to N, 27 Jun 08.
21. Savary 2, i, 279.
22. JN, iv, 389. JN to N, 28 Jul 08.
23. *Ibid.,* 418. JN to N, 11 Aug 08.
24. WD, iv, 29. Castlereagh to W, 15 Jul 08.
25. *Ibid.,* 19. Castlereagh to W, 30 Jun 08.
26. *Morning Chronicle,* 4 Nov 08.
27. Sherer, 43.
28. NC, xviii, 14,243. JN to Clarke, 3 Aug 08.
29. Cintra, 231.
30. NC, xvii, 14,243. N to Clarke, 3 Aug 08.
31. *Ibid.,* 14,244. N to JN, 3 Aug 08.
32. *Ibid.,* 13,929. N to Berthier, 18 May 08.
33. *Ibid.,* 14,239. N to JN, 30 Jul 08.
34. JN, iv, 343. Berthier to Savary, 12 Jul 08.
35. NC, xvii, 14,239.
36. Cau, 540.

37. NC, xvii, 14,275. N to JN, 27 Aug 08.
38. *Ibid.*, 14,243. N to JN, 3 Aug 08.
39. JN, iv, 425. N to JN, 16 Aug 08.
40. NC, xvii, 14,378. N to JN, 13 Oct 08.
41. Stuart to Moore, 18 Oct 08. Quoted in Oman i 365.
42. JN, iv, 406. JN to N 6 Aug 08.
43. JN, v, 103. JN to N, 22 Sep 08.
44. *Ibid.*, 35. JN to N, 23 Aug 08.
45. JN, iv, 430. JN to N, 23 Aug 08.
46. JN, v, 85–88. JN to N, 14 Sep 08.
47. *Ibid.*, 116. JN to N, 11 Sep 08.
48. *Ibid.*, 49. Berthier to Jourdan, 2 Sep 08.

Chapter 3 Personal Appearance
1. NC, xviii, 14,413.
2. *Ibid*, 14,440. N to JN, 4 Nov 08.
3. MM, ii, 273–74.
4. NC, xviii, 14,462. N to Dejean, 11 Nov 08.
5. *Ibid.*, 14,469. N to Dejean, 13 Nov 08.
6. *Ibid.*, 14,499. N to JN, 20 Nov 08.
7. JN, iv, 265. JN to N, 10 Nov 08.
8. NC, xviii, 14,537.
9. *Ibid.*
10. *Ibid.*, 14,580. N to Berthier, 17 Dec 08.
11. JN, v, 281. JN to N, 8 Dec 08.
12. *Ibid.*, N to JN, 12 Dec 08.
13. MM, ii, 294.
14. NC, xviii, 14,552. General Order, 12 Dec 08.
15. NC, xviii, 14,543. 9 Dec 08.
16. *Ibid.*, 14,581. N to Berthier, 10 Dec 08 (misdated as 17 Dec).
17. *Ibid.*, 14,550. N to Berthier, 12 Dec 08.
18. Castlereagh to Moore, 25 Sep 08. Moore Appendix 3.
19. Moore to Castlereagh, 9 Oct 08. Moore Appendix 16.
20. Moore to Hope, 28 Nov 08. Moore 114.
21. Moore to Castlereagh, 12 Dec 08. Moore Appendix 91.
22. Moore to Castlereagh, 13 Jan 09. Moore Appendix 132.
23. NC, xviii, 14,577. N to Berthier, 17 Dec 08.
24. *Ibid.*, 14,606. N to Josephine, 22 Dec 08.
25. *Ibid.*, 14,616. N to JN, 23 Dec 08.
26. *Ibid.*, 14,610. Maret to Cambacérès, 22 Dec 08.
27. *Ibid.*, 14,609. N to JN, 22 Dec 08.
28. Graham, 292.
29. TS, 53.
30. *Ibid.*

31. NC, xviii, 14,626. N to JN, 31 Dec 08.
32. Neal, 181.
33. Harris, 165.
34. NC, xviii, 14,620. N to JN, 27 Dec 08.
35. *Ibid.*
36. *Ibid.*, 14,640. N to JN, 2 Jan 08.
37. *Ibid.*, 14,656. N to JN, 5 Jan 09.
38. *Ibid.*, 14,692. N to Clarke, 13 Jan 09.
39. *Ibid.*, 14,626. N to JN, 31 Dec 08.
40. *Ibid.*, 14,672 & 14,699. N to JN, 9 & 13 Jan 09.
41. Gordon, 165.
42. Patterson, 281.
43. Colborne, 100.
44. Quoted in WV, i, 208–10.
45. JN, v, 375. Soult to Berthier, 17 Jan 09.
46. *Ibid.*

Chapter 4 The Dream of Valladolid

1. Thi. ii. 241.
2. NC, xviii, 14,625. N to Clarke, 31 Dec 08.
3. NC, xviii, 14,634 & 14,663. N to Clarke and Cambacérès, 8 Jan 09.
4. *Ibid.*, 14,640. N to JN, 2 Jan 09.
5. *Ibid.*, 14,712. N to Berthier, 15 Jan 09.
6. *Ibid.*, 14,717. N to JN, 15 Jan 09.
7. *Ibid.*, 14,730. N to JN, 16 Jan 09.
8. *Ibid.*, 14,671. N to JN, 9 Jan 09.
9. *Ibid.*, 14,657. N to JN, 6 Jan 09.
10. *Ibid.*, 14,731. N to Jerome, 16 Jan 09.
11. LIN, i, 391. N to Champagny, 8 Jan 09.
12. Jourdan, 170.
13. NC, xviii, 14,684. N to JN, 11 Jan 09.
14. LIN, i, 390. N to Caulaincourt, 7 Jan 09.
15. *Ibid.*, 397. N to Caulaincourt, 14 Jan 09.
16. NC, xviii, 14,699. N to JN, 13 Jan 09.
17. *Ibid.*, 14,672. N to JN, 9 Jan 09.
18. *Ibid.*, 14,692. N to Clarke, 13 Jan 09.
19. *Ibid.*, 14,771; LIN, i, 394 & 396. N to JN, 9, 10, & 12 Jan 09.
20. JN, v, 391. JN to N, 22 Jan 09.
21. MM, ii, 311.
22. JN, vi, 68. JN to N, 7 Mar 09.
23. *Ibid.*, 34. JN to N, 25 Jan 09.
24. *Ibid*, 54. JN to N, 14 Feb 09.
25. LIN, i, 401. N to JN, 16 Jan 09.
26. NC, xviii, 14,716. N to JN, 15 Jan 09.

27. JN, vi, 161. JN to N, 30 Apr 09.
28. *Ibid.*, 59. JN to N, 19 Feb 09.
29. LIN, i, 392, 394, & 396. N to JN, 9, 10, & 12 Jan 09.
30. MM, ii, 313.
31. JN, vi, 51. N to JN, 7 Feb 09.
32. NC, xviii, 14,910. N to JN, 16 Mar 09.
33. JN, vi, 150. JN to N, 6 Apr 09.
34. *Ibid.*, 54. JN to N, 14 Feb 09.
35. *Ibid.*, 78. JN to N, 19 Mar 09.
36. *Ibid*, 89. N to JN, 27 Mar 09.
37. NC, xviii, 14,798. N to JN, 21 Feb 09.
38. JN, vi, 68. JN to N, 7 Mar 09.
39. NC, xviii, 14,684. N to JN, 11 Jan 09.
40. JN, vi, 40. JN to N, 29 Jan 09.
41. Jourdan, 170.
42. *Ibid.*   ..
43. JN, vi, 199. JN to N, 20 Jan 09.
44. NC, xviii, 14,955. Clarke to Jourdan, 26 Mar 09.
45. JN, vi, 56. Berthier to Ney, 18 Feb 09.
46. *Ibid.*, 55. N to JN, 17 Feb 09.
47. *Ibid.*, 40. JN to N, 4 Feb 09.
48. *Ibid.*, 74. JN to N, 11 Mar 09.
49. NC, xviii, 14,936. N to JN, 21 Mar 09.
50. JN, vi, 153. JN to N, 12 Apr 09.
51. *Ibid.*, 153. N to JN, 12 Apr 09.
52. MM, i, 187.
53. Cau, 493.
54. JN, vi, 157 & 159. JN to N, 22 & 28 Apr 09.
55. *Ibid.*, 91. JN to N, 28 Mar 09.
56. *Ibid.*, 148. JN to N, 2 Apr 09.
57. *Ibid.*, 177. JN to N, 24 May 09.
58. *Ibid.*, 182. JN to N, 30 May 09.
59. *Ibid.*, 188. JN to N, 10 Jun 09.
60. *Ibid.*, 511. Proclamation of the Supreme Junta, 17 Apr 09.
61. MS. Letter of Major John Campbell to Marshal Beresford, 2 Apr 09.
62. WD, vi, 261. Memorandum on the Defense of Portugal, 7 Mar 09.
63. *Ibid.*
64. George III to Castlereagh, 3 Oct 09. Quoted in Maxwell i 134.
65. WD, iv, 303. W to Castlereagh, 6 May 09.
66. Leslie, 114.

Chapter 5 Battle Royal
1. Bigarré, 351.

2. NC, xviii & xix, 14,995, 15,038, 15,292, & 15,332.
3. NC, xix, 15,332. N to Clarke, 11 Jun 09.
4. *Ibid.*
5. JN, vi, 192. Clarke, 12 Jun 09.
6. NC, xix, 15,396. N to Clarke, 18 Jul 09.
7. NC, xix, 15,552. N to Clarke, 18 Jul 09.
8. Roederer, 234.
9. JN, vi, 158. JN to N, 10 Jun 09.
10. *Ibid.*, 274. JN to N, 18 Jul 09.
11. *Ibid.*, 269. JN to N, 3 Jul 09.
12. *Ibid.*, 183 & 197. JN to N, 1 & 23 Jun 09.
13. *Ibid.*, 274. JN to N, 18 Jul 09.
14. *Ibid.*, 270. JN to N, 9 Jul 09.
15. NC, xix, 15,340. N to Clarke, 12 Jun 09.
16. JN, vi, 270. JN to N, 9 Jul 09.
17. *Ibid.*, 266. JN to N, 1 Jul 09.
18. WD, iv, 270. W to Castlereagh, 24 Apr 09.
19. *Ibid.*, 412. W to Castlereagh, 11 Jul 09.
20. *Ibid.*, 526. W to Frere, 24 Jul 09.
21. Cammisc, 16. W to W. W. Pole, 25 Jul 09.
22. JN, vi, 274. JN to N, 18 Jul 09.
23. *Ibid.*, 419. Jourdan to Clarke, 15 Sep 09.
24. *Ibid.*, 278. Jourdan to Soult, 22 Jul 09.
25. WD, iv, 524. W to Frere, 25 Jul 09.
26. *Ibid.*
27. JN, vi, 474. General Deprez's account of Talavera.
28. *Ibid.*
29. MS. Letter of Asst. Surgeon W. Brookes, 22 Aug 08.
30. WD, v, 83. W to Castlereagh, 25 Aug 09.
31. Jourdan, 256.
32. Jourdan, 259.
33. JN, vi, 474. Deprez's account.
34. Jourdan, 258.
35. JN, vi, 474. Deprez's account.
36. *Ibid.*
37. JN, vi, 282. JN to N, 29 Jul 09.
38. *Ibid.*, 284. JN to N, 31 Jul 09.
39. *Ibid.*, 419. Jourdan to Clarke, 15 Sep 09.
40. Savary 2, ii, 156, & 160.
41. NC, xix, 15,694. N to Clarke, 21 Aug 09.
42. WD, iv, 536. W to Castlereagh, 29 Jul 09.
43. NC, xix, 15,711. N to Clarke, 25 Aug 11.
44. Jourdan, 261.
45. JN, vi, 387 15,864. Jourdan to Clarke, 22 Aug 08.

46. NC, xix, 15,864. N to Clarke, 26 Aug 09.
47. *Ibid.*, 15,871. N to Soult, 26 Sep 09.

Chapter 6 Conquering King
1. NC, xix, 15,926. N to czar, 10 Oct 09.
2. JN, vii, 43. JN to N, 15 Oct 09.
3. NC, xx, 16,301. Speech to Corps Legislatif, 3 Dec 09.
4. JN, vii, 73. JN to Clarke, 15 Nov 09.
5. *Ibid.*, 59. JN to Julie, 8 Nov 09.
6. St Chamans, 203.
7. Lamarque, ii, 182. Quoted in Oman, vi, 591.
8. Ellesmere, 139.
9. St. Chamans, 203.
10. JN, vi, 54. Soult to Clarke, 6 Nov. 09.
11. *Ibid.*
12. WD, v, 150. W to Roche, 14 Sep 09.
13. SD, vi, 343. W to Burghersh, 1 Sep 09.
14. *Ibid.*, 394. Roche to W, 10 Oct 09.
15. WD, v, 335. W to Frere, 6 Dec 09.
16. JN, vii, 107. JN to N, 3 Dec 09.
17. *Ibid.*, 206. Soult to Berthier, 3 Jan 10.
18. St. Chamans, 163.
19. Foy, 85.
20. JN, vi, 207. JN to N, 28 Jun 09.
21. NC, xx, 16,192. N to Berthier, 31 Jan 10.
22. *Ibid.*, N to JN, 11 Nov 09.
23. JN vii, 129. JN to N, 19 Dec 09.
24. *Ibid.*, 117. Soult to Berthier, 14 Dec 09.
25. *Ibid.*, 203. JN to N, 1 Jan 10.
26. *Ibid.*, 199. Soult to Berthier, 1 Jan 10.
27. *Ibid.*, 220. Soult to Berthier, 11 Jan 10.
28. *Ibid.*, 232. JN to N, 22 Jan 10.
29. *Ibid.*, 236. JN to N, 25 Jan 10.
30. Proclamation from Cordova. Quoted in GG, ii, 197.
31. JN, vi, 238. JN to N, 27 Jan 10.
32. MM, ii, 385.
33. MM, ii, 387.
34. JN, vii, 249. JN to N, 2 Jan 10.
35. *Ibid.*, 252. JN to N, 8 Feb 10.
36. *Ibid.*, 259. JN to N, 18 Feb 10.
37. Donaldson, 69.
38. Miot, ii, 351.
39. JN, vii, 259. N to Berthier, 28 Jan 10.
40. NC, xx, 16,175. N to La Forest, 28 Jan 10.

41. JN, vii, 265. JN to N, 2 Mar 10.
42. MM, ii, 397.
43. MM, ii, 413.
44. JN, vii, 266. JN to Julie, 5 Mar 10.
45. *Ibid.*

Chapter 7 The Shrinking Realm
 1. MS. Letter of Lt. Col. G. H. Duckworth, 14 May 10.
 2. JN, vii, 240. N to Berthier, 28 Jan 10.
 3. NC, xx, 16,229. N to Berthier, 8 Feb 10.
 4. *Ibid*, 16,275. N to Clarke, 21 Feb 10.
 5. MM, ii, 434.
 6. JN, vii, 272. JN to Julie, 12 Apr 10.
 7. LIN, ii, 13. N to Champagny, 18 Feb 10.
 8. MM, ii, 434.
 9. GG, ii, 210.
10. Massena to JN, 4 Aug 10. Quoted in MM, ii, 450.
11. JN, vii, 278. JN to N, 30 Apr 10.
12. La Forest to Champagny, 17 Aug 10. Quoted in GG, ii, 272.
13. Bigarré, 280.
14. *Ibid.*, 281.
15. JN, vii, 293. Berthier to Soult, 14 Jul 10.
16. *Ibid.*, 296. Berthier to JN, 14 Jul 10.
17. NC, xx, 16,678. N to Clarke, 19 Jul 10.
18. JN, vii, 316. Soult to Berthier, 20 Aug 10.
19. *Ibid.*, 322. JN to Berthier, 25 Aug 10.
20. *Ibid.*, 324. Soult to Berthier, 29 Aug 10.
21. JN, vii, 318. JN to Julie, 21 Aug 10.
22. *Ibid.*, 306. JN to Julie, 8 Aug 10.
23. *Ibid.*, 306. JN to N, 8 Aug 10.
24. LIN, ii, 77. Draft by N.
25. NC, xxi, 16,877. N to Champagny, 9 Sep 10.
26. JN, vii, 188. Miot's Diary for 7 Sep 10.
27. *Ibid.*, 354. JN to Julie, 12 Oct 10.
28. *Ibid.*, 357. JN to Julie, 17 Oct 10.
29. NC, xxi, 17,111. N to Champagny (for passing to La Forest), 7 Nov 10.
30. JN, vii, 192. Miot's Diary for 3 Dec 10.
31. JN, vii, 193. Miot's Diary for 10 Dec 10.
32. *Ibid.*, Miot's Diary for 11 Dec 10.
33. JN, vi, 240. N to Berthier, 31 Jan 10.
34. Foy, 110.
35. *Ibid.*, 100.
36. Hulot, "Reminiscences," 303. Quoted in Oman, iii, 208.

37. NC, xx, 16,504. N to Berthier, 27 May 10.
38. *Ibid.*, 16,732. Berthier to Massena, 29 Jul 10.
39. *Ibid.*, 16,519. N to Berthier, 29 May 10.
40. *Ibid.*
41. WD, vi, 214. W to H. Wellesley, 20 Jun 10.
42. Sprünglin, 445. Quoted in Oman, iii, 273.
43. Massena to Berthier, 22 Sep 10. Quoted in Oman, iii, 352.
44. Sprünglin Diary for 7 Oct 10. Quoted in Oman, ii, 412.
45. Massena to N, 22 Nov 10. Printed in Foy, 343.
46. JN, vii, 364. N to Berthier, 9 Nov 10.
47. Foy, 107–11.

Chapter 8 The Family Reunion
1. JN, vii, 374. JN to Julie, 12 Dec 10.
2. *Ibid.*, 372. JN to Berthier, 28 Nov 10.
3. NC, xxi, 16,967. N to Berthier, 29 Sep 10.
4. *Ibid.*, 17,131. N to Berthier, 14 Nov 10.
5. *Ibid.*
6. JN, vii, 449. Soult to Berthier, 22 Jan 11.
7. Hill, 150. Letter of 10 Nov 10.
8. Foy, 128.
9. JN, vii, 374. JN to Berthier, 15 Dec 10.
10. JN, vii, 376. JN to Julie, 25 Dec 10.
11. NC, xxi, 17,285. N to Berthier, 17 Jan 11.
12. La Forest to Champagny, 17 Dec 10. Quoted in GG, ii, 228
13. JN, vii, 463. JN to Berthier, 21 Feb 11.
14. *Ibid.*, 476. JN to Berthier, 9 Mar 11.
15. *Ibid.*, 466. JN to Julie, 5 Mar 11.
16. *Ibid.*, 483. JN to Berthier, 13 Mar 11.
17. *Ibid.*, 466. JN to Julie, 5 Mar 11.
18. *Ibid.*, 451. JN to N, 26 Jan 11.
19. La Forest to Champagny, 9 Feb 11. Quoted in GG, ii, 294.
20. *Ibid.*
21. *Ibid.*
22. JN, vii, 492. JN to Fesch, 24 Mar 11.
23. *Ibid*, 493. JN to N, 24 Mar 11.
24. *Ibid.*, N to JN, 20 Mar 11.
25. *Ibid.*, JN to Julie, 21 Apr 11.
26. MM, ii, 488.
27. La Forest to Champagny, 23 Apr 11. Quoted in GG, 303.
28. JN, viii, 15. Notes presented at Rambouillet.
29. *Ibid.*
30. NC, xxiii, 18,652. Bassano to Castlereagh, 17 Apr 12.
31. NC, xxii, 17,752. N to Berthier, 27 May 11.

32. *Ibid.*
33. *Ibid.*
34. *Ibid.*
35. MM, ii, 503.
36. LIN, ii, 137. N to Berthier, 11 Jun 11.
37. Masson, 165.
38. NC, xxii, 17,813. Speech of 16 Jun 11.
39. *Ibid.*, 17,824. N to Decrés, 19 Jun 11.
40. *Ibid.*, 17,965. N to Clarke, 29 Jun 11.
41. JN, viii, 38–42. JN to N, 2, 8, 11, & 17 Jun 11.
42. MM, ii, 511.
43. Bigarré, 289.
44. JN, viii, 101. JN to N, 29 Oct 11.
45. NC, xxii, 18,084. N to Berthier, 25 Aug 11.
46. JN, viii, 77. JN to Berthier, 3 Sep 11.
47. *Ibid.*, 66. JN to Berthier, 24 Aug 11.
48. *Ibid.*, 102. JN to N, 29 Oct 11.
49. Return of 15 Jul 11.
50. Return of 15 Sep 11.
51. SD, vii, 94. W to Liverpool, 11 Jun 11.
52. SD, xiii, 659. Bessières to Berthier, 6 Jun 11.
53. Berthier to Marmont, 21 Nov 11. Quoted in Oman, iv, 591.

Chapter 9 Supreme Commander
1. NC, xxiii, 18,487. N to Clarke, 8 Feb 12.
2. JN, viii, 272. JN to La Forest, 1 Jan 12.
3. NC, xxiii, 14,818. N to Berthier, 6 Jan 12.
4. JN, viii, 291. JN to Berthier, 25 Jan 12.
5. *Ibid.*, 290. JN to Berthier, 25 Jan 12.
6. *Ibid.*, 292. JN to Suchet, 26 Jan 12.
7. DMS. Letter of Capt. Dyneley, RHA, 22 Jan 12.
8. Berthier to Marmont, 13 Dec 11. Marmont, iv, 271.
9. Dorsenne to Marmont, 5 Jan 12. Quoted in Oman, v, 192.
10. Marmont to Berthier, 13 Jan 12. Quoted in Oman, v, 188.
11. JN, viii, 301. Marmont to Berthier, 6 Feb 12.
12. *Ibid.*, 303. JN to Berthier, 3 Feb 12.
13. NC, xxiii, 18,496. Berthier to Marmont, 11 Feb 12.
14. *Ibid.*
15. Marmont to Berthier, 26 Feb 12. Marmont, iv, 342.
16. Berthier to Marmont, 21 Feb 12. Quoted in Oman, v, 210.
17. Marmont, iv, 512.
18. JN, viii, 353. Soult to Berthier, 8 Apr 12.
19. *Ibid*, 368. Soult to Berthier, 14 Apr 12.
20. *Ibid.*

21. Bigarré 293.
22. JN, viii, 322. Berthier to JN, 2 Feb 12.
23. NC, xxiii, 18,583. N to Berthier, 16 Mar 12.
24. *Ibid.*, 18,632. N to Berthier, 3 Apr 12.
25. Jourdan, 386–94. Memorandum of 28 May 12.
26. *Ibid.*
27. *Ibid.*
28. *Ibid.*
29. *Ibid.*
30. *Ibid.*
31. Jourdan, 395. Clarke to JN, 9 May 12.
32. Thi, ii, 252.
33. JN, ix, 34. Deprez to JN, 13 Jun 12.
34. *Ibid.*
35. *Ibid.*, 32. Soult to JN, 12 Jun 12.
36. Fée, 135.
37. Jourdan to Marmont, 14 Jun 12. Marmont, iv, 411.
38. JN, ix, 38. JN to Marmont, 18 Jun 12.
39. Rapp, 145.
40. Cau, 122.
41. Jourdan to Marmont, 30 Jun 12. Quoted in Oman, v, 395.
42. JN, ix, 42. JN to Soult, 30 Jun 12.
43. *Ibid.*, 51. JN to Marmont, 21 Jun 12.
44. *Ibid.*, 58. Marmont to JN 25 Jul 12.
45. *Ibid.*, 54. Clausel to JN, 21 Jul 12.
46. Kincaid, 155.
47. WD, ix, 298. W to Bathurst, 21 Jul 12.
48. Marmont, iv, 21 Jul 12.
49. Greville, iv, 40.
50. WD, ix, 308. W to Bathurst, 24 Jul 12.
51. Cau, 191.
52. NC, xxiv, 19,175. N to Clarke, 2 Sep 12.

Chapter 10. On His Travels Again
1. JN, ix, 46. Soult to JN, 16 Jul 12.
2. *Ibid.*, 60. JN to Soult, 29 Jul 12.
3. *Ibid.*, 64. Clausel to Clarke, 29 Jul 12.
4. Reiset, "Souvenirs," ii, 358. Quoted in Oman, v, 507.
5. JN, ix, 64. JN to Clarke, 11 Aug 12.
6. Simmons, 248.
7. WD, ix, 355. W to Bathurst, 13 Aug 12.
8. Jourdan, 427.
9. Hugo, ii, 97.
10. Jourdan, 427.

343

11. GG, iii, 303.
12. MM, ii, 561.
13. JN, ix, 80. JN to Clarke, 29 Aug 12.
14. *Ibid.*, 65. Soult to JN, 12 Aug 12.
15. *Ibid.*, 73. JN to Soult, 17 Aug 12.
16. *Ibid*, 68. Soult to Clarke, 12 Aug 12.
17. *Ibid.*, 86. JN to N, 9 Sep 12.
18. *Ibid.*, 90. Deprez to JN, 22 Sep 12.
19. Clarke to Soult, 31 Aug 12. Quoted in GG, iii, 170.
20. JN, ix, 176. Deprez to JN, 3 Jan 13.
21. *Ibid.*
22. JN, ix, 94. N to Clarke, 19 Oct 12.
23. Kurz, "Der Feldzug von 1812," 125. Quoted in Brett James.
24. Jourdan, 436.
25. *Ibid.*
26. JN, ix, 93. JN to Soult, 12 Oct 12.
27. WD, ix, 93. W to Bathurst, 21 Oct 12.
28. MM, ii, 575.
29. JN, ix, 119. JN to Clarke, 23 Dec 12.
30. *Ibid.*
31. Jourdan, 444.
32. MM, ii, 580
33. WD, ix, 573. W to Liverpool, 23 Nov 12.
34. Rapp, 217.
35. Cau, 440–43.
36. Méneval, iii, 89.
37. Bigarré, 313.
38. JN, ix, 180. Deprez to JN, 3 Jan 13.
39. NC, xxiv, 19,411. N to Clarke, 3 Jan 13.
40. *Ibid.*, 19526. N to Clarke, 31 Jan 13.
41. *Ibid.*, 19546. N to Clarke, 7 Feb 13.
43. Jourdan, 455.

Chapter 11 Retreat
1. WD, x, 569. W to Liverpool, 23 Jul 13.
2. *Ibid*, vii, 102. W to Stuart, 3 Jan 11.
3. *Ibid.*, ix, 370. W to Bathurst, 18 Aug 12.
4. *Ibid.*, viii, 127 & 166. W to H. Wellesley, 20 Jul & 2 Aug 11.
5. *Ibid.*, ix, 617. W to Beresford, 10 Dec 12.
6. NC, xxiv, 19,549. N to Clarke, 8 Feb 13.
7. JN, ix, 240. JN to Clarke, 1 Apr 13.
8. *Ibid.*, 193. Clarke to JN, 12 Feb 13.
9. *Ibid.*, 274. Jourdan to Clarke, 16 May 13.
10. *Ibid.*, 290. Clarke to JN, 7 Jun 13.

11. Jourdan, 462.
12. JN, ix, 280. JN to Clausel, 27 May 13.
13. *Ibid.*, 285. JN to Clarke, 5 Jun 13.
14. *Ibid.*
15. Tomkinson, 232.
16. Wheeler, 112.
17. Simmons, 285.
18. Jourdan, 466.
19. JN, ix, 286. JN to Clarke, 5 Jun 13.
20. *Ibid.*, 271. Clarke to JN, 10 May 13.
21. *Ibid.*, 285. JN to Clarke, 5 Jun 13.
22. Jourdan, 468.
23. JN, ix, 468. Miot's Journal.
24. WD, ix, 429. W to Bourke, 10 Jun 13.
25. JN, ix, 468. Miot's Journal.
26. Croker, ii, 308.
27. Ellesmere, 150.
28. JN, ix, 468. Miot's Journal.
29. *Ibid.*
30. *Ibid.*, 294. Clausel to JN, 15 Jun 13.
31. *Ibid.*, 454. Clausel to JN, 30 Jun 13.
32. Foy, 207.
33. Kincaid, 206.
34. Pen Sketches, ii, 38.
35. SD.
36. Pen Sketches, ii, 40.
37. Leith Hay, ii, 178.
38. *Ibid.*
39. Jourdan, 472.
40. Lapène, 25.
41. MM, ii, 598.
42. *Ibid.*, 600.

Chapter 12 The Reckoning

1. Jourdan, 475.
2. Jourdan to Clarke, 20 Jun 13. Quoted in Oman, vi, 398.
3. Wyldmem. Gazan's report.
4. Fortescue, ix, 162.
5. Jourdan, 162.
6. Wyldmem. Gazan's report.
7. Sherer, 324.
8. Wyldmem. Gazan's report.
9. JN, ix, 426. D'Erlon's report.
10. Wyldmem. Orders of 20 Jun 13.

11. Cook.
12. Pen Sketches, ii, 46.
13. Wyldmem. Gazan's report.
14. *Ibid.*
15. Napier, v, 127.
16. MM, ii, 606.
17. Leith Hay, ii, 202.
18. Stanhope, 144.
19. MM, ii, 610.
20. NC, xxv, 20,070. N to Clarke, 2 Jun 13.
21. JN, ix, 343. JN to Julie, 1 Jul 13.
22. *Ibid.*, 310. JN to Clarke, 23 Jun 13.
23. NC, xxv, 20,208. N to Soult, 1 Jul 13.
24. LIN, ii, 254. N to JN, 1 Jul 13.
25. *Ibid.*, 257. N to Clarke, 1 Jul 13.
26. *Ibid.*
27. *Ibid.*
28. *Ibid.*, 265. N to Cambacérès, 11 Jul 13.
29. *Ibid.*, 271. N to Cambacérès, 20 Jul 13.
30. JN, ix, 344. Clarke to JN, 2 Jul 13.
31. LIN, ii, 265. N to Clarke, 11 Jul 13.
32. *Ibid.*, 256. N to Cambacérès, 1 Jul 13.
33. *Ibid.*
34. LIN, ii, 277. N to Clarke, 1 Aug 13.
35. Roederer, 304.
36. *Ibid.*
37. *Ibid.*
38. *Ibid.*
39. JN, ix, 404. JN to N, 12 Jul 13.
40. Soult's Order of the Day, 23 Jul 13.

Epilogue
1. LIN, ii, 265. N to Cambacérès, 11 Jul 13.
2. Gourgaud, 130.
3. JN, vi, 68. JN to N, 7 Mar 09.
4. MM, ii, 273.
5. LIN, ii, 272. N to Savary, 20 Jul 13.
6. Quoted in Oman, vii, 301.
7. NC, xxv, 21,039. N to Melzi, 25 Dec 13.
8. JN, x, 3. JN to N, 29 Dec 13.
9. LIN, ii, 306. N to JN, 7 Jan 14.

INDEX

Index

Index

Index

Index

Index